Gender and Information Technology:
Moving Beyond Access to Co-Create Global Partnership

Mary Kirk
Metropolitan State University, USA

INFORMATION SCIENCE REFERENCE

Hershey · New York

Director of Editorial Content:	Kristin Klinger
Director of Production:	Jennifer Neidig
Managing Editor:	Jamie Snavely
Assistant Managing Editor:	Carole Coulson
Managing Development Editor:	Kristin M. Roth
Assistant Development Editor:	Deborah Yahnke
Editorial Assistant:	Rebecca Beistline
Typesetter:	Sean Woznicki
Cover Design:	Lisa Tosheff
Printed at:	Yurchak Printing Inc.

Published in the United States of America by
Information Science Reference (an imprint of IGI Global)
701 E. Chocolate Avenue, Suite 200
Hershey PA 17033
Tel: 717-533-8845
Fax: 717-533-8661
E-mail: cust@igi-global.com
Web site: http://www.igi-global.com/reference

and in the United Kingdom by
Information Science Reference (an imprint of IGI Global)
3 Henrietta Street
Covent Garden
London WC2E 8LU
Tel: 44 20 7240 0856
Fax: 44 20 7379 0609
Web site: http://www.eurospanbookstore.com

Library of Congress Cataloging-in-Publication Data

Gender and information technology : moving beyond access to co-create global partnership / Mary Kirk.

   p. cm.

 Includes bibliographical references and index.
 Summary: "This book explores the decline in female involvement in technology and other discrimination related to the industry"--Provided by publisher.

 ISBN 978-1-59904-786-7 (hardcover) -- ISBN 978-1-59904-788-1 (ebook)
 1. High technology industries--Employees. 2. Sex discrimination against women. I. Kirk, Mary, 1955-
HC79.H53G46 2009
331.4'81004--dc22

                         2008022553

British Cataloguing in Publication Data
A Cataloguing in Publication record for this book is available from the British Library.

All work contributed to this book set is new, original material. The views expressed in this book set are those of the authors, but not necessarily of the publisher.

Table of Contents

Section II:
Perspectives on Dominator Social Institutions

Section III:
Perspectives on Partnership Social Institutions

Chapter XI

Foreword

Written with verve, compassion, and passion, *Gender and Information Technology* offers finely crafted tools for narrowing the digital divide that perpetuates inequality and injustice worldwide, marginalizing women and other socially disempowered groups. But in this much needed book, Mary Kirk does much more. She offers us a treasure trove of fascinating information that alternately enlightens, enrages, and empowers us to take an active role in creating a more just and caring future.

Sometimes what Kirk reveals about the male bias in science and technology is astonishing, as in her exposé of pornographic images in the critically acclaimed technology magazine *Wired* before was acquired by Condé Nast Magazines. Sometimes it is amusing, as when she notes how media accounts of female scientists who win Nobel prizes feel compelled to tell us the women are also wives, mothers, or grandmothers; information about family roles is notably absent when winners are male. Sometimes it is alarming, as when she shows how, despite years of efforts to change this, women and other marginalized groups such as African-Americans are subtly (and often not so subtly) discouraged from entering the IT field, and how even the language of the IT culture (terms like "hack," "blue screen of death," "boot," "crash") supports a stereotypically "masculine" culture of domination and violence, adding still another element to its inhospitality to women and the stereotypically "feminine." And sometimes it is shocking, as when she documents how IBM gave the Nazis the technological tools to identify and exterminate Europe's Jews, and how IBM head Tom Watson personally accepted a medal from Hitler for his support; it is a cautionary tale on the uses of technology unfortunately still all too relevant today.

Reading this book, I was constantly amazed by the wealth and breadth of Mary Kirk's knowledge (from video games for boys that no longer idealize violence and cruelty to "female" games such as "Barbie Fashion Designer," which reinforce gender stereotypes and consumerism) to her challenges to sacred academic cows, such as the notion of an apolitical, race- and gender-neutral science. And though serious, these challenges are often funny, as when she ridicules acclaimed writers who assert there is no discrimination by, so to speak, hoisting these "authorities" by their own petards, quoting their own uninformed and biased statements.

In this sense, Kirk gives us a primer for debunking pernicious myths about gender and race. But her main focus is not just on critique, it is on giving us positive examples and a vivid picture of what IT and our world can, and should, be. For instance, she gives us powerful examples of women who made important (though still generally ignored) contributions to science and technology, going back to Merit Path, an Egyptian physician around 2700 BC, from there to the great scientist Hypatia (370-415 AD), and then to Grace Murray Hopper (1906-1992), a still unrecognized pioneer computer programmer, and Shirley Ann Jackson and Jennie Patrick, who had to overcome both racism and sexism as pioneering women at MIT. Perhaps most important, and useful, Kirk gives us numerous real life illustrations of people, programs, and organizations that are today vigorously working for what she calls "partnership science and IT."

I want to here thank Mary Kirk for the excellent use she makes of my own work, of the new social categories of the *partnership system* and *domination system* and the cultural transformation theory introduced in my book *The Chalice and The Blade: Our History, Our Future*. It is a delight for me to see how Kirk not only uses but powerfully builds on my work, brilliantly applying it to her subject, imaginatively and always with great integrity taking it further. For instance, she details the dominator values still reflected and perpetuated in the powerful IT industry and uses the *partnerism* economic model introduced in my recent book *The Real Wealth of Nations* to show how IT can, and must, be used to create a *caring economics* worldwide.

In this connection, among the great strengths of this book are Kirk's creative proposals for change. She gives us instances from many world regions and adds to them her own proposals. An example is her detailed sketch of a new IT magazine she calls *connect!*, combining the best features of *Ms.* and *Wired* to give women a voice and images of themselves in the conversation about digital technology and culture.

As Kirk writes, the information revolution has created an unlocked gate allowing access into the "no trespassing zone" where the cultural conversation is defined, where the character and direction of IT is determined, and it is now up to traditionally marginalized groups to "co-create partnership language, communications, and media."

Gender and Information Technology provides guideposts to facilitate our entry into this important technological and cultural zone and to how we can provide leadership in shifting it from domination to partnership, thereby creating a *real* digital revolution.

Riane Eisler

Riane Eisler *is an eminent social scientist, attorney, and social activist best known as author of the international bestseller The Chalice and The Blade: Our History, Our Future, which is now in 23 languages, including most European languages and Chinese, Russian, Korean, Hebrew, Japanese, and Arabic. Her newest book, The Real Wealth of Nations: Creating a Caring Economics, has been hailed by Archbishop Desmond Tutu as "a template for the better world we have been so urgently seeking," by Gloria Steinem as "revolutionary," by Peter Senge as "desperately needed," and by Jane Goodall as "a call for action." Her other books include the award-winning The Power of Partnership and Tomorrow's Children, as well as Sacred Pleasure, a daring reexamination of sexuality and spirituality, and Women, Men, and the Global Quality of Life, statistically documenting the key role of the status of women in a nation's general quality of life. Dr. Eisler is president of the Center for Partnership Studies, keynotes conferences worldwide, and is a consultant to business and government on applications of the partnership model introduced in her work. She has received many honors, and is the only woman among 20 great thinkers including Hegel, Adam Smith, Marx, and Toynbee selected for inclusion in Macrohistory and Macrohistorians in recognition of the lasting importance of her work. Dr. Eisler can be contacted at center@partnershipway. org. Her website is www.rianeeisler.com.*

Preface

This preface describes both the need for and purpose of this book—an interdisciplinary, meta-analysis of the larger systemic issues related to women's underrepresentation as developers, users, and beneficiaries of technology. This chapter explores: the data on computer and Internet access for users and beneficiaries of technology as well as data on women's participation in higher education and the professions; the need for interdisciplinary scholarship such as this; the problem with the "science wars"; the organization of this text; and the need for complex multidimensional solutions to the problem of women's participation in IT.

THE DIGITAL DIVIDE

The exponential growth of technology is fostering a concurrent growth in information, but it is digital information, which is primarily accessible only to those with certain privileges. Dale Spender (1995) describes how the growth of written information as a result of the mass dissemination of the printing press around 1450 parallels the contemporary growth of digital information as a result of computer technology. Both events inspired tremendous social revolutions on a large scale. In 1450, a series of dramatic social shifts occurred when individuals (who due to their social and economic status did not have access to books) suddenly had access to the world of ideas previously only available to the wealthy. Today's digital revolution has the same dramatic potential for social change, and "it is the change in society—the shifts in power, wealth, influence, organization, and the environmental consequences—that matters to us all as individuals, and as communities" (Spender, 1995, p. xiv).

The issue of power, of who holds the power, and of how they exercise that power, is one of the most significant issues we face as a global technology community. We live in a world with great disparities in social conditions. "The United Nations

Human Development Report 1998 reported that the world's 225 richest people have a combined wealth of over $1 trillion, or equal to the combined annual income of the poorest 2.5 billion people—47 percent of the world" (Eisler, 2002, p. 141). A similar gap exists in the United States where "the richest 1 percent's share of reported income" grew from 9.6 percent in 1979 to 17.5 percent in 2003, while "the bottom 40 percent's share fell from 11.3 percent to 8.8 percent" (Eisler, 2007, p. 202). Further, the "United States has the highest rate of childhood poverty among" industrialized nations with twelve million children living in poverty, which equates to "more than one in five children" (Eisler, 2007, p. 258).

In a global environment of such massive human inequality, what purpose should technology serve? How might we use technology to close the existing (and rapidly growing) gap between the haves and have-nots worldwide? How might we use IT in service of human need instead of placing humans in service of the technology? What are the most critical global social concerns that technology might serve? What if we focused "economic investments not just on technologies that yield short-term corporate profits but on those that yield long-term social and environmental profits"? (Eisler, 2007, p. 185) What kind of social revolution might our technologies create?

The explosion of technology, especially information technology, has brought us to another historic social crossroads—one where we must consider the answers to questions like these because this time our decisions will not just influence our small corner of the world, they will impact our global human community. The ways in which technology (and access to technology) influences our lives is up to us. *If* we ensure that all have access to technology (as developers, users, and beneficiaries of it), and *if* we consider the social impact of our technologies, then we have the potential to rapidly and profoundly reshape our human lives for the better.

Unfortunately, we suffer from a growing digital divide both within the U.S. and between the technologically-developed nations and others worldwide. I use the term "digital divide" broadly here to refer to power and access gaps in relation to users, beneficiaries, and developers of technology. First, let us explore who uses and benefits from technology in the U.S. The well-documented numbers are familiar to anyone who has studied this issue. In 2003, only 62% of U.S. households had a personal computer and 55% had Internet access; that still left nearly half of the U.S. population without Internet access in their homes ("Computer," 2005, p. 1). Several studies (one by the National Science Foundation and another by Federal Reserve Bank economists) continue to show how differences in race, family income, and educational attainment influence computer usage in the U.S. One study shows that while 72.9% of Asian families and 63.9% of Whites own home computers, only 44.6% of Black and 44.3% of Hispanic families do[1] ("Computer," 2005, p. 2). Among those who own home computers, fewer have Internet access at home:

Asians (66.7%), Whites (57.0%), Blacks (36.0%), and Hispanics (36.0) ("Computer," 2005, p. 2). Another study shows that "while 61.2% of whites and 62.7% of Asians use computers at home, only 35.7% of blacks and 31.6% of Hispanics do" (Valletta & MacDonald, 2003, p. 2). In their survey of K-12 students, DeBell and Chapman (2006) found that 64% of Whites and 63% of Asians use computers in their own homes, while only 43% of Hispanics, 35% of Blacks, and 27% of American Indians do (p. 27).

Family income is another powerful determinant of computer ownership and usage. One study shows that "2.7% of families with incomes under $15,000 own computers compared to 77.7% of families with incomes over $75,000; and [*sic*] among all families with incomes under $35,000 computer ownership of white families was three times that of African-American families and four times that of Hispanic families" (Kirk & Zander, 2004, p. 171). A 2003 study shows the dramatic influence of family income on home Internet access: under $25,000 (30.7%), $25,000-$49,999 (57.3%), $50,000-$74,999 (77.9%), $75,000-$99,999 (85.8%), and $100,000 or more (92.2%) ("Computer," 2005, p. 2). Another study shows that the "usage rate is 21.1% for individuals with family income under $15,000 per year and 79.6% for individuals with family income of at least $75,000 per year" (Valletta & MacDonald, 2003, p. 1). A more recent study in 2006 shows little change in these earlier data related to family income and percentage of home computer use: under $20,000 (19%), $20,000-$34,999 (32%), $35,000-$49,999 (45%), $50,000-$74,999 (54%), and $75,000 or more (66%) (DeBell & Chapman, 2006, p. 26).

DeBell and Chapman (2006) show that race and income differentially influence whether or not K-12 students used computers at all, not just in the home. While 93% of White students and 91% of Asian students in their study use computers, only 86% of Blacks and American Indians, and 85% of Hispanics do (p. 6). Fortunately, schools have some positive influence on bridging the computer use gap, but the degree of impact is also affected by family income. Following are the data that DeBell and Chapman (2006) report on family income and the percentage of students who used computers at all (which included school, home, and work): under $20,000 (85%), $20,000-$34,999 (87%), $35,000-$49,999 (93%), $50,000-$74,999 (93%), and $75,000 or more (95%) (p. 66). The advantages accorded by having a home computer vs. only the limited access provided by work or school are still strongly differentially correlated with race and income.

Some research suggests that educational attainment has a stronger influence on home computer use than family income, while other research shows family income to be a stronger predictor of home computer use. One study shows that "home computer use ranges from 18.9% for those with no high school degree to 81.9% for those holding graduate degrees" (Valletta & MacDonald, 2003, p. 1). DeBell and Chapman (2006) echo these findings in their discovery that parental educational attainment directly and dramatically correlates with the percentage of K-12 students who use the Internet in their own home: less than high school (17%); high school credential (34%); some college (48%); bachelor's degree (56%); and graduate education (63%) (p. 26). U.S. Census data show a similarly strong correlation with educational attainment and home Internet access, but a slightly more powerful influence with regard to family income (cited in the previous paragraph): less than high school (20.2%); high school graduate/GED (43.1%); some college or associate's degree (62.6%); bachelor's degree (76.8%); and advanced degree (81.1%) ("Computer," 2005, p. 2).

Clearly, better access to education narrows the digital divide in relation to computer users, but who belongs to the exclusive club that actually develops the technology? Since IT is a professional field that increasingly requires formal academic training, one way to understand the demographics of those who develop technology is to look at the data on higher education. Table 1 lists data on the percentages of women and students of color who complete bachelor, master, and doctorate degrees in IT-related fields from two sources. The Taulbee Survey that is annually reported by the Computing Research Association (see www.cra.org) in *Computing Research News* shows the percentage of computer science and computer engineering degrees granted to women (Vesgo, 2007). The National Science Foundation report, *Women, Minorities, and Persons with Disabilities in Science and Engineering: 2007* (NSF 07-315), shows the percentage of women who receive engineering degrees as a percentage of all recipients, (see Table 1).

As this data evidence, while women degree recipients in computer science and engineering continue to make fairly steady progress, their numbers continue to grow slowly. They remain dramatically underrepresented in IT as compared to their numbers in the population as a whole. Another recent report shows:

That while the numbers of computer science majors at all levels of higher education has increased overall, there has also been a decline in the percentage of women and students of color at all levels. Of all computer science majors in the U.S., only 18.8% are women, 3.4% are African American, 3.6% are Hispanic, 21.7% are Asian/Pacific Islander (although this population is overrepresented, their percentage has still declined), and 0.4% are Native American. (Kirk & Zander, 2004, p. 169)

With this much inequity in a developed nation such as the U.S., how large is the digital divide on a global scale? Geographer Joni Seager (2003) reports that more "than 80% of Internet users are in the industrialized countries; Africa is the least wired" (p. 82). However, other data suggests that the numbers even in developed nations may not be as high. Balnaves, Donald, and Donald (2001) report the percentage of students who had access to the Internet from schools was 25% in France and

Table 1. Percentages of women who earned IT degrees

	Bachelor's (%)		Master's (%)		Doctorate (%)	
Year	Taulbee	NSF	Taulbee	NSF	Taulbee	NSF
1966		0.4		0.6		0.3
1967		0.5		0.6		0.3
1968		0.6		0.6		0.4
1969		0.8		0.7		0.3
1970		0.8		1.1		0.5
1971		0.8		1.1		0.5
1972		1.1		1.6		0.6
1973		1.2		1.7		1.4
1974		1.6		2.3		1.1
1975		2.1		2.5		1.7
1976		3.4		3.5		1.9
1977		4.9		4.4		2.8
1978		7.4		5.2		2.2
1979		9.1		6.1		2.5
1980		10.1		7.0		3.6
1981		11.1		8.1		3.9
1982		12.3		9.0		4.7
1983		13.1		9.3		4.5
1984		14.1		10.4		5.2
1985		14.5		10.7	11	6.3
1986		14.5		11.4	13	6.7
1987		15.3		12.6	10	6.5
1988		15.4		12.4	9	6.8
1989		15.2		13.0	13	8.3
1990		15.4		13.6	13	8.5
1991		15.5		14.0	12	9.0
1992		15.6		14.7	11	9.3
1993		15.9		14.8	14	9.2
1994	18	16.5	19	15.4	16	10.9
1995	18	17.3	20	16.2	16	11.6
1996	17	17.9	20	17.1	12	12.3
1997	17	18.4	23	18.1	14	12.3
1998	17	18.6	23	19.8	14	13.1

continued on following page

Table 1. (continued)

Year	Bachelor's (%)		Master's (%)		Doctorate (%)	
	Taulbee	NSF	Taulbee	NSF	Taulbee	NSF
1999	17	NA	26	NA	15	14.8
2000	19	20.5	26	20.7	15	15.7
2001	19	20.1	27	21.2	16	16.9
2002	18	20.9	25	21.2	18	17.5
2003	18	20.3	26	20.8	17	17.0
2004	17	20.5	25	21.1	18	17.6
2005	15	20.0	25	22.3	15	18.3
2006	14		23		18	

Germany, 28% in Italy and Japan, 59% in the U.K. and the U.S., 63% in Taiwan, 74% in Canada, and 78% in Sweden (p. 17).

Those who claim that access gaps are closing often point to public libraries as a solution. However, a few comparative numbers make clear that there is widely varying access to public libraries globally. In 1999, the number of people per public library was 6,000 per library in Germany, 11,000 per library in the U.K., 23,000 per library in France, 35,000 per library in Japan, 52,902 per library in Kenya, 337,000 per library in Egypt, and 1.5 million per library in Nigeria (Balnaves et al., 2001, p. 17). Language remains another barrier to Internet access today with English dominating the Internet, "although other languages, such as Spanish and Chinese, are expected to be equally widespread by 2020" (Balanves et al., 2001, p. 16). Further, since the vast majority of current Internet content is in English, we must ask exactly what members of other cultures have access to? The World Wide Web in its current manifestation has the potential to be a significant tool for spreading a new kind of cultural colonialism, diluting local values and beliefs in favor of those that reflect English-speaking industrialized cultures. Finally, all of these statistics on access assume a literate population. However, about "20 percent of the world's population and about 30 percent of women are illiterate" (Balnaves et al., 2001, p. 16). Given the deep-rooted causes of some of these barriers, how can we begin to increase the number of those who are developers, users, and beneficiaries of technology?

BRIDGING THE DISCIPLINARY DIVIDE

One important first step towards bridging the digital divide is to close the disciplinary gap between the social sciences (e.g., women's studies, ethnic studies, psychology, and sociology) and the "hard" sciences (e.g., math, engineering, and computer science); these two discourses rarely intersect, either theoretically or practically. In fact, traditional education is so narrowly focused on a single-discipline approach that ideas are often "taught as if they had nothing to do with each other—and often as if they had nothing to do with real life" (Eisler, 2002, p. 3). Given the rigid disciplinary boundaries within which most academic publishing occurs, scholars tend to write about their area of expertise for other experts in their field. Therefore, IT professionals tend to write about technology for technologists, and social scientists tend to write about social science for their colleagues.

There is little academic discourse that bridges these disciplinary gaps. This is the primary reason that although many scholars have recognized that there is a problem regarding the participation of women in IT, few have an adequate understanding of the complexities of the problem and its origins. Due to the narrow definition of disciplines and the emphasis on expertness, most educators, scholars, and administrators in education are only familiar with the discourse of their field of expertise. Feminist science studies scholars and other social scientists have spent decades researching and identifying the deep-rooted and systemic causes for the paucity of women and people of color in science and technology. However, their work is little known to those who are in the position to effect the greatest change, that is, IT scholars, educators, and administrators.

Existing books by women's studies and social science professionals tend to focus more deeply on the details of these systemic social influences, leaving out a broader overview of how these systems function that could be easily understood by anyone other than scholars in the field. Two books that attempt to offer broader overviews of feminism for a general audience are Allan G. Johnson's (1997) *The Gender Knot: Unraveling Our Patriarchal Legacy* and bell hooks'[2] (2000) *Feminism is for Everybody: Passionate Politics*. However, neither of these books explores how these issues manifest themselves in specific relation to science and technology.

In a 2002 paper, computer science educator Carol Zander and I first attempted to bridge the disciplinary gap and issued the following "call to action" to computer science educators:

Our task is also to bridge the intellectual divide between those who 'do' science and women's studies . . . When all of us better understand the challenges we face in recreating a more inclusive learning environment, we can collaborate towards even richer solutions together. (p. 123)

Two years later, we attempted to further narrow the disciplinary divide by reviewing two new books in the context of the question, "Which book might be most valuable to a computer science educator in higher education who is seeking a map to mend the gap created by the digital divide?" (Kirk & Zander, 2004, p. 169). *Unlocking the Clubhouse: Women and Computing*, written by a computer scientist and a social scientist, had already received a great deal of recognition among IT professionals. However, *Gender and Computers: Understanding the Digital Divide* (2003), written by social psychologists Joel Cooper and Kimberlee D. Weaver, was little known in the computer science community. Although the first book provides a good overview of the problem and proposes some solutions, the second book provides evidence of the deeper and often less well-understood influences of gender, race, and socioeconomic factors in terms of the negative impact of stereotyping, especially on the psychology of learning. Understanding the deeply-embedded nature of these problems and the ways in which they are woven into the fabric of all of our social institutions is critical to the creation of viable and lasting solutions.

This book proposes to further bridge the disciplinary divide by providing a "primer" on feminist science studies for IT scholars, educators, administrators, and all those who are interested in a deeper understanding of the large-scale, systemic, historical influences that have contributed to the dearth of women and people of color in IT today. I offer one feminist scholar's perspective on the root causes of women's poor representation as developers, users, and beneficiaries of technology. If computer scientists better understood the work of social scientists, they would not need to devote their energies exclusively to conducting research to further document a problem that is well-understood, but could also spend some energy in being creative change agents. Rushing to "solve" the problem using single-cause solutions, without a richer knowledge of the more complex, multifaceted social causes, will only ever lead us to partially successful results (if they are successful at all). I also propose a few strategies for addressing the problem from a variety of standpoints. However, my hope is that when equipped with a more thorough understanding of the problem's causes, we can all work together to devise even better, more complex solutions than those I propose here.

While most research focuses on documenting the details of a specific problem, often without any context at all, this book engages in an interdisciplinary, meta-analysis—engaging the results of many studies from diverse perspectives—in an attempt to help readers understand the issues in a broader social context and on a systems level. Mohanty, Russo, and Torres (1991) explain the value of interdisciplinary feminist scholarship that engages in "context-specific differentiated analysis"; feminist analysis must be context-specific by beginning with a *thorough* understanding of the context from which a social situation arises, and it must be differentiated by including issues and perspectives from multiple traditional disciplines, such as history, politics, and social science (p. 67). Eisler's (1987, 2000, 2002) systems science approach—"that analyzes how different parts of a system relate to each other and to the larger whole"—is central to the creative frame employed in the construction of this book (p. 3). Eisler (2007) describes our current social system as predominantly a "dominator" model (one based primarily on control) and offers suggestions for how we might move towards a "partnership" model (based primarily on respect); this text honors the concept of partnership by inviting readers to participate in knowledge creation with me, not merely to passively receive the information recorded on these pages (p. 5). My hope is that this broader interdisciplinary, systems-level perspective will help readers begin to participate in envisioning solutions—to inspire a multiplicity of voices and minds to start where they are to create change rather than wait for further expert scholarship to narrowly define the problem.

At its core, authentic feminist scholarship is about reorganizing hierarchical systems of power-over. However, like all human endeavors, this work is subject to the foibles of individual humans and their differing understandings of, or ideas about how to manifest, this new world vision. Therefore, this book is simply one attempt to describe the possibilities that I see in a new vision that places power in the hands of individuals rather than social institutions. The perspectives that I engage are just "a mapping of a terrain that has interested me and some others—not the mapping of it" (Harding, 1998, p. x). I do not pretend to present "THE" truth about these issues. I present the truth as I have come to know it, based on my social standpoint, and based on my scholarly expertise. As Harding (1998) wisely expressed, "truth claims all too often have the effect of closing down conversations, of asserting arrival at a final account" (p. x). My desire is to keep the conversation open, and I hope that readers will consider this the beginning of a dialogue "between peoples who rarely have occupied the same institutional locations" (Harding, 1998, p. x).

NEGOTIATING A CEASE FIRE IN THE "SCIENCE WARS"

In order to engage in a meaningful dialogue across what may be very different perspectives, it seems important to negotiate a cease fire with regard to the so-called "science wars."[3] Feminist scholars have spent decades asking and answering questions about how our social systems function, and feminist science scholars have focused on these questions in specific relation to science and technology. Unfortunately, feminism has become the new "F" word for many and as such feminist "perspectives are often charged with being biased, because they are overtly political" (Spanier, 2001, p. 370). However, this charge ignores the irrefutable fact that all knowledge creation is socially situated while many of those in the sciences worship the "cult of objectivity" which allows them to deny "social, cultural, and economic influences" on the production of scientific knowledge (Spanier, 2001, p. 370). To claim that scientific and technical knowledge is created in a social context that has some influence on that creation is tantamount to saying "the emperor has no clothes," which accounts (at least, in part) for the "outsider" status of feminist thought in relation to science. These issues are focused upon in detail in Chapter II in an exploration of dualisms and stereotypes.

The "science wars" are an example of how difficult it can be to even ask questions about how we think about and/or "do" science and technology; this is sacred territory and to challenge it risks accusations of scholarly sacrilege. However, this particular debate culminated in the publication of *Higher Superstition: The Academic Left and Its Quarrels with Science* (1994) by life scientist Paul Gross and mathematician Norman Levitt. Gross and Levitt sharply critiqued the work of social scientists exploring questions in science studies as inherently unscientific. Others chimed in on this debate. Many "hard" scientists supported Gross and Levitt while social scientists did not. In 1995, the New York Academy of Science sponsored a conference titled "The Flight from Science and Reason," inferring that social scientists were guilty of having "lost their sense" (Kleinman, 2000, p. 2).

In *Higher Superstition: The Academic Left and Its Quarrels with Science*, Gross and Levitt (1994) devote a chapter titled "Auspicating Gender" to critiquing the so-called "feminist attack" on science (p. 108). According to Gross and Levitt, sexist discrimination "is largely vestigial in the universities" and the only "*obvious* discrimination today is against white males" (p. 110). The authors also claim that women's studies and feminist criticism has "sacrosanct status" in the academy that provides "unprecedented immunity to the scrutiny and skepticism that are standard for other fields of inquiry" (p.110). This is most certainly not the case at my university where our women's studies program does not even have department status, is served by faculty housed in other "real" departments, and where it took me 4 years to get my course titled Women in Math, Science and Technology (the focus of my doctoral studies) through the curriculum approval process to meet a general education category in social science. My course proposal was exposed to a level of scrutiny far beyond that of other courses in more traditional disciplines. Feminists at universities nationwide are struggling with similar pressures and challenges to their credibility as scholars. In fact, there has been growing dialog at the National Women's Studies Association annual conferences in the past few years about how to help the discipline thrive in an environment of heightened "backlash" against the field. (See www.nwsa.org for more information.)

As further evidence of the favored status of women and the discrimination against white males, Gross and Levitt (1994) cite the increased numbers of women in certain areas of science, with a cursory acknowledgement of the low numbers of women in some areas; they cite no data to support this claim of increased female enrollment. They also cite the fact that job searches at universities have requirements in place to include women in their pool of candidates, but cite no data on the underrepresentation of women who actually occupy these faculty positions. The persistent disparity in women faculty salaries in relation to men is not examined in the text at all.

In 2004, the American Association of University Professors (AAUP) reported the following for women faculty positions in all areas: 58% (instructors), 54% (lecturers),

46% (assistant professors), 38% (associate professors), and 23% (full professors) (Curtis, n.d.). The ratio of women's salaries to men's in the same positions are less and these "ratios have changed very little over twenty-five years in the AAUP data" (Curtis, n.d.). In 2004, the AAUP reported the percentage of women's earnings in relation to men's in the same positions were: 96% (instructor), 90% (lecturer), 93% (assistant and associate professor), and 88% (full professor) (Curtis, n.d.). These data show that women occupy lower status and less permanent positions in higher numbers. The numbers of women in faculty positions in computer science and engineering follow a similar pattern with regard to rank and are much lower than women in other fields. The latest Taulbee Survey conducted by the Computing Research Association, reports that the share of women faculty in computer science and computer engineering has grown between 1990 and 2007, but women remain seriously underrepresented in these areas. In 1990 women were: 9% (assistant professors), 8% (associate professors), and 3% (full professors). In 2007 women were: 20% (newly hired tenure-track), 19% (assistant professors), 13% (associate professors) and 10% (full professors) (Vesgo, 2007, p. 2-3). However, Vesgo (2007) also notes that the National Science Foundation reported even lower data for women faculty during the same period in computer science and engineering: 14% (assistant professors), 13% (associate professors) and 8% (full professors) (p. 3).

Gross and Levitt (1994) also object to mathematical word problems with diverse subjects that try to avoid race, gender, and cultural stereotyping, but make no mention of the extensive literature from social psychology on the documented relationship between "stereotype threat" and academic performance. For example, they might have attempted to critique the extensive social psychology literature explored in Cooper and Weaver's *Gender and Computers: Understanding the Digital Divide* (2003). Gross and Levitt also object to questioning the use of sexist language and metaphor, but make no mention of a whole literature on how language as a social institution reifies beliefs and attitudes of all kinds. For example, for their argument to have weight, they would need to counter the extensive arguments made by scholars such as Evelyn Fox Keller (1985, 1992, 2002) and Dale Spender (1980, 1995) in multiple books and essays.

In making their case against feminism, especially feminist science studies, Gross and Levitt (1994) lump together diverse thinkers from a broad array of academic disciplines into a group they call "humanists and social scientists" and then redub "the academic left." With regard to questions and critiques of natural science, Gross and Levitt (1994) then accuse their self-defined "academic left" of "muddleheaded-ness," of not expressing a "self-consistent body of doctrine," of professing a variety of different doctrines "with no well-defined center," and "the absence of a central body of doctrine that can be said to constitute the quintessence of that view" (pp. 1-10). The problem with this approach is their method itself; if you define the terrain broadly enough, you might make a similar critique of any body of knowledge. For example, if I lumped together distinct disciplines such as applied mathematics, mechanical engineering, and nuclear medicine and labeled them "the academic right," I might make a similar critique that they have no central doctrine.

Gross and Levitt (1994) attempt to further support their claim by saying that these "misconceived attacks on science . . . grow out of a doctrinaire political position" (p. 9). The implicit message is that science as these authors do it has no such political position. However, the historical fact of research-funding alone weakens this position, even if you do not believe in seriously considering the ways in which the political, social, economic context in which scientific and technical knowledge is created may influence its creation.

Gross and Levitt (1994) also attempt to argue that recent critiques of natural science from the "academic left" stem from a "resentment" of science (p. 12). The authors claim that this resentment emanates from several sources: (1) a kind of scholarly envy of the hierarchical value placed on the sciences that makes social scientists want to "regain the high ground, to assert that the methods of social theory and literary analysis are equal in epistemic power to those of science" (p. 12); (2) "a lingering distrust of science and technology . . . [deriving] from the long tradition of fear and loathing toward the nuclear arsenals of the world"; and (3) "the misgivings of the environmental movement toward technology" (Gross & Levitt, 1994, p. 27-33). However, Gross and Levitt (1994) clearly have a political position (and seemingly deep-seated resentment) of their own. For example, how can a scholarly text, which claims to value scientific "objectivity," use a term like "fire-breathing feminist zealots" with implicit reference to respected scholars such as Sandra Harding and Evelyn Fox Keller, who they have explicitly included in their "academic left"? (p. 37). At the end of this same passage, they say, "Nor is this book in any sense an update of the *Malleus Maleficarum*; we shan't give our readers detailed instructions for finding the witch's mark" (Gross & Levitt, 1994, p. 37). Associating Harding and Keller with a medieval handbook for persecuting and burning "witches" does little to further dialogue. In the end, Gross' and Levitt's own biases are revealed in this passage:

If . . . the humanities department of MIT (a bastion, by the way, of left-wing rectitude) were to walk out in a huff, the scientific faculty could . . . patch together a humanities curriculum, to be taught by the scientists themselves . . . What the opposite situation—a walkout by the scientists—would produce . . . we leave to the reader's imagination. (p. 243)

I return to the accusation that Gross and Levitt make of the "academic left," that they are resentful of science and want to get back at scientists for the years of academic elitism that garners scientists more respect for their scholarship than social scientists. The passage above seems to suggest that it is Gross and Levitt who resent the voices of the "academic left" that are being heard in the discussion of science studies.

Gross and Levitt (1994) argue that only scientists are entitled to serve as *social* critics of science, and their key objection to others doing this work seems to be that "common to all of them is a failure to grapple seriously with the detailed content of the scientific ideas they propose to contest" (p. 235). They accuse their self-defined "academic left" of not bothering to "know science," but feeling entitled to critique it (p. 6). First, I might make the same accusation of these two authors; one is a life scientist and the other a mathematician. Using their own argument, I could claim that they are unqualified to critique a huge body of scholarship from a variety of disciplines that they admit themselves not to be expert in—the social sciences. There is a contradiction here. The authors simultaneously argue for the sanctity of disciplinary expertise, while they engage in an extensive critique of disciplines in which they are not expert. Further, their argument is simply inaccurate; most of the authors whose examples they critique are in fact scientists or mathematicians who do engage in a close critique of science. For example, Evelyn Fox Keller's academic training was in physics through to the doctoral level. However, lastly, and most importantly to this author, their argument misses the point that there is great value in interdisciplinary research and interdisciplinary dialogue. Perhaps if we could respectfully dialogue across the rigid confines of traditional disciplinary boundaries, we might have developed an even richer knowledge tradition by now. I believe that it is the perceived threats to the sanctity of the knowledge tradition itself that is at the core of Gross' and Levitt's concerns.

As Daniel Lee Kleinman points out in *Science, Technology and Democracy* (2000), it seems odd that this debate only arose in the mid-90s when the scholarship in science studies that first explored the social construction of knowledge was published in the 70s and 80s. Kleinman (2000) suggests that the debate arose partly due to significant changes in public policy that restructured research funding practices and heightened the competition for resources. After World War II and during the Cold War years, most funding was based on a "social contract with science" in which the government allowed scientists autonomy and control over their research if they would focus their research on "improvements in national social and economic well-being" (p. 3). As Kleinman (2000) reasons, several things have changed since then: (1) the Cold War is over and there is no longer a need to fund research that promotes "a vibrant democracy in contrast to the totalitarian world of our Soviet adversaries"; and (2) the promise of science's social contract has become a mixed blessing in the eyes of the public with some scientific research saving lives by curing human diseases while other research results in technologies that threaten lives by contributing to disasters such as Love Canal and Three Mile Island (pp. 3-4). Kleinman suggests that the primary reason that the science wars debate occurred was an "effort to reinforce a crumbling boundary: a wall that divided scientists and lay citizens, a barrier that legitimated scientists' autonomy on expert matters and dictated citizen silence" (p. 5). However, especially in a democracy, one question is at least worth asking: Why can't average citizens be involved in public policy with regard to science and technology that will impact their lives?

Although I endorse Gross and Levitt's right to disagree, the so-called "science wars" are a manifestation of the very climate (in which such unsubstantiated claims against feminist scholars can easily gain a large voice) that we need to better understand and address if we are ever to create a more inclusive science and technology. This "us v. them" attitude is ironically a pointer to the very problem itself. The fact remains that as of January 14, 2005, we still lived in a society where Harvard University President Dr. Lawrence Summers found it appropriate to build a case that women's underrepresentation in science and technology is primarily due to "issues of intrinsic aptitude" and that "socialization and continuing discrimination" are lesser factors (Bombardieri, 2005). Summers was speaking to a select group of 50 elite scholars attending an invitation-only conference titled "Diversifying the Science and Engineering Workforce" sponsored by the National Bureau of Economic Research (Bombardieri, 2005). Summers' remarks instigated a walk-out by some of the notable women in attendance, such as then chancellor designate (later chancellor) of the University of California, Santa Cruz Dr. Denise Denton[4], who held a B.S., M.S., and Ph.D. in electrical engineering from MIT and was the first woman in the U.S. to serve as Dean of a College of Engineering at an NRC-designated Research One university (She served 9 years as Dean at the University of Washington) ("Chancellor," 2006).

What makes these remarks even more difficult to comprehend is that Summers' scholarship is in economics, but he felt free to use "evidence" such as observing his own twin daughters to justify his argument that differences in aptitude are the primary reason why there is a shortage of women in science and engineering, ignoring the contradictory evidence of scholars who study these issues. Meanwhile, the percentage of tenured job offers made to women in Harvard's College of Arts and Sciences declined during his tenure; in 2004, only 4 of 32 tenured job offers went to women. To be fair, Summers denounced this as "unacceptable and promised to work on the problem." He also subsequently apologized for his comments at the conference, but this did not stop the Harvard faculty from passing a vote of no confidence in his leadership a few months later (Bombardieri, 2005). Unfortunately, Summers' sense of entitlement to comment on the causes of the problem without an adequate understanding is not uncommon, and it is one of the primary reasons that we all need a better understanding of the complexity of these issues if we are ever to create lasting change.

ORGANIZATION OF THIS BOOK

This book uses a feminist perspective to place what we know so far about the under-representation of women as developers, users, and beneficiaries of IT (from early education through to the workforce) in the context of the larger social institutions that influence our lives, and describes how shifting from a dominator to a partnership social system can make a difference in who participates in IT. Each chapter begins with a list of objectives that identify the broader understanding that readers should gain from that chapter and ends with a list of "Questions for Reflective Dialog." Rather than providing a summary, my hope is that these questions will inspire readers to reflect in dialog with others, enabling them to co-create knowledge in relation to the ideas I have shared in this book.

The book is organized in three sections. Section I: One Feminist's Perspective (Chapters I through III) lays the foundation for understanding the perspective that informs this book by exploring the ways in which the fundamental elements of a dominator social model undergird all of our social institutions, especially how they influence women's participation as developers, users, and beneficiaries of technology.

Chapter I: "Demyth-ifying Feminism: Reclaiming the 'F' Word" explores how and why feminism became a "dirty" word and offers my perspective on the feminist project. I also describe why I believe that feminism offers a useful perspective from which to examine power relations in terms of both individual identity and the beliefs and attitudes purveyed by social institutions. To further clarify the meaning of feminism, I explore the following six myths about feminism and the social system that we have created: (1) it's just the way things are; (2) it's just about women being equal to men; (3) men and women are just different by nature; (4) feminists want to be like men; (5) I don't have a race, I'm White; and (6) it's "their" problem, not mine.

Chapter II: "Dualisms and Stereotypes: Tools of Domination" explores the concept of gender as the ultimate dualism, and demonstrates the pervasive ways in which stereotypes are used as tools of domination in dominator societies. Dualistic thinking encourages us to organize knowledge in simplistic "either/or" terms, rather than considering the "both/and" complexities of our real human experience. Understanding gender, the ultimate socially-defined dualism, can help one begin to grasp the deeply-embedded nature of gendered attitudes and beliefs in the social institutions through which we learn about IT. The stereotypes (of gender, race, class, physical ability, etc.) that are purveyed by our social institutions are some of the most enduring and significant influences on our sense of individual identity as well as how we perceive (and are perceived by) others in the social hierarchy. An in-depth understanding of stereotypes, especially gender stereotypes, is critical to beginning to understand how to address the participation of women in IT as developers, users, and beneficiaries.

Chapter III: "Gendered Philosophy of Science: Science is Male, Nature is Female" lays the last few bricks of the foundation for this book by examining the gender dualism (science=male, nature=female) that is at the core of the philosophy of science and influences the ways in which we have learned to think about science, as well as the attitudes and beliefs about who can (or should) participate in science and IT.

Section II: Perspectives on Dominator Social Institutions (Chapters IV through VII) examines how four social institutions—media, language, education, and business—teach the values, attitudes, and beliefs of a dominator society in specific relation to IT. Each chapter begins with a few general themes representative of that social institution and then provides an in-depth example of how these themes are reflected in specific relation to science and IT.

Chapter IV: "Mass Media as Social Institution: The *Wired* Example" explores the role of mass media as a primary social institution that teaches us about ourselves and our world. In the U.S., and in the global IT field, media play an increasingly powerful role in terms of interpreting our world, and that interpretation also makes heavy use of stereotypes to convey a message. This chapter offers a few general examples of the ways in which this influences women's participation in IT as well as a more in-depth analysis of one form of mass media—the widely-read computing magazine, *Wired*. *Wired* offers an interesting ground for analysis of the influence of stereotypes in mass media since one of its founding purposes was to discuss technology in relation to culture.

Chapter V: "Language as Social Institution: The Male-Centered IT Culture" offers an analysis of the role of communication and language as another social institution that teaches us the values, attitudes, and beliefs of our culture and that uses stereotypes pervasively. I explore these issues by discussing why "political correctness" matters, our gendered communication style, the male-centered IT language and culture, and the influence of dominance, violence, and sex metaphors in IT on women's participation.

Chapter VI: "Education as Social Institution: Understanding Her-Story" explores the ways in which education as a social institution teaches us values, attitudes, and beliefs. Education plays a particularly key role since it is the social institution that defines the knowledge tradition itself—the bounds around what is known, what it is important to know, and who knows. This chapter offers a brief her-story of women in math, engineering, and IT, as well as describing trends in education and employment.

Chapter VII: "Business as Social Institution: Global Issues in IT" explores ways in which the global IT business operates as another significant social institution purveying attitudes, values, and beliefs that contribute to the underrepresentation of women as beneficiaries, users, and developers of technology. This chapter analyzes the following major issues: (1) the values reflected in the global IT business model; (2) the relationship between postcolonialism and U.S. participation in global economic development; and (3) the rising social and political significance of economic development in India and China with specific relation to the IT industry. As a way of asking questions about what values the global IT industry might be concerned about, we look through the lens of an in-depth example—IBM's global business relationships and the Holocaust.

Section III: Perspectives on Partnership Social Institutions (Chapters VIII through XI) offers ideas and examples for how we might develop and teach the values, attitudes, and beliefs of a partnership social model in specific relation to IT. These chapters offer examples in relation to the same four social institutions explored earlier: media, language, education, and business. I have separated a deeper exploration of the problem from suggestions for "solutions" for several reasons. One reason, and perhaps the most important one, is that I wanted to offer readers the opportunity to begin to envision their own solutions as we explore the problem more deeply together. Another reason is that although my suggestions emanate from my expert perspective on the available research in this area, they are not the only correct answers. My hope is that by allowing readers to begin to frame their own solutions as they read, my solutions will be viewed as less prescriptive and more as new perspectives from which to think about how to develop more complex, systemic solutions together.

Chapter VIII: "Partnership Language and Media: Creating a New IT Culture" offers ideas for how we might shift away from a dominator social model to a partnership model in relation to language and media. This chapter explores the following ideas for how we can co-create the conditions that encourage partnership language and media: (1) identifying core components of a partnership culture that are particularly relevant to language and media; (2) developing partnership language and communication by understanding the cultural components of voice and silence, focusing on linkages in relationships in IT, practicing dialogic process, and practicing nonviolent communication; and (3) offering an example of new partnership media—*connect!* magazine.

Chapter IX: "Partnership Science and Technology Education" explores strategies for redefining education as a social institution. This chapter explores the following suggestions for shifting education (especially science and IT education) towards a partnership model by: (1) exploring partnership ways of knowing; (2) considering the needs and perspectives of users and beneficiaries of science and IT in education; (3) educating teachers from kindergarten through college to better understand how our current system works as well as how to co-create partnership; (4) redefining student-teacher relationships in terms of partnership; (5) co-creating collaborative learning environments; (6) developing partnerships systems of testing, evaluating, and measuring learning; and (7) offering examples of partnership curricula and programs.

Chapter X: "Partnership Global IT Business" introduces a partnership economic model and attempts to envision answers to questions about our social responsibility to each other as a human community with regard to the direction of development efforts in the global IT industry. For example: How might we use technology to close the existing (and rapidly growing) gap between the haves and have-nots worldwide? What are the most critical global social concerns that technology might serve? To address some of these questions, this chapter explores the following topics in relation to co-creating a partnership global IT business: (1) U.S. economic dominance in IT; (2) "partnerism" a new economic model; (3) global IT development ideas between developed and developing nations; (4) partnership IT policy making; and (5) examples of partnership science and IT.

Chapter XI: "A Concluding Pledge: With Technology and Justice for All" recaps the main themes of this book and offers suggestions for (1) future research, and (2) where you can begin to co-create partnership and provides an epilogue from the author that demonstrates the ways in which social change is a lifelong learning experience.

Appendix: Recommended Resources offers a few resources for readers to educate themselves further about the issues raised in this book. This is not meant to be a comprehensive list, but offers a good starting point for further reading. As I suggested earlier, the work of understanding an issue whose roots are as deeply-embedded in our social structures as this one requires a long-term commitment. The readings are grouped in the following sections, which loosely relate to the structure of this book: feminism and partnership, feminist science studies (I have included a few things here, such as Cohoon and Aspray, that are not explicitly feminist, but are doing nonetheless important work to understand the problem of women's participation in IT), media studies, language and communication, education, her-story, global economics and partnership science, films, and organizations working toward change.

FINDING OUR COMMON GROUND WHILE CREATING COMPLEX SOLUTIONS

We cannot seek unidimensional solutions to such a multidimensional problem as the underrepresentation of women as developers, users, and beneficiaries of technology. There is no one-size-fits-all solution to the problem of increasing the participation of women in IT. We need complex multifaceted solutions for a complex multifaceted set of problems. And, it will take all of us, technologists and social scientists, educators and business leaders, women and men, working together to create the kind of change that will really make a difference in women's lives and in our world. In order for all of us to participate in envisioning and enacting more comprehensive, more complex, and more responsive solutions, we need a richer understanding of the problems in their complexities.

When addressing issues that are labeled as social concerns, some believe that it is enough to attend a diversity workshop or read a book or two about gender, race, and class. However, that is unlikely to lead one to the kind of deep understanding that is required to participate in constructive change on a larger scale. Understanding how systems of power and privilege work in our society is a real challenge because the nature of these systems is to teach those who are privileged by them to be blind to the ways in which they are privileged. With a limited understanding, which is all that many of us have, organizational change efforts can be too simplistic or too short lived. Johnson (2006) describes the problem:

Most organizations' failure in the area of diversity occurs not because they're run by mean-spirited bigots—few are—but because they deal with issues of privilege badly or not at all, unless a crisis forces the issue. Even then, they deal with it only enough to make it seem to go away, which usually doesn't include confronting the reality of privilege and oppression. (p. 65)

In their comprehensive edited collection *Women and Information Technology: Research on Underrepresentation* (2006), J. McGrath Cohoon and William Aspray explore the latest research on women in IT from early education through higher education to the workforce. Cohoon and Aspray support the point I am making here when they suggest that "[w]ell-intentioned interventions, based on the best intuition of pioneering activists, have not been able to reverse the downward trends, perhaps because more nuanced strategies based on the complexities of the situation were needed" (p. ix). The authors add that two things contribute to the continued underrepresentation of women in IT: (1) "inadequate understanding of the underlying and immediate causes" and (2) "inadequate intervention efforts" (p. 137).

Addressing the underrepresentation of women in IT is about helping more of those who are in positions of power to understand how deeply and tightly these problems are woven into the fabric of our society. It is a large-scale project that requires a long-term commitment by a group of well-informed change agents who are committed to ripping up the deeply buried roots of systemic oppression. Unfortunately, adopting a traditional scientific view may lead some to delay action because they believe that we do not understand the relationship between gender and participation in IT well-enough. I believe that social scientists do understand the relationship between gender and participation in IT very well, and that we simply need to talk and work across the disciplinary divide. In fact, regarding concerns such as the underrepresentation of women in IT, I would like to see us move away from an "either/or" argument altogether. We might be better served by adopting a "both/and" perspective; those who choose to continue to further document the problem in increasingly detailed levels of specificity can (and should) continue to do that kind of research, *and* those who feel that the problem is well-understood can begin to commit their energy to finding better, more creative, and more complex solutions to solving it. We can do both. Fortunately, there has been a recent shift away from research that simply seeks to understand the problem to more complex research efforts that seek to solve the problem. Cohoon and Aspray (2006) cite new NSF programs such as "the ITWF, the new Broadening Participation in Computing, and Gender Science and Engineering" as well as organizations such as the National Center for Women in IT, the Anita Borg Institute, and many others (p. 471).

Feminism has long supported the notion of linking theory and action, of not separating what we know from applying that knowledge to change our world. This is one reason that a feminist perspective may be particularly useful in addressing the underrepresentation of women as developers, users, and beneficiaries of IT. Interestingly, although they only mention feminism (or feminist perspectives) on a few pages of their nearly 500-page book, Cohoon and Aspray seem to share my perspective that it is time to act:

We cannot afford to wait to act until we have a perfect understanding of the issues; we are wasting too many resources by having so few women involved in computing—a waste for their own careers and for the nation as a whole. We can learn while we act . . . (p. 473)

In *Our Endangered Values: America's Moral Crisis* (2005), former U.S. President and Nobel Peace Prize winner Jimmy Carter said, "It is in America's best interests to understand one another and to find as much common ground as possible" (p. 5). This is as good a place as any to begin this book, because in the end, this is a story about finding our common ground and about cultivating a new society from that rich fertile soil. This is not another story about the so-called "battle of the sexes"—a violent metaphor which in itself reflects the dominator social system that we are all caught up in. This is not another story about "us" vs. "them." This is a story about the ways in which we are all one "us."

This is a story about using feminist perspectives to find common ground where we can better understand the ways in which the social system that we have co-created is not serving us. This is a story about how to shift from a dominator to a partnership society. This is a story about building a democratic society for the citizens of this globe. This is a story about how IT could play a major role in such a constructive social shift. As Spender (1995) explains, the digital revolution is creating a tremendous social shift, but the direction of that shift will be defined by those who participate in it. We are at a crossroads as a human species, and the road that we take will be determined both by the limits of what we already know and by our capacity to imagine the world we have yet to create. This book is my attempt to help us envision that new world in relation to IT, to help us envision moving beyond the simple notion of access to the richer notion of co-creating global partnership.

REFERENCES[5]

Balnaves, M., Donald, J., & Donald, S. H. (Eds.). (2001). *The Penguin atlas of media and information*. New York: Penguin Putnam.

Bombardieri, M. (2005, January 17). Summers' remarks on women draw fire. *The Boston Globe*. Retrieved on September 22, 2007, from http://www.boston.com/news/education/higher/articles/2005/01/17/summers_remarks_on_women_draw_fire/

Carter, J. (2005). *Our endangered values: America's moral crisis*. New York: Simon and Schuster.

Chancellor Denice D. Denton: A Brief Biography. (2006, June). *Remembering Chancellor Denton Web site at the University of California, Santa Cruz*. Retrieved on September 22, 2007, from http://www.ucsc.edu/administration/denice_denton/biography.asp.

Computer and Internet Use in the United States: 2003. (2005, October). U.S. *Department of Commerce Economics and Statistics Administration. U.S. Census Bureau (P23-208)*. Retrieved September 23, 2007, from http://www.census.gov/prod/2005pubs/p23-208.pdf

Cooper, J., & Weaver, K. D. (2003). *Gender and computers: Understanding the digital divide*. Mahwah, NJ: Erlbaum.

Curtis, J. W. (n.d.) Faculty salary and faculty distribution fact sheet 2003-04. *American Association of University Professors*. Retrieved September 23, 2007, from http://www.aaup.org/AAUP/pubsres/research/2003-04factsheet.htm

DeBell, M., & Chapman, C. (2006, September). Computer and Internet use by students in 2003. *U.S. Department of Education: Institute of Education Sciences, National Center for Education Statistics* (NCES 2006-065). Retrieved September 5, 2007, from www.eric.ed.gov.ezproxy.metrostate.edu

Eisler, R. (1987). *The chalice and the blade: Our history, our future*. San Francisco: Harper San Francisco.

Eisler, R. (2000). *Tommorrow's children: A blueprint for partnership education in the 21st century*. Boulder, CO: Westview.

Eisler, R. (2002). *The power of partnership: Seven relationships that will change your life*. Novato, CA: New World.

Eisler, R. (2007). *The real wealth of nations: Creating a caring economics*. San Francisco: Berrett-Koehler.

Gross, P. R., & Levitt, N. (1994). *Higher superstition: The academic left and its quarrels with science*. Baltimore: Johns Hopkins UP.

Harding, S. (1998). *Is science multicultural?: Postcolonialisms, feminisms, and epistemologies*. Bloomington: Indiana UP.

Keller, E. F. (1985). *Reflections on gender and science*. New Haven, CT: Yale UP.

Keller, E. F. (1992). *Secrets of life, secrets of death: Essays on language, gender and science*. New York: Routledge.

Keller, E. F. (2002). *Making sense of life: Explaining biological development with models, metaphors, and machines*. Cambridge, MA: Harvard UP.

Kirk, M., & Zander, C. (2002, December). Bridging the digital divide by co-creating a collaborative computer science classroom. *Journal of Computing in Small Colleges, 18*(2), 117-125.

Kirk, M., & Zander, C. (2004, December). Narrowing the digital divide: In search of a map to mend the gap. *Journal of Computing in Small Colleges, 20*(2), 168-175.

Kleinman, D. L. (Ed.). (2000). *Science, technology and democracy*. Albany: SUNY.

Mohanty, C., Russo, A., & Torres, L. (Eds.). (1991). *Third world women and the politics of feminism*. Bloomington, IN: Indiana UP.

Seager, J. (2003). *The Penguin atlas of women in the world*. New York: Penguin.

Spender, D. (1980). *Man made language*. London: Routledge.

Spender, D. (1995). *Nattering on the net: Women, power and cyberspace*. North Melbourne, Australia: Spinifex.

Valletta, R., & MacDonald, G. (2003). Is there a digital divide? *FRBSF Economic Letter, 2003-38*, 1-3. Retrieved December 19, 2007 from http://www.frbsf.org/publications/economies/letter/2003/el2003-38.html

Vesgo, J. (2007, July 31). CRA Taulbee trends: Female students and faculty. *Computer Research Association*. Retrieved September 18, 2007, from http://www.cra.org/info/taulbee/women.html

Women, Minorities, and Persons with Disabilities in science and engineering: 2007. (2007). *National Science Foundation, Division of Science Resources Statistics* (NSF 07-315). Retrieved April 3, 2008, from http://www.nsf.gov/statistics/wmpd/

ENDNOTES

[1] I have included the only four racial/ethnic categories (White, Black, Asian, and Hispanic) included in this study. Native Americans and biracial data were not gathered.

[2] Gloria Watkins chose not to capitalize her pseudonym "bell hooks" in order to give primacy to the ideas over the author.

[3] The description of this debate as a "war" is a classic example of how themes of dominance and violence pervade our society as well as science and technology. I will discuss these issues further in subsequent chapters.

[4] I met Denise Denton briefly when she participated in a conference that I organized on women in computing at the University of Washington, Bothell campus while I was teaching in the Computing and Software Systems program. She was personable, kind, and humble in a way that struck me as particularly remarkable given her history of exceptional achievement. Sadly, Dr. Denton took her own life on June 24, 2006 after serving 16 months as Chancellor of the University of California, Santa Cruz (UCSC). Certainly, there are many factors (most of which are mysterious to those of us who are still here) that might cause one to commit suicide. However, as a feminist science studies scholar, I know too much not to at least wonder whether the lifelong weight of the forces I explore in this book on her courageous soul had finally become too much to bear. If people only knew what carrying this burden really costs women, even great women.

[5] Some portions of this chapter may have appeared in, and are reprinted with permission from Kirk, M. (2006). Bridging the digital divide: A feminist perspective on the project. In G. Trajkovski (Ed.), *Diversity in Information Technology Education: Issues and Controversies* (pp. 38-67). Hershey, PA: Information Science Publishing.

Mary Kirk, Ph.D.

Acknowledgment

I owe a deep debt of gratitude to the many scholars whose thoughtful and insightful perspectives first shined the light in the dark. However, my special thanks go to the following: Riane Eisler, whose ideas about dominator and partnership societies are the spine around which the creature that I have given birth to here was shaped; Dale Spender, whose leading edge thinking on technology and social good gave me a broader perspective about the importance of this historical moment in IT; Alan Johnson, for clarifying the big picture framework of individuals in relation to social institutions; Sue V. Rosser, for helping me envision the pathways to include more women in science; and bell hooks, whose many ideas over many years of study have modeled how to write about feminism in an accessible way and whose persistent courage has helped me to manifest my own.

I originally germinated the sprouts of these ideas while completing my Ph.D. in Women's Studies/Women in Computing. Therefore, I want to thank the members of my doctoral committee for their contributions to the completion of my graduate degree and the development of my early thinking in this area. Dr. Judith Arcana, the best editor I have ever worked with, always helped to refine the lump of coal that was my writing into a diamond. Dr. Rita Arditti was among the first women scientists to write about gender in science and her perspective was invaluable. Dr. Jane Brem challenged me to "not forget about the men," which made me both a better teacher and a better women's studies scholar. Dr. Carol Zander shared her lived perspectives as a woman in computer science and as a gifted educator. Dr. Cindy Cone's research on the impact of single-sex learning environments in K-12 also contributed to my thinking in this area.

I am employed at Metropolitan State University where the emphasis for faculty is on teaching over research. Although the university did not have an infrastructure to support me in researching and developing this book, I was blessed with a few people who chose to help just because they believed in the project. Staff-member

Shelley Hunt eagerly advertised for students who might want to earn internship credit as student researchers. My deepest gratitude also goes to several of my undergraduate students who were so excited by the book that they volunteered their time as research assistants. Terry Bebertz spent months e-mailing me links to current research on women in IT. Trisha Gill thoroughly researched the Lawrence Summers incident for me. Mary Lee researched and synthesized essays on the philosophy of science for me to review.

The book might not be finished and the writing would certainly not be what it is without the editorial support that I was blessed with. IGI Global Editor Meg Stocking was very supportive about the possibilities for the book and some of my questions about audience, tone, and structure at a time when I was riddled with doubts, and IGI Global Editor Rebecca Beistline helped shepherd me to the finish line. I also want to thank the three anonymous reviewers that IGI assigned for their comments on my manuscript; most were incredibly positive (giving me the energy-boost I needed to complete final revisions), and the rest were supportive and constructive (helping me develop a much clearer final manuscript). Angel-Saint M. Laurel Walsh (she swears she is neither an angel nor a saint, but I do not believe her) was the editor of my dreams. She seemed to be inside my head and speaking with my voice, while simultaneously offering incisive assessments and observations that made for a far, far better book than I could have created without her. Laurel had unwavering confidence in the book's purpose from the moment that she read the first draft, and she eagerly waved her bright, colorful pom-poms to cheer me over the finish line when I was tiring from the writing marathon. I look forward to working on my next book with her soon.

I also owe a deep debt of gratitude to Dr. Catherine Warrick for her attentive ear, wise observations, and spiritual nurturance. She helped me see why I needed to write this book and I have no doubt that without her clear vision, there would be no book today. She also reminded me to read Riane Eisler's latest book on global economics which added tremendous clarity to my thinking about the global IT business.

There would be no book and I cannot imagine my existence without the support of the two most important people in my life. My best friend (and developmental psychologist) Dr. Carol Hawk introduced me to Uri Bronfenbrenner's work, spent countless hours on the phone with me sharing her unique insights about these ideas, and has shown me during our nearly 30-year friendship what empathy, caring, and partnership really look like. Bless you, Buddy. My sister (and lifelong friend) Kerry Kirk has steadfastly supported my every wish and dream, no matter how absurd or fantastic, since the moment I was born over 53 years ago. There are no words adequate enough to thank her for gracing me with a lifetime of such enduring faith and unconditional love. Thank you, sister-friend. Fixed the newel post!

To my readers, I want to thank you for reading this book and for having faith in our possibilities as human beings to manifest our greatest potential. I hope this book helps light the way to a brighter future for us all.

Mary Kirk, Ph.D.
Sister, friend, teacher, colleague, neighbor, global citizen

Section I
One Feminist's Perspective

Section I: One Feminist's Perspective (Chapters I through III) lays the foundation for understanding the perspective that informs this book by exploring the ways in which the fundamental elements of a dominator social model undergird all of our social institutions, especially how they influence women's participation as developers, users, and beneficiaries of technology.

Chapter I: "Demyth-ifying Feminism: Reclaiming the 'F' Word" explores how and why feminism became a "dirty" word and offers my perspective on the feminist project. I also describe why I believe that feminism offers a useful perspective from which to examine power relations in terms of both individual identity and the beliefs and attitudes purveyed by social institutions. To further clarify the meaning of feminism, I explore the following six myths about feminism and the social system that we have created: (1) it's just the way things are; (2) it's just about women being equal to men; (3) men and women are just different by nature; (4) feminists want to be like men; (5) I don't have a race, I'm White; and (6) it's "their" problem, not mine.

Chapter II: "Dualisms and Stereotypes: Tools of Domination" explores the concept of gender as the ultimate dualism, and demonstrates the pervasive ways in which stereotypes are used as tools of domination in dominator societies. Dualistic thinking encourages us to organize knowledge in simplistic "either/or" terms, rather than considering the "both/and" complexities of our real human experience. Understanding gender, the ultimate socially-defined dualism, can help one begin to grasp the deeply-embedded nature of gendered attitudes and beliefs in the social institutions through which we learn about IT. The stereotypes (of gender, race, class, physical ability, etc.) that are purveyed by our social institutions are some of the most enduring and significant influences on our sense of individual identity as well as how we perceive (and are perceived by) others in the social hierarchy. An in-depth understanding of stereotypes, especially gender stereotypes, is critical to beginning to understand how to address the participation of women in IT as developers, users, and beneficiaries.

Chapter III: "Gendered Philosophy of Science: Science is Male, Nature is Female" lays the last few bricks of the foundation for this book by examining the gender dualism (science=male, nature=female) that is at the core of the philosophy of science and influences the ways in which we have learned to think about science, as well.

Chapter I
Demyth–ifying Feminism:
Reclaiming the "F" Word

OBJECTIVES

This chapter aims to help you understand the following:

- Why feminism became the "F" word and why you need not fear it.
- How we created our dominator social system, an overview of its characteristics, and the characteristics of a partnership social system.
- How an understanding of privilege and oppression in our social systems will carry us further than simply emphasizing equality.
- How understanding the ways in which social institutions (such as family, media, language, education, and business) influence individual identity formation can reveal a richer understanding of gender than simply focusing on the nature/nurture debate.
- How social power and leadership are gendered.
- Why an understanding of race matters to us all.
- Why we all must be allies in co-creating a partnership society.

INTRODUCTION

One barrier to more people understanding the work of feminist scholars is a fallacious view of "feminism" that has transformed an entire area of scholarship into the "F" word. The term itself (as well as the purpose of feminist movement) is poorly understood, and in most cases *mis*understood, even in academic circles. In

Feminism is for Everybody: Passionate Politics, renowned cultural critic and feminist theorist bell hooks (2000) describes her experience of conversing with people about her work. Although most people are excited to ask questions about her work as a cultural critic of mass media since they participate in popular culture, hooks describes how the tone of the conversation typically changes when she mentions feminism:

I tend to hear all about the evil of feminism and the bad feminists: how 'they' hate men; how 'they' want to go against nature—and god; how 'they' are all lesbians; how 'they' are taking all the jobs and making the world hard for White men, who do not stand a chance. (hooks, 2000, p. vii)

When hooks asks these same people about feminist authors they have read, or feminist lectures they have heard, or feminist activists they know, she usually discovers that all of their knowledge about feminism has come to them third hand and largely through the messages of mass media. In "The 'F' Word: How the Media Frame Feminism," Debra Baker Beck (1998) supports hooks' suggestion that stereotypical images of feminists and feminism in mass media (including broadcast, print, and film) have affected "society's acceptance or rejection of the movement and its goals" (p. 139).

In her now classic work *Backlash: The Undeclared War Against American Women*, Susan Faludi (1991) engages in an in-depth exploration of the patterns in messages from mass media which are largely anti-feminist. Faludi documents how many forms of media (including movies, television programs, fashion magazines, political reporting, nonfiction writers and scholars in a variety of disciplines, and popular psychology) engage in a two-part process that both "blames" feminism for women's sense of distress in a time of great social change and systematically undermines women's progress in their own eyes. At best, mass media delivers a distorted message about feminism which contributes to a reticence, even on the part of women, to seek knowledge about the real work of feminist movement today. However, this backlash against feminism is ultimately good news according to Faludi who explains that backlash is a natural social pattern that results during times of great social change; when voices that are not usually part of the discourse begin to be heard, there is a concurrent attempt to silence them and return to the status quo. This means that a backlash is a sign that previously marginalized voices are actually becoming part of the dominant discourse.

The power of this false social perception about feminism is evidenced in the fact that many women reject feminism largely because they do not want to be viewed as "angry, man-hating, lesbians." Of course, they often qualify their rejection by stating their support for issues that have been championed by feminists such as equal pay, day care, anti-discrimination efforts in the workplace, and reproductive rights. While it is true that all women do not view feminism the same way, it is also true that the closer some women get to full access to social power, the more likely they are to consciously reject feminism. Unfortunately, this is the case with some women in technology.

For example, in the 70s at MIT, two women faculty created a joint organization of students, staff, faculty, and wives of faculty called the Women's Forum whose task was to increase gender awareness. The group developed "consciousness-raising skits" and voiced "concerns about women's health, athletic opportunities, day care, and career planning," but "forum leaders found it impossible to please everyone":

Some MIT women found the group too conservative and wanted more aggressive demands for change; others judged it too radical and worried about perceptions of 'women's lib.' As participants noted, merely attending such meetings got them branded as 'troublemakers.' (Bix, 2000, p. 35)

The tensions that arose among the MIT women reflect attitudes still present today. Many women in science just want to "do science" and do not want to be associated with "feminism" because of the negative connotation it often carries.

During this same period, MIT hosted a workshop (sponsored by major donors such as the Carnegie Corporation and General Electric) on women in science and engineering targeted at parents, schools, and national media to inspire them to participate in increasing women's numbers in education and the professions. However, a memo inviting industry representatives to attend reflected the implicit fears of associating with "feminism" and of feminism as "women's work": "This will not be an *ardent feminist* production, so please don't hesitate to include the names of men who would otherwise be *terrified* by an *onslaught of screaming females* [italics mine]" (Bix, 2000, p. 37). Though stories from 30 years ago may seem outdated to some, they are classic examples of how powerfully social expectations operate to keep women in their place. It will take generations to shift the power of these social forces. Eisler (2002) points out that the classification of social concerns as "women's issues" is really "a code phrase signaling that these issues should take second place to more important ones," and that this "is in itself a commentary on how entrenched the devaluation of the female half of humanity still is" (p. 137).

A more recent example of the ambivalence some women in technology feel towards feminism was evidenced the first time I taught Women in Computing, a course that I had developed at the University of Washington in the Computing and Software Systems program during Summer Quarter 1997. I was eager to provide my students with the lived perspectives of women who actually worked in technology to support the theories we were reading about. I invited several women from the Association for Women in Computing, fully expecting them to share real life stories about the challenges they had faced as women in technology. None of the presenters attributed any negative experiences to being female; none of them had any background in feminist thought, and they were all eager to downplay the fact that they were women. In fact, in a classically sexist remark, one woman described how she preferred working with men rather than women because "women always had to deal with their petty emotional problems."

It was a teachable moment. After the women left, I was able to help my students explore how we cannot name something that we have learned not to see. I was also able to talk about the "petty emotional problems" comment as a classic kind of internalized sexism. In a social environment where women receive persistent messages of inferiority, many women internalize those messages and view (usually unconsciously) both themselves and other women from that negative perspective. In male-dominated environments like technology, this causes some women to strive to disassociate themselves from being "female" (or associated with emotion, which is exclusively assigned to females) in order to be "one of the boys." Ironically, after their presentation, the woman who had made the sexist comment asked for a copy of my working bibliography for the course. She had clearly recognized an opportunity to expand her perspectives about feminism.

The problem with the word feminism (as well as all of the other "isms") is that the term itself inspires fear and negativity which makes it hard to move towards a meaningful dialogue about the issues. In *Privilege, Power and Difference*, Allan Johnson (2006) explains the difficulty:

You can't deal with a problem if you don't name it. Once you name it, you can think, talk, and write about it . . . When you name something, the word draws your attention to it . . . That's why most people have an immediate negative reaction to words like racism, sexism or privilege. They don't want to look at what the words point to. (p. 9)

Once the term has placed people in a negative emotional state, their response is often that talking about theses issues just pits groups against each other. Johnson clarifies that we are "*already* pitted against one another by the structures of privilege that organize society as a whole" (p. 12). The trouble does not lie with the F word, with feminists, or with feminism. "The trouble is produced by a world organized in ways that encourage people to *use* difference to include or exclude, reward or punish, credit or discredit, elevate or oppress, value or devalue, leave alone or harass" (Johnson, 2006, p. 16). Rather than ignoring our differences, or attempting to gloss over them with comments like "we're all human," Goldstein (2004) proposes that "we create an educational approach that dismantles fear of difference and promotes understanding, appreciation, and respect among all people" (p. 127).

There is no need to fear the F word because the work of feminism is at once incredibly complex and astonishingly simple. For the purposes of this book, I offer the following simple definition of the feminist project. As bell hooks (2000) said, "feminism is for everybody" since it is engaged in scrutinizing social systems with the express goal of ending all forms of institutionalized oppression. Feminism offers a perspective from which to examine power relations in terms of individual identity as well as the beliefs and attitudes purveyed by social institutions.[1] To further clarify the meaning of feminism, I have chosen to debunk the following six myths about feminism and the social system in which we live: (1) it's just the way things are; (2) it's just about women being equal to men; (3) men and women are just different by nature; (4) feminists want to be like men; (5) I don't have a race, I'm White; and (6) it's "their" problem, not mine.

MYTH #1: IT'S JUST THE WAY THINGS ARE

Nope. It's not just the way things are. Societies are comprised of people and people participate in creating their societies. In the United States, and in most countries worldwide, we have co-created patriarchal societies. Johnson (1997) defines "patriarchy" as a society that is "male-dominated, male-identified, and male-centered"; usually a hierarchical society organized around power and who holds it (p. 5). In a patriarchal society, "the dominant message is that the human experience equals the male experience" (Kesselman et al., 2003, p. 9). This core assumption is the foundation for the attitudes and beliefs that inform all of our social institutions. Individuals learn about their society and how to function successfully in it from social institutions such as law, medicine, business, language, education, and media. These social institutions teach the values of the dominant culture, and we all learn the rules of the game from them. In a hierarchical social organization, the game is organized around power and who holds it which makes it critical for individuals to learn their "appropriate" social location within the hierarchical structure. Individuals learn a sense of identity that is defined by their social location, that is, a series of factors inclusive of gender, race, socioeconomic class, physical ability, sexual identity, religion, age, and so forth. This social location determines our "rightful" place in the hierarchy (Kirk & Okazawa-Rey, 2004).

Most (but not all) societies today are patriarchal. However, in the span of human time, patriarchy is a relatively recent social system. For many thousands of years prior to the general adoption of patriarchy, the world was populated with peaceful, prosperous, equalitarian, and matrilineal (descent is traced through the mother) societies. In *The Creation of Patriarchy*, historian Gerda Lerner (1986) attempts to explain how this major shift in the organization of societies occurred. Lerner challenges the inadequacy of single-cause, either/or explanations, and documents the multiple, overlapping, sometimes simultaneous events that led to the creation of patriarchy. Lerner adds that the:

Period of the 'establishment of patriarchy' was not one 'event' but a process developing over a period of nearly 2500 years, from app. 3100 to 600 B.C. It occurred, even within the Ancient Near East at a different pace and at different times in several distinct societies. (p. 8)

In her historical analysis of how this shift occurred, Lerner (1986) describes three significant and simultaneous events that contributed to the development of patriarchy: "hunting/gathering or horticulture gives way to agriculture, kinship arrangements tend to shift from matriliny to patriliny, and private property develops" (p. 49).

In addition to these primary forces, Lerner also proposes the following factors that contributed to the gradual shift to patriarchy: (1) appropriation of women's reproductive capacity happened before there were class-based societies oriented towards private property; (2) states were organized in the form of patriarchies and so had an interest in patriarchal families; (3) men learned to extend dominance over women to dominance over others with institutionalized slavery; (4) women's sexual subordination was institutionalized in the early laws; (5) class for men became related to their ties to the means of production, while for women class was defined through ties to a man; (6) long after their subordination to men, women still played active roles in mediating between gods and humans; (7) dethroning of the goddess religions and replacement with a male god happened after the establishment of a strong kingship system; (8) covenant communities established the subordinate role of women (God, then man, then woman); and (9) the symbolic devaluation of women in relation to the divine is "one of the founding metaphors of Western civilization" (p. 9-10). In these nine propositions that Lerner hypothesizes, we can begin to trace the development of classism and racism (in addition to sexism). We can also see clear links between these ancient social institutions and some of the beliefs still purveyed by our social institutions today, notably religion and law.

For example, Lerner's (1986) discussion of Mesopotamian law and the Code of Hammurabi explains when some of the gender distinctions that we still struggle with today first became codified in the social institution of law. Some of the principles that arose at this time were as follows: "a man's class status is determined by his economic relations and a woman's by her sexual relations" (p. 105–106)—a precursor to the beliefs we have today where men are judged in terms of achievements and women are measured in terms of attractiveness; "Babylonian families value the birth of sons over the birth of daughters" (p. 106)—a belief less common in the US, but still common in many other societies today; marriage as a contract for purchase (p. 107)—a belief that is still reflected in the general social assumption that the bride's family pays for the wedding and that the father of the bride gives her away; "laws against rape all incorporated the principle that the injured party is the husband or the father of the raped woman" and it was legal for husbands to physically abuse their wives (p. 116-117)—in some states in the U.S., it is still legal for a husband to rape his wife; self-induced abortion is made a crime (p. 120)—women in the U.S. are still fighting for legal control of their own bodies; and, "the metaphor of the patriarchal family as the cell, the basic building block, of the healthy organism of the public consciousness was first expressed in Mesopotamian Law" (p. 121).

In *The Chalice and the Blade: Our History, Our Future*, Riane Eisler (1987) also examines "this cataclysmic turning point during the prehistory of Western civili-zation, when the direction of our cultural evolution was literally turned around" and we shifted from thousands of years of peaceful coexistence worshiping "the life-generating and nurturing powers of the universe" (symbolized by the chalice) to a more violent social orientation, worshiping the power to take life, "to establish and enforce domination" (symbolized by the blade) (p. xvii). Eisler's systems-level interdisciplinary analysis (which includes disciplines such as art, archeology, social science, history, and religion) of the prehistory of Western civilization documents thousands of years of peaceful and prosperous prepatriarchal civilization that fea-tured an equalitarian, communal social organization. Even though these cultures were matrilineal, Eisler (1987) does not believe that the evidence supports describing them as "matriarchies," which is the opposite of patriarchy, with women dominating men. Unlike patriarchy, these societies were "remarkably equalitarian" and:

although in these societies descent appears to have been traced through the mother, and women as priestesses and heads of clans seem to have played leading roles in all aspects of life, there is little indication that the position of men in this social system was in any sense comparable to the subordination and suppression of women characteristic of the male-dominant system that replaced it. (Eisler, 1987, p. 25)

Eisler (1987) describes these earlier societies as "partnership" societies "in which neither half of humanity is ranked over the other and diversity is not equated with inferiority or superiority" and our current societies as "dominator" societies in which superior men (and all aspects of so-called "maleness") are ranked over in-ferior women (p. 28). According to Eisler (1987, 2000, 2002, 2007), a dominator social system features a hierarchical, authoritarian social structure that emphasizes rigid ranking and is founded on fear; it is a control model. In contrast, a partner-ship social system features an egalitarian social structure that emphasizes linking and is founded on trust; it is a respect model. Table 1 (a composite compiled from several books) contrasts the characteristics of a dominator social model with a partnership model (Eisler, 1987, 2002, 2007; Eisler & Loye, 1990; Eisler & Miller, 2004), (see Table 1). Whether we live in a social environment that is more oriented to domination than partnership:

affects which of our large repertoire of human traits and behaviors are reinforced or inhibited. The partnership system brings out our capacities for consciousness, caring and creativity. The domination system tends to inhibit these capacities. It brings out—indeed, requires—insensitivity, cruelty, and destructiveness. (Eisler, 2007, p. 95)

It is critical that more of us understand how our dominator society works in action, what attitudes and beliefs are currently embedded in our social institutions, and how this effectively works for many men and women both in terms of their own individual sense of identity and sense of possibility, but also in terms of their views of each other. Lerner (1986) provides the following description of the society men and women have currently co-created:

Table 1. Characteristics of dominator and partnership social systems

Dominator	Partnership
Fear- and control-based	Trust- and respect-based
Hierarchies of domination	Hierarchies of actualization
Emphasis on ranking	Emphasis on linking
Win/lose orientation	Win/win orientation
High degree of fear, abuse, violence	Low degree of fear, abuse, violence, since they are not required to maintain rigid rankings
Value so-called "male" traits such as control and conquest over so-called "female" traits	Value traits that promote human development such as nonviolence, empathy, and caregiving
Images of heroic violence sanctified, institutionalized	Images of nurturance honored, institutionalized
Leaders imaged as men who give orders and have subordinate followers	Leaders imaged as anyone who inspires others to collaborate on commonly agreed upon goals
Planning is short-term with little thought for future generations	Planning includes short- and long-term concerns for present & future generations
Emphasis on scarcity, hoarding	Emphasis on sustainability, sharing
Society viewed as a machine with people as expendable cogs	Society viewed as a living organism with people as involved co-creators
Earth imaged as an object to be conquered, exploited	Earth imaged as a living organism of which we are all a part

Men and women live on a stage, on which they act out their assigned roles, equal in importance. The play cannot go on without both kinds of performers. Neither of them 'contributes' more or less to the whole; neither is marginal or dispensable. But the stage set is conceived, painted, defined by men. Men have written the play, have directed the show, interpreted the meanings of the action. They have assigned themselves the most heroic parts, giving women the supporting roles. (p. 12)

This leads me to Myth #2.

MYTH #2: IT'S ABOUT WOMEN BEING EQUAL TO MEN

The contemporary work of feminism is not about women being equal to men. There are several problems with exclusively focusing on equality as a goal. First, being treated equally is often conflated with being treated identically. However, there are some ways in which men and women have very different needs. One common example is the design of public restrooms that does not take into account the different needs men and women have due to differences in both biological anatomy and clothing. Women who menstruate monthly have additional objectives in the bathroom. Women do not typically urinate standing up (some have attempted to design female urinals with limited success due to the gender socialization of most women which teaches them that "nice girls are modest"). Women must remove clothing for all of their bathroom functions, while men only need to remove clothing for one function. One research study suggested that in order for restroom allocation to be fair, it should be different: "a fairer allocation of toilets would be 60-40, favoring women" (Tavris, 1992, p. 95). Since that study, some states have enacted legislation to require a fairer distribution of toilets in public facilities. Being treated identically to men will not achieve equality; treating women differently may.

Another reason that focusing on equality will not solve the problem is that equality theories often "focus on the 'differences' that are in women (it is women who do the differing from the norm), and because they mistakenly assume that social institutions . . . are already egalitarian and gender-neutral—it's just a matter of fitting women into them" (Tavris, 1992, p. 123). This is the result of establishing maleness as the standard; women become misfits by definition. Equality is not enough because it assumes that women just want what men want (or want to be like men).

The primary reason that focusing on equality will not solve the problem is that it leaves the existing attitudes and beliefs that underlie our social institutions unchallenged. Lerner's (1986) play metaphor (first cited at the end of Myth #1) continues by demonstrating this problem with equality:

As the women become aware of the difference in the way they fit into the play, they ask for more equality in the role assignments . . . The women finally, after considerable struggle, win the right of access to equal role assignment, but first they must 'qualify.' The terms of their 'qualifications' are again set by the men . . . Men punish, by ridicule, exclusion, or ostracism, any women who assumes the right to interpret her own role or—worst of all sins—the right to rewrite the script. It takes considerable time for the women to understand that getting 'equal' parts will not make them equal, as long as the script, the props, the stage setting, and the direction are firmly held by men. (p. 12-13)

Our (largely unexamined and unquestioned) social institutions define the script, props, stage, and directions for the play in very exclusive terms. One of the fundamental directions for our patriarchal play is the assumption of power as an organizing theme. The contemporary work of feminism is to shine the light on structural issues, such as social power.

In *Truth or Dare*, Starhawk (1987) defines three types of social power: "Power-over is linked to domination and control; power-from-within is linked to the mysteries that awaken our deepest abilities and potential. Power-with is social power, the influence we wield among equals" (p. 9). Our social institutions feature power-over as a core organizing theme. Riane Eisler (1987) defines this type of social system as a "dominator" model with a "generally hierarchic and authoritarian social organization, with the degree of authoritarianism and hierarchism roughly corresponding to the degree of male dominance" (p. 179). I began my explanation of our social system with the term "patriarchy" since that is how many scholars refer to it. However, I find Eisler's use of the term "dominator" society more useful since it focuses on structural assumptions that contribute to classism, racism, and many other "isms" in addition to sexism.

In *Privilege, Power, and Difference*, Allan Johnson (2006) also moves away from the term "patriarchy" and attempts to unpack the core assumptions of our society by referring to it as a system organized around privilege and oppression. Johnson writes:

Systems organized around privilege have three key characteristics. They are dominated by privileged groups, identified with privileged groups, and centered on privileged groups. All three characteristics support the idea that members of privileged groups are superior to those below them. (p. 90)

Johnson explains that we use our so-called differences to create artificial distinctions in order to include some and exclude others from access to power in our social institutions. Johnson says that "privilege exists when one group has something of value that is denied to others simply because of the groups they belong to, rather than because of anything they've done or failed to do" (p. 21). Harry Brod (1989) wrote that male privilege:

is not something I take and which I therefore have the option of not taking. It is something that society gives me, and unless I change the institutions which give it to me, they will continue to give it, and I will continue to have it, however noble and egalitarian my intentions. (p. 280)

The key idea here is that privilege is granted by others (or assumed by the individual) based on their perceptions of the social categories to which they belong, that is, their "place" in the social hierarchy, not based on individual achievement. We learn these perceptions from our social institutions.

In *Of Woman Born: Motherhood as Social Institution*, Adrienne Rich (1986) describes how privilege allows individuals to exert power over others (often unconsciously):

To hold power over others means that the powerful is permitted a kind of short-cut through the complexity of human personality. He does not have to enter intuitively into the souls of the powerless, or to hear what they are saying in their many languages, including the language of silence. (p. 65)

This explains some of the comments often made today such as claims of "reverse discrimination," complaints about learning what "they" want me to call "them" (encompassed under the now-pejorative term "political correctness"), and similar sorts of bitter resistance to change that are reflected in our daily social discourse. Johnson (2006) lists the following strategies that privileged groups use for getting themselves off the hook in terms of doing anything about systems of oppression: (1) deny and minimize; (2) blame the victim; (3) call it something else; (4) claim it's better this way; (5) say it doesn't count if you don't mean it (a conflation of intention and consequences which often are not the same, but it is the consequences that matter); (6) claim "I am one of the good ones" as if anyone can *not* participate in social systems; and (7) claim to be "sick and tired" of all this talk about "them"; my life is hard, too—"White defensiveness runs right past the fact that whatever it is that exhausts White people, it isn't the fact of being White" (p. 108-121).

Those in positions of privilege are rarely aware of the benefits that they often derive from it. Johnson (2006) lists the following reasons that dominant groups do not see their privilege as a problem: (1) they don't know it exists; (2) they don't have to; (3) they think it's just a personal problem; (4) they want to hang on to their privilege; (5) they are prejudiced; and (6) they are afraid (p. 69-71). Items 1 through

3 can be explained in part by the fact that our social institutions are centered on and identified with the characteristics of those in privileged groups. This makes it easy for those with privilege to be blind to it, to be unmotivated to seek solutions to problems they do not have, and to focus on individualistic rather than systemic explanations. A famous quote by world-renowned anthropologist Margaret Mead is as follows: "If a fish were an anthropologist, the last thing it would discover would be water." For those with privilege, the water represents the characteristics of their privilege; the attitudes and beliefs of our social institutions are simply the water in which they swim, just the way things are. Items 4 through 6 stem largely from fear and ignorance. Bigotry and prejudice are learned, and they can be unlearned.

The challenge to helping those with privilege recognize its existence is that privilege does not necessarily make you happy. Johnson (2006) explains that although being privileged "improves the odds in favor of certain kinds of advantages and preferential treatment," there are no guarantees (p. 37). This makes it easier for some to claim that they don't have privilege because their lives aren't so great, they aren't happy, and they've had it hard, too. However, this type of individual experience does not negate the fact that a wide array of systemic inequalities are embedded in our social institutions. For example, no matter how difficult an individual White man's life is, a Black woman with those same circumstances would face an additional set of systemic barriers. The contemporary work of feminism is less about equality than it is about identifying and eliminating the systemic forces that support our dominator society and prevent us from building what Riane Eisler (1987, 2000, 2002, 2007) calls a partnership society.

MYTH #3: MEN AND WOMEN ARE JUST DIFFERENT

The myth that men and women are just different is persistently explored in the nature/nurture debate. Is it nature (biological sex) or nurture (gender socialization in our environment) that makes men and women different? The interesting issue with this myth is that the question itself is a manifestation of the problem. It assumes that a simplistic, dualistic, either/or answer is available for the very complex question of what determines human characteristics.

Sex/gender is set forth as the ultimate dualism, which in itself might not be a problem. However, it is a short step from creating either/or's to making one side of the dualism good and the other bad. This is where the real trouble begins. In addition, many scholars have documented that the dichotomy itself is false in relation to both gender and sex. In terms of gender, groups of girls/women are actually more similar to groups of boys/men than they are different. In her 1792 treatise on education called *A Vindication of the Rights of Woman*, Mary Wollstonecraft suggested that girls and boys "would play harmlessly together, if the distinction of sex was not inculcated long before nature makes any difference" (p. 42).

Examining some of the research might clarify the issues regarding this myth. Clearly, there are some differences between men and women due to biological sex. However, Anne Fausto-Sterling (2000) has argued that even biological sex cannot be reduced to a simple either-or dualism. Fausto-Sterling says that there are not just two sexes and that biological sex may be more accurately described on a continuum of female to male. The fundamental problem with a focus on identifying differences between women and men based on biology is that since scientific research, research questions, and analysis of their results occur in a social context, as long as we socialize for gender as vigorously and pervasively as we do, it will be difficult to definitively answer the question of what behavioral differences may correlate with biological sex. The researchers themselves have been gender socialized, and it is difficult to identify the ways in which their "gendered" perspectives might influence their research.

The endless and contradictory studies of sex differences, gender, and the human brain offer another example of how this dualistic, either/or social context influences research. Carol Tavris (1992) says that "all polarities of thinking, like all dichotomies of groups, are by nature artificial, misleading, and oversimplified" (p. 288). Tavris adds that the "fact that the brain consists of two hemispheres, each characterized by different specialties, provides a neat analogy to the fact that human beings consist of two genders, each characterized by different specialties" (p. 45). Many researchers keep trying to gender-assign the different hemispheres of the brain in the same way that they gendered the biological behavior of ovaries and sperm.

Research resulting from this perspective highlights the significance of social context on the results when it comes to matters of sex/gender. For example, in 1980 Benbow and Stanley tried to prove that girls do not have the same spatial ability as boys. What purpose does such research serve? Is it even necessary when the assumption is so clearly embedded in popular beliefs about gender and innate ability? Nearly 20 years later, in 1998, that cultural myth was still being expressed by a talking Barbie that said "Math class is hard!" (Mundy, 1998). In 2002, Harvard psychologist Steven Pinker published a best-selling book *The Blank Slate* where he asserted:

Men and women are by nature suited to different roles. Men are inherently 'risk-taking achievers who can willingly endure discomfort in pursuit of success,' while 'women are more likely to choose administrative support jobs that offer low pay in air conditioned offices.' (Barnett & Rivers, 2004, p. 3)

In 2003, Simon Baron-Cohen's *The Essential Difference: The Truth About the Male and Female Brain* used decades old research (much of which has not been repeated with consistent results) to make sweeping and stereotypical statements about gender. He also raised no questions about the context in which that research was conducted. His research classified brains as E (individuals in whom empathizing is stronger than systemizing), S (individuals in whom systemizing is stronger than empathizing), and B (individuals in whom both are equally strong). Unfortunately, he then gendered his research by labeling E the "female" brain and S the "male" brain. There is no discussion of how Bs fit into his thinking (the transgender brain?). Nowhere in the book is there any data on the sex and numbers of subjects who tested as E, S, or B. There are only overlapping bell-curves (vaguely labeled low to high with no numbers) that show a slight tendency for there to be more female Es and male Ss. The charts contain no reference to the Bs; this is likely because either/or thinking offers no easy way to deal with the complexities of what lies between the dualistic extremes. His research is meant to establish a link between extreme S brains and autism. Ironically, he ends the book with the comment that society is "likely to be biased toward accepting the extreme female brain" which shows an increased psychic and intuitive ability while "stigmatizing the extreme male brain." However, Baron-Cohen finds "hope" in the fact that "the modern age of electronics, science, engineering, and gadgets means that there are more openings now for the extreme male brain to flourish and be valued" (p. 186). It is hard to deny the obvious sexist attributions of this work, as well as the fear and prejudice that Johnson described often characterizes the perspectives of those in positions of privilege such as Baron-Cohen. There is an undertone of fear that women are "taking over" that is unsupported by data on the participation of women in science and technology education and professions.

For most scientists, the effort to find a gendered "either/or" description of the human brain has effectively arrived at a "both/and" explanation. After decades of research into the functions of the lobes or hemispheres of the brain that attempted to associate them with "gendered" functions, today most "believe that the two hemispheres complement one another, to the extent that one side can sometimes take over the functions of a side that has been damaged" (Tavris, 1992, p. 49). In addition, there are only a few sex differences that are considered reliable and these differences are very small. The following sex differences in mental abilities and personality traits among boys and girls have been consistently documented: (1) verbal abilities (girls are advantaged in early language development and reading achievement); (2) spatial abilities (boys outperform girls early, and it persists as they age); (3) mathematical reasoning (boys do better than girls); (4) school achievement (girls get better grades in elementary school after which the difference declines); (5) achievement motivation (boys see themselves as more competent); and (6) empathy/emotion (girls see themselves as more competent) (Tavris, 1992, p. 43-56). However, I would caution that even though some of this research has been reliably repeated with similar results, it is no more immune from the influences of social context than any other experiments involving human subjects. Gender socialization begins very early (in fact, in the womb when the sex is known).

The dualistic, either/or effort to prove sex differences misses the more interesting and more revealing complexities of how we learn gender, which continues to divide men and women in their daily lives. Many scholars from different disciplines have talked about the importance of a complex interaction between individuals and their environment. Barnett and Rivers (2004) say that we are "an ever-changing product of continuous learning and interaction that builds on our genetic heritage," and claim that "those who endorse the nature-is-all position tend to ignore the immense variety among men and women" (p. 12). In *Intelligence of Apes and Other Rational Beings*, Duane M. Rumbaugh and David A. Washburn (2003) explain their position on the debate about nature vs. nurture in psychology as follows:

The argument of nature vs. nurture is fundamentally an impossibly flawed juxtaposition of sources for why things are as they are, either in individuals or in groups. Without biology (life), behavior cannot occur . . . Without experiences in diverse environments, the organism cannot achieve development, maturation, conditioning, and other kinds of learning. Interactions between biology and environment are inevitable. These interactions are where the action is and where the answers are to be found—not in the question, 'Is this attribute due to nature or nurture?' (p. 42-43)

The point is that gender identity is not static. "Gender identity varies within particular contexts and forms, is reinforced within relationships and situations, and interacts with other types of identities in ways that influence beliefs about who takes on those identities" (Barker & Aspray, 2006, p. 9). Gender is created in an ongoing interchange between individuals and their environments (especially the larger forces of social institutions).

Identity and social location are created in a complex negotiation between the individual and their environment. The social context matters just as much as the individual and their choices. The primary influence on one's sense of identity is the individual themselves; a few core characteristics that are unique to that particular individual. The next influence on identity is the family; a family that supports the core individual creates a different sense of possibility than a family that denies these core aspects. The next most powerful influence on identity is the culture or community which can also support or challenge the individual's sense of identity. Next are all of the social institutions (i.e., education, business, media, medicine, business, government, etc.); the individual may receive messages that support or challenge their sense of identity. Lastly, we learn a sense of national identity; for example, in the U.S., that includes a sense of global privilege in terms of being Americans as well as an emphasis on individualism over communalism, (see Figure 1).

Here is an example of how this complex negotiation might work in relation to gender. An African-American girl may come into the world as an individual with an innate sense of strength and assertiveness. If she is reared in a family environment that supports those characteristics in her, she is likely to develop those characteristics and be confident in them. If she is reared in a family that challenges or criticizes those traits as "unfeminine," she may not continue to exercise them and/or she may lose confidence in herself. Since African-American culture tends to support strength and assertiveness in women, this girl is likely find her sense of identity supported by her cultural community. However, when that innately strong, assertive girl enters school (her first major encounter with a social institution), she is likely to learn from her social institutions that she is not a "good" girl because strength and assertiveness are gendered "male." She is also likely to encounter further oppression due to race, and may be perceived as "an angry Black woman" for being too outspoken; racial oppression in our social institutions often takes the form of expecting invisibility and or silence from people of color. However, if that girl was supported by her family and culture for being strong and assertive, she is less likely to be negatively impacted by the messages from her social institutions. If she was not supported by her family and/or culture for being strong and assertive, she is much more likely to be profoundly negatively impacted by the gendered and racialized messages of her social institutions. This difference is one of the major factors that will determine whether she is happy personally, and successful academically and

Figure 1. Influences on identity formation and social location

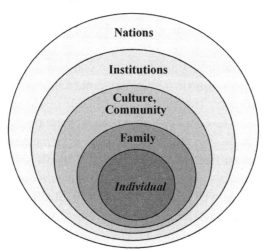

professionally. This complex, multilayered negotiation about identity happens in relation to race, class, and other social characteristics as well. It provides a useful lens through which to understand why we can have such different experiences of gender and race in our lives. Let us look at another example.

A White boy is born quiet, intelligent, and emotional. He is reared in a family environment that teaches him that it is "unmanly" to express emotion and that he should speak up more. Although he finds it uncomfortable to go against his nature, he learns to compete intellectually, and he suppresses his emotions. He moves around a great deal as a child and has no other ethnic heritage than White, which leaves him without a negative or positive support for his identity at the level of community and culture. When he begins his education, he finds his intellectual competitiveness supported and he learns to speak up more. However, he continues to suppress his emotions because education teaches him that "girls are sensitive" and "boys are strong." His intelligence continues to be an asset in education, and he works his way in business to be a multimillionaire. After a decades-long unhappy marriage, he goes into therapy to reclaim his emotional life buried long ago. Due to the complex interaction between this individual and his environment, he was unable to give full flower to his innate self until late in his life. It is not difficult to understand why this White man may have a difficult time understanding how his life was privileged by gender and race. This is also an example of how gender identity continues to be redefined in a complex negotiation between individuals and their environment over time. It is an ongoing dynamic process.

This idea of the dynamic development of identity that I have described above was also supported by developmental psychologist Urie Bronfenbrenner who proposed that we consider human development in terms of "the dynamic relationships between the developing individual and the integrated, multilevel ecology of human development" (Lerner, 2005, p. ix). His work also inspires hope for the potential to change our social institutions because he said that "individuals influence the people and institutions of their ecology as much as they are influenced by them" (Lerner, 2005, p. ix). He also supported the point that focusing on either nature or nurture is too simplistic because human development takes place in "the synergistic interaction between heredity and environment" (Bronfenbrenner, 2005, p. 1).

In the end, how will proving sex differences help improve our social situation? We might ask why some are so concerned with identifying and proving difference and who benefits from that pursuit and/or its answers. A focus on "proving" differences in large groups of human beings allows us to categorize people based on perceived social characteristics and to sustain systems of privilege and oppression. Attempting to prove sex differences is not likely to help us end deeply embedded views about gender that contribute to systems of inequality. Attempting to prove sex differences is not likely to alter the values and beliefs imbedded in our social institutions that contribute to systems of oppression. Attempting to prove sex differences is not likely to help us resolve the continued salary inequities between men and women in the U.S. Attempting to prove sex differences is not likely to help us build a society where women and children are not the largest numbers of poor U.S. Americans. However, the primary problem with research questions that are focused on difference is that it's too easy to take the next step and say that one sex/gender is better than the other based on these differences. As many early feminists who tried to valorize femininity discovered, saying that "women are better" is not the answer either. We must strive to create is a social system in which all human beings can manifest our best selves and live fully authentic lives. Bronfenbrenner (2005) suggests that instead of focusing our scientific research on proving difference, we could focus on:

a systematic effort to describe the ecological environment in which a given cultural group finds itself… Once such analyses are carried out, instead of regarding social class, ethnicity, and religion as attributes of the person, we shall come to see them for what they are, namely, structured aspects of the environment that function to enhance or inhibit the processes of making human beings human. (p. 47)

We must identify and remove institutionalized obstacles to making all human beings human.

MYTH #4: FEMINISTS WANT TO BE LIKE MEN

Firstly, feminists do not want to be like men; they do want to reveal the ways in which our social institutions are embedded with attitudes and beliefs that use "maleness" as the standard. For example, philosopher Elizabeth Minnich (1990) explains that you would never see the phrase "the White, male, philosopher Kant" because philosophers are assumed to be White and male. Minnich suggested that if you want to identify the normative standard, you simply need to look at the adjectives; they define who is assumed to be the standard and who is not. Secondly, women (feminist or otherwise) cannot be like men even if they want to due to an effect called the "double bind." The problem is that no matter how much some women may try to behave according to "male" standards, women are still generally *perceived* according to a gendered notion of "woman."

Barnett and Rivers (2004) explain that issues of social inequality are primarily due to power differences. These power differentials place more men in high-status roles and more women in oppressive low-status roles. This is true due to the ways in which we learn gender from our social institutions. It is usually easier for men to assume positions of power because we have organized our social institutions around so-called "male" characteristics of power, leadership, and so forth. A woman in a position of power (or leadership) faces the double-bind of being called a "bad woman" if she is not nurturing enough, and a "bad leader" if she is not aggressive enough; she must dance on the razor's edge, a bloody path to say the least. Johnson (2006) explains:

The standards used to evaluate men as men are consistent with the standards used to evaluate them in other roles such as occupations. Standards used to evaluate women as women are often different from those used to evaluate them in other roles. For example, a man can be both a 'real man' and a successful and aggressive lawyer, while an aggressive women lawyer may succeed as a lawyer but be judged as not measuring up as a woman. (p. 29)

In a dominator society, positions of power tend to be occupied by those with privilege. Therefore, "power looks 'natural' on a man [or a White person, or a wealthy person, or any other privileged group] but unusual and even problematic on a woman, marking her as an exception that calls for special scrutiny and some kind of explanation" (Johnson, 2006, p. 91). If we do not examine how attitudes about power and privilege are learned through our social institutions, we unconsciously continue to create a Darwinian social system in which only the strong survive; only those individual members of oppressed groups who are strong enough to take the constant criticism and abuse they will undoubtedly receive for assuming positions of power will survive. Or, as law professor Patricia Williams (1997) asked: "When will we stop turning America's most eloquent, intelligent, and committed women into test sites for the ability to endure abuse elegantly?" (p. 151).[2] What other natural talents and gifts might we be losing in positions of leadership because for a woman or a person of color to lead, they must have "thick skin"? What might our world look like if a few more sensitive souls (who may be women or men) were allowed to be considered good leaders? What kind of healthy organizational systems might evolve from this type of leadership?

"Maleness" is the standard for leadership as it is for many other attitudes and beliefs of our social institutions. We learn attitudes about leadership from our dominant social institutions (as well as our families and cultural communities). The predominant characteristics of what define a good leader are very strongly correlated with what defines a good "man." In one of my classes, I demonstrate the power of gender socialization by asking students to take an informal survey. The students all think they are getting the same survey, but there are actually two surveys. One asks them to "identify the characteristics that are associated with maleness or femaleness, as they are defined by the dominant society" and the other asks them to "identify the characteristics that are most strongly associated with leadership, as defined by the dominant society." Each semester, students overwhelmingly correlate "maleness" and "leadership" (with 100% correlation on most characteristics). It is a simple and powerful way to show students how most of us have learned to define gender and to reinforce it in our daily lives, usually without our conscious awareness. Table 2 lists the characteristics I use in my survey.

In several years of giving this survey, none of my classes have correlated even one female characteristic with leadership. This makes it easier to see the problem that women who aspire to positions of leadership (which grant them social power) face—the double bind. Any woman in a group of men will be acutely aware of her gender, and so will the men. No matter how she behaves, she is likely to be criticized, either for being too "feminine" or too "masculine." That is the double bind. That is why a woman can never be like a man.

Former Hewlett-Packard CEO Carly Fiorina's story serves as an example of the double bind women in leadership face. She was a woman in a high profile leadership position at a time when the number of women CEOs of any Fortune 500 business (never mind at a high-tech company) could be counted on one hand. It is not unreasonable to assume that there was some gender dimension to her story, but one does not have to look very far to find it deliberately ignored and/or discounted.[3] As an example of how the gender-dimension of Fiorina's situation and her decisions were ignored, I turn to a 2006 article in *Wired* magazine by Fred Vogelstein, a *Wired* magazine contributing editor, who was interviewing Fiorina about her book *Tough Choices*. Vogelstein (2006) asked Fiorina: "Why didn't you keep a lower profile?" The question itself belies either an ignorance of gender socialization in the U.S., or a deliberate determination to discount it as insignificant. In her answer, Fiorina admits that she wished she "had had the opportunity to be a low-profile CEO," but that one of the things she "learned the hard way" was that there was no way that her:

Table 2. Gender and leadership characteristics survey terms

Female	Male	Leader
caring	achiever	achiever
submissive	aggressive	aggressive
manipulative	confident	confident
passive	dynamic/active	dynamic/active
emotional/loving	rational	rational
weak/sensitive	strong	strong
soft	hard	hard
relationship-oriented	task-oriented	task-oriented
other-oriented	self-oriented	self-oriented

arrival at HP was going to be dealt with in a low-profile way by the media. I had
nothing to do with that other than to have to deal with it that first day. I was criticized
endlessly in the media for not being available enough. I was criticized endlessly in
the media for being too high-profile. (Vogelstein, 2006)

Certainly, the following factors may have also contributed to Fiorina's high profile
tenure as CEO: (1) the high tech industry itself is high profile; (2) HP was as an older
player in high tech and was floundering financially when she joined the company;
and (3) like some other large successful companies, HP had a particular culture and
Fiorina's management decisions appeared to some to threaten that culture.

There was a fourth factor—the proverbial elephant in the living room—the fact
that the new CEO was a woman. Unfortunately, because gender was not named as a
factor, the dynamics of its influence on the situation could not be openly discussed.
Further, who could mention gender as a factor? Fiorina could not or she might be
perceived as "whining," being a "victim," or wanting "special" consideration as
a woman. Vogelstein could not because male privilege has likely taught him that
gender is invisible, or he believes that technology is somehow immune from sexism, or some other such view that those with social privilege use to ignore gender.
So, the situation in this example is the kind of classic double bind that occurs for
women in leadership. The media focus special attention on Fiorina, in part because
she is a woman in a leadership role (which is unusual and therefore newsworthy),
and simultaneously criticize her for being "too high profile." I share this story about
Fiorina not in an effort to label her either a victim or a hero, though I am likely to
lean towards the latter. I share this story as an example of why we need to do the
conscious work of unpacking the complex assumptions about gender that negatively
influence all of our lives.

MYTH #5: I DON'T HAVE A RACE, I'M WHITE

The contemporary work of feminism is not just about ending gender discrimination;
it is about ending all systems of oppression. Once you understand that the feminist
project is about examining complex social systems, not just individual behavior, it
is easier to see how our social institutions are embedded with attitudes and beliefs
that foster all kinds of oppression. Therefore, sexism cannot be fully understood
without considering the concurrent social advantage or disadvantage of race. In fact,
some refer to sexism, racism, and classism (the big three oppressors) as interlocking
systems of oppression. Patricia Hill Collins (1990) explains that this notion actually
originated with Maria Stewart in the early 1800s:

Stewart's treatment of the interlocking nature of race, gender, and class oppression, her call for replacing denigrated images of Black womanhood with self-defined images, her belief in Black women's activism as mothers, teachers, and Black community leaders, and her sensitivity to sexual politics are all core themes advanced by a variety of Black feminist intellectuals. (p. 23)

Gloria Yamato (1998) refers to the interlocking systems of oppression as the "ism family." She describes these "isms" as parasites feeding off our lives and also defines the dangers of internalized "isms" that perpetuate the systemic "isms" and vice versa. The point is that we dwell in a social environment in which we are differently privileged and oppressed by different "isms."

Just as with sex/gender, there has been a persistent effort by researchers to prove that race is biological (the racial nature/nurture debate) and define racial difference. Peter Fryer (1989) offers a brief history of colonial, racist science, which included such "pseudo-scientific" pursuits as craniology, phrenology, and social Darwinism, all of which were used to "prove" the supremacy of whiteness as a racial category. Michael Vance (1989) raises the interesting question of why we chose skin/hair color as a signifier of difference:

In Europe people have differing skin colours, hair types and frequencies of gene for blood group A. Yet somehow Europeans manage to be presented as part of the same race—the Whiter and blonder members being slightly more pure, perhaps . . . there is more variation within a single 'racial' group than between them. (p. 118)

Biologically there is actually more variance between individuals of the same race than can be defined between racial groups. Vance points to the fact that we needed *visible* markers to socially differentiate. When you tie this concept to Lerner's (1986) hypothesis of how slavery evolved, it is a pretty powerful argument for the social construction of difference in order to oppress. Lerner says that one element of slavery was setting people apart as "different" and then "less than." It makes sense that in the historical framework in which this happened, people had to use outwardly visible markers. However, these outwardly visible traits do not establish the biology of race. Richard Lewontin (1989) explains that "there is no gene known that is 100 per cent of one form in one race and 100 per cent of a different form in some other race" (p. 203). Some of the latest genetic research establishes that "human genetic variation is geographically structured, in accord with historical patterns of gene flow and genetic drift . . . Analysis of many loci now yields reasonably accurate estimates of genetic similarity among individuals, rather than populations" (Jorde & Wooding, 2004). In fact, no "group is more hybrid in its origin than the present-day Europeans, who are a mixture of Huns, Ostrogoths, and Vandals from the east, Arabs from the south, and Indo-Europeans from the Caucasus" (Gill & Levidow, 1989, p. 207).

The idea of race as a social construction is further supported by the fact that definitions of "race" have changed over the years. For example, in the 19ᵗʰ century:

U.S. law identified those having any African ancestry as Black, a standard known as the 'one-drop rule,' which defined 'White' as a state of absolute purity in relation to 'Black.' Native American status, in contrast, required at least one-eighth Native American ancestry in order to qualify. (Johnson, 2006, p. 20)

These different standards for classifying race related to the ways in which they economically and legally disempowered Blacks and Native Americans in relation to Whites. This is a classic example of how law can operate as a social institution to support or challenge racism.

Just as maleness is used as a gender standard, "whiteness" is used as a racial standard. As with gender, our social institutions are designed with the assumption of whiteness. This means that to be White in the U.S. means to have race privilege, whether you want it or not. "When it comes to privilege . . . it doesn't really matter who we really are. What matters is who other people *think* we are, which is to say, the social categories they put us in" (Johnson, 2006, p. 35). Further, one of the markers of privilege is having choice about whether to acknowledge it or not. James Baldwin said, "To be White in America means not having to think about it" (Johnson 2006, p. 22). People of color have to think about race because they are reminded of their race in daily social encounters in a way that Whites are not.

Just as it may be difficult for some men to understand how they are privileged by gender, it may be difficult for some Whites to understand how they are privileged by race. In terms of awakening awareness and shifting the perspective of Whites with regard to race privilege, Peggy McIntosh's (1998) "White Privilege: Unpacking the Invisible Knapsack" provides one of the best roadmaps. Through a personal reflection on her own life in relation to an African-American woman peer, McIntosh offers a powerful lens through which to examine, define, and name the myriad ways in which our social institutions privilege Whites. The goal here is not to arrive at a simplistic "all Whites are bad, and all people of color are good" perspective. The goal is to begin to make conscious what has been largely unconscious to Whites, so that they can begin to make deliberate choices about how to use unearned race privilege to distribute power more fairly and ultimately end systems of oppression.

Just as not all women understand (or want to talk) about gender oppression, not all people of color understand about or want to name the systemic influences of racism. For those who are oppressed by institutionalized racism, the battle may be more of an interior one, to conquer internalized oppression. bell hooks gives this advice to people of color: "It is necessary to remember that it is first the potential oppressor within that we must resist—the potential victim within that we must rescue—otherwise we cannot hope for an end to domination, for liberation" (hooks, 1989, p. 21).

MYTH #6: IT'S "THEIR" PROBLEM, NOT MINE

Although I can probably assume that readers of this book have already grappled with this myth, I would like to briefly outline a few of the current costs of maintaining a dominator social model in an effort to underscore the importance of all of us working as allies to shift from a "dominator" to a "partnership" social system. (Eisler, 1987, 2002, 2007; Eisler & Loye, 1990; Eisler & Miller, 2004) These so-called "women's" issues matter to, and involve, us all.

What are the costs to society of perpetuating a dominator social system? After all, the dominator model has been the predominant social system worldwide for most of the last two millennia, and we have made pretty good progress as a human civilization, right? There is no doubt that human civilization as a whole has advanced astronomically. Nonetheless, the historical effect of centuries of patriarchy in women's lives has been to force women "to waste much time and energy on defensive arguments; it has channeled their thinking into narrow fields; it has retarded their coming into consciousness as a collective entity and has literally aborted and distorted the intellectual talents of women for thousands of years" (Lerner, 1986, p. 10). What knowledge might we have developed if the ideas and productive labor of half of our citizens had been fully engaged? What advances might we have made as a civilization? What more might we have learned about our world, about each other, and about how to be fully human? Similar questions could be raised about the contributions of people of color with one addition. Many people of color did contribute to social and scientific advances, but their stories have been largely excluded from the historical narrative.

If that concept of social cost is too broad, let us look at a more concrete and common example. Many people will say, "I'm not a feminist but, I agree in equal pay for equal work." That sounds great, but without understanding the deeply-embedded structural problems that contribute to our dominator social system, achieving salary equity will continue to progress very slowly. It has been over 40 years since The Equal Pay Act was passed (1964) in the United States and the following employment measures are still deeply impacted by gender and race: (1) types of employment; (2) percentage of unemployment; and (3) income inequity.

The type of employment that people pursue is still segregated by gender and race. Johnson (2006) claims that jobs "are so segregated by gender that half of all workers would have to change occupations in order for women and men to be equally represented across the U.S. economy" (Johnson, 2006, p. 59). The degree of unemployment and numbers of unemployed also show the influences of gender and race. Even among the upper strata of educated professionals, the negative impact of race contributes to greater unemployment for people of color, especially women of color. According to Johnson, "African-Americans and Latinas/os with four or more years of college are, respectively, 83 and 61 percent more likely to be unemployed than comparable Whites" (p. 59).

Income earned is still profoundly influenced by gender and race. The most common income measure comparing women's to men's earnings looks at the median annual income for full-time, full-year workers. This ratio has hovered around 76% since 2001, and the percentage of increase in the gender wage ratio has slowed in recent years. From 1980 to 1990, women's earnings increased 11.4% in relation to men, but only 5.4% over the next 15 years. In addition, a new report by the Institute of Women's Policy Research describes why this particular measure (median annual income for full-time, full-year workers) does not tell the whole story because it fails to capture the differences in lifetime earnings. Rose and Hartmann (2004) conducted a 15-year longitudinal study that looked at earnings from 1983-1998 and reported that "the average prime age working woman earned only $273,592 while the average working man earned $722,693 (in 1999 dollars)" which amounts to a gap of 62%, more than twice as large as the 23% gap reported by the more common annual measure (p. iii). There are multiple reasons for this salary gap, but they all relate to gender and race. Two of the most significant contributing factors are gender segregation in the labor market and time spent on family care. Rose and Hartmann developed a "three-tier schema of elite, good, and less-skilled jobs" and included in each tier sets of jobs that are predominantly male and predominantly female. They found the following:

Within each of the six gender-tier categories, at least 75 percent of the workers are of one gender. In each tier, women's jobs pay significantly less than those of their male counterparts even though both sets of occupations tend to require the same level of educational preparation. (Rose & Hartmann, 2004, p. iv)

In addition, they found that while 8% of men work in female occupations, 15% of women work in male occupations. However, these women still earn "one-third less than their male counterparts in male elite and less-skilled jobs" (p. iv).

Since we still have a gendered view of "care," time spent on family care has a significant impact on women's earnings over time resulting in both lower work hours and sometimes years with zero earnings. In terms of subsidized childcare and paid family leave, the U.S. lags far behind other industrialized nations. In terms of our social institutions in the U.S., family care (child care and elder care) is still largely viewed as the responsibility of individual women, rather than as a responsibility to be shared by society at large. The problem with that view is that both the quality of child care and the education children receive may suffer due to such a social system, both of which may contribute to other social problems in later years.

There is a significant relationship between the issue of family care and the issue of women's earnings in the work force. At the core of our gendered social system is the fact that we do not value family care as work; we *say* we value it in our social rhetoric which valorizes motherhood, but the *policies* in our social institutions do not support our rhetoric. This is true in large part because caregiving is "women's" work, but it is also because there is no dollar value attached to it. However, the "U.S. company Salary.com estimated that a fair wage for a typical stay-at-home parent would be $134,471 a year" (Eisler, 2007, p. 19). Since the 70s, scholars and politicians worldwide, notably Marilyn Waring, have tried to attach a dollar value to the caregiving that women do and to systematize this in social policy (Martin & Nash, 1997). These efforts seem to have finally raised the consciousness of some social policy organizations. For example:

There is now a satellite account in the U.N. System of National Accounts, or SNA (an international standard for national income accounting), that includes statistical data on household and other unpaid work . . . A 2004 Swiss government survey reported the value of unpaid work at 162 billion Euros or $190 billion—70 percent of the reported Swiss GDP. (Eisler, 2007, p. 37)

Undervaluing "women's" work (paid and unpaid) is also a contributing factor in terms of poverty statistics. Recent U.S. census data show the following percentages of these populations living in poverty: African-American, women 26.5%, Asian-American women, 12% (in spite of the fact that 42.7% hold bachelor's degrees or higher), Hispanic women, 10%, and White women, 4%. According to data from the National Organization for Women (n.d.), closing the pay gap between women and men would result in the following: women's annual family income would increase $4,000; poverty rates would drop 50%; and working families would gain $200 billion in family income annually.

In addition to these literal costs in income and more complex costs to society at large, continuing to support a dominator social model results in a myriad of internal costs to the human spirit of individuals. For women and people of color:

Little by little, day by day, the struggle to earn a living or a degree and maintain a sense of dignity and self-worth in the face of one sign after another that they do not really matter or belong wears people down, sapping morale and draining talent. (Johnson, 2006, p. 65)

Feagin and Sikes share the perspective of a Black college professor on what it is like to be Black in the U.S.:

It is . . . to lead 'lives of quiet desperation generated by a litany of daily large and small events that, whether or not by design, remind us of our 'place' in American society.' It is to experience a precarious balance between paranoia and the desire to live life simply as it comes, an endless struggle with humiliation, depression, and rage. (Johnson, 2006, p. 58)

In his groundbreaking work *A Different Mirror: A History of Multicultural America,* Ronald Takaki (1993) shares a personal story to illustrate a classic stereotype regarding what it means to be an "American." Takaki had just flown from his home in California to Virginia to attend an academic conference on multiculturalism. When he got into a cab and gave the driver directions, the driver asked how long Takaki has been in the U.S. because his English was excellent. Takaki explained that he was born here, and that his grandfather had come to the U.S. from Japan in the 1880s. It did not occur to the cab driver that someone who looked like Takaki was an American; Americans are White.

For men and Whites, there is a concurrent moral and emotional cost to individuals. In fact, hooks (1989) argues that "feminist struggle to end patriarchal domination should be of primary importance to women and men globally" because it negatively influences our private lives, our most intimate relationships with others, and "because it is that form of domination we are most likely to encounter in an ongoing way in everyday life" (p. 21). In a dominator system, we all learn to suppress parts of ourselves "to conform to externally imposed ideas about what men and women should be like" (Eisler, 2002, p. 9). Eisler (2002) explains the problem with gender socialization in a dominator system:

Contrary to Jungian masculine and feminine archetypes gaining renewed popularity, when a woman is assertive and logical, she is not accessing her masculine side; she is simply expressing qualities that are her own. In the same way, when a man is gentle and caring, he is not accessing his feminine side; he is expressing a part of his own inherent nature that's been stifled by a dominator culture. (p. 15)

Our authentic sense of identity is curbed by the forces of gender socialization, which results in a personal cost to most individuals.

In terms of creating institutional change, since male and White privilege cannot be disconnected from the oppression of women and people of color, those with social privilege must ally with the oppressed to be part of the change; we are all in this together. It is not useful for those with privilege to approach these issues from the standpoint of what to do about "them," making women and people of color the problem "other." We all need to approach these issues, asking what we can do "about us, so that our relationships, our work, our children, and our planet will flourish" (Tavris, 1992, p. 333). With regard to changing systems of privilege and oppression, those with privilege must have a sense of ownership of the issues in order to sustain their commitment to change. Everyone "is connected to a great deal of suffering in the world, and anyone who allows awareness of that to enter their consciousness is bound to feel something about it" (Johnson 2006, p. 75).

For centuries writers from Mary Wollstonecraft (1792) to bell hooks (2000) have called for the alliance of men with women in the struggle for social change. Wollstonecraft argues that educating women was not just about women, it was about bettering society:

Make them free, and they will quickly become wise and virtuous, as men become more so; for the improvement must be mutual or the injustice which one half of the human race are obliged to submit to, retorting on their oppressors, the virtue of men will be worm-eaten by the insect whom he keeps under his feet. (p. 182)

She also suggested that men could not sustain any sense of moral virtue while behaving as oppressors. hooks (2000) replaces the term "women's movement" (which she said implied that men could not be involved or that it was not relevant to them) with the term "feminist movement" (which she said better reflects the broad goals of eliminating all forms of oppression). In *Privilege Power and Difference* (2006), sociologist Allan Johnson explains why men must be allies in ending systems of male privilege and Whites must be allies in ending systems of race privilege:

Blacks and women and Asians, Latinos/as, Native Americans, lesbians, gay men, people with disabilities, and the lower and working classes . . . can't do it on their own, because although they certainly aren't powerless to affect the conditions of their own lives, they do not have the power to single-handedly do away with entrenched systems of privilege. If they could do that, there wouldn't be a problem in the first place. (p. 8)

Adding her voice to the call for allies, Jaleh Daie (1996) describes why the Association for Women in Science needs to include men as well as women. She says that men "should join AWIS for the same reasons women do: to advance diversity and equity in science and technology through programs in mentoring, career advancement, leadership development, coalition-building, and fund-raising" (p. 11).

Unfortunately, the force of our social institutions is deep and long-standing. The attitudes and beliefs that individuals learn from social institutions are remarkably deep-seated, and many of their origins are multiple centuries old. Our social institutions have taught us to see ourselves and our world in terms of differences (real or perceived), to categorize each other according to these differences, to rank each other according to these categorizations, to assume (or accede) power according to where we "fit" on the social hierarchy, and to dominate and oppress others "beneath" us on the social hierarchy. We are all players in this game, and it is a game where everyone loses in the end. That is why we all need to participate in creating social change.

WRITING A NEW STORY: SHIFTING FROM DOMINATION TO PARTNERSHIP

Now, the myths are exposed and maybe you are thinking: "Whoa! The problem is deeper and more complex than I thought. How can I possibly begin to make a difference?" Good question. It is true that one of the hardest things to do is to envision a new paradigm while standing in the old one (Johnson, 1989, p. 33). If the dominator values of gender socialization, hierarchical systems of power and privilege, and institutionalized oppression are so deeply embedded in our social institutions, how can we begin to envision and create the shift from a dominator to a partnership society?

First, it is important to liberate ourselves from the "either/or" thinking this is so pervasive in our dominator social system. Eisler and Loye (1990) suggest that while "differentiation is one of our most important thinking and learning tools, it is important to keep in mind that sometimes the differences between how these two models are manifested in actual practice is a question of degree or emphasis" (p. 181). To assume an either/or stance with regard to comparing a dominator society to a partnership society is too simplistic, and reveals the depth to which our current competitive paradigm is ingrained. The core elements of human society, such as competition and cooperation, may actually exist in both social models. However, the ways in which they manifest, and the degrees to which they manifest, are influenced by privileging different social values over others. A partnership society is:

not a utopian, ideal society free of problems, conflicts, disappointments, or grief. Conflict is a natural aspect of life . . . The difference . . . lies in how we are taught to deal with these givens. For example, in the dominator model, conflict is emphasized, but at the same time the violent suppression of conflict is institutionalized . . . in the partnership model, conflict is openly recognized, and dealing with it creatively in ways where both parties learn and grow is encouraged. (Eisler & Loye, 1990, p. 182)

Next, Eisler and Loye (1990) suggest many ways of envisioning the different values, attitudes, and beliefs that might emanate from the shift away from a dominator social system to a partnership system (p. 183-185). In the pervasive climate of fear that is perpetuated by dominator social systems, power over others is a central theme of our individual human interactions and of our social institutions. In the climate of trust cultivated by a partnership social system, the emphasis on power-over shifts to one of shared power, power-with, or empowerment. In a partnership social system it may even be possible to move beyond the notion of power to an emphasis on love and/or empathy as a central theme of our human interactions and ultimately of our social institutions. Eisler (2002) explains that "empathy and caring are not something we have to tack on to a brutal and callous 'human nature.' The capacity, and need for empathy and caring are biologically built into our species as part of our evolutionary heritage" (p. 36).

Eisler (1988) suggests that although a "suppressive dominator approach" still generally prevails, there is hope in the successful growth of contemporary movements for nonviolence as a means of conflict resolution (p. 192). Men like Gandhi, Martin Luther King, and Desmond Tutu and women like Mother Theresa, Rigoberta Menchu, and Wangari Maathai exemplify the potential that lies in using nonviolent means to resolve major social conflict and to inspire constructive social change. The contemporary rebirth of these ancient ideas first taught by Socrates and Jesus may suggest a current evolution and/or shift of emphasis away from a dominator to a partnership model. But, it is not only great leaders who can create change. Change can begin with us "with small acts and thoughts" (Eisler, 2002, p. 206). Eisler goes on to say:

I believe all of us are born with an inner voice that tells us to be caring, not cruel; that it is the essence of what makes us human. Unfortunately this empathic inner voice is often stifled, even silenced, by the dominator elements in our culture. (p. 182)

We can all contribute to the shift from a dominator to a partnership society simply by listening to that inner voice—the one that honors our essential, empathic, caring nature as human beings. This partnership perspective will help us shift away from "technologies designed to destroy and dominate" to "technologies that sustain and enhance life" (Eisler, 1987, p. xx). "In a world where technologies of communication and destruction span the globe almost instantaneously, creating a better world is a matter of enlightened self-interest" (Eisler, 2002, p. 125).

A feminist perspective can help us understand the values, attitudes, and beliefs that we have all learned from our current social system, and liberate us to make new choices about the kind of society that we want to co-create. In the end, perhaps the "F-word" that we really should resist and reject is not "feminism," it is "fear."

QUESTIONS FOR REFLECTIVE DIALOG

1. What does the word "feminism" mean to you? Make a list of the ideas and concepts that come to mind when you hear the word. Do you agree that "feminism" makes people withdraw from discussion? Why do you think we look away from feminism?

2. Do you agree with bell hooks that "feminism is for everyone"? Why or why not? Is there a group that feminism is not "for"? Describe those who are not served by feminism and why you selected that sub-set of individuals.

3. Consider Eisler's discussion of patriarchy as a "dominator model." How would you envision a shift to a partnership society in your work place? How might it look in a classroom? How might it look in government? Describe what shifts would need to take place and why these changes would be necessary.

4. Consider what elements of privilege intersect with your lived experience. Have you ever been excluded from an experience or opportunity because of a characteristic of your identity that you could not control (such as class, race, or gender)?

5. Do you agree that bigotry and racism are learned and can be unlearned? How would the process of "unlearning" racism begin? What could one individual do to help others "unlearn" their bigotry?

6. Consider your own gender socialization. Were you encouraged to do certain activities that suited your gender? Were you discouraged from participating in other activities that were not "appropriate"? Consider the clothes, toys, and other physical material that was special to you as a child. How much of it was gender specific? How does this early socialization inform our adult decisions?

7. The shift away from a dominator society requires that we move from a climate of fear to a climate of trust. How could you make that shift real in your own life? Where in your daily life could you move from using "power over" to one of shared power?

REFERENCES[4]

Barker, L. J., & Aspray, W. (2006). The state of research on girls and IT. In J. M. Cohoon & W. Aspray (Eds.), *Women and information technology: Research on underrepresentation.* (pp. 3-54). Cambridge, MA: MIT Press.

Barnett, R., & Rivers, C. (2004). *Same difference: How gender myths are hurting our relationships, our children and our jobs.* New York: Basic.

Baron-Cohen, S. (2003). *The essential difference: The truth about the male and female brain.* New York: Basic.

Beck, D. B. (1998, Spring). The 'F' word: How the media frame feminism. *NWSA Journal, 10*(1), 139-153.

Benbow, C. P., & Stanley, J. (1980). Sex differences in mathematical ability: Fact or artifact? *Science, 210,* 1262-1264.

Bix, A. S. (2000). Feminism where men predominate: The history of women's science and engineering education at MIT. *Women's Studies Quarterly, 28*(1/2), 24-45.

Brod, H. (1989). Work clothes and leisure suits: The class basis and bias of the men's movement. In M. Kimmel & M. A. Messner (Eds.), *Men's lives* (pp. 276-287). New York: Macmillan.

Bronfenbrenner, U. (Ed.). (2005). *Making human beings human: Bioecological perspectives on human development.* Thousand Oaks, CA: Sage.

Collins, P. H. (1990). *Black feminist thought: Knowledge, consciousness, and the politics of empowerment.* New York: Routledge.

Daie, J. (1996). Inclusion of women does not mean exclusion of men. *The Scientist, 10*(14), 11.

Eisler, R. (1987). *The chalice and the blade: Our history, our future.* San Francisco: HarperSanFrancisco.

Eisler, R. (2000). *Tommorrow's children: A blueprint for partnership education in the 21ˢᵗ century.* Boulder, CO: Westview.

Eisler, R. (2002). *The power of partnership: Seven relationships that will change your life.* Novato, CA: New World.

Eisler, R. (2007). *The real wealth of nations: Creating a caring economics.* San Francisco: Berrett-Koehler.

Eisler, R., & Loye, D. (1990). *The partnership way.* San Francisco: HarperSanFrancisco.

Eisler, R., & Miller, R. (Eds.). (2004). *Educating for a culture of peace.* Portsmouth, NH: Heinemann.

Faludi, S. (1991). *Backlash: The undeclared war against American women.* New York: Crown.

Fausto-Sterling, A. (2000). *Sexing the body: Gender politics and the construction of sexuality.* New York: Basic.

Fryer, P. (1989). Pseudo-scientific racism. In D. Gill & L. Levidow (Eds.), *Anti-racist science teaching* (pp. 178-197). London: Free Association.

Garreau, J. (1994). Conspiracy of heretics. *Wired, 2*(11), 98-158.

Gill, D., & Levidow, L. (Eds.). (1987). *Anti-racist science teaching.* London: Free Association.

Goldstein, L. S. (2004). Emphasizing variety rather than commonality: Educating young children for a culture of peace. In R. Eisler & R. Miller (Eds.), *Educating for a culture of peace* (pp. 127-135). Portsmouth, NH: Heinemann.

hooks, b. (1989). *Talking back: thinking feminist, thinking black.* Boston: South End Press.

hooks, b. (1992). *Black looks: Race and representation.* Boston: South End.

hooks, b. (2000). *Feminism is for everybody: Passionate politics.* Cambridge: South End.

Institute for Women's Policy Research. (2005, March 29). *African-American women work more, earn less.* Retrieved July 22, 2007, from http://www.iwpr.org/pdf/IWPRRelease3_29_05.pdf

Institute for Women's Policy Research. (2007, April). *The gender wage ratio: Women's and men's earnings.* Retrieved July 22, 2007, from http://www.iwpr.org/pdf/C350.pdf

Johnson, S. (1989). *Wildfire: Igniting the she/volution.* Albuquerque, NM: Wildfire Press.

Johnson, A. G. (1997). *The gender knot: Unraveling our patriarchal legacy.* Philadelphia: Temple UP.

Johnson, A. G. (2006). *Privilege, power and difference.* Boston: McGrawHill.

Jorde, L. B., & Wooding, S. P. (2004). Genetic variation, classification and 'race'. *Nature Genetics, 36*, S28-S33. Retrieved July 21, 2007, from http://www.nature.com/cgi-taf/DynaPage.taf?file=/ng/journal/v36/n11s/full/ng1435.html

Kesselman, A. et al. (Eds.). (2003). *Women images and realities: A multicultural anthology*. Boston: McGrawHill.

Kirk, G., & Okazawa-Rey, M. (2004). *Women's lives: Multicultural perspectives* (3rd ed.). New York: McGraw-Hill.

Lerner, G. (1986). *The creation of patriarchy*. New York: Oxford.

Lerner, G. (1993). *The creation of feminist consciousness: From the Middle Ages to eighteen-seventy*. New York: Oxford.

Lerner, R. M. (2005). Foreword: Urie Bronfenbrenner: Career contributions of the consummate developmental scientist. In U. Bronfenbrenner (Ed.), *Making human beings human: Bioecological perspectives on human development* (pp. ix-xxvi). Thousand Oaks, CA: Sage.

Lewontin, R. (1989). Are the races different? In D. Gill & L. Levidow (Eds.), *Anti-racist science teaching* (pp. 198-207). London: Free Association.

Martin, K. (Producer), & Nash, T. (Director). (1997). *Who's counting? Marilyn Waring on sex, lies & global economics* [Motion picture]. Oley, PA: Bullfrog Films.

McIntosh, P. (1998). White privilege: Unpacking the invisible knapsack. In P.S. Rothenberg et.al. (Eds.), *Race, class and gender in the U.S.* (pp. 165-169). New York: St Martin's.

Minnich, E. K. (1990). *Transforming knowledge*. Philadelphia: Temple UP.

Mundy, L. (1998, December 6). The doll's house. *Washington Post*. Retrieved August 30, 2007, from http://www.lexisnexis.com

National Organization for Women. (n.d.). *Facts about pay equity*. Retrieved July 22, 2007, from http://www.now.org/issues/economic/factsheet.html

Rich, A. (1986). *Of woman born: Motherhood as social institution*. New York: Norton.

Rose, S. J., & Hartmann, H. I. (2004). *Still a man's labor market: The long-term earnings gap*. Washington, D.C.: Institute for Women's Policy Research. Retrieved July 22, 2007, from http://www.iwpr.org/pdf/C355.pdf

Rumbaugh, D. M., & Washburn, D. A. (2003). *Intelligence of apes and other rational beings*. New Haven: Yale UP.

Starhawk. (1987). *Truth or dare: Encounters with power, authority, and mystery.* New York: Harper.

Takaki, R. (1993). *A different mirror: A history of multicultural America.* Boston: Little, Brown & Co.

Tavris, C. (1992). *The mismeasure of woman.* New York: Touchstone.

Vance, M. (1989). Biology teaching in a racist society. In D. Gill & L. Levidow (Eds.), *Anti-racist science teaching* (pp. 107-123). London: Free Association.

Vogelstein, F. (2006, October 9). Carly Fiorina tells her story. *Wired.* Retrieved July 20, 2007, from http://www.wired.com/science/discoveries/news/2006/10/71926?currentPage=all

Williams, P. (1997). *The rooster's egg: On the persistence of prejudice.* Cambridge, MA: Harvard.

Wolf, N. (1992). *The beauty myth: How images of beauty are used against women.* New York: Doubleday.

Wollstonecraft, M. (1996). *A vindication of the rights of woman. 1792.* Mineola, NY: Dover.

Yamato, G. (1998). Racism: Something about the subject makes it hard to name. In P.S. Rothenberg et al. (Eds.), *Race, class and gender in the U.S.* (pp. 150-153). New York: St Martin's.

ENDNOTES

[1]   When feminism is defined as broadly as I have defined it in this chapter, you may wonder about the difference between feminism and humanism. Feminism and humanism share the goal of affirming the "dignity and worth of all people" (en.wikipedia.org/wiki/Humanism). However, beyond that humanism is the product of a dominator Western philosophic knowledge tradition that emphasizes rationality over emotion and that (given its origins in the thinking of much earlier centuries) makes no specific reference to ending the institutionalized oppression of human beings based on gender, race, and class.

[2]   Professor Patricia Williams' book *The Rooster's Egg: On the Persistence of Prejudice* offers an insightful discussion of law as a social institution in relation to race.

3   Although you may have a carefully formed opinion about whether or not Fiorina's leadership of the company was good business, it is also true that your opinion (as well as the concrete results of her decisions as CEO) is likely to have been influenced by the fact that she was a woman in a position of leadership. At a minimum, your opinion was influenced by the social institution of mass media, which regularly "interprets" our world for us.

4   Some portions of this chapter may have appeared in, and are reprinted with permission from Kirk, M. (2006). Bridging the digital divide: A feminist perspective on the project. In G. Trajkovski (Ed.), *Diversity in information technology education: Issues and controversies* (pp. 38-67). Hershey, PA: Information Science Publishing.

Chapter II
Dualisms and Stereotypes:
Tools of Domination

OBJECTIVES

This chapter aims to help you understand the following:

- The gender boxes of male and female and why gender is the ultimate dualism.
- How dualisms such as gender and either/or thinking serve as tools of domination.
- How stereotypes influence our perceptions of ourselves and each other.
- Some classic gender and race stereotypes.
- Some ways in which stereotypes "keep us in our place" by influencing our self-concept, our academic performance (stereotype threat), our sense of possibilities, and our expectations of each other.

INTRODUCTION

Dualisms are a hallmark of dominator societies, and dualistic thinking is a deeply-embedded attitude that shapes our values and beliefs. The deficiency of dualistic thinking is that it encourages us to organize knowledge in simplistic "either/or" terms, rather than considering the "both/and" complexities of our human experience. Gender is socially-defined in dualistic terms; one is *either* male *or* female. Understanding gender, the ultimate dualism, can help one begin to grasp the ways in which gendered attitudes and beliefs are reflected in the social institutions through which we learn about IT.

The stereotypes (of gender, race, physical ability, age, etc.) that are purveyed by our social institutions are one of the most enduring and significant ways in which we all learn our sense of identity and "appropriate" location in the social hierarchy, as well as how we perceive and categorize others. Therefore, an in-depth understanding of stereotypes and their influence is critical to beginning to understand how we all continue to participate in recreating a dominator society.

Dualisms and stereotypes are two of the most pervasive and powerful tools of a dominator social system. Audre Lorde (1984) explains that "the master's tools will never dismantle the master's house" (p. 110). If we are ever to lay down these tools and construct a different house for our human community, we must understand how proficient we have all become at using the dominator tools of dualistic thought and stereotyping.

GENDER: THE ULTIMATE DUALISM

Understanding gender is not about saying "all men are this" and "all women are that." As described in Chapter I, the ways in which individuals understand and manifest gender is influenced by multiple factors—innate individual traits, family, culture and community, social institutions, and national ethos. In this book, my focus is on understanding the messages we receive about gender from our dominant social institutions in the U.S. Individuals may perceive gender slightly differently based on differences at other layers of influence, but they will also typically participate in reifying the dominant culture's notions of gender, at least to some extent.

Some of us begin to learn about gender before we are even born. Some researchers have shown that parents who know the sex of their babies will talk to them in the womb differently, beginning to teach boys to be "hard" and girls to be "soft." The sex of infants is often not easily identifiable, especially when they are all little round hairless lumps. So, our social institutions help us to make their sex (and implicitly gender) clearer with the blue-pink nature of baby clothes, toys, and even other functional items like blankets or bibs. However, few today know how recent this social development is to associate pink with girls and blue with boys. During the 1800s in the U.S., all babies wore little white dresses. This began to change at the turn of the 20th century "as plumbing, cloth diapers, and color-fast fabrics" were more available (Feinberg, 1996, p. 106). We did not settle on the blue=masculine and pink=feminine color scheme until after a debate in mass media over two paintings: Thomas Gainsborough's *Blue Boy* and Sir Thomas Lawrence's *Pinkie*. The problem with this color-coding is that few people easily fit one category. In *Transgender Warriors: Making History from Joan of Arc to Dennis Rodman*, Leslie Feinberg

(1996) explains how gender is better described on a continuum or circle than as a rigid either/or:

When I ride the subways or walk the streets of New York City, I see women who range from feminine to androgynous to masculine and men who range from masculine to androgynous to feminine. That forms a circle—a much more liberating concept than two poles with a raging void in between. (p. 107)

The problem with the dualistic construction of gender is that few of us completely fit into the gendered box of either "male" or "female" characteristics. Unfortunately, most of us learn that we are supposed to (degrading our confidence in our identity), and most of us learn to reinforce the boundaries of the gender box for others (leading to a kind of perpetual social abuse).

The Gender Boxes

What are the boundaries of the gender boxes? And, how do we learn the boundaries of the boxes? We learn about the gender boxes from our family, culture and community, and our social institutions. Although family and culture are the most intimate teachers, what we learn from social institutions about gender is sometimes more significant because it is so pervasive and so lasting. Table 1 describes the gender boxes to which human characteristics have been assigned in the U.S.

Table 1. Human characteristics and the gender boxes

Male	Female
Hard	Soft
Strong	Weak
Rational	Emotional
Active	Passive
Assertive	Submissive
Competitive	Cooperative
Domain is the outer world (public space)	Domain is the home (private space)
Subject	Object
Self-focused/Individualistic	Other-focused/Communalistic
Task-oriented	Relationship-oriented
Primary measure of worth is achievements, accomplishments	Primary measure of worth is appearance, attractiveness
Confident	Doubtful
Science	Nature

Based on our sex, we are assigned to the "appropriate" gender box. If you ever want to identify the boundaries of each gender box, just observe when women or men are censured for being "unfeminine" or "unmasculine." This will tell you where the boundaries of the box lie. For example, women may be criticized for being too "aggressive" because "assertiveness" is a male-defined characteristic, or men may be criticized for being too "emotional" because that is a female-defined characteristic. In fact, men are actually chastised for this type of behavior by being called "sissy" or "whimpy," which are both derogatory references to the female. As active participants in this either/or culture, men and women will reassert the gender boundaries for both men and women. We are all engaged in the socialization process.

In this dualistic model, it is extremely important to assign people to one box or the other in part because this so deeply informs how we behave towards each other. "We may not realize how routinely we form such impressions until we run into someone who doesn't fit neatly into one of our categories" (Johnson, 2006, p. 16). When we cannot make an immediate and obvious assignment, it creates a serious social discomfort. This was the idea behind the regular "Pat" sketches on the comedy show *Saturday Night Live* in the early 90s. Pat (a name used for men and women) was a sexually ambiguous, slightly overweight character, whose androgynous hair and clothing style made her/his gender identity ambiguous. Each sketch featured conversations with other people who were trying to figure out Pat's sex/gender without directly asking. Pat always delivered ambiguous or sometimes more confusing responses, and the stage was set for humor. For example, Pat might say, "Sorry if I'm a little grumpy, I have really bad cramps... I rode my bike over here, and my calf muscles are KILLING me!" The humor lay in the recognized discomfort people felt in not knowing whether they were talking to a man or a woman because that distinction is so fundamental to how we interact.

Perhaps you are asking, what is the big deal? The big deal is that we do not just rigidly define one gender as separate from other; we also consistently teach that one set of gendered characteristics is better than the other. Our social institutions are largely organized around "maleness" as the standard of behavior. This means that the human characteristics of the "male" gender box are the traits that are valued in our social institutions. I cite the example in Chapter I about how, as a culture, we have defined the characteristics of a good leader in relation to "maleness" and how difficult this then makes it for women to participate in leadership roles without persistent criticism of their behavior, no matter which characteristics they express. If they express concern for their staff, like a "good woman" should do, they are too emotional, too soft. If they are task-oriented and rational, like a "good man" should be, they are criticized with a variety of euphemisms for being too "hard."

To create a society in which all human beings are free to express the characteristics in both gender boxes—one in which it is acceptable for men to have emotion and women to have intelligence—we need a better understanding of how deeply rooted these attitudes are. Stereotypes are one of the most significant and pervasive tools used to teach about gender, race, class, culture, and so forth.

STEREOTYPES, INFLUENCE, AND PERSUASION

Educated people often claim that they are immune to the influence of stereotypes. Being aware of the existence of stereotypes does not make an individual immune to the pervasive nature of gender trait assumptions. A prime example of how these concepts are transmitted constantly is reflected in the fact that the U.S. advertising industry spends over $100 billion per year to sell us things. In newspapers and magazines, which were still the dominant advertising media in the U.S. (followed by TV and radio) in 1998, advertising expenditures were over $300 per person and represented 43% of the world's total expenditures on advertising (Balnaves, Donald, & Donald, 2001, pp. 72-73). Examining advertising is a great way to understand more about what stereotypes pervade our thinking; advertisers have very little space (in print) or time (on other media) to communicate a message that will persuade people to act. That means that they often purvey stereotypes to communicate in shorthand and to inspire emotional compliance.

In *Influence: The Psychology of Persuasion*, Robert Cialdini (1993) defines the psychology of compliance which examines the factors that cause people to say "yes" as well as techniques that advertisers and salespeople use to encourage compliance. The book, which is in its 25th printing since 1984, has garnered broad appeal from consumers to social psychologists to business people who study marketing principles (Kilduff & Krackhardt, 1994; Plous, 1993). Using evidence from many, now classic, psychological studies, Cialdini defines the following six principles of social interaction: consistency, reciprocation, social proof, authority, liking, and scarcity (p. xiii). He explains how humans living in societies together developed these social "shortcuts" to deal with increasingly complex interactions without having to separately evaluate each situation. Cialdini adds that as "the stimuli saturating our lives continue to grow more intricate and variable, we will have to depend increasingly on our shortcuts to handle them all" (p. 7). This raises serious questions about the increasing presence of mass communication in developed societies, and the potential effectiveness of efforts to address the negative impact of stereotypes. Stereotyping is an extension of this kind of shortcut thinking. If you can make certain assumptions about people based on limited information, you have seemingly accomplished a social shortcut. However, these shortcuts can have the same sort of negative social effects as the principles that Cialdini describes. So, the things that seem to "help" us may ultimately hurt us more.

The first principle of reciprocation "says that we should try to repay, in kind, what another person has provided us" (Cialdini, 1993, p. 17). The most common way this is used in marketing is to give people gifts or free samples in order to inspire a purchase or donation. This behavior is heightened if the person making the request makes a concession before coming to agreement; there is "an obligation to make a concession to someone who has made a concession to us" (Cialdini, 1993, p. 37). This takes on a particular character in a dominator social system where the emphasis is on fear and the goal is to have "power over" another.

The second principle of commitment and consistency describes the human need to be "consistent with what we have already done" and to be consistent with our own behavior once we have taken a stand on an issue (Cialdini, 1993, p. 57). One of the ways that salespeople use this principle is to get people to make minor commitments that set the stage for more significant commitments that are consistent with each other (p. 67). Another strong factor in the use of this social principle is that there seems to be an even greater urge to maintain the commitment if it is put in writing (p. 79). This is used in multiple ways such as goal setting for salespeople. The concept of cognitive dissonance also says that the more we have sacrificed to something, the more highly we will value it. One study showed that those who invested their energy waiting in line for a movie considered the movie better than those who did not have to wait to see it. In a social system where we have all learned discriminatory behavior, "commitment and consistency" suggests that we may be more invested in defending what we have already done than in being open to new ideas and behavior.

The third principle of social proof says that "one means we use to determine what is correct is to find out what other people think is correct" (Cialdini, 1993, p. 116). This is used in a variety of settings such as salting tip jars, collection baskets, and product advertisements that claim to be the "fastest-selling." This principle raises an interesting question in relation to the hegemony of patriarchal values in contemporary media. What does this mean in terms of helping people develop alternative views? Cialdini also adds that this principle is particularly effective in social situations where people are uncertain, or where the appropriate action is ambiguous (p. 129). Cialdini adds that the "principle of social proof operates most powerfully when we are observing the behavior of people just like us" (p. 140). Perhaps the most stunning evidence of social proof lies in the numerous studies that Cialdini cites to support the increase in suicides, plane crashes, and fatal car accidents after the publication of a suicide story (pp. 148-149). This may offer a key to answering the question of why the stereotypical characterizations of people represented in media matter so much.

The fourth principle of liking says that "we most prefer to say yes to someone we know and like" (Cialdini, 1993, p. 167). His stunning evidence of this in a common sales situation is the statistic that daily sales at Tupperware parties exceed $2.5 million (p. 168). Cialdini lists the following specific factors that contribute to likability: physical attractiveness, similarity, compliments, contact and cooperation, and conditioning and association. With regard to stereotypes about women, physical attractiveness is often associated with likability while women who are less physically attractive are often cast as less likable. In addition, physically attractive women are often stereotyped as less intelligent—the "dumb blonde" stereotype. Could it be that to be an attractive and intelligent woman is to hold too much power in a society centered on maleness?

The fifth principle of authority says that we feel a strong social duty to defer to authority, even just the perception of authority that is indicated by titles, clothes, or other trappings (Cialdini, 1993, pp. 213-229). The link between authority and the pervasiveness of stereotypes, and of the bigoted thinking that often accompanies them, should be easy to see. For example, if your boss tells sexist and racist jokes that make you uncomfortable, you are more inclined to laugh along than if a peer or subordinate told them. In fact, humor is another insidious way in which stereotypes are purveyed since it can be difficult to challenge a sexist or racist stereotype because it is "just a joke."

The sixth principle of scarcity says that "opportunities seem more valuable to us when their availability is limited" (Cialdini, 1993, p. 238). Businesses, or at least advertisers, in the free market, capitalist economy of the U.S. have an obvious reason to try to create the perception of scarcity. However, this is often also a characteristic of dominator societies; they tend to either have or focus on scarcity of resources rather than abundance (Eisler & Miller, 2004, p. 14). The concept that there is only so much to go around breeds an attitude of competition rather than cooperation. The focus is often on a win-lose approach to every problem since we have learned to be more worried about losing something than focusing on what might be gained by resolving a particular issue. The scarcity principle results in thinking, such as, "they are" taking all of the jobs when a truer description of the employment market is that it is constantly shifting and changing, and that these shifts and changes are influenced by far more complex issues in a global economy than a simplistic, dualistic "us-them" perspective will ever explain.

Stereotypes in Advertising

Advertising is one of the most prevalent and effective means of mass communication. It serves as an interpreter of cultural values that communicates immediately with consumers. One of the most dominant methods for establishing a connection quickly is the use of stereotypes that often reinforce limited, limiting, and injurious messages about people (Creedon, 1993). There is a behavioral advantage to categorizing information in terms of helping humans make judgments more easily in an increasingly complex society. However, when these systems are used exclusively to over-generalize and exaggerate, they become tools of prejudice rather than useful guides to human behavior; stereotypes serve no useful human behavioral purpose (Aries, 1996; Cialdini, 1993; Lester, 1996). Patricia Hill Collins (1990) further describes why these stereotypes are dangerous: "These controlling images are designed to make racism, sexism, and poverty appear to be natural, normal, and an inevitable part of everyday life" (p. 68). Hey, it's just the way things are, right? Nope. See Myth #1 in Chapter I.

Furthermore, communication scholars have explored the notion that "[v]isual images in the media can be seen as symbols of power" (McClelland, 1993, p. 229). Some of the most recent work on stereotypes in mass media has examined "content, image, and representation of gender in the mass media as discourses about power, rather than as issues of equal opportunity or sexist portrayals" (McClelland, 1993, p. 229). This may be one of the most significant issues in this analysis because it is a power that those who participate in the media—from media owners to reporters—understand well. Walter Lippmann is quoted as saying, "The power to determine each day what shall seem important and what shall be neglected is power unlike any that has been exercised since the Pope lost his hold on the secular mind" (Nelkin, 1995, p. 65).

Carolyn L. Kitch (1998) examined magazine covers during a 30-year period near the "first wave" of the women's movement and chronicled how the "ideal of a 'typical' American woman quickly came to stand for an ideal of a typical, middle-class American" (Kitch, 1998). This historical perspective helps to underline the integral ties between the ways in which women are represented in media and consumer culture, and a social backlash against feminism. Kitch says the "emergence of stereotypes" in U.S. American mass media took a once "progressive political concept, the New Woman of the 1890s" and "commercialized—commodified and contained" her by 1930 (Kitch, 1998, pp. 476-478). The two dominant stereotypes of the 1920s, "the flapper and the modern homemaker . . . recast feminist and other radical impulses in terms of personal fulfillment and competitive consumerism" (Kitch, 1998, pp. 476-478). This is a profound example of media's power to reshape our thinking about society and about ourselves.

Appropriating Cultures, Fragmenting and Commodifying People

This kind of cultural appropriation, commodifying ideas from the feminist movement into consumer-based values, is also reflected in mass media representations of people of color. bell hooks (1992) describes how mass media fosters race-based and class-based stereotypes by marking "encounters with Otherness . . . as more exciting, more intense, and more threatening" (hooks, 1992). She expands on this "commodification of difference" by analyzing several *Tweeds* catalogues, one of which featured images of Egypt where the people and their culture are commodities. In the catalog, Egypt becomes a "landscape of dreams, and its darker-skinned people background, scenery to highlight whiteness, and the longing of Whites to inhabit, if only for a time, the world of the Other" (hooks, 1992, pp. 26-31). She points out that in spite of the fact that the catalogue is filled with images of Egyptians, nothing is said in the text about them. The images also convey the placement of the Egyptians in relation to the Whites; there is "no mutual looking," and when "bodies contact one another, touch, it [is] almost always a white hand doing the touching." Not only does this commodification of otherness promote consumption, hooks (1992) also refers to it as a form of "consumer cannibalism that not only displaces the Other but denies the significance of that Other's history through a process of decontextualization" (pp. 26-31).

Robert M. MacGregor (1989) conducted a longitudinal study spanning 30 years of visible minority women in print advertising by examining *Maclean's*, one of Canada's major magazines. MacGregor defined "visible minorities" as including "aboriginal people, Canadians with origins in Africa, Arab countries, China, India, Pakistan, Japan, Korea, South East Asia, Latin America, the Pacific Islands, the West Indies, and the Philippines" (p. 137). The study showed that although the total representation of visible minorities had increased from 1.2 to 11.5%, the ways in which visible minorities are represented are extremely limited. First, "the category of tourism accounted for 46.9 percent of all advertisements for the thirty year period," which means that women were pictured as "exotics" decorating the landscape. By 1984, this trend was not much better with "33 percent of all visible minority women" pictured in "charity-related advertisements and 48.5 percent in tourism." Finally, in the tourism category three roles dominated the statistics, accounting for 83.7% of the total: decorative/idle (women are shown as atmosphere or background, not as actors), dancing (55% of these women pictured as entertainment were Latin/Mexican women, 45% were Black women), and poor/idle (92.3% of these women were Black) (p. 139).

Another aspect of stereotypical racist images and representations is the propensity for fragmenting people into parts. Jannette Dates and William Barlow (1993) documented the racist bias revealed in historical memorabilia of African-Americans in the United States where people are "portrayed as dismembered utilitarian objects, such as a Black man's head used as an egg cup and a Black woman's mouth used as a bottle opener" (p. 473). Dates and Barlow describe how these items and the advertisements are "an important vehicle for the transmission of ideologies related to Black inferiority and White supremacy" (p. 473). This issue of fragmenting people into parts has been a major dimension of feminist scholarship on stereotypical representations of women in advertising. In her now benchmark film on advertising, *Still Killing Us Softly: Advertising's Image of Women*, Jean Kilbourne describes how advertising first dehumanizes and sexually objectifies women ("turning a human into a thing is the first step toward violence") and then turns sexuality into "a dirty joke" (Lazarus, 1987).

The way in which stereotypical representations of White, middle class women in mass media operate in terms of turning women into consumers focused on "fixing" all of their fragmented body parts is one of the central themes of Naomi Wolf's (1992) *The Beauty Myth: How Images of Beauty Are Used Against Women*. The constant reflection of an impossibly perfect, airbrushed, thinner than normal, cellulite-free, wrinkle-free, hair-free, odor-free ideal, not only systematically lowers women's self-esteem, it does an excellent job of turning them into consumers; maybe this product will help her reach "perfection." According to Wolf, the real function that women serve as "aspiring beauties" in the mass media culture is "*to buy more things for the body*" (p. 66).

In *The Body Project: An Intimate History of American Girls*, Joan Jacobs Brumberg (1997) documents the historical and very personal origins of this process of turning girls into consumers during adolescence. Brumberg explains how contemporary U.S. American society provides fewer social protections for developing adolescent girls which leaves them "extremely vulnerable to the excesses of popular culture" (p. xvii). She also examines how the mass media have guided girls in turning their bodies "into an all-consuming project in ways young women of the past did not" (p. xvii). There is a double whammy here: the mothers of these adolescent girls are also indoctrinated by media images of what they should be, want, do, and consume. This means that traditional coming-of-age rites of passage such as lengthening skirts or wearing the hair up are acted out today in trips to the mall to purchase bras, lipstick, or high heels. Often led in part by their mothers, contemporary girls "establish a firm bond with the marketplace" (p. 33). This consumer-driven obsession with their outward appearance may limit girls' inner resources in terms of developing their characters and their intellects.

Dependent, Incompetent, Care-Giving, Sex Objects

In journalism, television programs, films, and advertising, women scientists are stereotypically depicted as: dependent on and supporters of others (especially men), incompetent and incapable of action (they must wait for men to take action), the primary caregivers (men are the breadwinners), and victims and sex objects (men are sexual aggressors) (Wood, 1999, pp. 304-315). Media have also created two images of women, that is, good and bad: "[g]ood women are pretty, deferential, and focused on home, family, and caring for others. As subordinates to men, women are usually cast as victims, angels, martyrs, and loyal wives and helpmates" (Wood, 1999, p. 305). Unfortunately, women's magazines are some of the most serious purveyors of these stereotypes. One scholar recently showed that although women's magazines have improved in recent years in terms of covering broader social issues, they continue to "emphasize how to look better, appeal to men, cook nice meals, maintain relationships, and care for families" (Wood, 1999, p. 306).

There is another much deeper dimension to this story. It is largely the story of White women. For example, an examination of news coverage in urban areas where diverse minority populations range between 23% and 26% of the total population showed that "photographic coverage of minorities was limited almost exclusively to African-Americans (who were not the largest racial minority group in their communities)" (Gist, 1993, p. 106). In addition, when minorities are pictured it is almost exclusively in association with negative events. In "neutral stories, ranging from politics to weather to housing or school issues, it was rare that professional or working class minorities were mainstreamed into the coverage in the way non-minorities are" (Gist, 1993, p. 107). When they are included at all, people of color are stereotyped in pervasively negative terms. The next few sections look more closely at these stereotypes.

Noble "Savages"

The Wild West shows of the late 1800s, and subsequently Hollywood today, characterize all indigenous peoples as "Indians," using a variety of stereotypical portrayals:

The lazy and shiftless drunk; the Indian as educated half-breed unable to live in either the red or White world; the Indian as noble hero; the Indian as friendly, loyal, trustworthy companion; the Indian as victim of the evil White man; the Indian as stoic and unemotional; and the Indian as vanishing American. (Robinson, 1996, p. 171)

Historically, the stereotypical choices were "bloodthirsty savage" or "noble warrior." Newer stereotypes are those of Indians as "spirit guides" or "protestors" (Lester, 1996, pp. 42-43). Women are notably absent from these images, other than as a loyal, stoic companion to the White man; a stereotype that mirrors the common racist legacy of women of color as the sexual property of White men.

Hot Mammas and Mammies

Collins (1990) describes how portraying "African-American women as stereotypical mammies, matriarchs, welfare recipients, and hot mommas has been essential to the political economy of domination fostering Black women's oppression" (p. 67). Collins adds that one of the first stereotypes—Black woman as mammy—served to justify the continued economic exploitation of Black women in domestic service as well as to reinforce the "ideal Black female relationship to elite White male power" (p. 71). The image of Black women as matriarchs (who are overly aggressive, unfeminine, and emasculating to men) also explains Black women's "place" in the context of race, class, and gender oppressions (pp. 73-74). Perhaps one of the most controlling and damaging images, because it is sometimes so implicit, is the role of a Black woman as Jezebel. Collins defines the Jezebel's function as relegating "all Black women to the category of sexually aggressive women," which helped justify the prevalence of rape during slavery and the expectation that Black women continuously bear children (p. 77). Most of these stereotypes remain active in one form or another today, and they continue to inform the exclusion of Black women in terms of standards of beauty.

These sexualized stereotypes of African-American women have a historical legacy going back to the display of naked African women in Paris in the early 1800s, most notably Sarah Bartmann (then referred to as "the Hottentot Venus") whose naked body was displayed for 5 years and whose genitals were put on display after her death (hooks, 1992; Schiebinger, 1993). According to hooks, Josephine Baker's popularity in the early 1900s was due in part to "White European fascination with the bodies of Black people" (1992, p. 63). Baker was known for calling attention to her "butt" by handling "it as though it were an instrument, a rattle, something apart from herself that she could shake" (hooks, 1992, p. 63). It's a tough call. Women today still tread the fine virgin-whore line when they display their bodies in an attempt to reclaim their own power around their sexuality.

In *Playing in the Dark: Whiteness and the Literary Imagination*, Toni Morrison (1992) examines the ways in which "whiteness" is defined against "blackness" and the ways in which these racialized meanings are embedded in our language. More specifically, she examines "how the image of reined-in, bound, suppressed, and repressed darkness became objectified in American Literature as an African-ist persona" (p. 39). She also points to a different price by examining what "racial ideology does to the mind, imagination, and behavior of masters" (p. 12). hooks also describes the way in which whiteness is defined against blackness: "Within commodity culture, ethnicity becomes the spice, seasoning that can liven up the dull dish that is mainstream White culture" (1992, p. 21).

"God's Brown Daughters"[1]

The subtitle of this section indicates the classic difficulty in trying to group people by race and culture because there are many variables. Although "Hispanic" has been used as a statistical category for years to refer to people whose heritage links to Spain and the Iberian peninsula, in the United States this term also refers to people who have immigrated from Cuba, Mexico, Puerto Rico, and many other countries in Central and South America. Economics scholars Teresa Amott and Julie Matthaei (1996) avoid using "the term 'Hispanic' because it reduces a complex, multi-racial and multi-cultural heritage to its European . . . component" and ignores the historical legacy of indigenous Central and South American peoples (p. 64). "Latino/a" and "Chicano/a" are the more contemporary terms that have emanated from the self-naming of scholars and activists who belong to these cultural groups; these terms refer to those whose heritage may be from anywhere in Latin America except Mexico, and to those whose heritage links to Mexico and its indigenous peoples, respectively. Obviously, the heritages of these many geographies and cultures may have more distinctions than similarities. Gloria Anzaldua (1987), who describes herself as a Chicana Tejana lesbian-feminist poet,[2] has written eloquently about the complexities of her multiple heritages:

What I want is an accounting with all three cultures—White, Mexican, Indian. I want the freedom to carve and chisel my own face, to staunch the bleeding with ashes, to fashion my own gods out of my entrails. And if going home is denied me then I will have to stand and claim my space, making a new culture—una cultura mestiza—with my own lumber, my own bricks and mortar and my own feminist architecture. (p. 22)

Unfortunately, stereotypes link all of the people from these rich and varied cultural heritages together into a misunderstood mass. Two broad stereotypes apply to both men and women: the wetback or illegal immigrant and the greaser, bandit, or gang member (Lester, 1996, p. 32). The wetback stereotype casts all immigrants with Hispanic origins as parasitic, poverty-stricken, drains on the welfare system. The greaser stereotype (whose origins lie in the California Greaser Act of 1855, an anti-vagrancy statute specifically "directed at the Mexican California citizens") casts Hispanics in terms of drugs, violence, and the growth of urban crime (Robinson, 1996, p. 127).

The female gender-specific flavors of these stereotypes are the funny Hispanic maid, "the devout, long suffering Hispanic mother," the Hot Tamale, spitfire, sexpot, or Mexican Jezebel, and the gangster's girlfriend (Cofer, 1998; Enloe, 1989; Robinson, 1996). It should not be surprising how much these stereotypes parallel those of the mammy, matriarch, and Jezebel for African-American women. Although not subject to the historical legacy of slavery, Latinas who often faced language and education barriers were also limited to employment as domestics, waitresses, or assembly line workers.

A Picture is Worth a Thousand Brides

Asian-Americans represent a similarly culturally pluralistic group as Latino/a's, historically including immigrants from China, Japan, Korea, and the Philippines, and more recently including immigrants from Vietnam, Cambodia, Thailand, and numerous other Asian countries. Asian stereotypes are as similarly monolithic as Latino/a stereotypes. However, they are informed by a slightly different history. Chinese and Japanese immigrants led the way in the late 1800s followed by Filipino/a and Hawaiian immigrants in the early 1930s and Southeast Asian immigrants in the late 1900s. Unlike some immigrant populations, the:

U.S. legal system denied Asian immigrants the legal rights which had been accorded their European counterparts, relying on the 1790 naturalization law that restricted the privilege of citizen ship to "free White persons" . . . [and] federal and state governments passed close to 50 laws specifically aimed at restricting and subordinating Asian immigrants between 1850 and 1950. (Amott & Matthaei, 1996, p. 194)

The early history of Chinese and Japanese immigration to the United States is gendered. Most men came independently to search for gold and build the railroad, but most women came via men by being sold into marriage (through marriages arranged by families or as picture-brides) or sold into prostitution. This set the stage in some small way for the stereotypes that took hold.

Since stereotypes for Asian-Americans are not very specific to their different histories, and all were ultimately lumped into the category of the "diabolical Yellow Peril," examining the history of Japanese-American stereotypes tells a representative story (Robinson, 1996, p. 132). In an albeit male-centered analysis, Dennis Ogawa (1971) documented the history of how Japanese-American stereotypes evolved from positive in the late 19th century to negative during and after World War II and returned to positive again during the postwar years. Early California newspapers such as the *San Francisco Chronicle* and the *Sacramento Bee* reflected a more positive editorial policy toward the Japanese than the Chinese, referring to the Japanese as "more docile and obedient than the Chinese" (Ogawa, 1971, p. 8). Of course, embedded in this "more positive" attitude was still an "appropriate" subservience in relation to the larger White community. However, the 1924 immigration law that banned "Orientals" was the beginning of the end of even these remotely positive stereotypes, and by the time Japanese-Americans were interred in camps in 1942, the transition to negative images was complete.

Ogawa (1971) names four primary stereotypes that evolved out of this period: highly un-American, inferior citizens, sexually aggressive, and part of an international menace. In the postwar years, Ogawa documents how these negative stereotypes were replaced with the more positive ones of highly Americanized and well-educated and superior citizens: "The men are thought to be quiet, shy, lovers of gardens and the women graceful, lovely, delicate, and servile" (p. 26). This emphasis on "gentleness" is another way of continuing to represent Japanese-Americans in "appropriately" nonthreatening roles, maintaining the traditional racial hierarchy. Another issue worth noting here is that Japanese-American women have not been subject to quite the same sexual aggressiveness that is characteristic of the stereotypes of other women of color. Although the "exotic" stereotype certainly makes Japanese-American women more sexually desirable, they are envisioned as appropriate prospective brides more often than other women of color, and there is a greater acceptance of "the marriage of a White man and a Japanese woman" (Ogawa, 1971, p. 59).

How Images Injure

I have chronicled some gender and race stereotypes that are purveyed through mass media. Now, let's look at the kind of damage they do in terms of perpetuating institutionalized and internalized "isms," such as racism, sexism, and classism. There is little debate among scholars about whether or not these stereotypical images influence how we feel about ourselves and others; the debate centers around just how they affect us.

Since the dawn of the second wave of the feminist movement in the late 1900s, scholars from a wide range of disciplines have examined the ways in which stereotypical representations of women have been injurious. Naomi Wolf (1992) describes how the White, middle class, U.S. American definition of beauty is exclusive of intelligence. Joanna Kadi (1996) discusses her sense of cultural exclusion as an Arab-American scholar in higher education with a working class heritage. Women's literature scholars Sandra M. Gilbert and Susan Gubar (1984) describe how negative gender stereotypes influenced early women writers by forcing them into a sense of split identity that often resulted in multiple internal identities that struggled against each other. Film scholar Patricia Erens (1990) looks at women as the object of the male gaze, where men are the actors and women are acted upon.

In examinations of mass media from news reporting to advertising stereotypes continue to ignore "the complexities of modern women's lives" while they fail to do their job of "selling solutions" (Lazier & Kendrick, 1993, p. 201). Stereotypes are also disappointingly stable and durable. One study that replicated a 1957 study of gender role concepts decades later "found that 62% of the adjectives used to describe men and 77% of the adjectives used to describe women remained unchanged" (Aires, 1996, p. 166). This study was supported by two more studies conducted 16 years apart that found a "high degree of similarity in sex role stereotypes . . . over the 16-year period" (Aires, 1996, p. 166).

Other scholars have shown that rather than improving in recent years, the situation may have even worsened. One 1986 study compared its data to a similar 1973 study and found that the newer advertisements were "slightly more sexist than those in the 1973 sample" (Lazier & Kendrick, 1993, p. 205). Mee-Eun Kang's (1997) study compared magazine advertisements in 1979 and 1991 and found few changes in the kinds of stereotypes, but found an increased stereotyping of women in the categories of "licensed withdrawal" and "body display." "Licensed withdrawal" is when the subject is "pictured engaged in involvements which remove them psychologically from the social situation at large, leaving them unoriented in it and to it, and dependent on the protectiveness of others who are present," and "body display" defines the relative degree of nudity (Kang, 1997, p. 985). So, according to Kang, there is an increase in picturing women in dependent or uninvolved positions (as models) and in less clothing than they wore in 1979.

Over the years, much of the scholarly discussion has centered around the influence of false, stereotypical, and idealized images of women's bodies on their sense of well-being. Two major studies documented (1) the prevalence of magazine ads and articles focusing on dieting, food, and (2) the body, and the ways in which bust-to-waist and hip-to-waist ratios have changed from 1901 to 1981. In 1901, the average bust-to-waist ratio was around 2.0; it declined steadily to a low of about 1.2 in 1925, rose steadily to a high of around 1.6 in the late 1940s, and has been steadily declining since then to its current low of 1.2 (Lazier & Kendrick, 1993, pp. 204-205). The U.S. media obsession with the female breast, and women's subsequent dissatisfaction, has led to the development of a multimillion dollar cosmetic surgery industry that has reshaped millions of women's breasts. Since this surgery invariably results in scar tissue and reduced erotic feeling, it might also be fairly considered "a form of sexual mutilation" (Wolf, 1992, p. 242).

Another example of the profound way in which these images can negatively influence women is evidenced in the work of recent scholars who have demonstrated connections between limited media images of women and the increasing prevalence of eating disorders among women (Rolf & Masten, 1990; Stice, 1998; Stice & Shaw, 1994; Striegel-Moore, 1986). Cusumano and Thompson (1997) recently examined the effects of media images in terms of portraying social ideals of body images and the internalization of these ideals on college women. They asked questions about body image, eating disorders, and overall self-esteem of college women who were "75% White, 7% Black, 10% Hispanic, 7% Asian or Pacific Islander, and 1% other" (Cusumano & Thompson, 1997, p. 701). Their work replicated the data of others on the negative effects of internalized body images and "found a direct effect of this risk factor on body dissatisfaction" (p. 718). In her work on body image, Brumberg (1997) describes how "middle-class White girls define" perfection in 1995 as "five feet seven inches tall and 110 pounds" (p. 119). According to U.S. Department of Health and Human Services, 110 pounds is in the "healthy weight range" for a woman who is four feet ten inches to five feet three inches tall. The healthy weight range for a woman who is five feet seven inches tall goes from a minimum of 121 pounds to 160 pounds (Northrup, 1998, p. 693).

Not only are the media standards of beauty nearly impossible to attain, they are also largely tied to being White and middle class. First of all, women of color are very rarely depicted at all. According to Lazier and Kendrick (1993), "[p]ast studies have confirmed that approximately 1% of ads use African-American or older models, regardless of their percentages in the population (12%-16%)" (p. 216). In the very rare instances when women of color are depicted, they are expected to conform to "White" standards of beauty. Historically, this has been true even in media that purport to represent specific ethnic interests. For example, until very recently, the middle-class magazine *Ebony* featured advertisements for skin bleachers and whiteners (Brumberg, 1997, p. 78). In addition, although there is some evidence to show that African-American women may be more accepting of different body sizes and styles, there is also evidence that this may be more class-based. *Essence*, another magazine that addresses African-American middle class women, "regularly runs stories on body-size anxiety and eating disorders, a fact which suggests that conventional 'White' standards become more relevant among women of color as affluence increases" (Brumberg, 1997, p. 119).

In another recent study, Natalie J. MacKay and Katherine Covell (1997) examined the impact of women in advertisements on attitudes towards women; their work replicated earlier data that showed a "relation between viewing sex image advertisements and reporting attitudes supportive of sexual aggression" (p. 573). Not only did these images contribute to male attitudes of sexual aggression, there was also a reduced male and female support for ideas that reflected more progressive views of women's roles in society (MacKay & Covell, 1997, p. 580-581). The images not only affect women, they also affect men's views of women.

In examining the ways in which media stereotypes breed racism, bell hooks (1992) eloquently describes the effects of these images by likening them to a media monster that breeds internalized racism. She describes the monster in action:

It rips and tears at the seams of our efforts to construct self and identity. Often it leaves us ravaged by repressed rage, feeling weary, dispirited, and sometimes just plain old broken hearted. These are the gaps in our psyche that are the spaces where mindless complicity, self-destructive rage, hatred, and paralyzing despair enter. (hooks, 1992, p. 4)

For many people of color, the result of the persistent negative messages about their identities is that these beliefs become internalized, leading them to turn on themselves with negative internal dialogue that mirrors the external world.

STEREOTYPE THREAT IN SCIENCE AND IT

Stereotypes project certain limitations in terms of women's perceived access to, interest in, and capabilities in computing as developers, users, and beneficiaries of technology. These stereotypes pervade all of our social institutions, especially media, education, and business. Many of these stereotypes are perpetuated in media that focus on the IT industry, and they influence how women are perceived by others as well as the possibilities that they perceive for themselves. Mary Catherine Ware and Mary Frances Stuck (1985) examined representations of women in popular computer magazines and demonstrated how they reinforce stereotypes. Their data showed that "men appeared in illustrations almost twice as often as women. . . . [M]en's most frequent roles were (in order) manager, other, expert, clerical, and repair technician." Women "were most often portrayed as (in order) clerical, other, sex object, manager, and learner" (p. 205). If women are pictured at all, they are pictured in largely subservient roles in relation to others (Ware & Stuck, 1985). In Chapter IV, I will provide a more current and in-depth example by exploring the way that women are imaged in the self-proclaimed "voice of the digital revolution," *Wired* magazine.

Another way in which an understanding of stereotypes is particularly important in terms of including more women and people of color in IT is that fear of being perceived negatively according to stereotypes can diminish academic performance; social psychologists call this "stereotype threat." Stereotype threat is likely to operate regardless of the individual's level of internalized oppression, because it has to do with the effect of an individual's expectation of how that individual is perceived by others more than that individual's own sense of identity. Studies on race and gender stereotypes in relation to test performance have documented the power of stereotype threat (Cooper & Weaver, 2003). Steele and Aronson (1995) gave a 30-question verbal test (designed to be similar to the verbal portion of the SAT) to Black and White Stanford undergraduate students who were told that their test was diagnostic (measuring their verbal "strengths and weaknesses") vs. nondiagnostic (no mention of measuring ability). Since one stereotype that African-Americans face is that of "poor academic performance," the researchers supposed that students who were told that their ability would be measured would perform more poorly. "Blacks in the diagnostic condition performed significantly worse than Blacks in the non-diagnostic condition," and than Whites in either the diagnostic or nondiagnostic condition (Steel & Aronson, p. 8). Blacks in the diagnostic condition also had lower accuracy (number correct over the number attempted) and completed fewer items than Whites (Steel & Aronson, p. 8).

Similar research on gender stereotypes confirms a similar pattern with regard to stereotype threat. The gender stereotype that women face is that they are "not as competent as men at technology, science or math" (Cooper & Weaver, 2003, p. 96). Spencer, Steele, and Quinn (1999) gave a computerized math test to men and women; one group was told that the tests had reliably proved gender differences in the past. No mention of gender was made to the control group. Men and women who were not reminded of gender prior to the test performed at the same level. Women who were reminded of gender prior to the test solved 1/4th as many problems correctly compared to men; while men who were reminded of gender prior to the test solved even more problems correctly than the men in the control group. Women performed down and men performed up according to gendered expectations with regard to their math abilities. (Keep these issues in mind as you read Chapter VI where I explore education as a social institution.)

Barbie and Hot Wheels PCs

Lastly, the IT industry itself perpetuates gender stereotypes in a variety of ways. One blatant example lies in the efforts to develop more colorful computers in the late 90s. In 1999, Mattel licensed their Barbie and Hot Wheels logos to Toronto-based Patriot Computer to develop Barbie and Hot Wheels PCs. The Barbie PC was a silver box with the classic Barbie-pink plastered all over in the form of giant daisies. The Hot Wheels PC was royal blue with bright yellow and orange flames shooting off its parts. Just in case you are thinking: So, what's the big deal? The really big deal was not just their "gendered" appearance, it was their "gendered" software. "Among the software titles offered with the Hot Wheels PC but not the Barbie PC were BodyWorks, a program that teaches human anatomy and three-dimensional visualization, and a thinking game called Logical Journey of the

Zoombinis" (Headlam, 2000, p. 1). The Barbie PC featured more design software than educational software which clearly would put girls at a disadvantage in terms of building the skills that might lead them to be developers of technology. However, a student in my Women in Computing course shared a story that highlights how this gendered approach might harm boys, too. My student was in Toys R Us with her seven-year old son, a budding artist, who really wanted the Barbie PC since it had more design software. Although my student was willing to buy it for him, her sobbing son was already gender socialized enough to understand that it was meant for girls, and he refused to accept it. Mercifully, Patriot Computer filed for bankruptcy in 2000, and Mattel quit making these computers. In 2007, the Barbie PC made *PC World*'s list of The 10 Worst Computers (Tynan, 2007). Unfortunately, the reasons it made the list had more to do with low-end technology and poor design than issues about gender.

CONCLUSION

Clearly, stereotypes matter in significant ways. They influence how individuals view themselves, how individuals expect others to view them, and how we view each other. Although the degree of impact that stereotypes have on an individual's life will be ameliorated by the messages that they receive about their identity from their family and culture of origin, the messages they receive from the dominant social institutions remain a powerful factor.

QUESTIONS FOR REFLECTIVE DIALOG

1. Draw two large boxes on a piece of paper. Label one male and the other female and place some characteristics in each box (at least 10 for each gender). On the opposite side of the paper, draw a box and put your name above the box. What characteristics are in your individual box that are not in your gender box? Where and when do you think outside of your gender box?
2. Do you feel immune to stereotypes? Have you ever had an assumption made about your abilities to perform a task because of your race or gender? Have there been times in your life when people thought that you should be capable of handling a situation better (or worse) based on gender assumptions?
3. Count the number of stereotypes that you find in one magazine's advertisements. In what ways are the advertisers using "shortcut thinking"? Are mental shortcuts helpful or hurtful in this age of information overload? When do you find yourself using mental shortcuts?

4. Consider the idea that humor is a major vehicle for reinforcing stereotypes. Would you be more likely to laugh at a joke that was demeaning to others if the joke was told by a person in authority? How can humor be used to deconstruct assumptions about race or gender?

5. Spend 2 days noting when and where you see women of color in advertisements. What are these ads selling and how are the women portrayed? After 2 days of making notes when you see an ad featuring a woman of color, consider the places and products that were advertised by these images. What trends or patterns did you notice? What surprised you?

6. Research has linked media portrayals of women's bodies to an increase in plastic surgery. Would you consider having part of your body modified through surgery? Because breast augmentation leads to decreased erotic sensation, some have called it a form a mutilation (Wolf, 1992). What is the argument for body modification? How do you believe that plastic surgery may be connected to stereotypical images?

7. Consider your own introduction to math and science. Did you consider yourself competent at math and science? What contributed to this self-perception? What aspects of math and science did you find difficult? Was your gender ever used as an explanation for your reaction to math and science?

8. Design an advertisement that employs powerful positive images. Select a product and describe how the ad would bolster and enhance a marginalized group. Could advertising create opportunities for partnership? What would such an advertisement look like? What would it sell?

REFERENCES[3]

Aires, E. (1996). *Men and women in interaction: Reconsidering the differences.* New York: Oxford UP.

Amott, T. L., & Matthaei, J. (1996). *Race, gender, and work: A multicultural economic history of women in the United States.* Boston: South End.

Anzaldua, G. (1987). *Borderlands/la frontera: The new mestiza.* San Francisco: Spinsters.

Balnaves, M., Donald, J., & Donald, S. H. (Eds.). (2001). *The Penguin atlas of media and information.* New York: Penguin Putnam.

Brumberg, J. J. (1997). *The body project: An intimate history of American girls.* New York: Random House.

Cialdini, R. B. (1993). *Influence: The psychology of persuasion.* New York: Quill.

Cofer, J. O. (1998). The myth of the Latin woman: I just met a girl named Maria. In P. S. Rothenberg (Ed.), *Race, class, and gender in the United States: An integrated study* (4th ed., pp. 292-296). New York: St. Martins.

Collins, P. H. (1990). *Black feminist thought: Knowledge, consciousness, and the politics of empowerment.* New York: Routledge.

Cooper, J., & Weaver, K. D. (2003). *Gender and computers: Understanding the digital divide.* Mahwah, NJ: Erlbaum.

Creedon, P. J. (Ed.). (1993). *Women in mass communication.* Newbury Park: Sage.

Cusumano, D. L., & Thompson, J. K. (1997). Body image and body shape ideals in magazines: Exposure, awareness, and internalization. *Sex Roles, 37*(9/10), 701-721.

Dates, J. L., & Barlow, W. (Eds.). (1993). *Split image: African-Americans in the mass media* (2nd ed.). Washington, D.C.: Howard UP.

Eisler, R., & Miller, R. (Eds.). (2004). *Educating for a culture of peace.* Portsmouth, NH: Heinemann.

Enloe, C. (1989). *Bananas, beaches, and bases: Making feminist sense of international politics.* Berkeley, CA: U of California P.

Erens, P. (1990). *Issues in feminist film criticism.* Bloomington, IN: Indiana UP.

Feinberg, L. (1996). *Transgender warriors: Making history from Joan of Arc to Dennis Rodman.* Boston: Beacon Press.

Gilbert, S. M., & Gubar, S. (1984). *The madwoman in the attic: The woman writer and the nineteenth-century literary imagination.* New Haven: Yale UP.

Gist, M. E. (1993). Through the looking glass: Diversity and reflected appraisals of the self in mass media. In P. J. Creedon (Ed.), *Women in mass communication* (pp. 104-117). Newbury Park: Sage.

Headlam, B. (2000, January 20). Barbie PC: Fashion over logic. *The New York Times.* Retrieved January 20, 2000, from www.nytimes.com/library/tech/00/01/circuits/articles/20barbie.html

hooks, b. (1992). *Black looks: Race and representation.* Boston: South End.

Johnson, A. G. (2006). *Privilege, power and difference*. Boston: McGrawHill.

Kadi, J. (1996). *Thinking class: Sketches from a cultural worker*. Boston: South End.

Kanellos, M. (2000). Bankruptcy crashes the Barbie PC. *Cnet News.com*. Retrieved December 16, 2007, from http://www.news.com/Bankruptcy-crashes-the-Barbie-PC/2100-1040_3-250222.html

Kang, M. (1997). The portrayal of women's images in magazine advertisements: Goffman's gender analysis revisited. *Sex roles, 37*(11/12), 979-996.

Kesselman, A. et al. (Eds.) (2003). *Women images and realities: A multicultural anthology*. Boston: McGrawHill.

Kilduff, M., & Krackhardt, D. (1994, February). Bringing the individual back in: A structural analysis of the internal market for reputation in organizations. *Academy of Management Journal, 87*. Retrieved April 26, 1999, from LEXIS/NEXIS

Kitch, C. L. (1998). *The girl on the magazine cover: Gender, class, and the emergence of visual stereotypes in American mass media, 1895-1930*. Diss. Ann Arbor, MI: Temple University. 9838498.

Lazarus, M. (Director). (1987). *Still killing us softly: Advertising's image of women* [Motion picture]. Cambridge, MA: Cambridge Documentary Films.

Lazier, L., & Kendrick, A. G. (1993). Women in advertisements: Sizing up the images, roles, and functions. In P. J. Creedon (Ed.), *Women in mass communication* (pp. 199-219). Newbury Park: Sage.

Lester, P. M. (1996). *Images that injure: Pictorial stereotypes in the media*. Westport, CT: Praeger.

Lorde, A. (1984). *Sister outsider: Essays and speeches*. Berkeley, CA: Crossing Press.

MacGregor, R. M. (1989). The distorted mirror: Images of visible minority women in Canadian print advertising. *Atlantis: A Women's Studies Journal, 15*(1), 137-143.

MacKay, N. J., & Covell, K. (1997). The impact of women in advertisements on attitudes toward women. *Sex Roles, 36*(9/10), 573-583.

McClelland, J. R. (1993). Visual images and re-imaging: A review of research in mass communication. In P. J. Creedon (Ed.), *Women in mass communication* (pp. 220-234). Newbury Park: Sage

Morrison, T. (1992). *Playing in the dark: Whiteness and the literary imagination.* New York: Vintage.

Nelkin, D. (1995). *Selling science: How the press covers science and technology.* New York: Freeman.

Northrup, C. (1998). *Women's bodies, women's wisdom: Creating physical and emotional health and healing.* New York: Bantam.

Ogawa, D. M. (1971) *From Japs to Japanese: An evolution of Japanese-American stereotypes.* Berkeley, CA: McCutchan.

Plous, S. (1993). *The psychology of judgment and decision making.* New York: McGraw.

Robinson, L. (1996). *Media myth, media reality: A primer of racism in America.* Diss. The Union Institute, Ann Arbor: UMI. 9633792.

Rolf, J. E., & Masten, A. S. (Eds.). (1990). *Risk and protective factors in the development of psychopathology.* New York: Cambridge UP.

Schiebinger, L. (1993). *Nature's body: Gender in the making of modern science.* Boston: Beacon.

Spencer, S. J., Steele, C. M., & Quinn, D. M. (1999). Stereotype threat and women's math performance. *Journal of Experimental Social Psychology, 35*, 4-28.

Steele, C. M., & Aronson, J. (1995). Stereotype threat and the intellectual test performance of African-Americans. *Journal of Personality & Social Psychology, 69*(5), 797-811. Retrieved July 24, 2007, from the EBSCOhost database.

Stice, E. (1998). Modeling of eating pathology and social reinforcement of the thin-ideal predict onset of bulimic symptoms. *Behaviour Research and Therapy, 36*(10), 931-944.

Stice, E, & Shaw, H. E. (1994). Adverse effects of the media portrayed thin ideal on women and linkages to bulimic symptomatology. *Journal of Social and Clinical Psychology, 13*(3), 288-308.

Striegel-Moore, R. H. et, al. (1986). Toward an understanding of risk factors for bulimia. *American Psychologist, 41*(3), 246-263.

Tynan, D. (2007, March 19). The 10 worst PCs of all time. *PC World.* Retrieved December 16, 2007, from http://www.pcworld.com/article/id,129857-page,10-c,desktoppcs/article.html

Ware, M. C., & Stuck, M. F. (1985). Sex-role messages vis-à-vis microcomputer use: A look at the pictures. *Sex Roles, 13*(3/4), 205-214.

Wolf, N. (1992). *The beauty myth: How images of beauty are used against women.* New York: Doubleday.

Wood, J. T. (1999). *Gendered lives: Communication, gender, and culture* (3rd ed.). Belmont, CA: Wadsworth.

ENDNOTES

[1] This title is in honor of Judith Ortiz Cofer's poem of the same name in which "Latin women pray 'in Spanish to an Anglo God/with a Jewish heritage'." Judith Ortiz Cofer, "The Myth of the Latin Woman: I Just Met a Girl Named Maria," *Race, Class, and Gender in the United States: An Integrated Study,* ed. Paula S. Rothenberg (New York: St. Martins, 1998) 296.

[2] Gloria Anzaldua, ed., *Making Face, Making Soul/Haciendo Caras: Critical Perspectives by Feminists of Color* (San Francisco: Aunt Lute, 1990) author's biography on last page.

[3] Some portions of this chapter may have appeared in, and are reprinted with permission from Kirk, M. (2006). Bridging the digital divide: A feminist perspective on the project. In G. Trajkovski (Ed.), *Diversity in information technology education: Issues and controversies* (pp. 38-67). Hershey, PA: Information Science Publishing.

Chapter III
Gendered Philosophy of Science:
Science is Male, Nature is Female

OBJECTIVES

This chapter aims to help you understand the following:

- How the historical philosophy of science, especially gendering science as male and nature as female, has influenced both how we think about science and who participates in science and technology today.
- How the "myth of objectivity" influences how we think about science, the knowledge we produce, and who participates in science and technology.
- How an emphasis on science and technology as purely "rational" (gendered male) domains devoid of "emotion" (gendered female) influences both how we create scientific and technical knowledge and who participates in its creation.
- How a new philosophy of science informed by the values of a partnership society might reshape scientific and technical knowledge and facilitate greater and more diverse participation in its creation.

INTRODUCTION

This chapter explores the ways in which the dualistic notion of gender is at the core of many fundamental ideas in the philosophy of science. The ways in which we have learned to perceive, think about, teach/learn, and conduct research in science and IT are deeply informed by a dualistic, gendered framework: science is associated with maleness, and nature with femaleness. This primary split supports a philosophy of science that envisions "good science" as purely rational and objective (male), devoid of emotion and subjectivity (female). These core values of a dominator society contribute to a climate that is not likely to be hospitable to those who are gender-socialized as women. In the end, I call for a new perspective on our philosophy of science and technology that embodies partnership values and ask: How might we proceed to reexamine our assumptions about science and technology to make the shift from a dominator to a partnership perspective? These ideas are explored in the following sections: (1) science is male; nature is female; (2) the myth of objectivity; (3) there's no crying in science; and (4) envisioning a partnership philosophy of science (democratizing science and technology, redefining what makes good science, and examples of partnership science and IT).

SCIENCE IS MALE, NATURE IS FEMALE

One could identify any number of points in previous centuries of patriarchal thought that explicitly and implicitly excluded women from the knowledge tradition. However, in relation to science and technology, one historic moment takes on a particular significance due to its emphasis on dualistic, "either/or" thinking, of which gender is one primary manifestation. Francis Bacon (1561-1626) is often referred to as the father of modern science, as "the originator of the concept of the modern research institute, a philosopher of industrial science . . . and as the founder of the inductive method" (Merchant, 2001, p. 68). Bacon's thinking helped reify the definition of science as male, and nature as female.

Many feminist science studies scholars have discussed the ways in which this particular dualism has influenced both the perception of science in society and our images of who participates in the world of science and technology (Bleier, 1991; Merchant, 1980; Schiebinger, 1993; Wajcman, 1995). In her now classic book *The Death of Nature: Women, Ecology and the Scientific Revolution*, Carolyn Merchant (1980) recounts the history of the Scientific Revolution and outlines ideas that have contributed to shaping science into a domain that privileges social definitions of "maleness": the notion of science gaining increasing domination over nature, the rise of mechanistic thinking, and power as the "mechanism." Historically, one of the most influential ways in which this split has been communicated is through artistic and literary imagery. As an example of this process in action, Merchant (1980) describes the way in which visual images fostered the view of science dominating nature:

The new image of nature as a female to be controlled and dissected through experiment legitimated the exploitation of natural resources. . . . [T]he image of the nurturing earth popular in the Renaissance . . . was superseded by new controlling imagery. . . . Natura no longer complains that her garments of modesty [sic] are being torn by the wrongful thrusts of man. She is portrayed in statues . . . coyly removing her own veil and exposing herself to science. From an active teacher and parent, she has become a mindless, submissive body. (p. 190)

These ideas alone may not have led to the development of science as a male domain. However, Merchant describes how coupling these attitudes (the domination of "female" nature) with the growing emphasis on mechanistic thought established a more gender-exclusive framework. Merchant explains how 17th century French and English scientists and philosophers developed a "new concept of the self as a rational master of the passions housed in a machinelike body" and how this concept began to "replace the concept of the self as an integral part of a close-knit harmony of organic parts united to the cosmos and society" (p. 214).

The third piece of Merchant's puzzle is that "mechanism" as a world view reorganized reality around order and power: "Order was attained through an emphasis on the motion of indivisible parts subject to mathematical laws and the rejection of unpredictable animistic sources of change. Power was achieved through immediate active intervention in a secularized world" (1980, p. 216). These fundamental elements—mechanistic thought, order, and power—deeply informed Western politics, religion, and science (as well as most other aspects of society) and at least contributed to the development of science as a domain that increasingly excluded women.

Riane Eisler (1987, 2000, 2007) traces our dominator philosophy of science emphasizing science (man) dominating nature (woman) back even further. Eisler (2007) describes a Babylonian creation myth in which "the war god Marduk created the world by dismembering the body of the Mother Goddess Tiamat" and includes this as one of many indicators of "a radical cultural shift . . . from earlier myths about a Great Mother, who created nature and *humans as part of nature* [emphasis mine], to a story where the world is created by the violence of a male deity" (p. 80). Later, in "Genesis 1:28, we read that man is to 'subdue' the earth and have 'dominion . . . over every living thing that moveth upon the earth" (p. 80). As one of our major social institutions, religion is a primary purveyor of values, attitudes, and beliefs. Gradually the development of scientific thought in Western civilization began to replace religion as the predominant influence on society. However, Eisler (2007) makes the point that the scientific perspectives of Baconian dualism, Newtonian mechanism, and Cartesian rationalism were "simply echoing a much earlier worldview" about science dominating nature (p. 80).

Regardless of when the shift occurred, in the end science was associated with a machine, scientists were the power, and nature was the entity to be dominated. Concurrent with the development of these ideas, women were more closely identified with the nature over which scientists sought to gain power. In the introduction to her book titled *Feminist Approaches to Science*, Ruth Bleier (1991), a scholar of the history and philosophy of science, examines the ways in which 17th century Baconian dualism "elaborated the metaphors of science in sexual and gendered terms, with science as male and nature as female, a mystery to be unveiled and penetrated" (Bleier, 1991, p. 6). This is also an example of how language operates as a social institution to teach values. Bleier explains that according to Bacon, woman was embodied in "the natural, the disordered, the emotional, the irrational," and man "as a thinker epitomized objectivity, rationality, culture, and control" (p. 6), a good example of how the gendered characteristics of maleness are embedded in institutionalized values over femaleness.

THE MYTH OF OBJECTIVITY

Another limiting factor in terms of women's participation in science is the myth of scientific objectivity. The problem, according to Bleier (1991), is that the unacknowledged biases that scientists hold "become part of a stifling science-culture, while scientists firmly believe that as long as they are not *conscious* of any bias or political agenda, they are neutral and objective, when in fact they are only unconscious" (p. 29). These unconscious biases influence the ways in which data are analyzed as well as the research questions themselves, and (in sometimes not so subtle ways) exclude diverse perspectives and experiences from consideration, effectively leaving women and other marginalized groups out of the discussion. Figueroa and Harding (2003) share ideas from scholars who questioned whether the study of science could be separated from social influences:

W.V.O. Quine (1960) proposed that scientific and everyday beliefs were linked in networks. How scientists theorized nature's order and chose to revise their hypotheses when faced with counterevidence depended in part on the ontologies, logics, and epistemologies they brought to their work, largely unconsciously, from their particular cultural contexts. Thomas Kuhn (1970) produced influential arguments claiming that to understand the history of scientific belief formation, one needed to focus not only on intellectual histories but also on the kinds of social histories of science that had begun to appear. (p. 2)

Harding (1998) adds that scientific process, questions, and topics are all imbedded in culturally specific notions that influence what we define as "good science." For example, the idea that there may be multiple ways of observing and multiple answers to a question is judged negatively in a traditional scientific framework. "Multiplicity is taken to be a sign of error from these conventional perspectives; or, at least, acceptance or appreciation of it is taken to reflect a damaging seduction by softminded relativists" (Harding, 1998, p. 74).

Feenberg (2003) offers a thought-provoking example of the significance of sociocultural context in the development of computer hardware. For most Westerners, the computer keyboard may seem to be "culturally neutral at first sight." However, Feenberg (2003) points out that if computers had "been invented and developed first in Japan, or any other country with an ideographic language, it is unlikely that keyboards would have been selected as an input device"; the early input devices would more probably have they been designed "with graphical or voice inputs of some sort" (pp. 242-243). Scientific research and IT development occurs within a social and cultural context, and the perspectives of researchers and developers are also informed by that context. In *Smaller is Better: Japan's Master of the Miniature*, O-Young Lee "argues that the triumph of Japanese microelectronics is rooted in age-old cultural impulses . . .to miniaturize, evident in bonsai, haiku poetry, and other aspects of Japanese culture" (Feenberg, 2003, pp. 242-243). These types of cultural values are so deeply embedded in our perspective that their influence on scientific and technological research will never be made explicit by the myth of scholarly objectivity.

Collins (1990) suggests that no "standpoint is neutral because no individual or group exists unembedded in the world" (p. 33). So, how do scientists and technologists begin to grapple with such a perspective? Harding (1998) offers a cure for the pre-existing blindness to the ways in which social context may influence science—a "strong objectivity" which "draws on standpoint epistemologies." To arrive at her definition, Harding (1998) first describes how the "demand for objectivity . . . becomes the demand for separation of thinking from feeling," which promotes moral detachment (p. 129). This moral detachment leads one to be blind to historical, political, and economic factors that may profoundly influence the selection of scientific problems and the resources that are committed to answering them.

Interestingly, one key to debunking the myth of scholarly objectivity may lie in science itself: the new world of quantum physics. John Lukacs (2001) explores the significance of Nobel Laureate Werner Heisenberg's work in physics, especially his uncertainty principle, on how we view "objectivity" in science. Heisenberg's uncertainty principle challenges the ideal of objectivity exclusive of context: "we can no longer speak of the behaviour [sic] of the particle independently of the process of observation" because "the very act of observing alters the nature of the object" (Lukacs, 2001, p. 226). This is quantum physics' way of naming the importance of context and interaction with what we observe and how we define it.

Harding (1998) also describes why relying on the "scientific method" of verifying results through experiment does not expose the problem: "When a scientific community shares assumptions, there is little chance that more careful application of existing scientific methods will detect them" (p. 135). However, duplicating another's research and taking it a step further is a largely unquestioned and standard practice in scientific research. This is frequently followed by a puzzled discussion about why repeated experiments do not come out like they are "supposed" to. This approach to research denies the fact that there is a complex set of interactions occurring, all of which may differ based on the circumstances and conditions of a new experimental environment.

THERE'S NO CRYING IN SCIENCE!

In 1992, Penny Marshall directed a film called *A League of Their Own* which is a fictional story inspired by the All-American Girls Professional Baseball League (AAGPBL). The AAGPBL was formed in 1943 in response to Chicago Cubs owner Phillip Wrigley's concerns about what would happen to major league baseball with so many healthy men off fighting World War II. Although top women athletes were recruited from across the country to play in the league, they were also caught in an odd double-bind: they were expected to maintain standards of femininity (including a regular beauty routine, etiquette training, and playing baseball in dresses) and to maintain standards of maleness as ball-players (All-American, 2007). One of those standards of maleness, to display no emotion, was immortalized in a now classic scene from the film where Jimmy Dugan (an unshaven, beer-bellied, baseball has-been who has been forced against his will to coach a women's professional baseball team) shouts at one of his sobbing women players, "There's no crying in baseball!" The same could be said of science and technology: "There's no crying in science!"

One of the founding assumptions that arises from gendering science as male and nature as female is the belief that science is the realm of pure rational thought and that "good" science should not involve emotion. Nobel Prize winning geneticist Barbara McClintock's story reveals the problem with this rigid, either/or, gendered view of science. Working with corn plants, McClintock made a major genetic discovery that it took decades for the scientific community to understand; they could not make the leap from what they currently understood about genetics to what she was describing until 25 years after she first published her research. Certainly, her gender was a factor in her lack of recognition, but another factor was that she was thinking beyond narrow, rigid concepts of genetics and suggesting a kind of flexibility that no one could conceive of. It was McClintock's "feeling for the organism"—the corn plants that she was studying—that led her to an insight beyond what any geneticists of the day could grasp (Keller, 1983).

McClintock's story is typical of many of the women who determined to "do science" at a time when it was a far less hospitable climate for them than it is today. In 1940, disappointed with her lack of advancement in academia, McClintock joined the Cold Springs Lab on Long Island where, sponsored by continuing grants from the Carnegie Institute, she researched and published until her death in 1992. In the 60s, the scientific community began to recognize the work she had been quietly publishing all along, and she received multiple honors for her work. In 1983, when she was 81, she was awarded the Nobel Prize in Physiology or Medicine (Keller, 1983). McClintock's story is one of an intelligent and independent woman who worked on the margins of science for most of her life in order to do the work she was compelled to do. She was a woman of unique character and courage, and she was a great scientist. Her story evokes the question: Must a woman be a heroic figure to sustain a career in science and technology? In the current social climate, the likely answer is "yes."

Since science and technology are considered objective domains that exist apart from any social influence, they are also often grounded exclusively in abstract thought and methods rather than concrete thought and methods; this influences assumptions about how science/technology should be taught and about the learning styles that are privileged in these teaching and learning environments. This is a classic example of the power of cultural context because most people would never question the validity of this education approach. However, the problem with this approach is founded in the dualistic thinking upon which it is based. Thelma Estrin (1996) clarifies: "The first term in the following pairs generally correlate with men, and the second with women: abstract/concrete, objectivity/subjectivity, logical/intuitive, mind/body, domination/submission" (p. 44). If "maleness" is associated with abstract, objective, logical, rational, and dominator behavior, and "femaleness" is associated with concrete, subjective, intuitive, emotional, and submissive behavior, which gender is likely to fit into science and technology as it is currently defined?

In fact, we have created a social system in which women who have been "appropriately" gender socialized will not fit easily into the study of science and technology, but most men will. Many scholars have documented why women may be "less comfortable" with the way science is taught (Estrin, 1996; Greenbaum, 1990; Keller, 1992; Riger, 1992; Turkle & Papert, 1990). Others have demonstrated that most women are more likely to be concrete learners while most men are more likely to be abstract learners (Belenky, 1986; Goldberger et al., 1996; Kramer & Lehman, 1990; Rosser, 1995; Turkle & Papert, 1990). Setting the inconclusive brain research on sex differences aside, one must consider how much gender socialization influences the predominant ways that women and men learn. In the U.S., most women learn best using concrete approaches that provide opportunities for negotiating connections rather than moving "abstractly and hierarchically from axiom to theorem to corollary" (Turkle& Papert, 1990, p. 136). More men learn best using abstract, linear approaches. Sherry Turkle (1990) calls for an "epistemological pluralism" that allows for multiple ways of learning about and developing computer systems.

In a dominator society that features either/or perspectives and hierarchical rankings, academic disciplines are gendered, too. Academic disciplines and professions carry a different social value based on whether they are: hard (masculine) or soft (feminine); mechanistic (masculine) or natural/human (feminine); and abstract (masculine) or concrete (feminine). If we look at both the history of women in science and the numbers of women in different disciplines today, the pattern is immediately apparent. Women are concentrated in the scientific disciplines most closely associated with softness, nature, and/or concreteness such as psychology, biology, and botany. Part of the reason for this is that these were the areas in which women had the least resistance historically, which meant that there were more women in those disciplines to serve as mentors and role models, contributing to a growing social perception that these might be scientific disciplines where women could thrive. (See Chapter VI, for a more detailed discussion of the history of women's participation in science and technology.) It takes time for women to reach a "critical mass" in a discipline that begins to contribute to developing a more hospitable climate. For many reasons which I hope this book will ultimately make clearer, IT has not reached that critical mass.

IT is categorized as a "hard" science, and the history of women's entry into IT bears this out. Some data have shown that more women major in computer science when universities name their programs "computer science" and house these departments in Colleges of Arts & Sciences (associating CS with "softer" sciences) rather than programs titled "electrical engineering" in Colleges of Engineering, (associating CS with "hard" sciences). There is also an obvious hard/soft "either/or" within IT itself; some education programs and businesses focus on "hard"ware and some on "soft"ware (or information). There are more women in the "soft" or information end of IT education and business. These hard/soft social perceptions of academic disciplines and professions are purveyed by all of our social institutions, and they contribute to a climate that keeps many women from entering these fields at all.

ENVISIONING A PARTNERSHIP PHILOSOPHY OF SCIENCE AND TECHNOLOGY

How might we proceed to reexamine the core philosophies of science and technology to make the shift from a dominator to a partnership perspective? Ruth Bleier (1991) suggests that we criticize "the many damaging and self-defeating features of science (the absolutism, authoritarianism, determinist thinking . . . ethnocentrism, pretensions to objectivity and neutrality)" and ask serious questions about the "values, opinions, biases, beliefs, and interests of the scientist" (pp. 1-3). Rita Arditti (1980) calls for an even more fundamental shift from a dominator to a partnership perspective on science:

Science needs a soul, which would show respect and love for its subjects of study and would stress harmony and communication with the rest of the universe. When science fulfills its potential and becomes a tool for human liberation, we will not have to worry about women 'fitting' into it because we will probably be at the forefront of the 'new' science. (p. 367)

To make the shift from a dominator to a partnership model of science and technology, one of the core assumptions that we must examine is the myth of objectivity as the only way to "do good science." Keller (1992) describes how "good science" is set up in opposition to so-called "value-laden science," and she challenges this commonly privileged practice of disassociating science from values:

[S]cientific knowledge is value-laden (and inescapably so) just because it is shaped by our choices—first, of what to seek representations of, and second, of what to seek representations for. Since uses and practices are obviously not value-free, why should we even think of equating "good" science with the notion of 'value free'? (p. 5)

In the traditional view, the "scientific method" has been the only valid pathway to "good science," and it includes "making observations, forming hypotheses . . . testing the validity of the hypotheses by further observations or experiments" (Bleier, 1991, p. 3). However, Keller (1992) says that the "[s]cientific 'method' is just the name we give to the assorted techniques that scientists have found effective for assessing, subverting, or exploiting" already agreed upon disciplinary boundaries and "more or less collectively endorsed" goals (p. 5). This is another effect of the narrow philosophical foundation upon which the scientific knowledge has developed. By its very nature, the claim to be "pure" truth, the "scientific method" eliminates serious consideration of and validation of diverse perspectives and their possibly "non-traditional" analyses. How might we create a more "democratic" science and technology?

Democratizing Science and Technology

Most who are concerned with the question of democratizing science make access their primary concern, but this "external" approach leaves the "internalized" core notions about science and technology unquestioned. Harding (2000) says that according "to the externalists, sciences are in society, but society is not *in* sciences, their best theories, models, methods or results of research" (p. 122). This is another way of expressing the myth of "objective" science which says that scientific and technological knowledge is created free from any social context or historical framework that shapes its values or core assumptions; real science is "value free." As an alternative, Harding (2000) proposes "cognitive democracy approaches . . . [which] are concerned with how social and political fears and desires get encoded in that purportedly purely technical, cognitive core of scientific projects" (p. 122). For those who fear that this is just a relativist "flight from reason," Harding suggests a "both/and" perspective that allows for the idea that new scientific and technological knowledge may represent social and political priorities "as well as more or less accurate pictures" of scientific and technological truths (p. 123). Further, she adds:

One can never be sure the sciences have arrived at absolutely true claims for two reasons: present claims must be held open to revision in case of the appearance of further empirical evidence, and they must be held open to the need for fruitful conceptual shifts. (2000, p. 123)

Ultimately, Harding argues that we cannot avoid the reality that science already does encode values, and the question we need to explore is whether they should be democratic values (p. 124).

Historically, education in science and technology has not been as democratic as it could be. In *Anti-Racist Science Teaching*, Dawn Gill and Les Levidow (1987) describe specific ways in which science teaching in the United Kingdom not only fails to reflect "pure truth," but also is implicitly embedded with racist attitudes. Gill and Levidow (1987) describe how science teaching:

Hides its appropriation of non-Western scientific traditions; often attributes people's subordination or suffering to nature . . . rather than to the way science and nature itself have been subordinated to political priorities; is permeated by an ideology of race . . . perpetuates assumptions about nature and human nature that support inequality; and is an alienating experience for many students. (p. 3)

The loss of diverse perspectives to the development of science and technology represents a major loss to our knowledge tradition and ultimately our human community. Incorporating diverse perspectives is another key to building a partnership model of science and technology. Multiple scholars have described the unique perspectives that those who operate on the so-called margins of our dominator social system might bring to their analysis of particular problems.

Patricia Hill Collins (1991) suggests that Black women who gain access to social institutions have a unique "insider-outsider" perspective by virtue of their status inside the system and their racial status as outsiders. Gloria Anzaldua (1987) shows how Chicana women share a similarly unique perspective because they exist on the "borderlands" between two social locations—the U.S. and Mexico. bell hooks (1984) demonstrates how the view "from the margins" can be much more complex and comprehensive than the view from the center. Part of our task as partnership scientists and technologists is to engage women and men of color who participate in science and technology in sharing their "insider-outsider" or "borderlands" perspectives, embodying Rosser's (1995) redefinition of science that is "reconstructed to include us all" (p. 4).

Redefining What Makes "Good" Science

Partnership science and technology requires us to renegotiate the notion of "good science" as being distinct from the environment, the social climate, in which it is produced. Robert Young (1987), a scholar writing about anti-racist science, calls for "a historical and social approach to knowledge" that examines "the social forces and connections (or articulations) of scientific and technological disciplines and research problems" (p. 22). Sandra Harding (1998) suggests that naming the social context in which science is done, taught, and learned, actually may allow us to come closer to "objectivity" because we can consciously work to identify the ways in which our standpoint may influence both the questions we ask and the answers we find. This underlines the tremendous significance of more scientists and technologists understanding the cultural values, attitudes, and beliefs that we learn from our social institutions.

Harding (1998) also recommends "we would do better to think of scientific and technological claims as located on a continuum where 'global' occupies one pole, 'local' the other, and 'universal' disappears as no longer useful." (p. 20) Harding names the ways in which environment, social context, has already influenced the science that we have done so far, and how honoring that truth (including the influences of global colonialism) might move us closer to producing better science and technology and to better meet real human needs. A better understanding of science and technology's social context might profoundly change the kinds of questions that scientists ask; we might also consider the broader social uses to which developing technology is applied.

The "universality ideal" has also played a key role in our beliefs about science and technology; this perspective explicitly excludes differing cultural contexts for how scientific knowledge is created:

According to this argument, there is one world, one and only one possible true account of it, and one unique science that can capture that one truth most accurately . . . there is just one group of humans, one cultural model of the ideal human, to whom nature's true order could become evident. (Harding, 2000, p. 129)

Harding (2000) names several problems with the universality ideal: (1) modern science is in fact plural in terms of there being different methods and models for understanding nature and the research process; and (2) different cultures ask different sorts of scientific and technological questions, and have different models (and concepts) for understanding nature that cannot be meaningfully conflated into one universal view. To achieve the universality ideal also has significant political and scientific costs: (1) politically, the attempt to fit vastly different priorities and perspectives into one universal view encourages devaluing certain cultural perspectives and their local knowledge traditions, potentially sacrificing "third world cultures to purported economic progress" ; (2) scientifically, "the universality ideal legitimates accepting less-well supported claims over potentially stronger ones in many cases," "legitimates resistance to some of the deepest and most telling criticisms of particular scientific claims" such as feminist or postcolonial analyses of science, and "promotes only narrow conceptions of both nature and science"; (3) "the ideal of one true science obscures the fact that any system of knowledge will generate systematic patterns of ignorance as well as knowledge"; and (4) "relativist epistemological positions start to look far too attractive as long as the universality ideal is the only alternative" (Harding, 2000, pp. 130-136).

These ideas underline the importance of expanding the focus beyond simply fostering the participation of women and other marginalized groups in science. The philosophy that informs science and technology must be redefined to reflect the actual pluralism of human perspectives. Without such a redefinition of perspective, we risk a new kind of technological colonialism especially with regard to the rapid and pervasive development of IT in a global context. In a partnership social context, the best technologies would be those that arise from the needs of specific cultural contexts in response to those needs, not those that are globally disseminated top-down by dominator cultures.

Eisler (2007) suggests that one first step towards a partnership technology is to begin to consider the potential uses of new technologies, as opposed to the "pure science" approach of developing ideas just because we can and ignoring possible social costs or benefits. "By focusing on ends, we can distinguish between positive and negative uses of the same technological base" (Eisler, 2007, p. 177). Further, Eisler proposes organizing our thinking about technologies into three basic types: (1) technologies of life support, (2) technologies of actualization, and (3) technologies of destruction. Technologies of life support include technologies for maintaining human health and well-being (e.g., farming, weaving, construction, communication, transportation, and healthcare) and environmental sustainability. Technologies of actualization are those "designed to help realize our highest potentials: our capacities for consciousness, reasoning, empathy, creativity, and love . . . [helping] us meet our deep human yearnings for caring connections, meaning, justice and freedom"; these include music, the arts, and "social technologies, such as public education, representative democratic politics, equitable economics, and other human inventions" (Eisler, 2007, p. 178). Technologies of destruction are those whose "aim is destruction rather than creation" such as "weapons for nuclear warfare and bacteriological terrorism." The challenge is that "in cultures orienting primarily to the domination system there's no way to prevent the use of technological breakthroughs for destruction" (p. 178). The solution is for us all to develop a concern for whether "new technologies are guided by an ethos of caring and responsibility" (p. 178), and for political and business leaders to focus their economic investments "not just on technologies that yield short-term corporate profits but on those that yield long-term social and environmental profits" (p. 185). This is the way to a partnership technology.

Examples of Partnership Science and IT

Some major shifts in perspectives about science and technology are already occurring in some areas of science. We may be building towards the kind of major paradigm shift in the philosophy of science suggested by Thomas Kuhn (1962), who argues that scientific thought does not develop in a strictly linear way. Kuhn suggests that we begin to build a set of ideas or questions that do not fit the current paradigm, and that a major shift occurs when a new paradigm answers those outstanding questions. One new paradigm or perspective that is increasingly shared in many areas of science relates to the importance of considering environment, or social context, in our understanding of science and in the production of scientific and technical knowledge.

In biology, some are shifting away from a traditional Darwinian view of evolution (which reflects a dominator social emphasis on competition in the core notion of "survival of the fittest") to Lamarck's earlier view of evolution (which reflects a partnership emphasis on interactive cooperation between organisms and their environments). French biologist Jean-Baptiste de Lamarck was actually the first to establish evolution as a scientific fact, and his theory (presented 50 years before Darwin) "suggested that evolution was based on an 'instructive,' cooperative interaction among organisms and their environment that enables life forms to survive and evolve in a dynamic world" (Lipton, 2005, p. 42). In fact, Darwin himself "went on from what we have been told for a century was the be-all and end-all for his theory of evolution to develop a 'higher' theory of evolution" (Loye, 2004, p. 42). In *The Descent of Man*, Darwin specifically states that "he is going beyond the 'survival of the fittest' theory of *Origin of Species*, which pertains mainly to prehumans, to complete his theory with a look at *human* evolution" (Loye, 2004, p. 42). David Loye (2004) conducted a close analysis of Darwin's *The Descent of Man* and documented a very different emphasis: "Darwin actually writes only twice of 'survival of the fittest'—and one of these times is to apologize for exaggerating the importance of this idea in *Origin of Species*" (p. 43). Darwin's thinking about human evolution was marked by much deeper concerns:

What Darwin was actually writing about in The Descent of Man is love (which he mentions ninety-five times), moral sensitivity (ninety-two times), and mind (ninety times). It seems that he was saying . . . that caring and the search for meaning are at the heart of human life. (Loye, 2004, p. 43)

In the context of a dominator society, it is not surprising that a core idea such as "survival of the fittest" (which justifies power-over and hierarchical rankings) predominated in our scientific thought in spite of Darwin's later work (which emphasized love and moral sensitivity). Unfortunately, the "survival of the fittest" vision of human evolution that has predominated in science contributed to an implicit acceptance of a "doctrine of selfishness as the primary motivation for everything" that became explicit in 20th century disciplines like sociobiology and evolutionary psychology. This belief in "the supposedly scientific certification that ultimately we are all driven solely by selfishness" diminishes our capacity to believe in basic human goodness motivated by love and trust. (Loye, 2004, p. 45). The good news is that contemporary biology is moving back towards a theory based less on dominance and more on partnership, that is, an interactive, systems view of evolution. There is a growing new field called systems biology that reflects this type of thinking. According to Lipton (2005), contemporary British scientist Timothy Lenton:

provides evidence that evolution is more dependent on the interaction among species than it is on the interaction of individuals within a species. Evolution becomes a matter of the survival of the fittest groups rather than the survival of the fittest individuals. (p. 46)

In psychology, Urie Bronfenbrenner (2005) described his bioecological theory of human development as "an evolving theoretical system" and "stressed that research should begin to focus on how children develop in settings representative of their actual world" (Lerner, 2005, pp. x-xxviii). Bronfenbrenner credited Kurt Lewin with "regard to the development of the link between basic science and social policy . . . [and his] stress on the connections between people and settings and his concept of action research" (Lerner, 2005, pp. xxi-xxii). Lewin viewed the perceived as more important than the actual and urged researchers to "investigate the environment and human activity as they appear[ed] in the minds of people" and to "be prepared to see a complex of differentiated regions, some embedded in others, some interconnected, others isolated, but all interacting to steer the behavior and development of the person" (Bronfenbrenner, 2005, p. 44). Ultimately, Bronfenbrenner developed the PPCT model which considered process, person, context, and time as interactive influences on human behavior and the study of human development (Lerner, 2005, p. xv).

In physics, a shift has occurred from the seemingly certain world of classical mechanics (based on the ideas of Isaac Newton and others) towards the far more contextual world of quantum mechanics (based on the work of Werner Heisenberg and others). Lipton (2005) states that:

Einstein revealed that we do not live in a universe with discrete, physical objects separated by dead space. The Universe is one indivisible, dynamic whole in which energy and matter are so deeply entangled it is impossible to consider them as independent elements. (p. 102)

Heisenberg's work suggests "the collapse of absolute determinism even in the world of matter" as he postulates the influence of both "mathematical uncertainty" and "observer effect" with regard to measuring atomic particles:

Modern physics now admits . . . that important factors may not have clear definitions: but, on the other hand, these factors may be clearly defined, as Heisenberg puts it, 'with regard to their connections.' These relationships are of primary importance: just as no 'fact' can stand alone, apart from its associations with other 'facts' and other matters, modern physics now tends to divide its world not into 'different groups of objects but into different groups of connections.' (Lukacs, 2001, p. 228)

Until recently, most scientists have typically operated based on the reductionist model which tries to find the source of a problem by linking it to one specific malfunction along the assembly line (Lipton, 2005, p. 103). However, in our increasingly complex and interconnected world, and in the face of quantum mechanics, this type of linear approach is far less likely to lead us to any type of authentic scientific certainty. The best physics today is not based on an *either/or* between classical and quantum mechanics, but on an honoring of what they *both* have to offer in relation to understanding atoms and the context in which these atoms exist.

A partnership philosophy of science would understand and respect the fact that the perspectives of researchers (and the social context of their research) can influence both the questions asked and their observable results. For example, Keller (2004) describes how long it took the field of reproductive genetics to connect the critical role of the cytoplasm of the egg prior to fertilization. The discovery did not depend on new techniques; they were available as early as the 1930s. Instead, researchers were confined by their perspective that the active sperm forcefully propelled itself into the passive egg to "deliver its genes"—a classic gendered, power-over, dominator metaphor for science and nature. Until extensive work was done by Christiane Nusslein-Volhard and her colleagues to shed light on the active influence the (gendered female) egg has in the field of fertility, questions about the role of the cytoplasm had simply never been asked. The new context for knowledge created by a different perspective allowed researchers to see the relationship between egg and sperm in a new light and research around this issue then grew rapidly. This story supports the importance of shifting away from the perspective of science dominating nature that is a deeply-embedded element of the philosophy of science, and shows the possibilities created by a partnership perspective. Viewing the egg and sperm in a biological partnership with each other established a perspective from which better science emerged.

CONCLUSION

Science and nature do not need to be gendered. It was a false paradigm that resulted from a dominator social system. However, it is important to bring these implicit assumptions into the light if we are ever to create a partnership philosophy of science. A new perspective seems increasingly critical to our survival as we face environmental destruction on a scale beyond what any humans have previously witnessed. Nature "should not just be a force to be tamed for the benefit of humanity; humanity is an integral part of the Nature it defines and equilibrium between the two should be the goal" (Lederman & Bartsch, 2001, p. 4). Science (and technology) should not just be a force of domination and control over nature. Our best new science and technologies will understand that "the Earth and all of its species constitute one interactive, living organism" (Lipton, 2005, p. 46).

As you try to move toward partnership, you may hear the Darwinian "survival of the fittest" argument. "A simple response is that survival of the fittest does not mean survival of the meanest," but a more thorough response is that "empathy and caring also play a crucial role in determining survival or extinction of many species" (Eisler, 2002, p. 35). These empathic and care-giving roles are not rigidly assigned by sex. There are many species of birds and mammals where fathers and mothers are caregivers (Eisler, 2002, p. 36). It is time for us all to recognize that "empathy and caring are not something we have to tack on to a brutal and callous 'human nature.' The capacity, and need for empathy and caring are biologically built into our species as part of our evolutionary heritage" (Eisler, 2002, p. 36). The rapid and pervasive global development of IT in the 21st century has presented us with one of our greatest opportunities for an evolutionary quantum leap as a human species. Technology could contribute to a major social shift from domination to partnership and foster the development of a more highly evolved humanity.

QUESTIONS FOR REFLECTIVE DIALOG

1.   Make a list of science traits and nature traits and then compare those lists to the gender-assigned trait list from the first chapter. Where do assumptions about nature intersect with perceptions of femaleness?

2.   Do you believe in objectivity? Describe an objective experiment from beginning to end. Who is involved? What questions are asked? How are the results displayed and explored? What marks the experiment as pure truth?

3.   In this chapter, the argument is made that "there's no crying in science" (or in professional baseball for that matter). Consider other settings. Is there "crying" in finance, law enforcement, management, or technical communication? In your chosen profession, is there "crying" or freedom to be emotional? Why or why not?

4.   "Survival of the fittest" is a foundational scientific theory that casts a long shadow. Consider examples of cooperation in nature. How does this interdependency challenge our "winner takes all" concept of evolution?

5.   Imagine that you are the head of a research and development firm, and one of your researchers has presented you with a new technology that could rapidly accelerate the rate at which groundwater could be decontaminated. Look at this discovery from a business perspective, what and where could a pure profit be made? Who could you sell this technology to? Now switch to a partnership philosophy of technology, how could your company collaborate with other groups to make this finding beneficial to humanity? Is there a middle road between the two? What does this path look like?

REFERENCES[1]

All-American Girls Baseball League. (2007). Retrieved on December 14, 2007, from www.aagpbl.org

Anzaldua, G. (1987). *Borderlands/la frontera: The new mestiza.* San Francisco: Spinsters.

Arditti, R. (1980). Feminism and science. In R. Arditti et al. (Eds.), *Science and liberation* (pp. 350-368). Boston: South End.

Bleier, R. (1991). *Feminist approaches to science.* New York: Teachers College.

Bronfenbrenner, U. (Ed.). (2005). *Making human beings human: Bioecological perspectives on human development.* Thousand Oaks, CA: Sage.

Collins, P. H. (1990). *Black feminist thought: Knowledge, consciousness, and the politics of empowerment.* New York: Routledge.

Daie, J. (1996). Inclusion of women does not mean exclusion of men. *The Scientist, 10*(14), 11.

Eisler, R. (1987). *The chalice and the blade: Our history, our future.* San Francisco: HarperSanFrancisco.

Eisler, R. (2000). *Tommorrow's children: A blueprint for partnership education in the 21st century.* Boulder, CO: Westview.

Eisler, R. (2002). *The power of partnership: Seven relationships that will change your life.* Novato, CA: New World.

Eisler, R. (2007). *The real wealth of nations: Creating a caring economics.* San Francisco: Berrett-Koehler.

Enloe, C. (1989). *Bananas, beaches, and bases: Making feminist sense of international politics.* Berkeley, CA: U of California P.

Estrin, T. (1996). Women's studies and computer science: Their intersection. *IEEE Annals of the History of Computing, 18*(3), 43-46.

Feenberg, A. (2003). Technology in a global world. In R. Figueroa & S. Harding (Eds.), *Science and other cultures: Issues in philosophies of science and technology* (pp. 237-251). New York: Routledge.

Figueroa, R., & Harding, S. (Eds.). (2003). *Science and other cultures: Issues in philosophies of science and technology.* New York: Routledge.

Garreau, J. (1994). Conspiracy of heretics. *Wired, 2*(11), 98-158.

Gill, D., & Levidow, L. (Eds.). (1987). *Anti-racist science teaching.* London: Free Association.

Goldberger, N., et al. (1996). *Knowledge, difference, and power: Essays inspired by women's ways of knowing.* New York: Basic.

Greenbaum, J. (1990). The head and the heart: Using gender analysis to study the social construction of computer systems. *Computers and Society, 20*(2), 9-17.

Harding, S. G. (1998). *Is science multicultural: Postcolonialisms, feminisms, and epistemologies.* Bloomington: Indiana UP.

Harding, S. (2000). Should philosophies of science encode democratic ideals? In D. L. Kleinman (Ed.), *Science, technology & democracy* (pp. 121-138). Albany: SUNY.

hooks, b. (1984). *Feminist theory: From margin to center.* Boston: South End.

hooks, b. (1992). *Black looks: Race and representation.* Boston: South End.

hooks, b. (2000). *Feminism is for everybody: Passionate politics.* Cambridge: South End.

Johnson, A. G. (2006). *Privilege, power and difference.* Boston: McGrawHill.

Kadi, J. (1996). *Thinking class: Sketches from a cultural worker.* Boston: South End.

Keller, E. F. (1983). *A feeling for the organism: The life and work of Barbara Mc-Clintock.* San Francisco: Freeman.

Keller, E. F. (1992). *Secrets of life, secrets of death: Essays on language, gender and science.* New York: Routledge.

Keller, E. F. (2004, March). What impact, if any, has feminism had on science? *Journal of Biosciences, 29,* 7-13. Retrieved September 8, 2007, from http://www.ias.ac.in/jbiosci/mar2004/7.pdf

Kilduff, M., & Krackhardt, D. (1994, February). Bringing the individual back in: A structural analysis of the internal market for reputation in organizations. *Academy of Management Journal, 87.* Retrieved April 26, 1999, from LEXIS/NEXIS

Kramer, P. E., & Lehman, S. (1990). Mismeasuring women: A critique of research on computer ability and avoidance. *Signs, 16*(11), 158-172.

Kuhn, T. S. (1962). *The structure of scientific revolutions*. Chicago: U of Chicago P.

Lederman, M., & Bartsch, I. (Eds.). (2001). *The gender and science reader*. London: Routledge.

Lerner, R. M. (2005). Foreword: Urie Bronfenbrenner: Career contributions of the consummate developmental scientist. In U. Bronfenbrenner (Ed.), *Making human beings human: Bioecological perspectives on human development* (pp. ix-xxvi). Thousand Oaks, CA: Sage.

Lipton, B. H. (2005). *The biology of belief: Unleashing the power of consciousness, matter and miracles*. Santa Rosa, CA: Elite.

Loye, D. (2004). Darwin's lost theory and the hidden crisis in Western education. In R. Eisler & R. Miller (Eds.), *Educating for a culture of peace* (pp. 42-55). Portsmouth, NH: Heinemann.

Lukacs, J. (2001). Heisenberg's recognitions: The end of the scientific world view. In M. Lederman & I. Bartsch (Eds.), *The gender and science reader* (pp. 225-230). London: Routledge.

Merchant, C. (1980). *The death of nature: Women, ecology and the scientific revolution*. San Francisco: HarperSanFrancisco.

Merchant, C. (2001). Dominion over nature. In M. Lederman & I. Bartsch (Eds.), *The gender and science reader* (pp. 68-81). New York: Routledge.

Morrison, T. (1992). *Playing in the dark: Whiteness and the literary imagination*. New York: Vintage.

Nelkin, D. (1995). *Selling science: How the press covers science and technology*. New York: Freeman.

Plous, S. (1993). *The psychology of judgment and decision making*. New York: McGraw.

Riger, S. (1992). Epistemological debates, feminist voices. *American Psychologist, 47*(6), 730-740.

Rolf, J. E., & Masten, A. S. (Eds.). (1990). *Risk and protective factors in the development of psychopathology*. New York: Cambridge UP.

Rosser, S. V. (Ed.). (1995). *Teaching the majority: Breaking the gender barrier in science, mathematics, and engineering*. New York: Teachers College.

Schiebinger, L. (1993). *Nature's body: Gender in the making of modern science.* Boston: Beacon.

Schiebinger, L. (1999). *Has feminism changed science?* Cambridge, MA: Harvard.

Turkle, S., & Papert, S. (1990). Epistemological pluralism: Styles and voices within the computer culture. *Signs, 16*(1), 128-157.

Wajcman, J. (1995). Feminist theories of technology. In S. Jasanoff et al. (Eds.), *Handbook of science and technology studies* (pp. 189-204). Thousand Oaks, CA: Sage.

Young, R. (1987) Racist science, racist society. In D. Gill & L. Levidow (Eds.), *Anti-racist science teaching* (pp. 16-42). London: Free Association.

ENDNOTE

[1]   Some portions of this chapter may have appeared in, and are reprinted with permission from Kirk, M. (2006). Bridging the digital divide: A feminist perspective on the project. In G. Trajkovski (Ed.), *Diversity in information technology education: Issues and controversies* (pp. 38-67). Hershey, PA: Information Science Publishing

Section II
Perspectives on Dominator
Social Institutions

Section II: Perspectives on Dominator Social Institutions (Chapters IV through VII) examines how four social institutions—media, language, education, and business—teach the values, attitudes, and beliefs of a dominator society in specific relation to IT. Each chapter begins with a few general themes representative of that social institution and then provides an in-depth example of how these themes are reflected in specific relation to science and IT. Although one might also consider other social institutions such as law, government, religion, and the family in such an analysis, I have focused on these four because they are four of the most influential and pervasive in their impact with specific regard to IT.

Chapter IV: "Mass Media as Social Institution: The Wired Example" explores the role of mass media as a primary social institution that teaches us about ourselves and our world. In the U.S., and in the global IT field, media play an increasingly powerful role in terms of interpreting our world, and that interpretation also makes heavy use of stereotypes to convey a message. This chapter offers a few general examples of the ways in which this influences women's participation in IT as well as a more in-depth analysis of one form of mass media—a computing magazine titled Wired. Wired offers an interesting ground for analysis of the influence of stereotypes in mass media since one of its founding purposes was to discuss technology in relation to culture.

Chapter V: "Language as Social Institution: The Male-Centered IT Culture" offers an analysis of the role of communication and language as another social institution that teaches us the values, attitudes, and beliefs of our culture and that uses stereotypes pervasively. I explore these issues by discussing why "political correctness" matters, our gendered communication style, the male-centered IT language and culture, and the influence of dominance, violence, and sex metaphors in IT on women's participation.

Chapter VI: "Education as Social Institution: Understanding Her-Story" explores the ways in which education as a social institution teaches us values, attitudes, and beliefs. Education plays a particularly key role since it is the social institution that defines the knowledge tradition itself—the bounds around what is known, what it is important to know, and who knows. This chapter offers a brief her-story of women in math, engineering, and IT, as well as describing trends in education and employment.

Chapter VII: "Business as Social Institution: Global Issues in IT" explores ways in which the global IT business operates as another significant social institution purveying attitudes, values, and beliefs that contribute to the underrepresentation of women as beneficiaries, users, and developers of technology. This chapter analyzes the following major issues: (1) the dominator values reflected in the global IT business model; (2) the relationship between postcolonialism and U.S. participation in global economic development; (3) the rising social and political significance of economic development in India and China with specific relation to the IT industry; and (4) as a way of asking questions about what values the global IT industry might be concerned about, we look through the lens of an in-depth example—IBM's global business relationships and the Holocaust.

Chapter IV
Mass Media as Social Institution:
The *Wired* Example

OBJECTIVES

This chapter aims to help you understand the following:

- How mass media operates as a social institution to teach the attitudes, values, and beliefs of a dominator society.
- How much power mass media and IT have over defining social norms, and how much of that power is held by just a few individuals and a few companies.
- The common stereotypes that media purvey about women in science and technology.
- The pervasiveness of violent and sexual metaphors in one popular technology magazine.
- How these negative images influence the participation of women in science and technology.

INTRODUCTION

Communication is generally understood as a two-part process consisting of messages that convey content and the interpretation of that content by the receiver. Meanings are conveyed through words, images, and symbols. In the U.S., mass media serve as one of the most significant social institutions shaping communication since media act as gatekeepers of information using stereotypes as one of the primary tools to communicate the values of the dominant culture (Creedon, 1993; Wood, 1999). As I discussed in Chapter II, stereotypes circumscribe the boundaries around where we "belong" and what is "possible" for us in our lives. We learn both about how to view each other (which teaches us to "discriminate" and rank by category), how to view ourselves (which teaches us to internalize views of being "less than" in relation to gender, race, class, and other systems of ranking), and how to organize our society (which teaches us who belongs where). These representations have a powerful influence on the possibilities that people perceive for themselves and impact the behaviors through which they manifest these possibilities.

Contemporary mass media play a pivotal role in defining the "appropriate" cultural boundaries around such factors as gender, race, and class. In *Playing in the Dark: Whiteness and the Literary Imagination* (1992), Toni Morrison states: "Eddy is White, and we know he is because nobody says so" (p. 72). It is only necessary to "define" those who are outside of the dominant social center. In the end, every "aspect of our culturally mediated identity . . . is challenged or altered by the hypnotic power of mass media" (Miller, 2004, p. 2). This chapter explores these issues in the following sections: (1) mass media and its power to influence; and (2) and in-depth analysis of *Wired* magazine.

MASS MEDIA AND ITS POWER TO INFLUENCE

In our dominator social system, men still hold the primary "power to define" and in contemporary industrialized societies that power is often exerted via the mass media and information technology. In the U.S., men are still the primary owners of media/communications and technology companies. In a recent *Forbes* report "The 400 Richest Americans," which ranks people by their net worth, 16 of the top 50 own technology or media companies and only one was a woman (Anne Cox Chambers owns Cox Enterprises which includes 17 newspapers, 15 TV stations, and 80 radio stations). Table 1 highlights the technology and media owners among the top 50 of the *Forbes* 400 richest Americans (Miller, 2007).

The tremendous development of new technologies and electronic communication combined with the 1996 Telecommunications Act (which permitted consolidation of media ownership) has instigated a rapid consolidation of various types of media into single megacorporations. When Ben Bagdikian first published *The Media Monopoly* in 1983, the former dean of the Graduate School of Journalism at the University of California at Berkeley cited 50 companies as owners of most media in the U.S. In *The New Media Monopoly* (2004), he explains how the principal media outlets in the U.S. are now owned by five global conglomerates: "Time Warner, by 2003

Table 1. Wealthiest American technology and media company owners

Rank	Name	Company	Net worth in $billions
1	Bill Gates	Microsoft	59
4	Larry Ellison	Oracle	26
5	Sergey Brin	Google	18.5
5	Larry Page	Google	18.5
8	Michael Dell	Dell	17.2
11	Paul Allen	Microsoft	16.8
16	Steve Ballmer	Microsoft	15.2
24	Anne Cox Chambers	Cox Enterprises	12.6
25	Michael Bloomberg	Bloomberg	11.5
27	Charles Ergen	Echostar	10.2
31	John Kluge	Metromedia	9.5
33	Rupert Murdoch[1]	News Corp	8.8
35	Jeffrey Bezos	Amazon	8.7
37	Donald Newhouse	Advance Publications (subsidiary Condé Nast owns *Wired* magazine)	8.5
37	Samuel Newhouse, Jr.	Advance Publications (subsidiary Condé Nast owns *Wired* magazine)	8.5
41	Sumner Redstone	Viacom	7.6
48	Eric Schmidt	Google	6.5
50	James Kennedy	Cox Enterprises	6.3

the largest media firm in the world; The Walt Disney Company; Murdoch's News Corporation, based in Australia; Viacom; and Bertelsmann, based in Germany" (Bagdikian, 2004, p. 3). These companies own most U.S. "newspapers, magazines, book publishers, motion picture studios, and radio and television stations . . . and the owners prefer stories and programs that can be used everywhere and anywhere" (Bagdikian, 2004, p. 3). On *Forbes* 2007 list of "The World's 2,000 Largest Public Companies," they rank as follows: #67 Time Warner ($131.67 billion in assets); #107 Disney ($60.99 billion); #134 News Corp ($59.17 billion); and #352 Viacom ($21.8 billion) (DeCarlo, 2007). Since Bertelsmann is not a public company, it is not included in the *Forbes* list. It is safe to say that in a capitalist economy, those with the money are also those who influence the information. And, when the sources of information (both print and digital) are consolidated into so few hands, they own even more social power to define our perceptions of our world. "As Gutenberg's movable type was in his day, the new electronic media as a social force remain in a still-uncertain balance" (Bagdikian, 2004, p. 26). With the primary image and information systems of our society in so few hands, and with the business need to appeal to a broad general audience, the new electronic media are likely to continue to purvey the pre-existing views of our dominator society even more efficiently.

Media Messages: Technology as Frontier and Journalism as Objective

The media also participates in "selling science" to the U.S. American public. Dorothy Nelkin (1995) characterizes the features of scientific journalism as follows: "imagery often replaces content," emphasis on "drama" and "hyperbole," and "focus on scientific and technological competition" (Nelkin, 1995, p. 5-6). Metaphors are also a common tool of journalists who must explain complex concepts to a broad audience, and metaphors are often informed by social stereotypes. Nelkin documents how the metaphors journalists use in science coverage heighten or diminish the importance of events, while they "marginalize some groups [and] empower others" (p. 11). One common metaphor in discussions of technology is that of the "frontier," which in the context of U.S. history suggests competition, war, winners, and losers. The new scientific frontier is perpetually promoted in terms of "cutting edge" technology that will "transform our lives" (p. 31).

There are several problems with the frontier as a metaphor for technology. One problem is the implicit assumption of power-over and of conquering, both hallmarks of a dominator society. For those who are already disenfranchised by the dominator social model, there is an implicit perception that the world of technology and its tools are "not for them," but the conqueror metaphor pushes those "conquered" groups even further towards the social margins. Another problem with the frontier metaphor is that it precludes any meaningful discussion of how science and technology might actually help us address deep-seated structural dilemmas in our social systems. These are the conversations that might uncover institutionalized values such as the male-centered ways in which science is defined.

Further, "the media has encouraged the widely held belief that science is distinct from politics and beyond the clash of conflicting social values" (Nelkin, 1995, p. 63). The mass media perpetuate the false notion that their discussion of science and technology is completely objective, without any social context or social influence. Journalists' claim to objectivity, to reporting that is unbiased by any social context, mirrors the scientific claims to objectivity that I discussed in Chapter III. These long-standing and deep-seated attitudes pervade dominator social systems and media as a social institution reflects them. Nelkin (1995) shares this historical quote about objectivity from an 1884 handbook for journalists which "states the imperative of separating facts and values in reporting and relates this imperative to American democratic values: 'It is as harmful to mix the two in journalism as it is to combine church and state in government'" (p. 86).

The problem lies in the fact that, as many feminist scholars have shown, it is nearly impossible to achieve true objectivity; our perceptions are influenced by our own social standpoint. Further, as quantum physicists and anthropologists have also suggested, just the act of our observation changes the things we observe. So, the pretense of separating facts from the social context in which they occur is a claim to something that is not possible. However, most of us have bought the myth; the emperor is marching past us naked, but we all "see" he is clothed. The fact is that journalism and science are both created in a social context, and that social context influences journalism and science in sometimes subtle, but largely powerful ways. A truer stance would be to admit that we are influenced by the social (and political) climate in which we create ideas, and to attempt to consciously name the ways in which this climate may influence our perceptions.

Images of Women in Science and Technology

One relevant example of the power of media (and stereotypes) to purvey cultural values and limit our perceptions lies in the media coverage of several women Nobel Prize winners in science. In 1966, headlines announcing Maria Goeppart Meyer's Nobel Prize reflected the stereotypical expectations placed on women: "The first woman to win a Nobel Prize in science is *a scientist and a wife*," and "British *Grandmother* Wins the Prize" [italics mine]. In 1977, when Rosalyn Yalow won the Nobel Prize in medicine, the coverage was not much better: "She Cooks, She Cleans, She Wins the Nobel Prize." And, in 1983, when corn geneticist Barbara McClintock won the Nobel Prize, "*Newsweek* called her 'the Greta Garbo of genetics.' At 81 she has never married, always preferring to be alone'" (Nelkin, 1995, p. 18-19). In all cases, their marital status and roles as child bearers are highlighted, and "oh, by the way" they are also smart. These historical examples of the stereotypes conveyed by stories on Nobel Prize-winning women in science are classic representations of the gender stereotypes still used today in mass media: "women's place is in the home; women are dependent upon men; women do not make independent and important decisions; women are shown in few occupational roles; women view themselves and are viewed by others as sex objects" (Lazier & Kendrick, 1993, p. 202).

Bix (2000) reports on the history of women's science and engineering education at one of the top engineering universities in the United States—the Massachusetts Institute of Technology. Her research shows similar stereotypes of women engineers as those reflected by the mass media. In 1940 a student newspaper introduced a "class member as a New York 'glamour girl' who wanted to work on cancer research and had won a hundred-dollar bet from fellow debutantes in gaining admission to MIT" (Bix, 2000, p. 25). In 1963, national media reports of the first woman's residence at MIT included these headlines: "Hardly anyone imagines girls attending mighty MIT," *Time* reported, but "Tech girls have 'brains' plus 'looks'" (Bix, 2000, p. 29). In 1967, MIT began an exchange program with Wellesley College that allowed students to take courses at either school. MIT women were characterized as "less than feminine, a girl five feet tall and equally wide, a slide rule hanging at her belt, who can speak only in differential equations" (Bix, 2000, p. 33-34). Wellesley women were stereotyped rather differently; the student newspaper hailed the new program by including a cartoon showing two men staring at "a woman in a miniskirt and high-heeled boots" walking by; "the caption read, 'Coeducation comes to the 'tute',—ignoring the fact that MIT women had been there all along" (Bix, 2000, p. 33-34).

These images of women technologists are not surprising in light of the fact that one of the most persistent stereotypes in relation to science and technology is the image of a "scientist" as male. Nearly 50 years of data from the Draw a Scientist Test show the remarkable persistence and pervasiveness of stereotypes. Researchers have now tested many populations including elementary students, college students, and teachers of math and science in the U.S. and internationally with woefully consistent results (Fung, 2002; Rubin & Cohen, 2003; Thomas, Henley, & Snell, 2006). Draw a Scientist Test participants have repeatedly imaged "a scientist as a middle-aged or older man wearing glasses and a white coat and working alone in a lab" (Sadker & Sadker, 1994, p. 123). These types of stereotypes begin to influence girls' and boys' attitudes about science and technology at very early ages and their costs are exponential over time.

Joanna Goode, Rachel Estrella, and Jane Margolis (2006) conducted interviews about participation in computer science with over 200 high school students and teachers in the racially diverse Los Angeles Unified School District. Their research corroborated the power of stereotypes learned from mass media; for many students "their images of who works in computer science comes largely from popular culture" (p. 99). Students mentioned that in media ranging from magazines and books to television and film, the most persistent stereotype is that of an antisocial, lone programmer, staring at a computer screen 24 hours a day, 7 days a week (the computer geek). It is not hard to understand how girls who have been gender-socialized to be relational would find this image, and the lifestyle it suggests, more unappealing than boys. Of course, like all stereotypes, this unidimensional depiction of a lone computer geek is inaccurate since most computer science professionals must work in teams to develop ideas and products. The fact that the stereotype persists in spite of its inaccuracy is a testament to the power of media to convey beliefs.

Dale Spender (1995) corroborates that what most girls turn away from is not the technology; what "they turn away from is the image of the scientist or the computer hacker" (p. 173). In comparison to boys, this leads to many girls being unprepared in math and science by the time they are ready for college. Multiple scholars have documented the predictable self-esteem slide that occurs for most girls during adolescence as they begin to feel increasing social pressure to be "feminine" (Brumberg, 1997; Pipher, 1994; Sadker & Sadker, 1995). Since girls shy away from the image of "scientist" as "unfeminine" in those pivotal adolescent years, this leads them to take fewer advanced math and science courses in junior high and high school (Goode et al., 2006; Sadker & Sadker, 1995). In addition, "girls are significantly underrepresented in after-school computer clubs, as computer participants, at free-access times using the computers, and in advanced computer electives" (Rosser, 1995, p. 147). This leads even fewer girls to make successful transitions from high school to college in terms of being either users or developers of technology.

The stereotypes perpetuated in technology magazines provide one example of the ways in which women and people of color are depicted in relation to technology. These stereotypes often project limitations in terms of perceived access to, interest in, and capability in technology, which influence social perceptions of who may be developers, users, and beneficiaries of the technology (Ware & Stuck, 1985). "Media images more frequently depict computer programmers and developers as males, and women as users. For example, in advertisements of technology products, women are often presented as passive and inexpert users . . . Men . . . are characterized as deep thinkers concerned with the future" (Barker & Aspray, 2006, p. 38).

Zarrett, Malanchuk, Davis-Kean, and Eccles (2005) conducted a longitudinal study of 1,482 adolescents, of whom 61% were African-American and 35% were European American, over a 9-year period from 1991 through 2000 to examine sociopsychological factors that influence computer-related occupational choices inclusive of race, gender, and socioeconomic class. Their findings demonstrate that individuals' choices to pursue IT careers are related to their "perceived ability or mastery of the field," their experiences with the subject (classes in math and computer programming), and "cultural norms and stereotypes" (Zarrett et al., 2005, pp. 75-76). Black males and females, and White females shared one key predictor of interest in IT careers—self-concept. For White males, what mattered most with regard to "IT aspirations was others' encouragement and, importantly, valuing math at an early age" (p. 75). Since stereotypes often contribute negatively to the self-concept of women and people of color, especially in relation to technology, this study underlines the potential social significance of understanding and reimagining our social images. bell hooks (1992) argues that there "is a direct and abiding connection between the maintenance of White supremacist patriarchy in this society and the institutionalization via mass media of specific images, representations of race" (hooks, 1992, p. 2). We need images and representations of women and people of color that are as rich, vivid, and varied as people themselves.

In this discussion, I have attempted to offer a brief overview of mass media's influence with regard to who participates in IT as developers, users, or beneficiaries of technology. Stereotypical images and ideas can be found in all mass media including advertising, newspapers, magazines, books, television, films, and the Internet. I have chosen to focus on one example from print media in part because print is one of the oldest forms of information media, and in part because it most closely parallels the information media now available via the Internet. For the remainder of this chapter, I provide a more in-depth analysis of how stereotypes have been purveyed by one magazine in the technology industry—*Wired* magazine.

WIRED: DO I HEAR STATIC ON THE LINE?

Picture this. You are a woman who excitedly picks up a technology magazine that's garnered high praise from the critics for putting technology in a social context. You eagerly look inside to find a nude image of a female body with its parts fragmented. On another page, you see another nude image of a female body with its legs spread apart and the word "SLUT" emblazoned over its head. On another page, you see an image of a female "warrior woman" with lasers shooting out of her genitals. These are some of the images in *Wired*. How do you imagine you might feel? Would you feel that the world of technology is for you? Would you feel safe or even comfortable in that world? Would you feel that this was a world in which you could participate in any other role than that of a sex object? If this were the only place that you encountered such stereotypes, perhaps you might not be so negatively influenced by them. The problem lies in the pervasiveness of such images and in the additive effect that this has on our psyches, for both women and men.

Why choose *Wired*? In February 1999, I reviewed over 20 computing magazines, including such biggies as *MacWorld*, *Dr. Dobbs*, and *PC Magazine*, and found that *Wired* had the most images and articles about women. During its highly lauded early years of publication (before the sale to Newhouse-owned Condé Nast), *Wired* included a few feature articles on notable women in technology. Among technology magazines, *Wired* appeared to be doing the best job in terms of attempting to represent women positively. I researched issues from *Wired*'s inception in January/February 1993 through April 1999, a few months after the sale to Condé Nast. Since the Condé Nast ownership resulted in new editorial directions, my research on images in *Wired* focused primarily on the early years when it was still being run by its independent founders. The following discussion explores: (1) a brief history of *Wired* up to the sale; (2) the covers of *Wired*; (3) how much male and female writers wrote about women, and how they wrote about women; and (4) interviews with women who wrote for *Wired*. The results show that images of women in *Wired* are at best a mixed bag. There are a few clear, positive images and messages about women in relation to technology. However, there is still the pervasive presence of negative stereotypes, some of which are sexualized and violent.

A Brief History of *Wired*

At its inception, *Wired* claimed to be the voice of the digital revolution and attempted to be the first computer magazine to place technology in a cultural context. Unfortunately, the "culture" tended to be a White, male, educated, and economically advantaged subculture, and the images of women and people of color in *Wired* were sometimes dubious. In *Cracking the Gender Code: Who Rules the Wired World?*, Melanie Stewart Millar (1998) comprehensively names the rich diversity of issues in relation to women, computing, and culture that were missing from *Wired* magazine:

Wired . . . negates difference by excluding positive images of women and minorities and denying that digital culture is the creation of a particular dominant elite. In so doing, it presents a particular set of gender, race and class constructions that reflect an underlying ideology characterized by a strong belief in technological progress and the conservation of hegemonic power relations. Whether Wired is excluding, reconstructing or eliminating difference, women and minorities continue to be subordinated in the digital world it creates. Thus, although Wired comes wrapped in a dazzling, novel package, like much of the discourse of digital culture, it continues to sell a very old, all-too-familiar ideology: one that serves to perpetuate inequality. (p. 112)

Millar (1998) elaborates on how *Wired*'s approach not only excludes and masks difference, but redefines "White masculinity in a new, quintessentially hypermodern form . . . [that] combines the mainstays of the emerging digital culture with very traditional constructions of masculine power, frontier mythology and technological transcendence" (p. 113). Thus, *Wired* echoed the historical attitude that science is male by defining computer culture in male terms and purveying the conquering, power-over, dominator frontier metaphor.

Was this what *Wired* wanted to be? In his November 1993 column announcing *Wired*'s new monthly status, co-founder Louis Rossetto stated *Wired*'s mission, which was "to cover the biggest story of the decade—the convergence of computing, telecommunications, and the media—for the most powerful people on the planet today, the people making this Digital Revolution" (Rossetto, 1998a). Jane Metcalf, the other co-founder, described *Wired* this way: "There are a lot of magazines out there about computers and the Internet. We never actually talk about the technology . . . We talk about how technology is changing the landscape of our lives and the effect it has on all of us" (Copilevitz, 1996). Metcalf certainly privileges the social context of technology in terms of her perspective on the publication's purpose. This is clear not only from comments she has made, but also from activities that she has involved herself with, such as leading the fight against regulation of the Internet by supporting industry rather than government solutions, and serving as a board member for the Electronic Frontier Foundation (Copilevitz, 1996). Serving as the voice of social conscience, Metcalf warns: "There's a danger of being enamoured [*sic*] with the technology and forgetting why it's here—to put information and power in the hands of everyone" (Copilevitz, 1996). However, John Plunkett, *Wired*'s Creative Director, reflected a slightly different view of *Wired*: "At once captious doyenne and encouraging confidante to aspiring members of a new socially insecure elite. *Wired* works . . . by tweaking its readers' anxieties, constantly reminding them that they are hopelessly behind the times" (White, 1996). Although a sense of a broader cultural purpose emerges from these three visions (most notably from the woman in the trio), they also reveal an emphasis on an insider-outsider view of technology, on the power-over dimensions of technology, and on the world of technology as a club to which only the privileged can belong. How did this vision emerge? How did *Wired* begin?

Wired was the brainchild of Louis Rossetto (Editor/Publisher) and Jane Metcalf (President), two innovators who spent years trying to bring the publication to fruition. The idea for *Wired* was born while the two were living and working in Amsterdam on a European computer magazine. Rossetto says, "The idea was based on the premise that we were entering a new era, and this new era was being created by the convergence of computing, telecommunications, and media" (Rossetto, 1998b). According to Rossetto, the concept originated in 1987 and was developed into a formal business plan by 1991. He says, "We would have loved to have done it here in Holland, but it was our belief that the culture that we're describing in *Wired* hadn't developed sufficiently in Europe to support a magazine like *Wired*." So, in spite of the fact that he and Metcalf had spent most of their adult lives outside the United States, they moved to San Francisco to begin the magazine (Rossetto, 1998b). Early financial contributors included MIT Media Lab magnet Nicholas Negroponte, who also had a regular column in the early years of *Wired*, and Dutch software tycoon Eckart Wintzen who gave Metcalf and Rossetto $36,000 to develop a 120-page prototype of a new consumer technology magazine in Europe. Although Wintzen did not directly invest in *Wired*, his support of an early prototype in 1991 paved the way for *Wired* (Copilevitz, 1996).

After years in the making, when *Wired* finally hit the market, it was an instant success with circulation topping 100,000 per issue and 23,000 subscribers by the end of the first year (Rossetto, 1998b). In fact, *Wired* sales took off so quickly that it transitioned from being a bi-monthly to a monthly publication after only two issues; the original plan called for that transition at the end of the first year. *Wired* won numerous awards from advertising, marketing, and magazine organizations, most notably the National Magazine Award for General Excellence in 1994 and 1997, which is awarded by the American Society of Magazine Editors (ASME). *Wired* earned the respected National Magazine Award for General Excellence in 1994 when it was barely a year old. *Time* claimed that "*Wired* invented geek mystique and made the promise of the wired world palpable" (Quittner, 1996). *Newsweek* labeled *Wired* the "Rolling Stone for the Computer Generation" (White, 1999). *The Seattle Times* dubbed *Wired* the "Digital Age's bible" (Clark, 1994; Copilevitz, 1996; White, 1999). And, it was not just the professionals who raved about *Wired*. This comment from a London reader typifies reader's responses: "I'm prepared to spend time reading *Wired* because it never fails to leave me with a sense of optimism and excitement about how the communications revolution is going to make the world a better place" (Offen, 1996).

Wired's success drew the attention of Condé Nast Magazines, a division of the $9 billion media conglomerate Advance Publications, and *Wired* was sold in 1998 for $80 to 85 million (Corcoran, 1998; Harmon, 1998). The story of the sale of *Wired* Ventures seems to be the classic story of a new business expanding too rapidly before it had the necessary capital to support the expansion. Rossetto had envisioned *Wired* Ventures as a new kind of media company; the magazine was only one, albeit very successful, aspect of the vision. But, as early as January 1994, Condé Nast bought a 15% interest in *Wired* for $3.5 million (Clark, 1994; Manly, 1996). In 1996, *Wired*'s financial death-knell began tolling loudly when *Wired* Ventures began increasing involvement in numerous projects such as "*Wired* UK, *Wired* Japan, a consumer design magazine, and an MSNBC TV talk show called Netizen" (Corcoran, 1998). In 1996, Rossetto failed twice to take the company public, which he attributed to "bad timing" and most investors attributed to overvaluing *Wired*. In June of 1996, *Wired* Ventures filed with the SEC to sell 6.3 million shares (17% of the company) for $10 to $12 per share, which would have earned the company $75.9 million and signified a valuation of $450 million (Manly, 1996). In October 1996, *Wired* filed another IPO at $293 million, still much more than investors had ever paid for a company *Wired*'s size.

Unfortunately, the Condé Nast sale meant that Rossetto ended up selling the magazine to precisely "the kind of 'old media' conglomerate that he had long decried" (Corcoran, 1998). Advance Publications was built by three brothers—Samuel I., Norman, and Theodore Newhouse. By the time of the sale in 1998, the three founders had died (Samuel in 1979, Norman in 1988, and Theodore in 1998), but the company was still run by Si Newhouse's sons; Samuel I., Jr. was chairman and Donald was president of Advance Publications (Associated Press, 1998). Around the time of the sale, the two brothers' estimated net worth of $4.5 billion each ranked them among the top 25 wealthiest U.S. Americans.

The Condé Nast group publishes numerous magazines on diverse topics with long-standing popularity: *allure, Architectural Digest, Bon Appetit, Brides, Condé Nast Traveller, Glamour, Gourmet, GQ, House & Garden, Mademoiselle, The New Yorker, SELF, Vanity Fair, Vogue*, and *Women's Sports & Fitness*. Condé Nast has been called the "supermodel of magazine publishing" (Condé Nast, 1999). At the time of the *Wired* sale, Advance Publications owned multiple cable TV stations, newspapers and Web sites, in addition to Condé Nast magazines. Until 1998, Advance also owned Random House, one of the largest trade book publishers in the U.S. (the Newhouses sold Random to Bertelsmann AG for $1.4 billion, after purchasing it for $60 million in 1980) (Fabrikant, 1998).

In May 1998, when *Wired* Ventures sold the magazine to Condé Nast, the *New York Times* claimed that "there would be little cash left for the pair whose vision and persistence created a new genre of magazine where traditional media companies said it could not be done" (Harmon, 1998). *Editor & Publisher* claimed that *Wired* Ventures would use the money to pay down debt and bolster its online operations such as the HotBot search engine, Hot*Wired*, and *Wired* News, "which have grown from 7% of the company's revenues in 1996 to about 30% in 1997" ("Newhouse," 1998; "Patriot-News," 1998). At the annual *Wired* anniversary party in January 1998, Rossetto announced that the magazine was undergoing its first major redesign which included three new people at the top: publisher Dana Lyon, editor-in-chief Katrina Heron, and managing editor Martha Baer. Evidently, Rossetto had been asked by *Wired*'s new corporate investors to step aside (Corcoran, 1998). Shortly after Condé Nast took over, Heron stated her intention to "broaden *Wired*'s focus" by including "more general stories on medicine, politics, and fashion, but isn't targeting women (or men) in particular" (Corcoran, 1998).

The Covers of *Wired*

My research on the magazine's front covers showed a predominance of male images and of power-over, domination-oriented values in the sex, death, and war language used on the headlines. Only nine women were pictured on the front cover from January/February 1993 through April 1999. Of these, eight were apparently White or light skinned (one was a cartoon) and one was racially ambiguous. There were two additional images that may have been female, but were pictured in such a way that distinguishing their gender would have been difficult or impossible to determine.

Language that emphasized sex, war, and/or death was used in the headings on the covers of 41 issues out of 71, sometimes multiple headings in one issue. One notable example of death language and imagery exclaimed, "Buy this magazine, or we fry this magician" on a cover with an image of a White man, in his 30s, sitting with legs spread in an electric chair, wearing a black all-leather outfit, and smiling down at the reader (September 1994). Other examples of sexually-oriented headlines are the painfully obvious: "Sex Sells!" (December 1997), and the insulting "Sex vs. Equity? Are you kidding?" (September 1998). These covers depict *Wired*'s attempt to discuss computer technology in the context of culture as male-centered and money-motivated with little or no real social context. The dominance of male images and of sex, death, and war language contributes to what Millar (1998) describes as the "building of the hypermacho man" (p. 113). This implicitly and explicitly casts the actors and their actions in the digital world as *Wired* defines it—they are male, they are White, and they are dominators.

Articles about Women

I began examining articles in *Wired* by developing a database that included the following: issue, author, article title, topic/gender, size/location, type of story [photo & sidebar (signified one full page), short (signified two to three page articles), feature (signified articles over four pages)], freelance or *Wired* staff, and contact information. Next, I categorized the content into three broad groups—positive, mixed, and negative—based on whether they challenged existing stereotypes (positive), contained mixed images/ideas, or reified existing stereotypes (negative).

By Men

Of the articles that I identified as containing positive images of women, there were six articles written by women and 26 by men. Of the six articles by women, two were written about men, one was written about a woman, and the rest were on general topics. Of the 26 articles by men, 25 were about women. In other words, there were *more men writing about women* than women writing about women. This may be one of the most interesting issues in thinking about images of women in *Wired*. In the rare moments when women are discussed, they are being discussed by men. So, what was the tenor of that discussion?

Kevin Kelly's writing about women makes an interesting subject for analysis since he was an Executive Editor of *Wired* with the authority to shape the direction of the magazine. According to the "Who is *Wired*?" listing on the Hotwired Web site, Kelly was with *Wired* since its inception, was a former editor/publisher of *Whole Earth Review*, co-authored a book on communication tools titled *Signal*, and served on the board of the WELL ("Who," 1999). Kelly wrote three stories about women, all of which fell in my "short" category, which means that they only covered two to three pages of the magazine each. The three women that he wrote about were Miss Manners ("Manners Matter" in the November 1997 issue), Martha Stewart ("I Do Have a Brain" in the August 1998 issue), and Hazel Henderson ("Win-Win World" in the February 1997 issue).

First, let us look at the choice of subject, that is, the women he chose to write about. Certainly, Judith Martin (Miss Manners) and Martha Stewart have shaped culture, which is one of the dimensions of analysis that *Wired* claims to focus on. They have also been very successful businesswomen. However, the focus of their work lies in etiquette and homemaking, both domains that are gendered "female" and they have little to do with computer technology (a domain that is gendered "male"). Stories about Judith Martin and Martha Stewart in a magazine that purports to be about the intersections between culture and computers do little to alter our stereotypes about women in relation to technology. In fact, highlighting these particular women in a magazine about technology may support traditional gender roles for women, reinforcing the social stereotypes that girls are supposed to "be polite" and "take care of the home." To paraphrase Martha Stewart, "that's a good thing!"

Renowned global economist and futurist Hazel Henderson is a more suitable topic in relation the stated focus of *Wired*. Her work is fundamentally about culture, focusing on reframing the discussion of global economics to be more representative of women and of social, cultural and economic values that differ from the colonialist structures implicit in a dominator social organization. Her views, if heeded, certainly might reshape the development of our global technologies in positive ways.

Wired's contents pages from January/February 1993 through April 1999 listed 23 other stories that were written by men about women. In terms of content, these writers wrote about women who were more directly related to issues that actually linked computers and culture, that is, women who have developed new computing technology, built successful companies, shaped how technology is being used, or created art working in digital media. These stories generally offered more positive and nonstereotypical views of women in relation to technology. Table 2 lists articles about women, written by men, organized alphabetically by author.

The issue with these stories is not about their stereotypical content, but about how little space was devoted to positive images such as these notable women. Only nine of the stories were what I have classified as feature length, consuming over four pages in the magazine. The remaining 13 stories fell into my short category, stories that spanned two to three pages each. Overall, although there was at least some conscious effort to include women and their achievements in *Wired* during the 6 years of issues that I examined, both the way in which they were discussed and the degree to which their accomplishments were covered tended to display and reinforce dominant cultural views regarding gender.

Table 2. Articles about women, written by men

Issue	Author	Title	Topic/Gender	Size/Loc
Feb-99	Bayers, Chip	Push Comes to Shove	F/Gerry Laybourne & Candace Carpenter	Feature 110
Apr-95	Berkun, Scott	Agent of Change	F/Pattie Maes	Short 116
May-96	Blume, Harvey	Touchstone	F/Mary Modahl	Short 126
Jan-96	Blume, Harvey	Zine Queen	F/Pagen Kennedy	Short 132
Feb-99	Bronson, Po	On the Net, No One Knows You're a Maxwell	F/Isabel Maxwell	Feature 82
Jul-97	Daly, James	Gunn Club	F/Moira Gunn	Short 136
Dec-96	Davidson, Clive	Christine Downton's Brain	F/Christine Downton	Feature 170
Sep-96	Diamond, David	Adventure Capitalist	F/Ann Winblad	Short 142
Nov-96	Freund, Jesse	Tuning in to Marimba	F/Kim Polese	Short 122
Sep-94	Goldberg, Michael	CamNet: Those Who Cam, Do	F/CamNet founders	Feature 74
Oct-94	Heilemann, John	CyberRep Sinks Clipper!!!	F/Maria Cantwell	Short 35
Jul-95	Katz, Jon	The Medium Is the Medium	F/Helena Blavatsky	Feature 108
Feb-97	Kunzru, Hari	You Are Borg	F/Donna Harraway	Feature 154
Sep-96	Levy, Teven	Clipper Chick	F/Dorothy Denning	Feature 162
Jul/Aug 93	Meeks, Brock N.	Privacy is My Life: ACLU's Janlori Goldman	F/Janlori Goldman	Short 40
Jun-96	Sand, Michael	Fashion Nerd	F/Jhane Barnes	Feature 132
Jun-96	Schwartz, Peter	R-Tech	M/F, Catherine Distler	Short 138
Jun-96	Shine, Jerry	Herd Mentality	F/Maja Mataric	Feature 98
Feb-95	Snider, Burr	Jenny Holzer: Multidisciplinary Dweeb	F/Jenny Holzer	Short 76
Jan-94	Steinberg, Steve	Ada, The Enchantress of Numbers	F/Ada Lovelace	Short 128
Mar-96	Weinberger, David	One-on-One with One-to-One's Martha Rogers	F/Martha Rogers	Short 152
May-95	Whalen, John	Super Searcher: Cybrarian Reva Basch	F/Reva Basch	Short 153

By Women

Some might assume that women journalists do a better job of covering women's stories. However, as I explained in Chapter I, many women deliberately disassociate themselves from being "female" or from so-called "women's issues" because they fear the ways in which they may be professionally marginalized by association with the feminine. My research showed that to be the case with most of these women writers. *Wired*'s contents pages from January/February 1993 through April 1999 listed 120 stories that were written by women. Most of those stories were on general computer topics such as copyright, intellectual property, and virtual reality. However, of the stories that focused on people, 49 were about men and 17 were about women. What is notable here is that of the 120 stories that women wrote, only 17

Table 3. Articles about women, written by women

Issue	Author	Title	Gender/Topic	Size/Location
May/ Jun 93	McCarthy, Susan	Techno-soaps and Virtual Theatre: Brenda Laurel Can Blow anything up	F/Brenda Laurel	Short 40
Apr-94	Guglielmo, Connie	Coco's Channel	F/Coco Conn	Short 58
Jul-96	Rumsey, Tessa	Un-Still	F/Corinna Holthusen	Sidebar 119
Sep-98	Borsook, Paulina	Damsels in Distress	F/Cornelia Hesse-Honegger	Photo & sidebar 134
Apr-97	Bennion, Jackie	r-r-r-rip	F/Dee Breger	Photo & sidebar 120
Nov-93	Borsook, Paulina	Release	F/Esther Dyson	Feature 94
Feb-94	Guglielmo, Connie	Class Leader	F/Jan Davidson	Short 44
Feb-95	Cross, Rosie	Modem Grrrl	F/Jude Milhon	Short 118
Mar-94	McCorduck, Pamela	America's Multimediatrix	F/Laurie Anderson	Feature 79
Apr-98	Speedie, Anne	Star Warps	F/Margaret Geller	Photo & sidebar 158
Oct-94	Richmond, Wendy	Murial Cooper's Legacy	F/Muriel Cooper	Photo & sidebar 100
Dec-97	Holloway, Marguerite	Pattie	F/Pattie Maes	Feature 237
May-96	Stryker, Susan	Sex and Death Among the Cyborgs	F/Sandy Stone	Feature 134
Apr-96	McCorduck, Pamela	Sex, Lies, and Avatars	F/Sherry Turkle	Feature 106
Apr-94	Garner, Rochelle	The Mother of Multimedia	F/Sueann Ambron	Feature 52
Jan-97	Parisi, Paula	The Teacher Who Designs Videogames	F/Susan Schilling	Feature 98
Oct-96	Schibsted, Evantheia	Lifeform	F/Thecla Schiphorst	Feature 173

focused on women and their achievements. Women writers spent more time writing about men than about women, living proof of the power of patriarchy to keep men at the center of discussion. Table 3 lists the articles about women, written by women, organized alphabetically by gender/topic.

The good news is that eight of the articles that women wrote about women were feature length (over four pages), four were short (two to three pages), and four were photos and sidebars (one full page). What follows is a close analysis of some of the more positive stories that women wrote about women and the kinds of images that they purveyed.

Susan McCarthy (1993) wrote about Brenda Laurel in a short titled "Techno-soaps and Virtual Theatre: Brenda Laurel Can Blow Anything Up" in the May/June issue. Laurel exemplifies many of the non-traditional pathways that involve women with computers. In the late 70s, she was working on a Ph.D. in theatre at Ohio State when a friend showed her computer graphics for the first time. "She later put her Ph.D. on hold and moved to Atari, where she produced videogames" (McCarthy, 1993, p. 42). Ultimately, her dissertation became a description of the ways in which theatrical theory and practice could be used to approach computer interface design. Laurel also makes a blatantly feminist statement that was included in the story:

I've been beating my head against the wall of adolescent-male-stereotype content for a very long time. And the interfaces that we've had have disenfranchised a very large number of people, because they are based around a set of cognitive abilities and learned skills that many of us aren't very good at. (McCarthy, 1993, p. 42)

Laurel also describes her feelings as an industry outsider, not a stance that is typical in most "technically-oriented" stories.

Paulina Borsook (1993) wrote about Esther Dyson in a feature titled "Release" in the November issue. Dyson is portrayed as a powerful woman from the opening tag line: "Some have called Esther Dyson the most powerful woman in computing" (Borsook, 1993, p. 95). She is also described as "a one-woman think tank...one of the very few people in the industry of true creativity," and "like Shakespeare's Puck, magically appearing at the right moment" (Borsook, 1993, p. 95). Dyson, who majored in economics at Harvard at 16, sells her advice about the computer industry. Although Dyson is clearly powerful, and certainly independent, she does not align herself with feminism. She raises the usual objections such as being compared with successful male computer analysts instead of female ones, or being judged by who she is (or more importantly is not) involved with. But she also comments that being a woman has given her an overall advantage, by saying, "Especially when I was younger and cuter . . . people spent lots of hours explaining things" (p. 125). And she describes herself as more like a man because she "measures her success by what she's achieved, rather than by more personal and conventionally female measures of love and family" (p. 125). As a reader, I am left with the impression that Dyson is typical of many of the women who were early entrants into IT. She has learned to play a male-defined game better than the men who designed it, but it is not clear how she has changed IT by being female. So, she is the kind of woman that *Wired* may find "safe" to call powerful.

Pamela McCorduck (1994) wrote about Laurie Anderson in a feature titled "America's Multimediatrix" in the March issue. The strong feminist tone of the piece is established in the introduction:

The females who clutter videos and films are airhead, baby dolls, bimbos, bitches, earth mothers, martyrs, madonnas, material girls, morons . . . and n-factorial re-combinations of those dreary roles. Any and all of them are interesting, apparently, only insofar as they relate to men . . . So, how is it that Laurie Anderson, nobody's mom or sweetheart, nobody's victim, nobody's predator . . . has broken through? (McCorduck, 1994, p. 79)

Laurie Anderson, the subject of the piece, is set up as a "disquieting undocu-mented alien among all those cliches" (p. 79). The author does not shy away from Anderson's power as a multimedia artist, nor does she shy away from an explicit discussion of power. She quotes Anderson as saying that "technology today is the campfire around which we tell our stories" and that there is a particular kind of attraction to "this kind of power, which is both warm and destructive . . . Many of the images of technology are about making us more powerful, extending what we can do" (p. 136).

McCorduck tells the story of Anderson's first experiment with voice filters in Germany where she turned her mezzo into a basso in order to get people to listen to what she wanted to say. Anderson says, "When I spoke as myself, their reaction was politely interested. When I spoke as a man, and was bossy, they listened up" (McCorduck, 1994, p. 136). One of the more stunning accolades in the article in relation to strong, powerful women comes from artist and musician Brian Eno who produced Anderson's 1994 record. He describes her "extraordinary energy to do things well," to not only have original ideas, but to realize them. And, he compli-ments Anderson on the feeling that "runs through everything she does; none of her work is based on humiliation or sneering, even when it's being angry or critical" (McCorduck, 1994, p. 137). In a social climate in which anger is the emotion most denied to women, and even the slight taint of feminism will cause a woman to be labeled as "angry," this comment seems particularly enlightened.

Pamela McCorduck (1996) also wrote about Sherry Turkle in a feature titled "Sex, Lies, and Avatars" in the April issue, making her the only woman to write two feature-length articles on women during the years that I examined. Like many other women featured, Turkle had a non-traditional entry to computer science, through psychology. McCorduck says, "For postmodernists like Turkle, no unitary truth resides anywhere . . . Postmodernism celebrates this time, this place; and it celebrates adaptability, contingency, diversity, flexibility, sophistication, and relationships" (McCorduck, 1996, p. 108). These are not the terms characteristically used to describe those who work in computer science, or for that matter, any kind of science traditionally concerned with finding "the truth." Turkle's vision of the future is one in which we are constantly dealing with profound states of change:

We are dwellers on a threshold, poised in the liminal moment, 'a moment of passage when new cultural symbols and meanings can emerge. Liminal moments are times of tension, extreme reactions, and great opportunity. '(McCorduck, 1996, p. 109)

Examining this space "betwixt and between" is Turkle's passion and her commitment to interdisciplinary scholarship nearly cost her tenure at MIT. She fought the decision by pointing out among other things that she had produced the required "two well-received books." She says that she loves MIT, but that "you might say that I am at it, but not completely of it . . . I am in some ways marginal, liminal" (McCorduck, 1996, p. 164). The primary focus of her work in recent years has been to look at the relationships between humans and computers, and the ways in which we use the machines to define who we are.

Paula Parisi (1997) wrote about Susan Schilling in a feature titled "The Teacher Who Designs Videogames" in the January issue. The article focuses on good contemporary pedagogy such as learning by discovery, engaging learners to have fun, and developing materials that support multiple learning styles. The interview is structured in a question and answer format which makes it easy to access Schilling's words directly. Schilling says that the edutainment industry needs people "who think visually, people who think with light—instead of the text-based learning style now prevalent in schools" (Parisi, 1997, p. 98). She also makes the important point that throughout history "most people have been oral and visual learners, rather than text learners" (Parisi, 1997, p. 98). This becomes particularly interesting in terms of actually creating a "world wide" Web. So, ultimately, the "best educational software will include text, visual images, and active participation" (Parisi, 1997, p. 98).

Schilling shares one especially engaging success story to support the power of this type of interactive learning approach. While testing a product called World Geography with African-American youth, one learner asked to see "'all of the countries of the world that have majority populations with people of color,' and the whole world lit up" (p. 98). This engaged students in an energetic discussion that spanned world wide history, economics, and geography. This is the type of article that demonstrates the best that *Wired* has to offer. It features a woman working in the computer industry, and the discussion is focused around technology in the context of positive and constructive social change.

Women Writers' View of *Wired*

In spite of the effort by some to include positive stories about women in the conversation linking computers and culture, for the years that I researched *Wired,* the presence of women remained limited. For example, the 1999 *Wired* Web site listed the *Wired 52—Wired*'s list of the top 52 most interesting people in technology. That list only contained the following nine women (one of which was a musician): Laurie Anderson, Esther Dyson, Donna Haraway, Brenda Laurel, Robyn Miller, Kim Polese, Sandy Robertson, and Sherry Turkle. In *Wired Women: Gender and New Realities in Cyberspace* (1996), former *Wired* contributing writer Paulina Borsook described how the magazine claimed to be for readers who were "with-it one-planet high-tech high-touch global citizens of the 1990s, but turned out 'to be largely by guys and for guys' (pp. 25-26). Borsook wrote with fearless honesty about her experience as a woman writing for *Wired* and detailed the ways in which gendered roles influenced her participation in the magazine. Her lucid description of the climate for "wired" women writing about technology inspired me to conduct interviews with other women who had written for *Wired* to see how their perspectives might add to my analysis.

I began my search for interviewees by using my database to identify women who had written more than one article for *Wired.* There were 26 and about half of these women were freelancers and the other half were on the *Wired* staff (in various positions from editors to interns). Next, I researched each of the 26 women to learn more about their interests and to locate other things they had written. Based on the results of that research, I considered the following factors to narrow the interview list to 18 women: (1) achieving a balance of freelancers and *Wired* staffers; (2) availability of information about the writers; and (3) achieving a diversity of perspectives. Finally, I e-mailed these 18 women to describe my project and request an interview. Most declined to be interviewed, some did not respond at all, and five consented to be interviewed on condition of anonymity. As it turned out, all five of the interviewees were freelance writers.

I developed the following list of questions to ask these five writers: (1) How do you think the publishers would describe *Wired*'s purpose as a publication?; (2) How do you think the managing editors would describe *Wired*'s purpose as a publication?; (3) How would you describe *Wired*'s purpose as a publication?; (4) Do you think that *Wired* has fulfilled its purpose?; (5) How would you describe your role in relation to *Wired*?; (6) How did writing for *Wired* relate to your fulfilling your own professional goals? OR What interested you in writing for *Wired*?; (7) Did you like writing for *Wired*? Why or why not?; (8) Who chose your story ideas?; (9) Do you currently read *Wired*?; (10) Can you describe any changes you have noticed in *Wired* since Condé Nast purchased it last fall?; (11) How do you feel that being a woman has influenced your choice in careers and the development of your career?; (12) How would you define the purpose of feminism?; (13) How would you define a woman feminist?; and (14) Do you consider yourself a feminist?

What follows is a brief analysis of their answers to the questions that I considered most relevant to issues explored in this chapter: (1) How would you define the term feminism? Do you consider yourself a feminist?; (2) Do you feel that being a woman has influenced your choice in careers and the development of your career? If so, how?; (3) How would you describe your relationship with *Wired*? Have you liked working with *Wired*?; (4) What was the editing process? Who had the final edit? Who chose your story ideas?; (5) How would you describe the purpose of *Wired*, and do you think they've fulfilled that purpose?; and (6) Can you describe any changes you have noticed in *Wired* since Condé Nast purchased it in 1998?

How Would You Define the Term Feminism?

When I asked, "How would you define the term feminism? Do you consider yourself a feminist?", their answers reflected the diversity of understandings that an average group of women have of feminism as well as the diversity of their beliefs about its purpose. As these writers demonstrate, just being a woman does not mean that you have insight into how institutionalized sexism operates or into the work of feminism:

You know that bumper sticker 'Feminism is the radical notion that women are people.' Feminism is women being actors in their own lives, not just acted upon. For example, I try to find the smart interesting women to use as sources in my stories. It's definitely strategic. I identify myself as a feminist, but I tend not to use the term, so that I won't be associated with it. I can't stand political correctness. (Interviewee 1, personal communication, May 21, 1999)

Very old fashioned. I'm for equality of opportunity in every sense, and that doesn't mean men and women are the same. I'm an unreconstituted feminist—fundamentalist feminist. (Interviewee 2, personal communication, May 24, 1999)

Feminine has delicate, positive connotations. Feminism is harsher, more serious, aggressive. I'm trying to think about whether women I work with at Wired are feminists. I'm sure they are to the extent that they're making their way, but they aren't really crusading. I'm not big into gender and drawing too many conclusions. I don't consider myself a feminist—I'm a person who's thrilled to be a woman. I haven't encountered a lot of sexual discrimination. (Interviewee 3, personal communication, June 4, 1999)

Have women be treated as equals. Most women are feminists—they want to be treated as equals. Almost every woman I've ever talked to is a feminist. I can't think of anyone who isn't. (Interviewee 4, personal communication, June 8, 1999)

Feminists are people who think men and women should have equal opportunities and not be excluded from certain opportunities because of their gender. And the responsibilities and privileges of life need to be more equitably distributed. Feminism pushes for us to better care for women and children as a society. Issues of poverty and unequal distribution of wealth and power in our society. Feminism is getting at who has power and why. Yes, I'm a feminist. (Interviewee 5, personal communication, June 7, 1999)

All of the writers suggest some association between feminism and the notion of equality. However, as I explored in Chapter I, equality is not enough because it leaves larger systemic, institutionalized forces unscrutinized. Interviewee 1 clearly sees herself as a feminist, but is also ambivalent about being associated with the term. Interviewee 3's response reflects a woman who (as she says) has not "encountered a lot of sexual discrimination" since her definitions are informed by very stereotypical thinking about "feminine" as "delicate, positive" and "feminist" as "harsher" and "more aggressive." Interviewee 5 is the only one who mentions the larger systemic issue of power and who holds the power.

Do You Feel that Being a Woman has Influenced Your Choice in Careers and the Development of Your Career?

When I asked: "Do you feel that being a woman has influenced your choice in careers and the development of your career? If so, how?", their answers reflected a range of the issues that I have described in earlier chapters related to gendered roles in women's private and professional lives:

It's hard to say. I wanted to be a writer, but Dad wanted me to be a doctor. I'm the bridge generation where career was taken for granted, but also were expected to marry and have children. I remember in one of the snotty girls schools I attended, one of my classmates made a comment 'Why are we getting all of this good educa-

tion, and competing to get into good schools, just to get a better husband?' So, I felt a bit more of a struggle and a conflict between career and traditional roles. I stumbled into technical writing and it was heaven—a way to use my brains, make mistakes, and be creative. Technical writing was 50:50 male:female. It wasn't a pink collar ghetto. But, other people have said the kind of thing that I do is so unusual for a woman, that that is why I have trouble publishing some of my stuff. Boys can be snotty, girls should be nice. (Interviewee 1, personal communication, May 21, 1999)

It's central—absolutely central. My first book topic was really a kind of accident. I didn't realize it until 15 years later, but one of the reasons I found such an affinity for artificial intelligence (AI) was growing up in a culture that said that women shouldn't have brains. And AI is about separating the mind from the machine. There are a tremendous number of women in AI. I made the connection with why I'd been interested in AI when I was talking to a male friend. I told him that I had this theory that everyone I've known in AI has an issue with their body. When he said to me, 'but you don't have a problem with your body.' In that moment, I discovered that being a woman in this society presented the same sorts of issues for me. I grew up hating being female and not wanting to be part of this body. (Interviewee 2, personal communication, May 24, 1999)

I think it has in terms of giving me more confidence. It influenced me to write a book. It gave me experience writing longer pieces. It opened my eyes as a reader and writer. It shifted the cultural landscape. Wired writers were also sought after by book publishers. (Interviewee 3, personal communication, June 4, 1999)

I started off to be a lawyer, and when I went to law school in 1967 there were three women. I was put down and treated with disrespect by my colleagues and professors. Including one who wouldn't ask me questions, wouldn't talk to me in class, and told me that women didn't belong in law. I worked my way up the ranks as a writer, became co-producer of a TV show on science, and was subsequently fired over a woman's issue. The union took it to court, and I lost after about six years. I've found that the computer industry is pretty good toward women, at least if you're in marketing and sales. But, when I worked for a small startup in the late 70s, I talked them into hiring a women programmer—we got the top woman from a local college. The guys ridiculed her the whole time. It wasn't working since they had to work as a team. So, they put her on tech support. People would hang up when they called. She went to work somewhere else. (Interviewee 4, personal communication, June 8, 1999)

I don't think that being a woman has influenced my choice, but it has influenced my development. Right now for example, I'm working part time because I just had a baby. And, try as I might to not fall into traditional gender roles, my husband is working full time while I work part time. I've taken myself off the fast track. In terms of earlier in my career, there are probably things like starting as an Editorial Assistant (essentially a secretary). I worked for New York magazine as an Editorial Assistant to the Managing Editor. More men start as Fact Checkers; they go back over a piece and check the research. Fact checking puts you more in touch with writers and establishes a different relationship. (Interviewee 5, personal communication, June 7, 1999)

Four of the five women named ways in which being female has created professional challenges that are examples of the issues I have explained in previous chapters, including: the tensions women face between traditional expectations about parenting and their professional lives; the cost of gendered stereotypes in relation to body image (Interviewee 2 mentions "hating being female and not wanting to be part of this body"); and numerous incidents of explicit sex discrimination in IT (Interviewee 4).

What was the Editing Process?

When I asked: "What was the editing process? Who had the final edit? Who chose your story ideas?", their answers revealed a genuine mix of editorial experiences that may reflect their differing expectations about these relationships in terms of who holds (or should hold) the power:

My experience was different than many. I was in the elite. They basically decided that what I did was OK from the very beginning. I was John Battelle's pet for a year or two, then, the last two I wrote for Martha Baer. Working with Battelle as my editor was one of the best experiences I've had. He made my work better. Mostly, the editing process revolved around: How do we make this good? How do we get this by Kevin? Many other writers were jerked around, by lots of rewrites and lots of passing their pieces back and forth. Basically, editorially, the personalities really mattered. It wasn't just another faceless media organization. What's weird about Wired, is that it's like a lot of Hollywood. It attracts all of these really smart, intelligent women, but there's phenomenal sexism. They seem to put up with it because the experience of being part of it is so exciting. Louis, Kevin, and John Battelle all had relationships with women that made us all cringe. It was weird. We thought, here's this leading edge thing that has all of this embedded sexism in it. It's a real disconnect from what you'd expect. I proposed a story recently about an accomplished woman scientist, but the editor's response was 'well, what's the news hook?' I said, what do you want to do, wait for her to get the Nobel before you write about her? The old Wired would have grabbed the story with the 'Catch her before she's famous' attitude. So, they say they want more women, but couldn't there be a little affirmative action? (Interviewee 1, personal communication, May 21, 1999)

Good. Compared to writing for other national magazines. If anything, I thought they were making articles too long. I'd hand in 3,000 words and they'd say make it 5,000. They'd push me on various points. They'd ask very different questions than I was used to in New York journalism: Can you probe this? Can you explain why? In New York, the questions were more like: Can you make this punchier? Wired's editorial approach was so contrary to the New York style. It was very much a collaboration. In relation to why more women didn't write for Wired, or write about women, it may just be a reflection of the fact that there were so few women writing about computing in the whole industry. Most of us were overextended and writing for Wired wasn't always at the top of the list. It was my experience that they were very eager for stories about women. They were very eager for anything I suggested or proposed. (Interviewee 2, personal communication, May 24, 1999)

It's a mystery to me. On each piece I dealt with an editor. I get the impression that it goes through many hands. There's no shortage of eyeballs going over this stuff. Sometimes I work with the Section Editor, and then it goes through other hands and bounces back a lot. Wired is not afraid to kill pieces that don't make the grade. In terms of story ideas, it's shifted more to them dictating ideas and less of me proposing them. I guess I need to get more systematic and aggressive in presenting my story ideas. (Interviewee 3, personal communication, June 4, 1999)

At first it was fine. They'd hardly change anything. After a year, they started changing everything without even asking. So, I just quit. Also, I spent about two months trying to talk to a reclusive interviewee for another story. Then I wrote it up, and they offered a kill fee, but didn't tell me why. I sold it to another publication. I quit writing for them because they were changing my meaning and not letting me see it. That was about three years ago. A couple of people have told me that every article is reviewed by Battelle, Kelly, Rossetto about a week before publication. If one of them doesn't like a piece, they kill it. They always had more than they needed, so they could afford to do this. (Interviewee 4, personal communication, June 8, 1999)

The questions that they've had have been right on, they don't try to do weird things with a piece and try to push it into something. In terms of choosing story ideas, it's been a little of both them proposing and me suggesting. (Interviewee 5, personal communication, June 7, 1999)

Interviewee 1 admits that she was "in the elite" and therefore had some additional authority over her work. However, she also names explicit sexism that was pervasive among the magazine staff. Interviewee 2 had a largely positive experience that she describes as "collaborative" and explicitly says that the editors were eager for more stories about women because there were not enough of them. Interviewee 3 (whose answer to an earlier question included the comment that she has never experienced sex discrimination) seemed the most "powerless" of the five in that the editorial process was "a mystery." Ironically, this Interviewee who earlier referred to feminists as harsh and aggressive, ends her response by pondering whether she should be more aggressive in presenting story ideas. All of these answers reflect the importance of power dynamics, and of personal authority in terms of creating the kinds of professional relationships that can challenge existing gender stereotypes.

How would you Describe the Purpose of *Wired*?

When I asked "How would you describe the purpose of *Wired*, and do you think they've fulfilled that purpose?", their answers supported the idea that although the magazine attempted to be about computers and culture that it rarely (or only briefly) accomplished that goal:

It was a publication that saw itself as describing and chanting digital culture. I worked at a technology trade magazine for five years and it about killed me. I was eager to have the chance to think and write about this technical stuff in a literary and cultural way. There was a huge pent up demand for this kind of writing. But, I think there was an opportunity lost in terms of real social analysis. Now, you don't have anything. (Interviewee 1, personal communication, May 21, 1999)

I thought they were doing something different. My career for the past 20 years has been to say that computing isn't just this box. It signifies an enormous cultural change, and let's participate, let's mold it the way we want it to be. Along comes Wired and they're saying the same thing, in a jazzy way, and I thought: 'Great! We have parallel goals.' I think that in the first two or three years, Wired fulfilled its purpose. It was clear that Wired wasn't run by people with pocket protectors, that they were hip and fashionable. Then there was a shift and suddenly the world caught up. Suddenly, everyone and their grandmother is on the Internet. Of course, there is also an enormous hostility against Wired among women who know a lot about computing, I pick it up in various places. But, I say, if you don't like it, change it. (Interviewee 2, personal communication, May 24, 1999)

It think Wired's purpose is to make technology look fun and interesting. Prior to Wired, all of the technology magazines were hardware oriented. Wired was called 'The Rolling Stone of the digital generation' because they defined the popular culture of our day. Technology went from unfashionable to incredibly hip, chic, and relevant. I think Wired fulfilled a need that wasn't being met in the marketplace. I'd like to see Wired maintain its wilder essence. It's like independent film, the minority appreciates that stuff. I would like to see them shake themselves up a little and get a little more adventuresome again. More conservatism is taking hold. (Interviewee 3, personal communication, June 4, 1999)

I think the magazine was a great idea, but it wasn't run very well as a business. Louis couldn't delegate power. The big problems with Wired don't have that much to do with women—just poor management. Women weren't part of running the magazine. Jane had nothing to do with editorial. Marketing was her thing and Louis exploited that. Some think that she's the business brains behind the company and they wouldn't have made it without her. She became one of his chief fund-raisers. She went to conferences and gave speeches—the PR front role. You could always find Jane at all the trade shows. Louis would never go, even if the magazine won an award. (Interviewee 4, personal communication, June 8, 1999)

I think it's really changed from when I first wrote for them. It was more of an insider magazine then—one part of a world talking to another part of a world. Now they're trying to talk to a broader audience and trying to expand to talk to those who don't know about it. Wired is more of a traditional magazine now. At the time I was first involved with Wired, I thought it fulfilled its purpose. Now I'd say, it's not. (Interviewee 5, personal communication, June 7, 1999)

All five writers reflect a similar view that the original idea for the magazine—to link technology and culture—was exciting but short lived. They all suggested that the current version (which was after the sale to media giant Condé Nast) is more conservative and traditional. Interviewee 1 is the only one of the five who felt that the original *Wired* represented "an opportunity lost in terms of real social analysis."

Can you Describe Changes in *Wired* Since the Condé Nast Purchase?

When I asked "Can you describe any changes you have noticed in *Wired* since Condé Nast purchased it in 1998?", their answers are slightly mixed, but most supported the notion I proposed earlier in this chapter that the core purpose of the magazine changed significantly with the change in ownership:

*I think that it's a 40th as interesting now as it was. Louis had passion and original-
ity. He was enraging, but thrilling. Now it's like a bad version of Fast Company.
Wired is following trends vs. leading trends. I'm on the Well, where there's a huge
Wired conference. It's become more and more deserted in the last year. No one is
talking about Wired anymore. Nobody seems to care about it anymore. Condé Nast
seems to have thrown away what made people love it, be loyal to it, and care about
it.* (Interviewee 1, personal communication, May 21, 1999)

No, I haven't noticed any. (Interviewee 2, personal communication, May 24,
1999)

*Condé Nast has added more of an entertainment influence. It's a little bit glossier,
slicker, straightforward, less zany and wild. It's improved for the better as an editorial
product. It's more defined in what its purpose is—landing on the reader's doorstep
as a coherent package of information.* (Interviewee 3, personal communication,
June 4, 1999)

*Condé Nast has brought in their own writers, and over the years Wired has angered
enough writers that they've quit writing for them. But they don't pay well either.
There was a certain caché about writing for them in the beginning. They used to have
people and ideas on the cover that were really far out, and now their cover stories
are what's already out there. They've become followers, not leaders.* (Interviewee
4, personal communication, June 8, 1999)

*I think it's moved more into trying to talk to those who don't know, an insider to
outsider conversation. I guess they're trying to broaden their market, subscriptions
and ad base. They're now calmer. For example, there hasn't been day glow in the
magazine since Condé Nast took over. They've tried to make it more journalistic,
and, as a result, some of the reported pieces feel really thin to me.* (Interviewee 5,
personal communication, June 7, 1999)

Interviewee 3 is the only one who sees *Wired* as having "improved for the better
as an editorial product" since the Condé Nast purchase. Interviewees 1 and 4 say
that since the change in ownership, *Wired* is "following trends vs. leading trends"
and that they've "become followers, not leaders." I see this as evidence of the power
of mass media as a social institution. Once *Wired* was owned by a major media
company like Condé Nast, it became even more difficult to push back against the
status quo in terms of exploring technology in relation to culture, and in terms of
a more explicit place for women in that new imagining.

CONCLUSION

A consideration of how to address the underrepresentation of women as developers, users, and beneficiaries of technology often begins with improving access to education and the professions. This is an important first step, but it is only a first step. It may be even more vitally important that women and men have a better understanding of how deeply gendered stereotypes are embedded in our consciousness as well as in our social systems. As the interviews with these writers suggest, it is not enough to simply have more women at the table. We need more women (and men) at the table that are educated about the explicit and implicit ways in which our social systems operate; they will be better equipped to challenge these systemic forces that keep gendered stereotypes in place. These five women writers were at the table as a new magazine about computer culture was being birthed. However, the magazine still could not give a prominent voice to women as writers or as subjects of discussion.

In this chapter, I have offered an analysis of one example of mass media—a computing magazine whose stated purpose was to talk about the links between technology and culture—in an attempt to show how deeply negative stereotypes about women are embedded in media as a social institution. I have also attempted to reveal some of the power structures that prevent these deeply embedded attitudes and beliefs from being seriously challenged. Although *Wired* offered some positive images of women in relation to technology, they were too brief and too few to counter the negative weight of the advertising images and magazine covers that I recounted at the beginning of this analysis. When you consider that we have just examined one social institution, and that these stereotypes are also purveyed by other social institutions, the sinking weight of their negative impact becomes even more unbearably heavy.

QUESTIONS FOR REFLECTIVE DIALOG

1. Do an online search regarding the "new frontier" and "science" or "technology." What scientific findings are revealed through this use of language by the media? How does the media use these deeply embedded conquest metaphors to direct our interpretation of science and technology? What metaphors could be used that promote inclusion?
2. Consider the "draw a scientist" research that shows a vast majority of children drew a White male. How might schools help to reshape a partnership vision of science and scientists that was more diverse? On a more personal level, how

might we positively reinforce the younger people in our lives to consider the career potential of science and technology?

3. Can you recall an event during high school that shaped your relationship with science or technology? Were you ever steered toward or away from certain fields of study? How did you feel about your scientific or technical abilities? How do you feel today?

4. Select a magazine that you enjoy reading and scan for concepts, articles, images, advertisements that focus on sex, war and/or death. What do you notice?

5. The famous adage "sex sells" has proven true time and again. What new adage could we promote that includes more positive images? What else might we sell besides sex?

6. Consider the concept of "nontraditional pathways" to technology and science that are more common among women. What pathways has your educational journey taken?

7. Compare your academic pathway to an actual physical highway. What exits have you taken? What rest stops have you visited? What accidents did you have? Physically draw a map of what that road looked like and then write a few paragraphs describing your academic pathway.

8. Laurie Anderson describes technology as "the campfire around which we tell our stories." What stories are being told today? What stories might we tell? In an era where 25% of all Internet searches are for pornography, who is invited to sit around the campfire and what stories will they hear?

REFERENCES[2]

About us. (1999, Apr 26). Retrieved May 11, 1999, from http://www.wired.com/wired/about.htm

Associated Press Writer. (1998, Nov 30). *Fox Market Wire*. Retrieved May 17, 1999, from http://foxmarketwire.com/wires/1130/f_ap_1130_33.sml

Bagdikian, B. (2004). *The new media monopoly*. Boston: Beacon.

Barker, L. J., & Aspray, W. (2006). The state of research on girls and IT. In J. M. Cohoon & W. Aspray (Eds.), *Women and information technology: Research on underrepresentation* (pp. 3-54). Cambridge, MA: MIT Press.

Bix, A. S. (2000) Feminism where men predominate: The history of women's science and engineering education at MIT. *Women's Studies Quarterly, 28*(1/2), 24-45.

Borsook, P. (1993) Release. *Wired, 1*(5), 94-126.

Borsook, P. (1996). The memoirs of a token: An aging Berkeley feminist examines *Wired*. In L. Cherny & E. R. Weise (Eds.). *Wired women: Gender and new realities in cyberspace* (pp. 24-41). Seattle: Seal.

Brumberg, J. J. (1997). *The body project: An intimate history of American girls.* New York: Random House.

Cherny, L., & Weise, E. R. (Eds.). (1996). *Wired women: Gender and new realities in cyberspace.* Seattle: Seal.

Clark, T. (1994, March 7). Year-old '*Wired*' so cool, it's hot. *Advertising Age*. Retrieved March 1, 1999, from http://proquest.umi.com/

Condé Nast. (1999). Hoover's company capsule. *1999 The Industry Standard: The Newsmagazine of the Internet Economy*. Retrieved April 5, 1999, from http://www.thestandard.net/companies/

Copilevitz, T. (1996, March 3). *Wired*: Read all about it—just don't call it a computer magazine. *Seattle Times*. Retrieved March 1, 1999, from http://proquest.umi.com

Corcoran, C. T. (1998, Apr). Re-*Wired*. *San Francisco Magazine*. Retrieved April 27, 1999, from http://www.diablopubs.com/focus/aRCHIVES/SF9804/SF9804wired.htm

Creedon, P. J. (Ed.). (1993). *Women in mass communication*. Newbury Park: Sage.

DeCarlo, S. (Ed.). (2007, March 29). The world's 2,000 largest public companies. *Forbes*. Retrieved December 16, 2007, from http://www.forbes.com/2007/03/29/forbes-global-2000-biz-07forbes2000-cz_sd_0329global_land.html

Fabrikant, G. (1998, March 24). Streamlining Newhouse for the next generation. *The New York Times*. Retrieved 11 May, 1999, from http://www.econ.yale.edu/~clerides...t/032498random-house-newhouse.html

Fung, Y. H. (2002, November). A comparative study of primary and secondary school students' images of scientists. *Research in Science & Technological Education*, *20*(2), 199-213.

Goode, J., Estrella, R., & Margolis, J. (2006). Lost in translation: Gender and high school computer science. In J. M. Cohoon & W. Aspray (Eds.), *Women and information technology: Research on underrepresentation*. (pp. 89-114). Cambridge, MA: MIT Press.

Harmon, A. (1998, May 11). Digital culture pioneer sold to Condé Nast. *New York Times*. Retrieved March 1, 1999, from http://proquest.umi.com/

hooks, b. (1992). *Black looks: Race and representation*. Boston: South End.

Lazier, L., & Kendrick, A. G. (1993). Women in advertisements: Sizing up the images, roles, and functions. In P. J. Creedon (Ed.), *Women in mass communication* (pp. 199-219). Newbury Park: Sage.

Maloney, J. (1998, March/April). Why *Wired* misfired. *Columbia Journalism Review*. Retrieved April 27, 1999, from http://www.cjr.org/year/98/2/

Manly, L. (1996, July). *Wired* creates stir with IPO. *Folio: The Magazine for Magazine Management*. Retrieved March 1, 1999, from http://proquest.umi.com/

McCarthy, S. (1993, January). Techno-soaps and virtual theatre: Brenda Laurel can blow anything up. *Wired*, *1*(2), 40-42.

McCorduck, P. (1994, February). America's multi-mediatrix. *Wired*, *2*(3), 79-137.

McCorduck, P. (1996, April). Sex, lies, and avatars. *Wired*, *4*(4), 106-165.

Millar, M. S. (1998). *Cracking the gender code: Who rules the wired world?* Toronto: Second Story.

Miller, R. (2004). Introduction. In R. Eisler & R. Miller (Eds.), *Educating for a culture of peace* (pp. 1-10). Portsmouth, NH: Heinemann.

Miller, M. (Ed.). (2007). *The 400 richest Americans*. Retrieved December 15, 2007, from http://www.forbes.com/2007/09/19/richest-americans-forbes-lists-richlist07-cx_mm_0920rich_land.html

Morrison, T. (1992). *Playing in the dark: Whiteness and the literary imagination*. New York: Vintage.

Nelkin, D. (1995). *Selling science: How the press covers science and technology*. New York: Freeman.

Newhouse gets *Wired*. (1998, May). *Editor & Publisher*. Retrieved March 1, 1999, from http://proquest.umi.com/

Offen, B. (1996, May). Media choice: *Wired*. *Marketing*. Retrieved March 1, 1999, from http://proquest.umi.com/

Parisi, P. (1997, January). The teacher who designs videogames. *Wired*, *5*(1).

Patriot-News parent buys *Wired* magazine. (1998, June). *View Source: A publication for Pennsylvania Newspaper Publishers' Association new media personnel*. Retrieved April, 1999, from http://www.pnpa.com/newmedia/viewsource/

Pipher, M. (1994). *Reviving Ophelia: Saving the selves of adolescent girls.* New York: Putnam.

Quittner, J. (1996, November). Don't diss the digerati. *Time.* Retrieved April 26, 1999, from http://proquest.umi.com/

Rigdon, J. I. (1996, October). *Wired* reflects the quirks of its founder. *Wall Street Journal.* Retrieved April 26, 1999, from http://proquest.umi.com/

Rosser, S. V. (Ed.). (1995). *Teaching the majority: Breaking the gender barrier in science, mathematics, and engineering.* New York: Teachers College.

Rossetto, L. (1993a). Get *Wired* (monthly). *Wired, 1*(5), 12.

Rossetto, L. (1993b). The story of *Wired. Doors of Perception.* Retrieved April 26, 1999, from http://www.doorsofperception.com/doors/doors1/transcripts/rosset/

Roy, A. (2004). *An ordinary person's guide to empire.* Cambridge, MA: South End.

Rubin, E., & Cohen, A. (2003, July). The images of scientists and science among Hebrew- and Arabic-speaking pre-service teachers in Israel. *International Journal of Science Education, 25*(7), 821-846.

Sadker, M., & Sadker, D. (1995). *Failing at fairness: How our schools cheat girls.* New York: Touchstone.

Spender, D. (1995). *Nattering on the net: Women, power and cyberspace.* North Melbourne, Australia: Spinifex.

Tavris, C. (1992). *The mismeasure of woman.* New York: Touchstone.

The wealthiest of America's wealthy. (1998, September). *The News Times.* Retrieved May 11, 1999, from http://www.newstimes.com/archive98/sep2898/bzd.htm

Thomas, M. D., Henley, T. B., & Snell, C. M. (2006, March). The draw a scientist test: A different population and a somewhat different story. *College Student Journal, 40*(1), 140-148.

Ware, M. C., & Stuck, M. F. (1985). Sex-role messages vis-à-vis microcomputer use: A look at the pictures. *Sex Roles,* 13(3/4), 205-214.

White, K. (1999, April). The killer app: *Wired* Magazine, voice of the corporate revolution. *The Baffler.* Retrieved May 11, 1999, from http://www.leb.net/~mmhamze/infobahn/wired1.htm

Who is *Wired*? (1999, April). *Wired.* Retrieved on May 11, 1999, from http://www.hotwired.com/Lib/PR/1.1/who.is.wired.htm

Wood, J. T. (1999). *Gendered lives: Communication, gender, and culture* (3rd ed.). Belmont, CA: Wadsworth.

Zarrett, N., Malanchuk, O., Davis-Kean, P. E., & Eccles, J. (2006). Examining the gender gap in IT by race: Young adults' decisions to pursue an IT Career. In J. M. Cohoon & W. Aspray (Eds.), *Women and information technology: Research on underrepresentation* (pp. 55-88). Cambridge, MA: MIT Press.

ENDNOTES

[1]   Australian-born Rupert Murdoch is a naturalized U.S. citizen.

[2]   Some portions of this chapter may have appeared in, and are reprinted with permission from, Kirk, M (2006). Bridging the Digital Divide: A Feminist Perspective on the Project. In G. Trajkovski (Ed.), *Diversity in information technology education: Issues and controversies* (pp. 38-67). Hershey, PA: Information Science Publishing.

Chapter V
Language as Social Institution:
The Male–Centered IT Culture

OBJECTIVES

This chapter aims to help you understand the following:

- Why paying attention to "political correctness" matters in our dominator social system.
- Ways in which both language and communication style are gendered and maleness is privileged over femaleness.
- How the communication style that predominates in IT contributes to an IT culture that may not be hospitable to many women.
- How the predominance of violence in language, metaphors, and video games contributes to an unfriendly climate for women in IT.
- How the IT culture is not immune from the sexual objectification of women that predominates in the larger society and the toll that can take on women in IT.

INTRODUCTION

Language as a social institution is the primary symbol system through which we teach/learn about our dominator culture. The assumptions, values, attitudes, beliefs, and behaviors that are considered "normative" are deeply embedded in our language and communication style. The "language of domination" features "shoulds and musts, blame and criticism, [and] judgment and demand," all of which privileges certain groups and suppresses others according to their "appropriate" social rank (Hart, 2004, p. 114). Language is also one of the powerful mechanisms for teaching and conveying stereotypes; the significant impact of which we have already explored.

Further, without a great deal of mindful effort, the average person conforms to stereotypes of language and communication style without even being aware of it. Johnson (2006) describes how most of us learn to take the "path of least resistance" with regard to social expectations of ourselves and of others. This also points to the necessity for what feminist activists and scholars have called "consciousness raising." Once we become conscious of the ways in which our language and communication style reflect dominator stereotypes that have taught us false models for how to think about ourselves and each other, we can make conscious choices to do things differently. This chapter explores the following concepts in an effort to chart the map down the "path of resistance" to a dominator social system: (1) why political correctness matters; (2) gendered communication style; (3) male-centered IT communication style and culture; and (4) dominance, violence, and sex metaphors in IT.

WHY POLITICAL CORRECTNESS MATTERS

One common and clear example of how values, attitudes, and beliefs are taught via language is the notion of "political correctness." In the 60s and 70s in the U.S., a variety of previously marginalized groups gained a louder social voice, and one of the social institutions that they began to challenge was language. In a dominator social system, those in power hold the power to name; the words of one group are privileged, while the words of the subordinate group are "lacking in authority, forcefulness, effectiveness, persuasiveness" (Spender, 1980, p. 10). Therefore, for subordinate groups, investing the dominator language with their own different and positive meanings is a priority (p. 6). However, when previously subordinate groups reclaim the power to name, they also explicitly disrupt the system of rankings that is a primary element of dominator societies. So, groups who are privileged by the system of dominance will naturally resist since they perceive these changes as representing a loss of power. With regard to language, the result has been the invention of a concept now referred to as "political correctness."

The claim from those with social privilege and social authority is that they should not have their beliefs, attitudes, and words defined by others; they often invoke "libertarian principles of freedom of expression" (Herring, 1999, p. 151).

This claim denies the fact that in a dominator social system many are not free to speak without repercussions. Spender (1995) states:

Free speech often amounts to free speech for the White man . . .women and people of color, for example, have always had to watch what they say. They have had to see which way the wind is blowing before they can express an opinion. (p. 225)

Another problem is that this demand for "freedom of expression" denies the fact that many of our beliefs, attitudes, and words were not so freely chosen in the first place. They are reinforced daily by our social institutions and learned by individuals in the context of the largely unexamined assumptions of a dominator society. However, this is often less noticeable to those with social privilege because the beliefs, attitudes, and words of a dominator social system are organized by and for them.

Why should "political correctness" matter? First, there is the moral argument. Most would agree that our actions have consequences. I argue that our words also have consequences. The old aphorism "sticks and stones may break my bones, but names will never hurt me" is false. Words have the power to harm because they are one of the primary ways in which we receive, perceive, and define our world. In a hierarchical social system, those with unearned social privilege hold a higher degree of social power. As many philosophers have argued, power also should come with a unique social responsibility to use that power wisely. Is it too much to ask that we work as a society to stop harming each other by not doing the things that many have previously said they find harmful? If you were in a relationship with someone and they told you something hurt them, wouldn't you try to stop engaging in the offensive behavior? We live in a human community where whole groups of people have said something hurts them. We have a moral responsibility to listen and at least try to stop doing those things. I will paraphrase Bill Cosby who said: "I find it a pitiful commentary on our society that we have lumped a group of ideas that were fundamentally about demonstrating respect for each other under the now pejorative term 'political correctness'."

There is another reason that political correctness should matter. In *Feminist Theory: From Margin to Center*, bell hooks (1984) explains that those who are oppressed by the dominator social model, who are marginalized and outside the social centers around which our system is organized, often have a much clearer view of the workings of the system. Patricia Hill Collins (1990) reflects a similar idea that she describes as the "outsider-within." Collins said that those who are disenfranchised as outsiders, such as African-Americans, but who also dwell within a particular social institution, may have a uniquely clear perspective on how things work. This makes a different case for the importance of learning to listen to all of the voices in our society. Their perspective can help us have a richer, clearer understanding of the current social system. This understanding has the potential to help us build a truly democratic society.

Let us look at a few other examples of the power of language to define culture. Most academic disciplines have adopted a policy of non-sexist language and those who are formally educated have some exposure to this. However, for most their understanding is limited to the gender pronoun problem. Sexism in language goes much deeper. Scholars such as Spender (1980) and Eisler and Loye (1990) explain how certain human characteristics are persistently gendered and how the characteristics associated with the feminine carry a negative connotation. Here are a few examples of how shifting our use of words can create opportunities for new social attitudes and beliefs. Using the term "emasculated" to refer to a man whose behavior is weak or nonassertive, explicitly suggests that men can never be weak or nonassertive and that they must always be strong. Using the term "effeminate" to refer to a man whose behavior is weak or nonassertive explicitly suggests that the man is not being "manly" and implicitly carries a negative connotation. Another example is the use of the term "brotherhood" which easily conjures the image of groups of men, rather than groups of people. Eisler and Loye (1990) suggest disassociating human behavior from gender altogether and simply describing the behavior itself. For example, the following terms are more descriptive of the attitudes and beliefs that "brotherhood" intends to convey without also being exclusive of gender: community, kinship, friendship, unity, or partnership (Eisler & Loye, 1990, p. 190). I will return to this idea about disassociating gender from behavior later in this book.

GENDERED COMMUNICATION STYLE

The words themselves are only one part of communication. The ways in which we communicate, our communication style, is also influenced by gender, race, and cultural socialization. In fact, Mulvaney (1994) suggests that gender socialization is so strong that it might be more useful to view cross-gender communication as a form of intercultural communication. She also sees communication as both "the medium by which we come to know things" and the medium by which we teach/learn values, which makes gender "both an influence on and a product of communication" (Mulvaney, 1994). The ways in which individuals choose to communicate are influenced by gender socialization (via social institutions), and our perceptions of the communication itself are also influenced by learned ideas about gender. However, consciousness of these learned ideas can empower individuals to behave differently and thus begin to scrutinize and alter social institutions. The cultural perspective we learn regarding gender and communication influences both the way a message is communicated and the way in which it is received. Miscommunication can occur across this cultural divide when we assume that one does not exist.

bell hooks (1989) describes how the style of expression in Black culture can often lead to misinterpretations when communicating with different races/cultures and how the "dominant culture" asserts the "appropriate" communication style. She explains how frequently reactions from White readers describe her as sounding angry when from her cultural perspective she is simply being direct (hooks, 1989, p. 15). I often observe this reaction to her work from White students in my classrooms. Both the style of hooks' writing and the issues that she addresses are outside of White readers' experiences, and they frequently act with resistance and/or anger. I believe that this reaction also reflects the assumption that academic writing should be purely "rational" and not "emotional," terms that are gendered.

Gender socialization is a powerful influence on our communication styles. In a dominator social system, most women are socialized to be subordinate, and most men are socialized to be dominant. The implicit awareness of our presumed or perceived place in the social order is often reflected in the ways in which women and men communicate. In *Talking Power: The Politics of Language*, Robin Lakoff (1990) says men's language is the "language of the powerful" since it is "direct, clear, [and] succinct, as would be expected of those who need not fear giving offense," while women's language reflects their lack of social authority since they must "listen more than speak" and "agree more than confront" (p. 205). This gendered power differential is reflected in male conversational style which is typically character-ized by focusing on the goal of "winning" the conversation and talking in terms of abstract ideas and rational argument.

Women's conversational style is typically characterized by focusing on the goal of "connecting" via conversation and talking in terms of personal story and emo-tions (Wood, 1999, p. 123-129). In addition, in mixed sex conversation, men talk more, interrupt more (especially women), direct the topic of conversation more, and define what qualifies as a "worthwhile" topic (Spender, 1980; Van Fossen, 1996). Interrupting is both a marker of social status and a tool for exercising dominance. For example, studies of faculty meetings showed that speakers of "higher rank tend to interrupt speakers of lower rank, even when all speakers are men" (Schiebinger, 1999, p. 81).

The conversational style that dominates in our day-to-day interactions in the U.S. is the "male" style, which makes it difficult for women to fully participate without repercussions for stepping outside of socially-accepted gender boundar-ies. As discussed in Chapter I, for women, the double-bind comes into play here. Women may have to pay a social price for communicating too much like "men." A woman may be perceived as arrogant if "she does not engage in what is considered appropriate womanly behavior—smiling, qualifying her statements, and tilting her head in deferential fashion" (Schiebinger, 1999, p. 81).

Since those in subordinate roles are aware of how the social system operates, some researchers have shown that their conversational style may sometimes be more influenced by the gender of the person to whom they are speaking rather than by their own gender. Psychologist Linda Carli (1990) observed pairs of men, pairs of women, and pairs of men and women discussing an issue on which they disagreed. Her research showed that:

when interacting with men, women spoke more tentatively than when interacting with women ... Men were influenced to a greater degree by women who spoke tentatively than by those who spoke assertively. It may be important for a woman not to behave too competitively or assertively when interacting with men in order for her to wield any influence, even if she may risk appearing incompetent. (p. 946)

This communication double-bind is a contributing factor to the persistent gender-based wage gap in the U.S. One area of research has focused on the issue of negotiation in terms of gendered communication. When negotiating salaries, women face a double-bind. If they are too competitive or assertive when negotiating salary, women may pay a social cost by being viewed negatively as women or a more literal cost by not being offered the job because they are too "aggressive." If they do not negotiate on salary, they may be offered the job, but are likely to be offered less money (Babcock & Laschever, 2003).

The following table shows the general emphases in communication in relation to gender. As with other aspects of identity, the way that these styles are expressed by individuals will be influenced by individual character, family environment, and

Table 1. Gendered communication styles

Men	Women
Dominant	Subordinate or submissive
Low-context	High-context
Goal of conversation is to win, accomplish tasks, exert control	Goal of conversation is to connect, build relationships
Emphasis is on superiority or uniqueness	Emphasis is on understanding
Style of speech is direct and definitive	Style of speech uses qualifiers, tag questions & fillers to soften message
Tend to ask directly for needs	Tend to hint at needs, using context and story
Content focuses on work, accomplishments	Content focuses on personal needs (self, others)
Interrupt other speakers more, especially women	Consider it a sign of poor listening to interrupt
To bond with others, use sarcasm & teasing	To bond with others, use compliments and sharing of personal information

unique cultural norms. However, Table 1 shows the ways in which we socialize for gender in our social institutions, and the characteristics that these institutions tend to value are "male" (Daft, 1997; Tannen, 2001).

Another core distinction between the ways in which most men and women in the U.S. learn to communicate is linked to the relative importance of social context. While most men learn to be low-context, most women learn to be high-context. In low-context cultures, communication is used "primarily to exchange facts and information; meaning is derived primarily from words; business transactions are more important than building relationships and trust; and individual welfare and achievement are more important than the group" (Daft, 1997, p. 475). In high-context cultures, communication is used "primarily to build personal social relationships; meaning is derived from context—setting, status, nonverbal behavior—more than from explicit words; relationships and trust are more important than business; and the welfare and harmony of the group are valued" (Daft, 1997, p. 475). Most business environments in the U.S. are low-context; the IT industry is no exception. As the IT industry becomes increasingly global, this offers additional incentive to understand and adapt to differing styles of communication.

MALE-CENTERED IT COMMUNICATION STYLE AND CULTURE

How can women in science and IT navigate gendered expectations about communication style? Ruth Bleier (1991) documents some ways in which communication about science has been gendered according to maleness in terms of the "public demeanor of scientists." She says that "the patterns of words they choose . . . almost invariably project an image of impersonal authority and absolute confidence in the accuracy, objectivity, and importance of their observations" (Bleier, 1991, p. 23). However, women scientists, who have been gender socialized not to "brag," exhibit very different behavior when delivering scientific papers. They tend to "call attention to the limitations of their data, to potential flaws in their experimental design, to control experiments that remain to be done," all of which certainly cast doubt on the credibility of their work in the male-identified scientific community (Bleier, 1991, p. 23).

There is some debate about whether computer-mediated communication may offer the opportunity for a more democratic conversation; it provides more people with access to information, removes the social context within which stereotypical judgments can be made, and there is little overt censorship of ideas (Spender, 1995, p. 2). Since communication is not face-to-face, the Internet offers women the opportunity to "pass" as men if they choose to deliberately challenge assumptions about gender roles and communication styles. Unfortunately, few women are aware enough of how institutionalized sexism operates to consciously make such a choice.

Susan Herring (1993) examined online communication to determine whether it was in fact "more democratic" with regard to gender and found that it was hard for her subjects to remove themselves from the forces of social context without very conscious effort. Those who have not recognized the constraints placed upon them by the social context that surrounds them (like the water surrounding Mead's unaware fish), can find it especially difficult to remove themselves from these corrosive forces. Herring's (1993) study of male and female participants in two electronic lists demonstrates gendered patterns of communication similar to traditional research, and shows the dominance of male conversational style online. Women's online messages were characterized by a more personal orientation, supportive language, and questions or apologies. Men's messages were characterized by a more authoritative orientation, challenging language, and self promotion (Herring, 1993, p. 7).

One of the more troubling findings in Herring's data was the pressure exerted on women to conform to the "male" conversational style. As with earlier data about mixed-sex conversation, Herring's study shows that when "women's rate of posting increased gradually to where it equaled 50% . . . men wrote in to decry the discussion, and several threatened to cancel their subscription to the list." Their objections said that the tone of the messages had become too "vituperative" and that the topics were "inappropriate" (Herring, 1993, p. 5). Far from being the "democratic" world it is depicted to be, online conversation appears to be subject to the same gendered communication patterns evidenced elsewhere. Other research has supported Herring's findings:

As long as men overwhelmingly dominate the conversation, the participation of women and men is perceived as roughly equal. But if women's talk rises to as little as a quarter or a third of the total interaction, men tend to perceive the women as taking over. (Johnson, 2006, p. 104)

Dale Spender (1995) finds that the male-identified conversational style that is privileged in daily interactions has dominated on the Internet as well:

The studies that have been done on communication on the net make it clear that it's more a male monologue than a mixed-sex conversation. The discourse is male; the style is adversarial. The premises are winning or losing. Despite the enormous potential of the net to be a network—to promote egalitarian, cooperative communication exchanges—the virtual reality is one where aggression, intimidation and plain macho-mode prevail. (p. 198)

One obvious example of a dominator communication style is the concept of "flaming," that is, the adversarial, aggressive, and often vitriolic style of dealing with conflict on e-mail.

In another study, Herring (1999) compared two extended interactions on the Internet, one from a recreational Internet relay chat (IRC) channel and another from an academic listserv discussion group called Paglia-L (dedicated to a discussion of "anti-feminist feminist Camille Paglia's work"). Herring (1999) observed "male participants employing more aggressive tactics than female participants in both samples" and identified the following stages of escalation in relation to gender-based harassment: "(1) initial situation; (2) initiation to harassment; (3) resistance to harassment; (4) escalation of harassment; (5a) targeted participants accommodate to dominant group norms and/or (5b) targeted participants fall silent" (p. 156). Once gender harassment began, men tended to "stick together" and women who resisted being silenced were stereotyped as "hysterical" and "not to be taken seriously," no matter how rational and reasonable their arguments were. Further, women were caught in the double-bind of being criticized if they were too "adversarial" while men were free to be as aggressive as they chose without repercussion. A quote from one of the women participants reflects the character of these dynamics: "Sure enough, the rule seems to be that when a male makes nasty, personal, sexist comments, he considers this a demonstration of proper macho aggressiveness. When a female responds in kind, she is hysterical and a man-hater" (Herring, 1999, p. 160).

One of the more discouraging findings from Herring's research was that "participation by women decreased as aggression by male participants increased in each sample" (p. 161). After an incident of harassment, women's messages decreased 33% in the IRC and 41% in the Paglia-L listserv. On the Paglia-L listserv, 71% of all active female participants "complained about the manner in which the discussion was carried out; of those who complained, fully 80% fell silent, posting no further messages. In contrast, only 11% of male participants complained about the discussion, and none stopped posting" (p. 161). Herring's research shows that online communication is not the democratic space that some claim it to be. It is subject to very similar influences of gendered power and status as face-to-face communication. In Herring's study, male participants were "entitled to express themselves freely," while women were labeled "censors" if they disagreed with men. This occurred despite the fact that the women:

did not attempt to exclude other views, and despite the fact that they explicitly conceded the dominant male (and Paglian) position that a free speech violation had occurred. Meanwhile, males hypocritically represented themselves as heroic defenders of freedom of expression, even as their behavior showed them to be intolerant of even partial disagreement with their views. (p. 163)

As Laura Gurak (2001) describes, clearly "cyberspace is gendered space. No technologies are value-neutral. They carry the marks of their makers and the ethos of the culture in which they arise" (p. 5).

These gendered differences in communication style often result in situations like that described by women graduate students and technical staff in electrical engineering and computer science at MIT. Bix (2000) describes how some women at this top-tier engineering school considered leaving due to being made to feel invisible, excluded from discussions, ignored in meetings, interrupted and talked over, and mistaken for secretaries (p. 41). Women are expected to tolerate such behavior without complaint (for fear of social censure), while they simultaneously navigate the pressures of trying to be "one of the boys" (while still being perceived as "girls"). Sound complicated? It is. Bix (2000) describes the complexities of dancing on this razor's edge that women at MIT faced in the 1950s:

Civil engineering majors learned surveying and other field technologies at a rough camp, with accommodations judged unsuitable for females. Mechanical engineering class required round-the-clock observations of engine performance; generations of male students turned the 'twenty-four-hour boiler tests' into beer parties. The prospect of women hanging out overnight with men in the lab seemed inappropriate. (p. 27)

Although MIT had been coed since 1871 and had an average of 50 women on campus each year (with 5,000 men), women students were still a "curiosity." And the school medical director questioned whether it was worthwhile to take positions away from men when there was such a need for male engineers. He added that although women might "bring 'pleasure and ornamentation' to campus," they "usually proved unable to hold their own against MIT men's competitiveness and 'high-grade intellects'" (Bix, 2000, p. 27). Another obvious example of the double-bind is evident in these comments. If women were competitive, they might be criticized for being unfeminine, which in fact is a stereotype of women scientists, or accused of using "feminine wile" and not earning their grades based on merit. Unfortunately, as long as we do not educate about gender socialization, women can purvey sexist attitudes just as easily as men. Comments by Florence Stiles' (a 1923 MIT graduate and later adviser to women students) on the status of women at MIT in 1947 mirror those made by the male medical director cited above:

The women . . . learn to work with men—not in competition ["nice" girls don't compete, they cooperate] . . . Women in general do not make acceptable engineers, although they have the intellectual ability to be proficient academically. However, they are acceptable in the so-called 'White apron' jobs in foods and hospitals. (Bix, 2000, p. 26)

The perceptions that people have of what they participate in and observe can be just as important as the actual situations themselves. Those perceptions are learned from our social institutions and are profoundly influenced by stereotypes. Given this early history of women in science and engineering, as well as the persistent influences of other social institutions in the intervening years, it should not be hard to understand why studies today continue to "indicate that women perceive the IT work environment as male-dominated and not welcoming to women" (Bartol & Aspray 2006, p. 396). One recent survey of randomly chosen students (275 women) at a large public university reported that about one-third of the women respondents expected not to experience a welcoming atmosphere if they pursued IT careers, while none of the men expressed this concern. Further, nearly "20 percent of the female respondents also believed that they would not fit in with their coworkers if they pursued an IT career. More than 80 percent of the women in the survey felt that they would not enjoy a career in IT" (Bartol & Aspray 2006, p. 396). Other studies have "identified masculine values and practices as an important reason for the lack of women in both computing education and computing professions," and many women reject computing in the first place because they consider it a "masculine" domain (Bartol & Aspray, 2006; Faulkner, 2000; Wilson, 2003).

Perceptions of capability in different domains are learned from social institutions (such as media and education) and the stereotypes they purvey are persistent enough to begin taking a serious toll on many girls by the time they reach adolescence when they must more narrowly define their "gendered" identity. "In their 1998 review article, Kirkpatrick and Cuban (1998) say that in early grades, the gap between males and females in achievement and attitude is minor, but the gap increases as they get older, as does the confidence gap" (Barker & Aspray, 2006, p. 29). Other scholars have also documented the fact that even though their academic performance stays the same as, or better than boys, girls confidence in their ability declines as they move through education (Pipher, 1994; Sadker & Sadker, 1995). If a learning environment or field of study is defined in male terms, girls/women are less likely to see themselves as suited to it, especially if they have a strong gender-identification as "female."

DOMINANCE, VIOLENCE AND SEX METAPHORS IN IT

Johnson (2006) explains that in a dominator social system most "high-status occupations . . . are organized around qualities culturally associated with masculinity, such as aggression, competitiveness, emotional detachment (except for anger), and control" (p. 98-99). Indeed, male-identified language and dominance metaphors are pervasive in science and technology. In *Secrets of Life, Secrets of Death: Es-*

says on Language, Gender and Science, Evelyn Fox Keller (1992) describes the significance of metaphors in terms of how they influence our perceptions as well as the questions we ask:

Different metaphors of mind, nature, and the relation between them, reflect different psychological stances of observer to observed; these, in turn, give rise to different cognitive perspectives—to different aims, questions, and even to different methodological and explanatory preferences. (p. 31)

Since power-over is a key theme in a dominator social system, the metaphors of IT embody violence and sexual dominance. Computer jargon—the language of the daily discourse in technology—is one example of this. The field is embedded with metaphors and language that implicitly support themes of dominance and/or violence including such terms as: boot, crash, abort, kill, hacking, blue screen of death, brute force, killer app, and number crunching (Cohoon & Aspray, 2006, p. 145; Spender, 1995, p. 200). Although violence is a predictable element of dominator societies, the prevalence of violence against women results "in patterns of chronic fear and avoidance as women and girls learn to circumscribe their lives in order to reduce the odds of being singled out for harassment or attack" (Johnson 2006, p. 58). In that broader social context, it should not be surprising that an IT culture that emphasizes violence in its metaphors is not considered hospitable by most women and some men.

Video Games: "Fun" with Sex and Violence

The gaming branch of the IT industry offers the most extreme example of this culture of domination, violence, and sex. One does not have to look farther than the annual E3 video-game industry expo which features girls in scanty clothes—amidst the sounds of gunfire, bombs exploding, and fake blood spraying across screens—to understand the culture of the gaming industry. Clearly, tall buxom women in bikinis are welcome in this culture, but what about the rest of us? Unfortunately, stereotypes of both men and women abound. "The shouting and swearing in arcades, war and sports games, focus on speed, images of men on software packaging, and utilitarian computer labs were all characteristics of the computer culture that fit masculine stereotypes" (Cohoon & Aspray, 2006, p. 147). "Likewise, computer games commonly feature competition, destruction and carnage" (Cohoon & Aspray, 2006, p. 145). Women characters, if they are included at all, are almost exclusively tall, thin, and abnormally large-breasted. Further, Eugene Provenzo (1995), author of *Video Kids: Making Sense of Nintendo*, reported that 13 of the 47 most popular video games featured the rape or abduction of a female character.

Although it may seem obvious that this type of violence would not appeal to girls/women, scholars have documented the fact that video game violence does indeed alienate girls/women (Cooper et al., 1990; Subrahmanyam & Greenfield, 1998). In the late 90s, this explained why "75 to 85 percent of the sales and revenues generated by the $10 billion game industry" were from male consumers (Cassell & Jenkins, 1998, p. 11). However, since video games were one of the early entreés to the world of technology, many began to be concerned that this was another factor that disadvantaged girls from an interest in IT at an early age. There were also concerns that the culture of domination and violence might discourage women from studying and working in IT since the implicit message is that it may not be a safe place for women.

This climate has meant that the majority of developers in the gaming industry are male, and that they have a "tendency to orient product development toward male users" or make an inadequate effort to "obtain the input/involvement of representative potential users" (Bartol & Aspray 2006, p. 410). In recent years, researchers and developers have attempted to address these concerns from the standpoint of "what to do to make software and Web sites more attractive to girls" (Bartol & Aspray 2006, pp. 410-411). These efforts can be grouped into three main categories: (1) "appeal to more traditional gender interests in collaboration, relationships, negotiation, glamour, and creative design"; (2) "mimic aggressive game software for boys in versions showing female assertive heroines"; and (3) create "gender-neutral content oriented to the common nonviolent interests of both boys and girls" (Bartol & Aspray 2006, pp. 410-411). Let us look more closely at examples of these three approaches.

Developing "Female" Games

Many of the companies that attempted Approach #1, developing games that appeal to traditionally female gender interests, are now out of business. Here is what happened. Women developers and entrepreneurs such as Brenda Laurel began to establish companies that attempted to build games that considered the needs of girls with "more psychologically nuanced characters, softer color palettes, more richly-layered soundtracks . . . and more complex stories" (Jenkins & Cassell, 2007). Sadly, in a testimony to the power of stereotypes (and market brand), "Barbie Fashion Designer was a top-seller in the 1996 Christmas season, and continued throughout the year to outsell industry standards, such as those set by Quake or Myst" (Jenkins & Cassell, 2007). However, the success of the Barbie game exemplified the problem that immediately arose—whether to develop games that pandered to existing gender stereotypes (and would be more likely to be a financial success) or whether to develop games that challenged and transformed existing gender stereotypes (in a male-centric gaming industry, who could possibly believe *that* could make money?).

Her Interactive is one example of a company still in business today that successfully designed award-winning interactive CD-ROM games targeted to girls and "that offer role-playing mysteries and adventures." According to the company Web site (www.herinteractive.com), the "Nancy Drew series offers exciting adventure game play without violence or gender stereotypes." Her Interactive president Megan Gaiser says that the company originally targeted girls from 10 to 15 years old, but expanded their audience to include women when they realized that market was not being tapped. Gaiser credits their success to the fact that they sought "female perspectives on everything we did, from playing style and mechanics to marketing." On the other hand, she also describes the obstacles she faced with distributors (who could not believe, in spite of Gaiser's research, that "female gamers could be a lucrative market") and with the "risk averse" interactive entertainment industry (that prefers to stick with the "sex and violence" formula and to target their games to boys and men) (Gaiser, n.d.). Designing games "for girls" is one viable solution to the problem of sex and violence in video games. However, the drawback to this approach is that it may problematize girls/women as the "other" that does not fit in, and it may leave the existing social premises about gender unquestioned.

Developing Games with "Boy-Like" Female Heroes

Approach #2, to mimic aggressive game software for boys with versions that have assertive female heroines, has also had some success. One of the best examples of this approach is Tomb Raider's Lara Croft. Aleah Tierney (n.d.) is a freelance writer and female gamer who characterizes her experience as being "a stranger in a strange land," playing in "male-created virtual space" that embodies the "fantasy women men want," but falls short of filling her desires. She explains her disappointment with the Lara Croft character whose "gargantuan breasts" and "tiny clothes" made her hard to take seriously:

the giant twin pyramids mounted onto her chest look like something she could use to impale her enemies. In many ways her kick-butt presence is a triumph, but the designers' decision to sexualize her to the point of deformity angered me. I couldn't get past her proportions, so I put the game away. (Tierney, n.d.)

Tierney shares another story of her husband introducing her to Super Nintendo's Super Metroid game. She was initially impressed that the main character Samus was a "powerful, versatile, physically tough" woman with a "weapon-loaded space suit." However, excitement turned to disappointment when her husband beat the game and his reward was that Samus removed her space-suit to reveal "a small, pixilated woman in a bikini." She goes on to say, "I was sad and mad at the denigration of my new video game superhero." Fortunately, as the Metroid series developed, so did Samus; the "new games lack 'rewarding' images of Samus sans suit" (Tierney, n.d.).

These types of characters may seem like a step forward, but they still define women as sex objects and heroism in "male" terms as strong, aggressive, and dominating others. The underlying and unquestioned assumption of these characters is that women want what men want—to have large breasts and to have power over others. So, as with Approach #1, Approach #2 does not raise questions about the fundamental assumptions of a dominator social system. It just gives women better access to be dominators, too.

Developing Nonviolent, Gender-Neutral Games

Approach #3, creating "gender-neutral content oriented to the common nonviolent interests of both boys and girls" (Bartol & Aspray 2006, pp. 410-411), comes closest to an approach that does not problematize girls. This approach necessitates asking questions about deeper cultural beliefs such as: "What is the social cost for women *and for men* of so-called 'games' that emphasize dominance, violence, and the sexual objectification of women?" In fact, Justine Cassell's latest research looks in this very direction. Cassell (in press) argues "that girls were for a long time not taken into account in the design of computer games; however designing games 'specially for girls' risks ghettoizing girls as a population that needs 'special help'." Cassell proposes what she calls "underdetermined design," which "encourages both boys and girls to express aspects of self-identity that transcend stereotyped gender categories."

Today, most of these woman-owned start-up companies have been bought by larger gaming companies, and the emphasis on placing girls/women at the center of the design process has died down tremendously from where it was several years ago. This is a classic example of the power of stereotypes to be reasserted, especially when they are unexamined. Huff and Cooper (1987) show this in their study that asked 75 technologically-savvy women school teachers to design software under three conditions: (1) design software for girls; (2) design software for boys; and (3) design software for students (without specifying sex). Under condition #3, the all-female developers designed software "for students" that was nearly identical to the programs written for boys. This demonstrates the powerful, and usually subconscious, influence of gendered assumptions about technology; it is really for "the boys."

Another common dynamic that operated to tamp down the development of games with girls in mind is an explicit backlash against placing girls/women at the center of the discourse about gaming. In a male-centered social environment, that is heresy. Jenkins and Cassell's (2007) comments on reactions to their landmark book *From Barbie to Mortal Kombat: Gender and Computer Games* offer an interesting example of this phenomenon:

It was clear that a large segment of the men who worked inside the games industry, not to mention the guys who played the games, had no interest in thinking seriously about gender . . . Much of the popular press response drew a wall around "real gamers": One could be a feminist or a gamer but not both. (p. 4)

The good news is that thanks to the determination of many developers and entrepreneurs who appreciate the growing market for girls/women in gaming, we have at least a few games that are both successful and appealing to broader audiences. Studies by:

technology consulting company XEODesign have shown that women—and a surprisingly large number of men—find games fun when they are social, not too violent and full of creative opportunities. Games such as The Sims and Myst, which draw on these principles, have been smash cross-gender successes. (Stites, 2006, p. 62)

There are also many more women involved in gaming as users, especially casual gaming. However, this has had no impact on the numbers of women in IT, and we still have to deal with the effects of the stereotyped images of large-breasted narrow-hipped female characters in gaming. This is no small matter (no pun intended). Just as violence in media cannot be directly correlated with violence in society, sexual objectification of women in media cannot be directly correlated with the sexual objectification of real women. However, at the very least, it contributes to a climate in which certain words, metaphors, attitudes, beliefs, and behaviors are viewed as acceptable. Eisler (2002) makes a similar argument with regard to television:

The average child is likely to have watched 8,000 screen murders and more than 100,000 acts of violence by the end of elementary school. So by the time they are adults, violence seems natural, and uncaring and abusive relations seem acceptable, even entertaining. (Eisler, 2002, p. 100)

This is one of the ways in which we learn the values of a dominator society.

Sexual Objectification of Women: The Sad, the Bad and the Uglier

When discussing the importance of gendered communication and the male IT culture, the implicit sexual objectification of women (which is at least contributed to by video games that feature sexualized stereotypes of women) cannot be ignored. It is perhaps the most insidious social force that operates against women in science and technology, and it relates to the legacy of Baconian science. Yes, I just made a connection between the sexual objectification of women and the philosophy of science that originated with Francis Bacon's ideas. Here is how it works.

As I discussed in Chapter III, maleness was associated with science while femaleness was associated with nature and the goal of science was to dominate nature. Female/nature was viewed as the creator over which male/science sought to gain control. These nearly 500-year old deeply embedded beliefs influence the ways in which individual men and women interrelate today. If you place the legacy of Baconian scientific thought in the context of our gendered social model—in which men are primarily judged in terms of their accomplishments and women are primarily judged in terms of their appearance—it is not surprising that women are sexually objectified to the extent that they are. Unfortunately, the IT environment is not immune to these broader social forces of our dominator social model.

The sexual objectification of women also can make it difficult for women to be taken seriously, or to take themselves seriously, as scientists and technologists. Sexual objectification may range from implicit to explicit. For example, Rosser (1995) shares examples of some sexual metaphors that dominate contemporary quantum physics. Terms such as "charm, beauty, and strangeness" describe the attributes of elementary particles, and terms such as "topless, naked bottom, and exotic hermaphrodite states" are used in the titles of seminars. On a more personal level, Bix (2000) describes what happened at MIT when obscene mail was:

sent over the computer system and Playboy-type pictures posed in the department. 'We were treated as potential dates instead of as colleagues . . . . I always feel as if I am being pursued.' Women who rejected unwelcome sexual attention were slandered for a lack of femininity, nicknamed 'Mrs. Attila the Hun.' (p. 41)

This is also an example of the price women often pay if they resist being sexually objectified and ask to be treated as professionals.

Sexual Objectification in the Workplace: Three Lose-Lose Stories

My own experience during my 7 years as a contract technical writer in the software industry offers another example of the pervasiveness of the problem, and of the price women often must pay. I left three technical writing positions in the software development industry because of behavior that sexually objectified women and created an inhospitable professional climate. These stories are meant to expose the uneven terrain that women must navigate in many IT workplaces. All three represent the classic lose-lose situation that women face. I could have tried to "be one of the boys," but I would have felt like a loser for selling myself out, thus internalizing the shame and objectification. Or, I could have said something (that was bound to be perceived negatively, no matter how unemotional and rational I was) which would have resulted in making me "the problem." These three stories exemplify the lose-lose choices many women face on a daily basis in the IT workplace.

One incident occurred at a large international IT company. I went to gather technical information from an engineer for the documentation that I was writing. I arrived at his office to find numerous images of nude women posted on the walls. He was not in his office, and I decided not to wait for him. I told my supervisor that he would have to gather the information that I needed from this man to complete my project because I would not be exposed to the images in his office again. My supervisor's reply was "Oh, he's a good guy. He doesn't mean anything by it." I repeated my request. He repeated his defense of the guy. I left the job when my contract ended a few months later.

Another man at a smaller start-up software company (later bought by the same international IT company referenced above) had a screen saver that featured rotating images of nude women. He shared an office with a female technical writer, who had no choice but to be exposed to these images daily. The day he posted the screen saver, she told me about it and we discussed potential resolutions. Since it was a small company, I suggested that she talk to the president of the company. The next day, before she had a chance to speak to the president, I overheard the president walk by the screen saver with the nude images, glance at it and say, "Hey! Cool screen saver." I left that job when my contract ended a few weeks later.

A few years later, I was employed at a small, growing software company. I was one of the first dozen employees when I joined the company, and within 6 months we had grown to over 80 employees. The president of the company regularly touched me (and other women) in ways that I found uncomfortable. He also included lascivious comments about women in his weekly postings to our company newsgroup about our company's growth and financial status. Since he had always told me how much he respected me, I decided to schedule time with him to discuss these issues. I said that I was taking a chance and banking on his respect for me that he might hear what I had to say and alter his behavior. I explained what I found uncomfortable. I explained that as the president of the company he had the power to establish the climate of the organization. I explained that this was not a hospitable climate for the women who worked there, and that I was not the only one who felt that way.

I explained that other men would gauge their behavior against his, and that this behavior would eventually put the company in jeopardy since it was grounds for a harassment law suit. I explained that I was not the "litigious" type, and that I would be more likely to just leave one day if things did not change, but that some other woman might file a law suit. He listened thoughtfully, thanked me for talking to him, and for a few weeks he stopped touching me inappropriately. However, the day he began his weekly company bulletin on our newsgroup with "I'm taking time out from bikini-watching on the beach here in LA to update you on our upcoming IPO" was my last day at the company.

The point of these stories is to highlight the pervasiveness of male-identified culture of IT. Certainly, all women do not find the same things offensive. Certainly, some women may have "thicker skin" than others. However, the question remains: "Why should they have to have thick skin in the first place?" (Never mind the irony that while gender stereotypes reinforce the notion that women are supposed to be soft and sensitive, if they respond in ways that are soft and sensitive in professional environments they are accused of being too soft and sensitive).

Why can't we work together to create a more hospitable, a more respectful, and a more collaborative climate for women and for men? The answer is that we can if we choose to.

CONCLUSION

It is possible to create a more hospitable and diverse IT culture. It is possible to change our social institutions. The bad news is that, as Jo Sanders (1995) describes it, our current IT culture has created a kind of "chicken and egg" dilemma: "Because mostly boys and men use computers, girls conclude that computing is not appropriately feminine, which leads them to decline computing opportunities available to them, which leaves computing environments male, which leads girls to conclude..." (p. 149). The chicken-and-egg construct is a useful one in terms of taking the onus off of "men as the bad guys keeping women out" and pointing to the systemic, institutionalized processes in which we all participate.

The good news is that a study by Blum and Frieze (2004) shows that as the "gender composition of the computing program became more balanced, the culture changed" (Cohoon & Aspray, 2006, p. 146). This research supports the notion that institutionalized systems of oppression are not static; individuals interact with their institutional environments in ways that reshape them. The interaction between gender and computing culture co-operates in both directions. As more women become part of the culture, the culture is changed by their presence to some extent. However, I would also add that the extent to which the computer culture is changed is dependent on the consciousness of the individuals who comprise that particular community. The more conscious they are of the pervasiveness and significance of the gendered ideologies of computer culture, the more likely they are to participate in asking more fundamental questions about the day-to-day climate of that culture.

QUESTIONS FOR REFLECTIVE DIALOG

1. Language is the primary method for conveying stereotypes. Consider the most hurtful word that has ever been used to describe you (for some of us grade school supplies adjectives galore). Write the word on a piece of paper and then free write about all the possible definitions of the word. Why did this word work to diminish your self-image? How is this word used in the media? What assumptions are embedded in the word? What images are attached to these assumptions? What is the opposite of the word that hurt you? Describe the concepts attached to that opposite word.

2. What does it mean to be "politically correct"? If you were to create a fictional character who was "politically correct," how would you describe this individual? Is "politically correct" language a form of dishonesty or could it be viewed as a modern form of politeness?

3. In your family of origin, what is the communication style? Is there an attempt to "win" conversations? Does dialogue occur between generations and between genders, or do women and men seem to congregate separately? Consider your closest friend's conversation style. Is there a free exchange of ideas between you and this person, or is it a verbal contest? Spend a day observing your own listening skills. How much time do you talk compared to the time spent listening?

4. Are you a member of any online community? What is your observation of the communication styles that predominate there? How do you think gender may influence communication online? Do you feel the move away from face-to-face communication erodes the gender assigned roles for men and women?

5. How can people actively promote healthy online communities? Laura Gurak (2005) observed that "cyberspace is gendered space." Go online and look at a "male" magazine Web site and a "female" magazine Web site. Make a list of the article titles and advertisements on each site. Compare the two homepages. What images are featured? At a glance, could you guess the gender of the Web site's target audience? Why or why not?

6. Write a list of your top 10 dream jobs and explain why you would like to pursue these jobs. Write a list of the types of jobs that you would enjoy doing (regardless of income) and name specific skills or aptitudes that you need for

each job. Are any of your dream jobs also jobs that you would enjoy doing? How many of the dream jobs are traditionally held by members outside of your gender?

7. Consider a recent conflict that you had with someone of a different gender. If possible, try to recall the exact phrases and words that you both used. In what ways does this conversation fit with or diverge from the gendered communication styles described in this chapter? Describe the role that gender played in the interaction.

REFERENCES[1]

Babcock, L., & Laschever, S. (2003). *Women don't ask: Negotiating the gender divide*. Princeton, NJ: Princeton.

Bartol, K. M., & Aspray, W. (2006). The transition of women from the academic world to the IT workplace: A review of the relevant research. In J. M. Cohoon & W. Aspray (Eds.), *Women and information technology: Research on underrepresentation* (pp. 377-419). Cambridge, MA: MIT Press.

Bix, A. S. (2000). Feminism where men predominate: The history of women's science and engineering education at MIT. *Women's Studies Quarterly, 28*(1/2), 24-45.

Bleier, R. (1991). *Feminist approaches to science*. New York: Teachers College.

Carli, L. L. (1990, November). Gender, language, and influence. *Journal of Personality & Social Psychology, 59*(5), 941-952. Retrieved August 12, 2007, from www.ebscohost.com

Cassell, J. (in press). Genderizing HCI. In J. Jacko & A. Sears (Eds.), *The handbook of human-computer interaction*. Mahwah, NJ: Lawrence Erlbaum. Retrieved July 30, 2007, from http://web.media.mit.edu/~justine/publications.html

Cassell, J., & Jenkins, H. (Eds.). (1998). *From Barbie to mortal kombat: Gender and computer games*. Cambridge, MA: MIT.

Cohoon, J. M., & Aspray, W. (2006). A critical review of the research on women's participation in postsecondary computing education. In J. M. Cohoon & W. Aspray (Eds.), *Women and information technology: Research on underrepresentation* (pp. 137-180). Cambridge, MA: MIT Press.

Collins, P. H. (1990). *Black feminist thought: Knowledge, consciousness, and the politics of empowerment*. New York: Routledge.

Conduct Problems Prevention Research Group. (1999). Initial impact of the fast track prevention trial for conduct problems: I. The high-risk sample. *Journal of Consulting and Clinical Psychology, 67*, 631-647. Retrieved August 13, 2007, from www.ebscohost.com

Cooper, J. et al. (1990). Situational stress as a consequence of sex-stereotyped software. *Personality and Social Psychology Bulletin, 16*, 419-429.

Daft, R. L. (1997). *Management.* New York: Dryden.

Eisler, R. (2002). *The power of partnership: Seven relationships that will change your life.* Novato, CA: New World.

Eisler, R., & Loye, D. (1990). *The partnership way.* San Francisco: HarperSan-Francisco.

Faulkner, W. (2000). Dualisms, hierarchies and gender in engineering. *Social Studies of Science, 30*(5), 759-792. Retrieved on January 16, 2007, from www.jstor.org

Flannery, D. J., et al. (2003, March). Initial behavior outcomes for the PeaceBuilders Universal school-based violence prevention program. *Developmental Psychology, 39*(2), 292-309. Retrieved August 13, 2007, from www.ebscohost.com

Gaiser, M. (n.d.). *Solving the mystery of the missing girl games.* Retrieved January 28, 2007, from http://www.pbs.org/kcts/videogamerevolution/impact/girl_games.html

Gurak, L. (February 2001). Is this the party to whom I am speaking? *The Women's Review of Books, XVIII*(5), 5-6.

Hart, S. (2004). Creating a culture of peace with nonviolent communication. In R. Eisler & R. Miller (Eds.), *Educating for a culture of peace* (pp. 113-125). Portsmouth, NH: Heinemann.

Herring, S. C. (1993). Gender and democracy in computer-mediated communication. *EJC/REC, 3*(2). Retrieved on November 12, 1998, from http://dc.smu.edu/dc/classroom/Gender.txt

Herring, S. C. (1999). The rhetorical dynamics of gender harassment on-line. *The Information Society, 15*, 151-167. Retrieved on August 12, 2007, from www.ebscohost.com

hooks, b. (1984). *Feminist theory: From margin to center.* Boston: South End.

hooks, b. (1989). *Talking back: Talking feminist, thinking black.* Boston: South End.

Huff, C., & Cooper, J. (1987). Sex bias in educational software: The effect of designers' stereotypes on the software they design. *Journal of applied social psychology, 17*, 519-532.

Jenkins, H., & Cassell, J. (2007). From quake grrls to desperate housewives: A decade of gender and computer games. In Y. Kafai, C. Heeter, J. Denner, & J. Sun (Eds.), *Beyond Barbie and Mortal Kombat: New perspectives on gender and computer games.* Cambridge, MA: MIT Press. Retrieved September 1, 2007, from http://www.soc. northwestern.edu/justine/publications/Jenkins_Cassell%20BBMK_Forward.pdf

Johnson, A. G. (2006). *Privilege, power and difference.* Boston: McGrawHill.

Keller, E. F. (1992). *Secrets of life, secrets of death: Essays on language, gender and science.* New York: Routledge.

Lakoff, R. T. (1990). *Talking power: The politics of language.* New York: Basic.

Mares, M., & Woodard, E. (2005). Effects of television on children's social interactions: A meta-analysis. *Media Psychology, 7*(3), 301-322. Retrieved on August 13, 2007, from www.ebscohost.com

Mulvaney, B. M. (1994). *Gender differences in communication: An intercultural experience.* Retrieved on August 9, 2007, from http://www.cpsr.org/prevsite/cpsr/ gender/mulvaney.txt

Pipher, M. (1994). *Reviving ophelia: Saving the selves of adolescent girls.* New York: Putnam

Provenzo, E. (1995). Interview. *Minerva's machine* (Videocassette). Association for Computing Machinery.

Roldan, M., Soe, L., & Yakura, E.K. (2004, April 22-24). Perceptions of chilly IT organizational contexts and their effect on the retention and promotion of women in IT. *'04*, Tuscon, Arizona.

Rosenberg, M. B. (2005). *Nonviolent communication: A language of life.* Encinitas, CA: PuddleDancer.

Rosser, S. V. (Ed.). (1995). *Teaching the majority: Breaking the gender barrier in science, mathematics, and engineering.* New York: Teachers College.

Sadker, M., & Sadker, D. (1995). *Failing at fairness: How our schools cheat girls.* New York: Touchstone.

Sanders, J. (1995). Girls and technology. In S.V. Rosser (Ed.), *Teaching the majority: Breaking the gender barrier in science, mathematics, and engineering* (pp. 147-159). New York: Teachers College.

Schiebinger, L. (1999). *Has feminism changed science?* Cambridge, MA: Harvard.

Spender, D. (1980). *Man made language.* London: Routledge.

Spender, D. (1995). *Nattering on the net: Women, power and cyberspace.* North Melbourne, Australia: Spinifex.

Stites, J. (2006, Summer) More than a game: Move over geekboys: Feminists reclaim video gaming. *Ms.*, 61-62.

Subrahmanyam, K., & Greenfield, P. M. (1998). Computer games for girls: What makes them play? In J. Cassell & H. Jenkins (Eds.), *From Barbie to Mortal Kombat: Gender and computer games* (pp. 46-71). Cambridge, MA: MIT.

Tannen, D. (2001). *You just don't understand: Women and men in conversation.* New York: Quill.

Tierney, A. (n.d.). *What women want.* Retrieved January 28, 2007, from http://www.pbs.org/kcts/videogamerevolution/impact/women.html

Van Fossen, B. (1996). Gender differences in communication. *Institute for Teaching and Research on Women, Towson University.* Retrieved August 5, 1997, from http://midget.towson.edu/itrow

Walker, H. M., Colvin, G., & Ramsey, E. (1995). *Anti-social behavior in schools: Strategies and best practices.* Pacific Grove, CA: Brooks/Cole.

Wilson, F. (2003). Can compute, won't compute: Women's participation in the culture of computing. *New Technology, Work, and Employment*, 18(2), 127-142.

Wood, J. T. (1999). *Gendered lives: Communication, gender, and culture* (3rd ed.). Belmont, CA: Wadsworth.

ENDNOTE

[1]   Some portions of this chapter may have appeared in, and are reprinted with permission from Kirk, M (2006). Bridging the digital divide: A feminist perspective on the project. In G. Trajkovski (Ed.), *Diversity in information technology education: Issues and controversies* (pp. 38-67). Hershey, PA: Information Science Publishing

Chapter VI
Education as Social Institution:
Understanding Her–Story

OBJECTIVES

This chapter aims to help you understand the following:

- How our knowledge tradition has been influenced and limited by those who were able to participate in its creation.
- That there have been educated women who generated ideas and inventions for centuries in spite of their exclusion from systems of formal education.
- A brief her-story of some of the women who have contributed to scientific and technical knowledge creation in spite of the many barriers they faced.
- How the historical legacy of women's intermittent access to and exclusion from scientific and technical education (and the professions) influences women's participation in science and technology today.

INTRODUCTION

Education is another of the primary social institutions from which we learn the values, attitudes, beliefs, and behaviors of a dominator culture. A discussion of education as a social institution embraces: (1) how we come to know (epistemologies); (2) the methods of teaching and learning (pedagogies); and (3) what we know, the content of our knowledge tradition. In Chapter III, I explored some ideas about epistemological barriers to women in IT education related to our philosophy of science. For example, some scholars have argued that since more women tend to be concrete learners, and more men tend to be abstract learners, women may be less comfortable with the abstract approaches that predominate in science and IT education (Belenky, 1986; Estrin, 1996; Goldberger, 1996; Greenbaum, 1990; Keller, 1992; Kramer & Lehman, 1990; Riger, 1992; Rosser, 1995; Turkle & Papert, 1990). In Chapter IX, I will address questions of epistemology and pedagogy in more depth as I propose a partnership model of education. In this chapter, I would like to focus on the third issue, that is, the content of our knowledge tradition. This chapter explores: (1) our incomplete knowledge tradition; (2) a brief her-story of women in math, engineering, and IT; and (3) the ins and outs of women's education and employment in these fields.

OUR INCOMPLETE KNOWLEDGE TRADITION

The Western knowledge tradition reflects the dominator social system from which it has emerged. Education as a social institution purveys the message that only certain people have accomplished anything and only certain perspectives are "worth" learning about. The disciplines and their "ways of knowing" were created by a group of people whose circumstances and experiences of their world were not reflective of the broader population. Therefore, the questions considered relevant for study, the proposed methods of study, and the content of today's academic disciplines are the result of a narrowly informed set of perspectives. "Other groups, with a different set of experiences—in this case, women—were largely excluded from the identification of problems and the creation of disciplinary knowledge and tools of analysis" (Bucciarelli, 2004, p. 138). The histories that we record, the literatures that we consider classics, the disciplines that we consider important, the ways in which we come to know, and the ways in which we teach and learn originate from giving primacy to a singular set of perspectives for centuries. This has led to the development of an incomplete, and perhaps even distorted, knowledge tradition.

The truth is that numerous women have contributed to our human knowledge as religious scholars, as artists and writers, as educators, and as scientists. Unfortunately, only the most exceptional of the exceptional women—those who braved far more oppressive times to contribute new knowledge and perspectives to our human experience—have actually become part of the canonical knowledge tradition in a variety of fields. This leaves the impression that there simply "were not any women" artists, writers, scientists, or other women of achievement before the 20th century. However, as 20th century feminist scholars worldwide have shown, there were in fact many women (and men from communities of color), who have made remarkable contributions to our knowledge tradition. It is simply that in a dominator social system their often unique perspectives and the products of their labor were implicitly and explicitly marginalized and therefore excluded from our knowledge tradition.

In *The Creation of Feminist Consciousness* (1993), Gerda Lerner shares centuries of histories of women's intellectual and creative achievements. Lerner's chapter titled "One Thousand Years of Feminist Bible Criticism" offers a compelling illustration of "the lack of continuity and the absence of collective memory on the part of women thinkers"—the price of excluding their perspectives from the knowledge tradition (p. 139). Lerner explains how convents served as a kind of educational oasis for women, but only for those whose families could afford a dowry; the church would pay to educate poor men who wanted to pursue the ministry (p. 26). While education was historically denied to most women, there were several "islands of privileged space for women":

The double monasteries of the 7th and 8th centuries, the nunneries . . . in the 8th–13th centuries, the urban centers of Holland and the Rhineland . . . in the 12th century, the course of some of the cities of Renaissance Italy and France, and centers of the Protestant Reformation. (Lerner, 1993, p. 28)

This also meant that women who wanted a scholarly life were channeled into religious writing while other forms of expression were "discouraged or foreclosed" (p. 139). However, the fruits of their religious scholarship were excluded from the knowledge tradition, so that each subsequent generation of Biblical scholars had to begin anew.

Here is the legacy of a few of these women, most of whom never heard of each other. Christine de Pizan (1365-1430) wrote *The Book of the City of the Ladies* in which she examined all of the misogynist charges against women in a dialogue with Lady Reason who answered each with a Biblical excerpt. Isotta Nogarola (1418-1466) dialogued with a male humanist over who was responsible for the Fall. Marguerite d'Angouleme (1492-1549) wrote *Mirror of the Sinful Soul* which expressed feminine/feminist theology. Anne Askew (daughter of a courtier and Henry VIII) was burned at the stake in 1546 for asserting her right to reinterpret St. Paul. Jane Anger (1589) engaged in a pamphlet war over misogynist comments by reinterpreting the Biblical creation story to favor women instead of condemn them. Rachel Speght (1615) also engaged in a pamphlet war using elaborate Biblical arguments. Sarah Fyge (1669-1722) answered a misogynist attack with a long poem titled "The Female Advocate" that argued Eve's superiority and caused her father to throw her out of the house. Poet Aemilia Lanyer wrote a volume of religious poems in 1611 that attempted to explore the active and positive role that women played in Christ's passion. Mary Astell (1666-1733) wrote of women's authorization to prophesy and made one of the first arguments that women have been denied their right to interpret scripture due to lack of education in the original languages. Julia Smith (1792–1878) repeated Erasmus' work by translating the Bible five times in 7 years with the help of her four sisters. Sarah Grimke (1792-1873) wrote *Letters on the Equality of the Sexes* in 1838, 10 years before Margaret Fuller, and said: "I ask no favors for my sex. All I ask our brethren is, that they will take their feet from off our necks and permit us to stand upright on that ground which God designed us to occupy" (Lerner, 1993, p. 162). Some may know Elizabeth Cady Stanton as one of the two key figures (the other was Susan B. Anthony) who spent decades fighting for women's suffrage. However, fewer know that along with Matilda Joslyn Gage, Stanton published *The Woman's Bible* in 1895, and argued that "the Bible and the orthodox church were the two greatest obstacles in the way of women's advancement"—a position that ultimately forced her out of the suffrage movement (Lerner, 1993, pp. 138-166).

In sharing these histories, Lerner (1993) systematically reports on how few of the women referenced each other, which she cites as probable evidence that they had no access to earlier women's writings. Lerner shares the sentiment that Bernard of Chartres first expressed (but later became an aphorism of Isaac Newton) in reflecting on his own accomplishments: "If I have seen further, it is by standing on the shoulders of giants"—women scholars have had no such experience (p. 166). They have had to recreate an intellectual tradition anew with each generation because earlier "women's creations sank soundlessley into the sea, leaving barely a ripple, and succeeding generations of women were left to cover the same ground others had already covered before them" (Lerner, 1993, p. 220).

Without knowing their history, each generation of women believes that they are the "first" and that they face their numerous obstacles to success alone, without literal or historical mentors to lead the way. However, every generation has had its heroes, those who have gained access to education and employment when no one else could, and overcome systemic barriers to success. What these inspirational stories do not tell us is how many others who might have had the talent to make it, but did not because they had no guidance from those who had gone before.

In previous chapters, I have described some of the obstacles that women face in a dominator society, most of which women themselves are unaware of. If women are to succeed on pathways that are not readily open to them, if they are to continue the climb up a mountain littered with rocks, crevasses, and the potential for landslides, we might at least give them the proper climbing gear. We might at least place the occasional plaque marking the spot where another woman successfully made the climb. We might at least let them know that they are not alone. That is the primary purpose of this chapter—to share a brief "her-story" of women in science and technology.

A BRIEF HER-STORY OF WOMEN IN MATH, SCIENCE, AND ENGINEERING

Merit Path, an Egyptian physician around 2700 B.C. whose picture is in a tomb in the Valley of the Kings, may be the earliest woman scientist. "Medicine seems to have been a well-established field in Egypt, with many women working as doctors and surgeons" (Ambrose, Dunkle, Lazarus, Nair, & Harkus, 1997, p. 4). Tapputi-Belatekallim, a Babylonian perfume maker, might be considered the earliest woman chemical engineer since "she devised several new methods for preparing perfumes." Theano (end of 6th century B.C.), a student and later wife of Greek mathematician Pythagoras, is said (along with her daughters) to have continued Pythagoras' school and teachings after his death (Arditti, 1980, p. 351).

Hypatia (370-415 A.D.), unlike most women of her day, was educated by her father Theon who was an astronomer and mathematician. Since she was accomplished in mathematics, physics, astronomy, chemistry, and medicine, Hypatia held a chair in philosophy at the University of Alexandria and is credited with several inventions, including the astrolabe (for measuring the positions of celestial bodies), the planesphere (for distilling water), and a hydrometer (for measuring the density of liquids) (Ambrose et al., 1997; Arditti, 1980).

There is little documented participation by women in science in Europe during the Dark Ages, but women continued to participate in science in Arabic cultures and in China. During the Middle Ages, "the Church monopolized centers of learning, and almost all intellectual activity took place in convents and monasteries" (Arditti, 1980, p. 352). A number of German nuns achieved prominence during this time, most notably Hildegarde of Bingen (1098-1179) who wrote extensively in a variety of scientific areas including medicine, botany, zoology, and geology, and whose writing explored questions about the nature of the cosmos, the soul and God. Arditti (1980) says this of Hildegarde of Bingen:

She recognized that the stars are of different sizes and of different brightness and made a comparison between the movement of the stars and the movement of blood in the veins—an idea that predated the discovery of the circulation of the blood. Other ideas also anticipated later discoveries. She put the sun at the center of the firmament and speculated about the seasons. She argued that if it is winter and cold in one part of the planet, then the other side of the earth should be warm. (p. 353)

The participation of women in science during the Middle Ages waxed and waned. Arditti (1980) says, "The suppression of the convents in England by Henry VIII signaled the end of organized efforts to educate women" (p. 353). Ambrose et al. (1997) cite the closing of convents in many countries as a result of the Protestant Reformation in the 1500s as one contributing factor, but name the "witch hunts that swept across Europe between about 1300 and 1700" as "the greatest deterrent to women's involvement in scientific pursuits" (p. 6).

Emilie de Breuteuil Marquise de Chatelet (1706-1749) is most noted for her translation of Newton's *Principia Mathematica* from Latin to French, and to which she added her own scholarly commentary. She devoted much of her scientific research to the nature of fire. Maria Agnesi (1718-1799) wrote a widely acclaimed textbook on differential and integral calculus called *Analytical Institutions* that was published in 1748, but she was nonetheless turned down for membership in the French Academy of Science (Arditti, 1980; Osen, 1974).

Augusta Ada Byron Lovelace (1815-1852) was the daughter of the poet Byron and Annabella Millbanke. When she was 18, Ada heard a lecture by Charles Babbage (1791-1871) on his automatic mechanical calculator, the Difference Engine. He invited her to translate an article summarizing his work from Italian to English. They began exchanging letters as she developed her thinking and added substantially to Babbage's original concept. Ada's suggestions to Babbage regarding how to use his calculating machine are now regarded as the first "software program." In 1979, the U.S. Department of Defense named its new software language Ada in her honor (Stanley, 1995; Toole, 1992).

Marie Pape-Carpantier (1815-1878) was a French educator who invented "a boulier numerateur, an educational calculator using colored balls to make the calculations" that was "shown at the Paris Exhibition of 1878" (Stanley, 1995, p. 436-437). Emily Duncan (1849-1934) was a U.S. American who received two patents for calculators; "her 1903 calculator makes it easy to calculate interest on any amount of money at 6-8%; and her 1904 invention allows one quickly to calculate the number of days a note has to run" (Stanley, 1995, pp. 436-437). Another contemporary was Edith Clarke (1883-1959), an electrical engineer who spent many years with GE and whose first patent in 1925 was for a "calculating device that allowed engineers to monitor or predict the performance of electrical transmission lines and systems without laboriously solving many complicated equations" (Stanley, 1995, p. 438).

Grace Murray Hopper (1906-1992) is considered one of the most significant pioneering women in computing. While completing her Ph.D. in mathematics at Yale in 1934, she taught at Vassar, her undergraduate alma mater. In 1943, she joined the U.S. Navy Reserve and worked on the Mark I computer. In 1946, she joined the Harvard faculty as a research fellow and worked on the Mark II and III computers. In 1949, she became a senior scientist at Eckert-Mauchly, later the Univac Division of Sperry-Rand. In 1967, she was recalled to active duty in the Navy and spent the next 20 years working on programming languages at the Pentagon. Among her contributions include: creating the first computer language consisting of words, Flow-Matic (from which COBOL evolved); inventing virtual storage, "allowing data and program segments to be swapped between peripheral and central storage in such a way that the effective storage capacity of a given computer is vastly increased"; and working to develop the concept of parallel processing, a concept that rapidly changed computing as we know it (Reynolds, 1999; Stanley, 1995).

THE INS AND OUTS OF EDUCATION AND EMPLOYMENT

Kim Tolley's *The Science Education of American Girls: A Historical Perspective* (2003), and Margaret Rossiter's landmark volumes on the history of women in science, *Women Scientists in America: Struggles and Strategies to 1940* (1982) and *Women Scientists in America: Before Affirmative Action 1940–1972* (1995), lay a strong foundation for understanding the structural and cultural influences on girls' and women's participation in science education in the United States. Tolley (2003) compares the experiences of adolescent girls and boys in 19th century "higher schools," which include "private venture schools, incorporated seminaries and academies, boarding schools, the preparatory departments of colleges and universities . . . and publicly funded high schools" (p. 6). Rossiter (1982) details the "series of limited stereotypes, double binds, resistant barriers" and other "no-win situations" that women historically faced in colleges and universities (p. xvii). Together they describe the varying historical climates that sometimes encouraged girls and women in to science and technology, and alternately pushed them out. This historical legacy of uneven and inconsistent access to education and employment can help us to better understand why women remain underrepresented in most areas of science and technology today.

Free Public Education

Historically speaking, the system of free public education that we have in the U.S. today is a new phenomenon. Until the 1840s and the beginning of the common school movement, education was the province of local governments and states, which meant that it was largely available only to those with money. Prior to the U.S. Civil War, there was virtually no public school education available for Black girls and very little available for White girls except those who were privileged by socioeconomic class. "Rural women, immigrants and African-American women were illiterate longer than native-born, White and middle-class women" (Lerner, 1993, p. 43).

By the end of the 19th century, free elementary education was available for Whites in most areas and compulsory attendance laws had been passed by most states. The types of "higher schools" open to middle- and upper-class White girls ages 12 to 18 included day schools, boarding schools, and female seminaries. "These schools educated the majority of the nation's secondary students before 1880, and many were single-sex rather than coeducational schools" (Tolley, 2003, p. 8). The movement to establish free public high schools did not gain ground until after the Civil War, but there was still poor access to education beyond the first few years of school for Black girls that lasted until the 1950s. In 1954, the U.S. Supreme Court decision in Brown v. Board of Education of Topeka federally mandated an end to legal segregation in schools; the Court ruled that "separate but equal" educational facilities are "inherently unequal" making segregation in public education uncon-stitutional. Free access to education through high school was not available to all women in the U.S. until well into the 1960s.

Access to College for Some

In terms of college education for women, a few institutions were coeducational in the early 1800s. Gradually, the social climate began to change thanks to the efforts of Emma Willard and other women pioneers who began to the make the convincing argument that women must be better educated because they were responsible for the moral and cultural education of the next generation of citizens. Willard opened the Troy Female Seminary in 1821 as the first endowed institution for the education of women (Arditti, 1980). This led to the founding of many female "seminaries" where women were trained to be teachers (and expected never to marry if they pursued that profession). Then, in 1837, Mary Lyon founded Mount Holyoke Seminary, which became a model for many of the women's colleges founded later in the 1800s. Like many other women-only colleges, Mount Holyoke became an early leader in science education for women. That legacy continues today with nearly one-third of their undergraduates majoring in science and math, and more of their graduates earning "doctorates in the physical and life sciences (356 and 109, respectively)" than any other liberal arts college ("Science leadership," 2007). Still this was only a begin-ning, and most women in the U.S. had extremely limited access to college-level education (let alone education in the sciences) until the late 1800s when a few of the now nationally-renowned women's colleges were founded (e.g., Smith College [1871], Wellesley College [1875], and Bryn Mawr College [1885]).

The establishment of women's colleges, which provided a single-sex learning environment, was a significant contributor to the success of women in science. Many scholars, as well as women in science, have documented the importance of single-sex learning environments in relation to women in science (Barker & Aspray, 2006;

Rossiter, 1982; Sadker & Sadker, 1995; and Warren, 1999). The reasons for this are many, but a few of the most significant are: the presence of female role models and mentors; smaller classes that offer students more attention from faculty; the documented fact that women talk more (and talk more freely) in single-sex learning environments; curricular content that tends to contain more "female-friendly" material; and peer dynamics that are more cooperative (without male peers to push toward a competitive model) (Rosser, 1997; Sadker & Sadker, 1995).

Access to College for African-American Women

The existence of these women's colleges still only offered access to a socially- and economically-privileged few, not to all women. Due to the historical legacy of slavery and legalized racism, African-American women were often limited to studying at segregated colleges and universities (now called Historically Black Colleges and Universities or HBCUs). Many HBCUs were founded as a result of the Morrill Land-Grant Act of 1890, which gave federal land to states who would open colleges and universities to educate farmers, scientists, and teachers. Although many states had taken advantage of the earlier Morrill Land-Grant Act in the 1860s to establish state schools, most were closed to Black Americans. So, the 1890 act specified:

that states using federal land-grant funds must either make their schools open to both Blacks and Whites or allocate money for segregated Black colleges to serve as an alternative to White schools. A total of 16 exclusively Black institutions received 1890 land-grant funds. ("Origination," 2007)

Like the women's colleges, many of these colleges and universities were successful in producing scientists. However, their facilities were often under-funded and the professional opportunities for graduates were mostly limited to teaching within the HBCUs. So, although it was a start, the existence of HBCUs did not rapidly open the doors of access to a professional life in the sciences. There were many more social barriers to overcome (Rossiter, 1982).

There was one unusual social dynamic due to race that actually positively influenced Black women. Lerner (1993) explains that from 1890-1970 African-American women actually exceeded men in access to education due to their families' eagerness to help daughters find a way out of domestic service. They were privileged over Black men in terms of education, because even with degrees Black men were largely relegated to menial jobs. Evelyn Boyd Granville, who along with Marjorie Lee Browne tied as the first Black woman to earn a doctorate in mathematics in 1949, supported this idea in comments from a 1983 interview: "Black women have always had to work . . . [and] because Black women have had a long history of work outside the home, Black females tend to be better educated than their male counterparts" (Warren, 1999, p. 106). That gender "advantage" did not sustain itself through the changes brought by the Civil Rights Act of 1964. "Ironically, one of the few gains of the 20th century civil rights movement which has remained in place is that the educational advantage of Black men over Black women now follows similar sexist patterns as that of White men over White women" (Lerner, 1993, p. 44).

Although African-American women had access to college-level study, access to any type of doctoral degree was difficult and it took many decades longer to begin to have access to doctorates in math and science. According to Scott W. Williams (1999), professor of mathematics at the State University of New York in Buffalo:

The first American woman to earn a Ph.D. in Mathematics was Winifred Edgerton Merrill (Columbia U. 1886). . . however, it was not until 1949, 25 years after the first African-American [man] earned a Ph.D. in mathematics that a Black woman reached that level.

That woman was Evelyn Boyd Granville who earned her Ph.D. in mathematics at Yale. Other sciences, such as physics, were even harder to gain entry to; the first Black woman to earn a doctorate in physics was Shirley Ann Jackson in 1973. These notable women are two of only 10 doctoral "firsts" among African-American women in science and medicine between 1933 and 1973 (Rossiter, 1995, p. 83). Of the few who managed to hurdle all of the barriers to doctoral education, most of these "pioneers spent their entire career teaching at Black colleges" (Rossiter, 1995, p. 83). There is no question that racism and segregation limited career options for African-American women in a way that it did not for European-American women. Rossiter speculates that this may have been the reason that many of these pioneers taught at HBCUs, but it may also have been out of a desire to serve their communities and mentor other Black women (p. 82).

Inhospitable Climate in Science Education

Although some women began to gain access to college and university education by the late 1800s, they were largely White middle- and upper-class women. In addition, the climate that they found once they arrived was less than ideal. Amy Bix's (2000) examination of the history of women in science and engineering at MIT from 1871 until 2000 provides a sense of the types of barriers that limited women's entry to and success at this elite engineering institution. The story is a common one: women were present in very small numbers all along, but their experiences typically ranged from marginalization to outright sexism. Ellen Swallow was the first woman allowed to study at MIT in 1871. However, she already had a bachelor's degree from Vassar and was admitted to MIT as a "special" student which meant that she did not have to pay tuition. This may sound like a good deal, but it was actually an institutional strategy that allowed administrators to hide her presence if necessary. Swallow (later Richards after she married an engineering professor at MIT) built a career at MIT where she volunteered her services and even raised money to found the MIT Women's Laboratory which served to prepare women for successful scientific study. Between 1880 and 1910, Richards' leadership was critical to the development of a new field that allowed women entrée to scientific study and a new vocabulary to accompany it (e.g., home economics, domestic science, and nutrition education).

Like many other women scientists, Richards' strategy was not to deny traditional gender roles nor to align herself with "feminists," but to capitalize on women's role as homemakers with the addition of scientific training, most especially chemistry. The field of home economics became one of the major entry points for women into the sciences. Richards' work forever altered the landscape for women in scientific education and employment. In spite of these achievements, most of her work was unpaid and unacknowledged by the scientific community. She was one of three women chemists (the others were Lydia Shattuck and Bessie Capen) who attended an 1874 meeting that led to the formation of the American Chemical Society. However, the women were denied admittance to the organization and were not even included in the "official photograph" of the organization. A rare exception to employment barriers was the access women had to state boards of public health. Ellen Richards was the first woman to serve on the Massachusetts State Board of Public Health. The field grew rapidly at the turn of the 20th century due to a series of epidemics of infectious diseases such as tuberculosis, diphtheria, typhoid, and poliomyelitis. The state agencies needed many bacteriologists, and could not afford to hire men. These organizations could pay significantly lower salaries to women, which made this a rapidly growing employment opportunity for female scientists (Bix, 2000; Rossiter, 1982).

Bix (2000) recounts the history of women at MIT, and the narrative of the university corroborates the types of barriers (some subtle, some overt) that Rossiter outlines in her more extensive history. Although a few women were allowed to study, by the late 1800s their numbers remained very low. The total number of women admitted to MIT was about 45 per year in the 1920s, 50 per year in the 1930s, 65 per year in the early 1940s, and by 1958-59 there were 125 women among more than 5,000 men. One common excuse for not admitting more women was the "lack of adequate facilities" both on campus and in terms of housing. This inspired debate about equal treatment, with some arguing that women who chose to come to a "man's school" should not ask for special treatment and others arguing that women's "educational and personal needs differed from those of male students"

(Bix, 2000, p. 27). What often goes unscrutinized in these types of debates is the fact that women face institutional (and interpersonal) barriers that men do not face. Since these barriers make their experience different by definition, fairness may necessitate different accommodations of all types from housing to pedagogy.

In 1939, following decades of debate, MIT appointed librarian "Florence Stiles, a 1923 MIT graduate, to the semiofficial post of adviser to women students" (Bix, 2000, p. 25). In 1945, MIT established housing for women, but it was a half-hour commute to campus via subway and only allowed space for 14 new admits per year. So, rather than helping to increase enrollment, space limitations in fact allowed admissions staff to discourage women applicants and to evaluate women more selectively than men. "In 1960, philanthropist Katharine McCormick (MIT class of 1904) pledged $1.5 million to build MIT's first on-campus women's dorm" (Bix, 2000, p. 25). This was the beginning of the end of the space-limitation argument as an excuse for not admitting women. However, gaining access was not enough; there were still many other discriminatory barriers for women to overcome to successfully complete their studies.

African-American Pioneers: Shirley Ann Jackson and Jennie Patrick

Two stories of two courageous women pioneers who graduated from MIT in the 1970s illustrate the challenges women faced. Shirley Ann Jackson (born in 1946) began her elementary education riding the bus from the predominantly White neighborhood of Washington, D.C., where she and her social worker mother and postal worker father lived, to a Black elementary school across town. By the time Jackson attended Roosevelt High School, times were beginning to change. She completed an accelerated math and science program as valedictorian of her 1964 class. Jackson attributes her success in part to both parents' persistent emphasis on the value of education and to her supportive high school math and science teachers. Jackson studied physics at MIT where she was one of "about forty-three women" including one other African-American female and one of "about ten African-Americans" in the 900-member freshman class (Jordan, 2006, p. 124; Warren, 1999, p. 128).

As a member of two socially-subordinate groups, Jackson had to navigate both racism and sexism that left her working (and even eating) alone; neither the White women nor the Black men viewed her as part of their group. Jackson completed her degree in physics in 1968 and was accepted to the graduate physics programs at Harvard, Brown, and the University of Chicago. However, she chose to stay at MIT where she "had already been active in urging the university to admit more minorities" (Warren, 1999, p. 129). In 1973, she became the first Black woman to earn a Ph.D. at MIT, and the first Black woman in the nation to earn a doctorate in physics. Dr. Jackson has since spent her career as a researcher in particle physics (at such places as the Fermi Lab, CERN, Bell Labs), chair of the Nuclear Regulatory Commission, and now president of Rensselaer Polytechnic Institute (RPI) (the oldest nonmilitary engineering school in the U.S.) (Ambrose et al., 1997; Warren, 1999). As president of RPI, Dr. Jackson initiated *The Rensselaer Plan*, a strategic blueprint for institutional transformation that included hiring more than 180 new faculty (allowing reductions in class size and student/faculty ratios), completing $500 million in renovations and additions for research, teaching, and student facilities, and innovations in curriculum, undergraduate research, and student life initiatives. Dr. Jackson's story is even more remarkable given the fact that physics remains one of the most underrepresented sciences for women and for students of color ("Shirley," 2007; Warren, 1999).

The second story is of Jennie Patrick, who was the first Black woman to earn a Ph.D. in chemical engineering in the U.S. Patrick benefited from the love and encouragement of her parents. However, due to their own lack of formal education, they were not even able to help her with her school work. Patrick was among the first generation of Blacks to integrate Southern schools in Alabama, and this experience shaped her in significant ways. She comments: "Not only did I have to survive academically, but also emotionally, psychologically, and physically . . . I made a commitment to succeed. Perhaps even more important was my commitment to myself, my forefathers, and African-American people" (Warren, 1999, p. 220). Patrick was true to her commitments, completing a B.S. in chemical engineering at the University of California, Berkeley (1973) and a Ph.D. in chemical engineering at MIT (1979). She experienced explicit racism and sexism at both universities. At UCB, where she was the first African-American in chemical engineering in 10 years, Patrick recounts how the professor of her senior chemical engineering design class forced her to do her design project alone while "other students worked in teams of four persons" (Jordan, 2006, p. 167). At MIT, Patrick encountered more African-Americans in general, and "four or five Black graduate students, including African graduate students" (Jordan, 2006, p. 167). However, Patrick also described her experience at MIT as follows:

MIT is known for its challenging and rigorous academic program. For an African-American, the challenge was even greater. Not only did I have to conquer the academic challenge, but I also had to be emotionally and psychologically strong enough to overcome the racism. (Warren, 1999, p. 200)

Patrick spent about a decade as a research scientist at GE and the Phillip Morris Research Center; she is now a 3M Eminent Scholar Professor in chemical engineering at Tuskegee University, formerly known as the Tuskegee Institute (Jordan, 2006).

These two stories raise some important questions. How different might the experiences of these two women at MIT have been if they had been there at the same time (Jackson completed her graduate work the year that Patrick was entering graduate study)? What happened to those who did not have the internal courage to face such obstacles as these alone? How many women and students of color were lost to science and technology not because they were not smart enough, but because they could not endure the emotional and social isolation (or in some cases overt abuse) caused by sexism and racism? What if either of these women had also known the history of other Black women in science who had succeeded before them against even greater obstacles?

The MIT story is a good example of what was happening nationwide. Although some women had begun to gain access to undergraduate degrees in the 1800s, they did not gain full access to doctoral degrees in the U.S. until as late as the 1960s at some institutions, notably Princeton. "Many graduate schools were reluctant to accept women in the late 1960s, and the reason, they said, was that women were so unpredictable, idiosyncratic, and unreliable—so, in a word, unmasculine" (Tavris, 1992, p. 37). Christine Ladd-Franklin's story surely reflects the experience of many women who went ahead and completed doctoral work in spite of the fact that their institutions would not award them a degree. Ladd-Franklin completed her doctoral studies at Johns Hopkins in 1882 at a time when the university did not grant Ph.D.s to women. "Finally, in 1926, at its fiftieth anniversary celebration, The Johns Hopkins University awarded a long overdue doctorate... Christine Ladd-Franklin... now a sprightly seventy-nine-year-old, made it a point to attend the ceremonies and collect her degree forty-four years late" (Rossiter, 1982, p. 46).

Historical Barriers to Employment

For those few women who managed to scale the barriers to education, there were new barriers in terms of access to employment in academics, the private sector, and the government. In the 1800s, the primary "career" option for educated women was teaching. Even in teaching, women were already experiencing the ghettoization of the only real profession that was accessible to them. In New England in the late 1830s, about one-half of all public school teachers were women, and they were being paid only 40% of what their male peers earned (Rossiter, 1982, p. 5). For another 50 years, teaching would remain one of the few professions open to women, but it would provide barely a subsistence living. The privilege to work at less than half pay as teachers was reserved almost exclusively for European-American women. Few African-American women were allowed to teach; those who did served entirely minority populations for even less money.

In higher education, women scientists were increasingly hired to teach at the newly forming public universities, but those women rarely rose above the rank of associate professor even "after decades of service teaching heavy loads of introductory courses" (Rossiter, 1995, p. 130). Women were channeled into low (or *no*) paying research jobs in part due to the anti-nepotism rules that prohibited husbands and wives from being employed on the same faculty. There were occasional token women in some of the science programs. Some, such as Nobel Prize winner Maria Goeppart Meyer, even filled the "new category of 'volunteer professor'" and taught without pay (Rossiter, 1995, p. 141). The fact that many women scientists were willing to work without pay in order to do their research is another factor that contributes to the gender differences in salaries and employment in the academy that is still evident today.

World War II created tremendous employment opportunities for women in general, and especially for women scientists. Many were employed at the newly developing government organizations such as the Bureau of Labor Statistics and agricultural research units. But, the government had no qualms about paying women less money than they paid men in equivalent positions. In fact, the government was eager to hire women into certain positions because they *could* pay them less. In 1938, while the average salary for men in one Civil Service category was $3,214, women in the same category earned an average salary of $2,299—almost $1,000 or 40% less (Rossiter, 1982, p. 235).

The Navy WAVES, Army WAACS, and Coast Guard SPARS created some of the best opportunities for women in science because they "could receive the advancement denied to them elsewhere" by becoming veterans and reaping all of the postwar benefits that this implied (especially education and home loans) (Rossiter, 1995, p. 8). However, there was also a quota on the number of women who could be "in the highest ranks of military and naval officers" (p. 294). There were "separate lists for men and women 'eligibles'" that allowed "the appointing officer to specify which sex he (rarely she) preferred for any position" (p. 294). According to Rossiter (1995), "a spot survey . . . showed that for 94 percent of the jobs at the GS levels 13–15 the requests were for men only" (p. 294).

Women in industry faced far more limiting employment environments than those in the academic or government sectors. They were prey to many of the same sort of limitations we still see today. Women could only advance so far and were channeled into certain positions more than others, such as librarians, technical writers, and research assistants. One notable exception is the small group of women with undergraduate degrees in mathematics that were hired as early "computers" to work on the first general purpose computer, the ENIAC (Electronic Numerical Integrator and Computer) from 1942 to 1955 (Fritz, 1996; Stanley, 1995).

Ultimately, the tremendous economic growth in the 40s through the 60s "that could have made room for more and better-trained scientists of both sexes did not benefit the two equally; in fact, it generally unleashed certain forces that hastened the women's exit and subsequent marginalization and underutilization" (Rossiter, 1995, p. xv). Gradually, due to such factors as post-war displacement and demotion, anti-nepotism rules (especially at universities), and the emphasis on "prestigious research" even at women's colleges, many of the women who had entered the sciences in the first half of the century were forced out and replaced by men in both the academy and in industry (Rossiter, 1995, p. xv).

Education, Employment, and Earnings Today

In spite of the somewhat positive influence of Affirmative Action, this historical legacy of barriers to scientific education and the professions informs the degree to which, and the ways in which women participate in technology today both as users and developers. In 1994, although women in the United States earned over 50% of the awarded bachelor's degrees, they earned only 28% of the undergraduate degrees in computer science and engineering, and this number has been steadily declining since a high of 37.1% in the early 80s (Camp, 1997, p. 105). In 1996, the number of women who earned doctoral degrees in computer science and information science was even lower, only 15.1% (Schiebinger, 1999, p. 199). The number of women of color who earned computer science and information science doctorates in 1996 is so low that percentages have not even been calculated by researchers. The *actual number* of women in the United States who earned doctorates in computer and information science in 1996 (including European Americans for comparative purposes) is as follows: 3 African-Americans, 16 Asian/Pacific Islanders, 61 European Americans, 7 Hispanic, and 2 Native American (Schiebinger, 1999, pp. 201-202).

Women's salaries have not improved much either. In a report titled "The Gender Wage Ratio: Women's and Men's Earnings," (2007) the Institute for Women's Policy Research reports that women's median annual earnings in relation to men's remained "constant from 1955 through the 1970s" ranging from 63.9 to 58.8 and then began to steadily increase through the 80s, grow modestly through the 90s, and reach an "all-time high of 76.6" in 2002, but the ratio fell back to 75.5 in 2003. Data on median annual income in 2003 from the U.S. Census Bureau adds to this picture: White men $30,732; White women $17,422; Black men $21,986; Black women $16,581; Asian men $32,291; Asian women $17,679; Hispanic men $21,053; Hispanic women $13,642 (U.S. Census, 2003). This census report did not include data on other cultural or ethnic groups, such as Native American. These data together show that women still earn less than men overall and that when race is also as a factor, the additive differences are profound.

If you think that women are doing better in terms of median annual earnings in information technology jobs, you are partially correct. The overall earnings picture for women in technology is much brighter than in the female population as a whole, but there is still a gender gap. Some of the overall increase in annual median income is accounted for by education, since income increases in direct correlation with number of years of education. Several recent reports demonstrate that there is still a gender gap in annual salaries. For example, a 1999 survey in *Network World* reported that while men's earnings averaged $67,237 (base salary) and $77,322 (total compensation), women's earnings averaged $51,789 (base salary) and $55,596 (total compensation); men are earning 23% more than women in base salary and 28% more than women overall (Weinberg, 1999). A 2003 survey of 21,000 technology professionals by Dice, Inc. reports that the average salary for technology professionals is $69,400 and that the gender gap decreased for the first time in this survey's history and is down to 11%. "When segmenting by age, women over 50 had the largest gap, earning 13.5% less than their male counterparts" and, the "gender gap remained lowest (8%) in the Mountain region and was highest in the south an mid-Atlantic states (15%)" ("Technology salaries rise," 2004). Clearly, education makes a difference, as does working in technology, but the point is that there is still a difference.

CONCLUSION

This may seem like a bleak history, one whose legacy weighs heavily on possible solutions. It is true that the historical legacy of women's poor access to science and technology education and employment influences their participation today. However, it is also reasonable to assume that one reason why we repeat the mistakes of our historical past is that we have only known part of our history. Part of the solution lies in telling all of our stories. We need to know about all of the women and people of color who have gone before, who managed to thrive in science and technology in times far more oppressive than these, who managed to study, who managed to do the work that they loved, and who managed to invent things in spite of living as second-class citizens in a sexist and racist society. The potential that lies in knowing our true history as a human species is limitless.

QUESTIONS FOR REFLECTIVE DIALOG

1.   Consider the metaphor of mountain climbing in relation to science education. Imagine a sign posted at a high elevation that directed climbers to reach higher

because others had attained this height before. How might that feel? Did you have an individual whose accomplishments inspired you to higher education or inspired you to seek new professional challenges? Describe individuals who have been mentors to you either educationally or professionally. How did they encourage you to grow? Have you been a mentor to others?

2. One of the early reasons offered by women pioneers for including women in public education was because of their responsibility to create a moral culture through childrearing. Draw a family tree and look at the level of education obtained by the members of your family of origin. Compare the male and female degree completion levels and make a list of observations. What did you discover?

3. What does it mean to be educated? Consider your experiences in education to date. What learning environments help you learn? Think about the worst class that you ever had to take. What made that learning environment difficult? How did other students react to the class? How would you describe the perfect educational environment? What would the classroom look like? How would the teacher behave?

4. Consider some of the women in this chapter who have contributed to science and technology. How many of the inventors and scientists were you familiar with before reading this chapter? Are you aware of many female trendsetters in your chosen professional field?

5. Think of your early introduction to scientific and technical education. What was your reaction? Did you enjoy creating scientific experiments when you were younger? Did you enjoy dabbling on the computer? Did you ever pursue scientific research as a child (a fascination with dinosaurs would be an example)? Did you ever take things apart and put them back together? Was there any encouragement by members of your family to become interested in science or technology outside of the classroom?

REFERENCES[1]

Ambrose, S. A., Dunkle, K. L., Lazarus, B. B., Nair, I., & Harkus, D. A. (1997). *Journeys of women in science and engineering: No universal constants*. Philadelphia: Temple UP.

Arditti, R. (1980). Feminism and science. In R. Arditti et al. (Eds.), *Science and liberation* (pp. 350-368). Boston: South End.

Barker, L. J., & Aspray, W. (2006). The state of research on girls and IT. In J. M. Cohoon & W. Aspray (Eds.), *Women and information technology: Research on underrepresentation.* (pp. 3-54). Cambridge, MA: MIT Press.

Belenky, M. F., et al. (1986). *Women's ways of knowing: The development of self, voice, and mind.* New York: Basic.

Bix, A. S. (2000). Feminism where men predominate: The history of women's science and engineering education at MIT. *Women's Studies Quarterly, 28*(1/2), 24-45.

Bucciarelli, D. (2004). If we could really feel: The need for emotions of care within the disciplines. In R. Eisler & R. Miller (Eds.), *Educating for a culture of peace* (pp. 136-159). Portsmouth, NH: Heinemann.

Camp, T. (1997). The incredible shrinking pipeline. *Communications of the ACM, 40*(10), 103-110.

Estrin, T. (1996). Women's studies and computer science: Their intersection. *IEEE Annals of the History of Computing, 18*(3), 43-46.

Fritz, W. B. (1996). The women of ENIAC. *IEEE Annals of the History of Computing, 18*(3), 13-28.

Goldberger, N., et al. (Eds.). (1996). *Knowledge, difference, and power: Essays inspired by women's ways of knowing.* New York: Basic.

Greenbaum, J. (1990). The head and the heart: Using gender analysis to study the social construction of computer systems. *Computers and Society, 20*(2), 9-17.

Jordan, D. (2006). *Sisters in science: Conversations with black women scientists on race, gender, and their passion for success.* West Lafayette, IN: Purdue UP.

Keller, E. F. (1992). *Secrets of life, secrets of death: Essays on language, gender and science.* New York: Routledge.

Kramer, P. E., & Lehman, S. (1990). Mismeasuring women: A critique of research on computer ability and avoidance. *Signs, 16*(11), 158-172.

Lerner, G. (1993). *The creation of feminist consciousness: From the Middle Ages to eighteen-seventy.* New York: Oxford.

Origination of the HBCU concept. (2007). *Historically Black Colleges and Universities Network.* Retrieved on August 15, 2007, from http://www.hbcunetwork.com

Osen, L. (1974). *Women in mathematics.* Cambridge: MIT P.

Reynolds, M. D. (1999). *American women scientists: 23 inspiring biographies, 1900-2000.* Jefferson, NC: McFarland & Co.

Riger, S. (1992). Epistemological debates, feminist voices. *American Psychologist, 47*(6), 730-740.

Rosser, S. V. (Ed.). (1995). *Teaching the majority: Breaking the gender barrier in science, mathematics, and engineering.* New York: Teachers College.

Rosser, S. V. (1997). *Re-engineering female friendly science.* New York: Teachers College.

Rossiter, M. W. (1982). *Women scientists in America: Struggles and strategies to 1940.* Baltimore: Johns Hopkins.

Rossiter, M. W. (1995). *Women scientists in America: Before affirmative action 1940–1972.* Baltimore: Johns Hopkins.

Sadker, M., & Sadker, D. (1995). *Failing at fairness: How our schools cheat girls.* New York: Touchstone.

Schiebinger, L. (1999). *Has feminism changed science?* Cambridge, MA: Harvard.

Science leadership. (2007). Retrieved August 16, 2007, from http://www.mtholyoke.edu/acad/science.shtml

Seymour, E., & Hewitt, N. M. (1997). *Talking about leaving: Why undergraduates leave the sciences.* Boulder, CO: Westview.

Shirley Ann Jackson, Ph.D. (2007, May 8). Retrieved August 16, 2007, from http://www.rpi.edu/president/profile.html

Sonnert, G. (1995). *Gender differences in science careers: The project access study.* New Brunswick, NJ.

Stanley, A. (1995). *Mothers and daughters of invention: Notes for a revised history of technology.* New Brunswick, NJ: Rutgers UP.

Tavris, C. (1992). *The mismeasure of woman.* New York: Touchstone.

Technology salaries recover and gender gap narrows, according to Dice annual salary survey of 21,000 technology professionals. (2004, February 3). Retrieved March 7, 2005, from http://marketing.dice.com/releases/salaryrelease.html

The gender wage ratio: Women's and men's earnings. (2007, April). *Institute for Women's Policy Research.* Retrieved July 12, 2007, from www.iwpr.org

The rise of women's colleges. (2007) Retrieved August 15, 2007, from http://www.womenscolleges.org/history/

Tolley, K. (2003). *The science education of American girls: A historical perspective.* New York: RoutledgeFalmer.

Toole, B. A. (1992). *Ada, the enchantress of numbers: A selection from the letters of Lord Byron's daughter and her description of the first computer.* Mill Valley, CA: Strawberry.

Turkle, S., & Papert, S. (1990). Epistemological pluralism: Styles and voices within the computer culture. *Signs, 16*(1), 128-157.

U.S. Census. (2003). *Federal records pertaining to median wage by race and gender.* Retrieved August 15, 2007, from www.census.gov

Warren, W. (1999). *Black women scientists in the United States.* Bloomington, IN: Indiana UP.

Weinberg, N. (1999, July 26). Shortchanged by sex. *Network World.* Retrieved March 10, 2005, from InfoTrac database

Williams, S. W. (1999, January 1). *History of black women in the mathematical sciences.* Retrieved October 16, 1999, from http://www.math.buffalo.edu/mad/wohist.html

ENDNOTE

[1]   Some portions of this chapter may have appeared in, and are reprinted with permission from Kirk, M. (2006). Bridging the digital divide: A feminist perspective on the project. In G. Trajkovski (Ed.), *Diversity in information technology education: Issues and controversies* (pp. 38-67). Hershey, PA: Information Science Publishing.

Chapter VII
Business as Social Institution:
Global Issues in IT

OBJECTIVES

This chapter aims to help you understand the following:

- The values that inform dominator economics and how the process for funding scientific and technical research in the U.S. guides those values.
- The shifts in global economic wealth (historically and today) and how those shifts have influenced the development of scientific and technical knowledge.
- The power that trans-national corporations (TNCs), many of which are wealthier than some nations, wield to influence changing fortunes in the global IT business.
- The relationship between economic globalization and global poverty.
- Why the global IT industry cannot afford to continue to operate as a dominator institution—the social costs.

INTRODUCTION

The global IT business as a social institution reflects the same dominator values as other social institutions in the U.S. Since IT is a large and increasingly powerful industry worldwide, the question of what kinds of values the business purveys holds growing significance to our human community. Further, our ways of doing business are defined by the economic models that we adopt. The term "economics" can be used in two ways: (1) in reference to the academic discipline "that deals with the production, distribution, and consumption of goods and services"; and (2) in popular reference to describe "economic systems, policies and practices" (Eisler, 2007, p. 11). In this chapter, I refer to the latter—economic systems, policies, and practices—as we explore the following topics: (1) the dominator economic values reflected in the global IT business; (2) the relationship between postcolonialism and U.S. participation in dominator global economic development; and (3) the rising social and political significance of economic development in India and China with specific relation to the IT industry. I end this chapter with an in-depth example of a global IT giant to demonstrate the effects of dominator economic decisions on the Holocaust during World War II.

WHAT VALUES INFORM DOMINATOR ECONOMICS?

In *The Real Wealth of Nations: Creating a Caring Economics*, Riane Eisler (2007) explores the features of our current dominator economic systems.[1] "During the last five hundred years of Western history, different technological phases gave rise to different economic systems. Gradually, as we shifted from mainly agricultural to primarily industrial technologies, feudalism was replaced by capitalism and in some areas, socialism" (Eisler, 2007, p. 15). Capitalism emerged because it was preferable to the earlier feudal systems where nobles and kings owned most resources. Capitalism also contributed to the development of representative constitutional monarchies and republics and was a major factor in the creation of the middle class.

Marx and Engels developed their thinking about scientific socialism in the 19th century "when it was clear that capitalism was not fulfilling Smith's vision of an economics that works for the common good" (Eisler, 2007, p. 142). Eisler (2007) demonstrates how neither the capitalist free market (envisioned by Adam Smith) nor the scientific socialism (envisioned by Karl Marx and Friedrich Engels) could be realized in a dominator social system. "Smith's assumption that competition would counter self-interest did not factor in the emergence of ferocious financiers, men like J.P. Morgan and Cornelius Vanderbilt, who ruthlessly used chicanery, bribery, and force to smash both competitors and union organizers" (p. 147). Similarly, Marx and Engels' vision of a "just and egalitarian system" was also difficult to manifest in the midst of dominator values about control "by ruthless men from the top" (p. 147). In the end, neither economic system fully manifested their vision due to the "underlying dominator beliefs, structures, and habits we've inherited" (p. 117).

The global IT business operates largely within a capitalist economic model. One way in which capitalism reflects dominator values is the emphasis on individualism over the community, specifically the sense of entitlement for individuals and corporations to earn whatever they can without consideration of any social good. The explicit and deliberate separation between profit and not-for-profit businesses in this system is both completely acceptable and largely unquestioned. It is another classic example of a kind of "either/or" that could just as easily be a "both/and." What if a business could both make money and serve a greater social good? It is a question that is rarely asked as the familiar dominator constructs of power-over and competitiveness take on new forms in relation to the global IT business. However, as global economist Marilyn Waring suggests in a film on global economics, "the system cannot respond to values it does not recognize" (Martin & Nash, 1997). So, it is important to understand the values that inform the global IT business if we are to create change.

The dominator model for economic development that we operate under today is narrowly conceptualized "as increased economic productivity, bereft of concern for the preservation and improvement of natural resources, local community relations, non-western cultures, or women's conditions" (Harding, 1998, p. 81). It is precisely this attitude that has contributed to a rapidly growing gap between the haves and the have-nots in our global economy. Eisler (2002) adds that "the terms *free enterprise* and *free market* are often code words for economic predation, worker exploitation, and environmental degradation—and that these practices are mainly the result of bad economic rules and models rather than bad people" (p. 115). Eisler (2007) explains the fallacies of our dominator economic model:

As current economic theory has it, what is valued is a matter of supply and demand, with scarce goods and services more valued than abundant ones. But this ignores two key points. The first . . . is that current economic policies and practices often artificially create scarcities. The second point . . . is that demand is largely determined by cultural beliefs about what is and is not valuable. (p. 16)

If, as Eisler suggests, cultural beliefs about what we value shape economics, how can we identify the cultural beliefs in the U.S. that shape the global IT business?

Research Funding in the U.S.

One way to identify the values guiding the global IT business in the U.S. is to examine the recent history of how academic scientific and technological research is funded. Federally-funded research has profoundly influenced the kind of science and technology we develop. Between the end of World War II (1945) and the Soviet launch of Sputnik (1957), "80% or more of all federally funded research was justified in terms of national security needs" (Sarewitz, 2000, p. 87-88). By 1965, the burgeoning space program had contributed to the development of a myriad of technologies that supported national defense. This established a research organization that was dominated by physical science, and fostered a dependent relationship between academic research universities, research scientists, and the government agencies that funded them. Sarewitz (2000) comments:

The persistence of this organization can be seen in the continued dominance of three agencies—the Department of Defense, NASA, and the succession of energy research agencies—which peaked at nearly 90% of the federal R&D budget at the height of the Apollo program in 1965, and today still constitutes 66% of all federal research and development spending. (pp. 88-89)

Many IT-related fields, such as electrical engineering and computer science, continue to receive much of their research funding from the Departments of Defense and Energy (a descendent of the Atomic Energy Commission). Therefore, the IT research policy agenda has exacerbated the top-down, science-over-nature approaches to science and technology that were intrinsically established by a dominator philosophy of science. Although this agenda may have once been justified as fulfilling a human need, the costs of actually trying to "control nature" without consideration of how these technologies may impact complex human organisms and global ecosystems has inspired many to challenge the efficacy of this power-over approach. Marilyn Waring (Martin & Nash, 1997) and Vandana Shiva (1997) offer examples of the negative effects of global economics in agriculture; both describe how this live-for-today approach to economics has moved entire countries into an unceasing battle with starvation and malnutrition as they give up land to large agricultural concerns that grow crops for export, while eliminating the small subsistence farms that used to operate in their place.

Daniel Sarewitz (2000) names a series of problems that have arisen as a result of this research funding model. Scientific and technological developments have not equally benefited the rich and poor globally, and the proliferation of technology has introduced a new kind of instability to the notion of community, a critical component of a functioning democracy. He proposes that scientific researchers, governments, and other funding sources re-envision their notion of what it means for science to serve human well-being in terms of both individual and collective needs for survival, human dignity, and the leveling of the civic and moral playing field (Sarewitz, 2000, p. 87). In short, he suggests that we consider the context in which science and technology operate in terms of making decisions about what knowledge to pursue. These ideas directly challenge dominator economic values.

Robert Young (1987) asked the following questions about the direction of scientific research: "Where do scientists' questions come from? What leads to the priorities, agendas, assumptions and fashions of science?" (p. 18). Young offers the example of U.S. pharmaceutical companies to demonstrate ways in which commercial interests in the global economy influence scientific research. Young explains that "the vast sales of vitamins in metropolitan countries bears no relationship to the real need . . . this same drug industry does not develop cheap vaccines against malaria and other diseases because the potential purchasers of such products cannot afford them" (p. 25). Young's long term solution to this issue is to broaden science education to encompass "a historical and social approach to knowledge . . . examine the social forces and connections (or articulations) of scientific and technological disciplines and research problems" (p. 22).

The history of research on sickle cell anemia offers another example of the ways in which research funding is influenced by dominator social values. Michaelson (1987) shares the story of a disease that was not high on the research agenda while it was killing far more people than the "hot" diseases were. In the U.S. in 1979, 1 in 500 Blacks had sickle cell anemia and about 50,000 were dying from it, while another 2 million carried the trait (pp. 61-62). Only a few years earlier in 1967, "there were an estimated 1,155 new cases of sickle cell anemia and 1,206 of cystic fibrosis" (p. 62). In spite of the fact that the numbers of new cases of both diseases were similar, volunteer organizations only raised $100,000 for sickle cell anemia and $1.9 million for cystic fibrosis (p. 62). Sickle cell anemia is directly tied to African ancestry; 98% of those with cystic fibrosis are White. It seems difficult to deny that there was a racial dimension influencing which research was better funded.

The vast funding discrepancy demonstrates the different value placed on human lives according to race. However, there is another factor in this story that adds further weight to the argument that social context matters with regard to scientific and technical research. More current research has shown that the sickle cell trait is actually an adaptive trait for Blacks in Africa where it gives them a certain protection from malaria (p. 65). The colonial institution of slavery forcibly transported people from their native land where they had developed biological advantages for survival, and placed them in a new environment where their adaptive advantage became biologically maladaptive, resulting in a life-threatening physical ailment. A scientific community that considered social context might have made the link to the increased importance of sickle cell research as a form of recompense for the moral obscenity of slavery, and its very literal physical cost. Unfortunately, our "beliefs about what is or is not valuable are largely unconscious" and in our current dominator economic system we fail "to give real value to caring and caregiving, whether in families or in the larger society" and this "continues to lie behind massive economic inequities and dysfunctions" (Eisler, 2007, p. 15).

Dominator or Caring Economics?

A conscious consideration of social concerns rarely plays a role in the technology that is developed today. A story about Bill Gates, who became the wealthiest man in the world by founding and building Microsoft into a worldwide IT corporate giant, illustrates my point. Recently, he and Melinda Gates (his wife), founded a non-profit organization whose mission is to improve conditions related to health and education worldwide. The Bill and Melinda Gates Foundation is guided by the following "two simple values": (1) "All lives—no matter where they are being led—have equal value"; and (2) "To whom much has been given, much is expected" ("Our values," n.d.). In addition, one of the 15 Guiding Principles for the foundation is: "Science and technology have great potential to improve lives around the world" ("Our guiding," n.d.). These statements of the foundation's values and principles reflect a positive step in the direction of linking technology with larger social concerns. However, in practice, there is a huge chasm between the work of the non-profit foundation and development decisions at for-profit global IT giant Microsoft.

Two recent examples support my point. In a 2006 interview with PBS-journalist Charlie Rose, Gates discussed the work of the foundation, and then shared new development ideas planned at Microsoft. While Gates discussed the global health and education concerns that his foundation was working to address, I was impressed with his intelligent, data-supported, serious, and caring demeanor. However, as he began to discuss new ideas under development at Microsoft, Gates' shifted into a much more animated here's-the-latest-cool-toy tone and made no apparent connection between the large scale social concerns that he had just discussed and the development of new technologies at Microsoft. Although moments earlier Gates seemed to clearly understand the depth and dimension of some of the global social concerns we face (including the growing global technology gap), he made no explicit connection between those issues and the development decisions being made at Microsoft.

A few weeks later at the 40th International Consumer Electronics Show, Gates's keynote speech touted the "connected experience" that is the centerpiece of Microsoft's latest technology linking personal computers, stereos, TVs, and cell phones. Gates described how one new software product (Sports Lounge) will deliver "Fox Sports news and statistics around a TV broadcast of a game," and another product (Sync) will link cell phones with car stereos and "allow users to beam their address books and music files from cell phones to their cars" (Pegoraro & Noguchi, 2007). In a global environment where Gates' own foundation clearly understands that having enough clean water to drink and being able to read are still major issues worldwide, how vital is it to link user's cell phones with their car stereos?

The point is not that "toys" are bad, or that people in the richest country in the world should not be free to spend their earnings in whatever way they choose, or that Microsoft should convert itself into the world's largest social service organization. I am making a both/and argument here, not an either/or. The issue I want to raise is one of balance and scale. How many people will benefit from these types of innovations? How many people worldwide *need* to be able to see sports statistics on their TV screen while they are watching the game? Even in the U.S., how many people can afford the bandwidth to make this product accessible? What might happen if we devoted *some* of our IT resources (by this I mean creative human capital as well as research dollars) towards developing technology that served a broader social need? What if the resources spent on developing a product that allows a wealthy U.S. American to listen to an incoming text message from their cell phone on their car stereo, were instead spent on an issue with broader social significance? What global human concerns might our IT business contribute to solving then? These are the questions that rarely get asked in a dominator economic system.

POSTCOLONIALISM AND DOMINATOR ECONOMICS IN IT

Postcolonial studies offer a valuable lens through which to observe and identify the core assumptions that support dominator economics in relation to the development of science and IT in the U.S. In *Is Science Multicultural: Postcolonialisms, Feminisms, and Epistemologies*, Sandra Harding (1998) describes how the end of "formal European colonial rule in the 1960s" spawned a new field of knowledge called postcolonial studies from which "a new kind of global history . . . emerged—one that has charted the continual encounters and exchanges between cultures from the beginnings of human history through the present" (p. 23). She explains that contrary to the tunnel vision that charts Western science from the Garden of Eden to the present, these new perspectives acknowledge that many scientific developments occurred "rapidly due to the need for scientific and technological information to speed along the Voyages of Discovery" (p. 27). Harding (1998) argues that scientific development in Western Europe was assisted by "borrowings from the scientific and technological traditions of the cultures that expanding Europe encountered" (p. 27). Unfortunately, this information flow was largely one way, which meant that while European cultures benefited from vast amounts of knowledge from other cultures, the other cultures did not benefit equally in return. Further, these other cultures were rarely credited as the source of the scientific idea or innovation. A few examples follow:

The principles of pre-Columbian agriculture, that provided potatoes for almost every European ecological niche and thereby had a powerful effect on the nutrition and subsequent history of Europe was subsumed into European science. Mathematical achievements from India and Arabic cultures provide other such examples. The magnetic needle, rudder, gunpowder, and many other technologies useful to Europeans . . . were borrowed from China. (Harding, 1998, p. 35)

Harding (1998) documents how Western Europe developed quite literally at the expense of other cultures and argues that this is at least a partial explanation for why many remain "underdeveloped" economically today. Harding (1998) identifies six main ways in which this "de-development" occurred: (1) extracting raw materials from foreign lands that supported the growth of European societies; (2) extracting labor from other cultures (sometimes involuntary or slave labor); (3) extracting local scientific and technological knowledge (many of the botanical gardens in Europe were the result of specimens collected overseas); (4) destroying local trades/industries, some of them deliberately, to make room for European replacements (such as the Indian and African dying and weaving markets); (5) annihilating local populations through disease, warfare, and slavery (small pox rapidly decimated indigenous populations in the Americas in numbers ranging from 50 to 100% in some communities); and (6) devaluing and destroying local cultural traditions (pp. 39-50).

Eurocentrism both contributed to and was reified by the historical legacy of colonial scientific and technical development. Harding (1998) defines the following primary features of Eurocentrism: (1) the concepts, practices, and creations of peoples of European descent "express the unique heights of human development"; and (2) these concepts, practices, and creations are "fundamentally self-generated" and owe nothing to "the institutions, practices, conceptual schemes, or peoples of other parts of the world" (p. 14). This Eurocentric approach to science and technology in the West has made us prisoners of our "own historical 'tunnels' back through the centuries" (p. 8). Our view of the development of scientific and technical knowledge is inaccurately narrowed to exclude everything outside of the Eurocentric lens that proscribes it; there is a blindness to other historical and cultural influences that fall outside of this tunnel view. Gill and Levidow (1987) claim that the effects of such a Eurocentric view of science are that it:

masks the real political and economic priorities of science; hides its appropriation of non-Western scientific traditions; often attributes people's subordination or suffering to nature—be it biological or geographical factors—rather than to the way science and nature itself have been subordinated to political priorities; is permeated by an ideology of race, both racist in origin and racist in effect; plays a key part in an exploitative economic and political system; perpetuates assumptions about nature and human nature that support inequality; and is an alienating experience for many students. (p. 3)

The Eurocentric perspective also results in an emphasis on "modernity" where modern always equals better. There are several problems with this belief. One is that "women's knowledge, in both northern and southern cultures, is invariably conceptualized as premodern and therefore not socially progressive. It is represented as a kind of folk belief" (Harding, 1998, p. 106). The unquestioned belief in modernity also implicitly means that "development" is often gendered. With regard to the shift from primarily agrarian to primarily industrial economies, men move into new educational and job opportunities, while women lose status as land rights shift. However, paying attention to the status of women in a society "can be an even better predictor of quality of life than conventional indicators such as GNP or GDP," according to a study titled *Women, Men and the Global Quality of Life* conducted by the Center for Partnership Studies (Eisler, 2007, p. 89). Another problem with the unquestioned valuing of modernity as it relates to IT is that it often means purveying technological innovations from one sociocultural context to another. This transference proceeds without regard for whether or not the technology is relevant or meaningful in a different social context. Disregarding cultural context in IT development has the potential to turn the global IT industry into a neocolonial business sustaining the unequal relationships between nation states that were established during colonial history.

Although dominator societies have been prevalent worldwide for several thousand years, the West (historically just Europe, now including the U.S. and other industrialized nations) did not always dominate global economics. In *Three Billion New Capitalists: The Great Shift of Wealth and Power to the East*, economist Clyde Prestowitz (2005) shares a brief history of how the map of global wealth has been (and is now being) redefined. Prestowitz (2005) explains that in 1415 "China and the area we now call India produced about 75 percent of the global GDP. America was still undiscovered, and the countries of Europe were insignificant and backward" (p. 8). Prior to the voyages of discovery, the world's wealth was concentrated largely in the East. The first wave of globalization in 1415 began shifting that wealth to Western Europe via Portugal whose "sailing, navigational, and naval warfare technology . . . was superior to anything in Asia" (p. 9). Over the next 400 years, the Spanish, Dutch, English, French, U.S. Americans, and Japanese, "comprising less than 2 percent of the earth's surface and less than 20 percent of its population, exploited these advantages to create world-girdling empires that gave the West both economic and geopolitical dominance" (p. 10). The Industrial Revolution both cemented Western dominance and began to tie the world together "tighter than ever before" (p. 10).

Prestowitz (2005) defines the "second wave" of globalization as the period from 1947-2000 and argues that this was "orchestrated" by the U.S. with a different focus, that is, "instead of expansion, the focus was to rebuild areas devastated by the war and regain living standards and opportunities for a new generation" (p. 10). There was also an emphasis on creating a better trading system both to "avoid the pitfalls of the past" and to provide "an attractive alternative to the expanding communist model" thus defending against the threats of the Cold War (p. 10-11).

In July 1944, representatives from 44 nations attended a meeting in Bretton Woods, New Hampshire to forge a vision for a new global economy that would unite the world in economic interdependence and "preclude nations taking up arms" (Korten, 1995, p. 160). The result of these conversations was to establish the International Bank for Reconstruction and Development (the World Bank) and the International Monetary Fund (IMF); subsequent meetings led to the formation of the General Agreement on Tariffs and Trade (GATT). Although "these organizations were formally designated as 'special agencies' of the UN, the Bretton Woods institutions function nearly autonomously from it. Their governance and administrative processes are secret—carefully shielded from public scrutiny and democratic debate" (p. 160). Today, these practices and others have led some scholars to view the World Bank and IMF as purveyors of earlier "colonial" relationships between nations since they serve as "secret" administrators of "economic development" policies that never seem to adequately meet the needs of populations in developing countries (Harding, 1998; Henderson, 1996; Korten, 1995).

In a postcolonial context such as this, Harding (1998) suggests two important questions for those engaged in scientific and technological development to answer: (1) "To what extent does so-called development reverse at all the direction of the flow of resources that colonialism established in a one-way stream"; and (2) "To what extent are the benefits of modern sciences and technologies that reach developing countries distributed below the level of their small middle classes and the already wealthy aristocracies" (p. 50). One example supporting the value inherent in answering the second question is explored in *Hell to Pay*, a documentary film by Anderson and Cottringer (1988), that features Bolivian (among the poorest South American countries) peasant women discussing their country's economic debt burden. The women (who include miner's wives, teachers, and garment workers) discuss the ways in which government austerity programs (enacted by wealthy leaders who borrowed money from the World Bank for failed enterprises and now must pay it back) have negatively impacted their lives. One poignant scene features women knitting sweaters to earn a subsistence living while they discuss their country's economic situation with an intelligent awareness far surpassing that of most U.S. Americans (many of whom might have difficulty locating Bolivia on a map) about U.S. economic issues.

Indeed, knowledge of global economics is a key factor in understanding the varying social and political conditions that exist worldwide. Therefore, economics is especially important in the context of examining women's place as developers, users, and beneficiaries of IT globally. However, due to the legacy of colonialism, most Westerners have a limited understanding of "third world" or developing nations, especially regarding economics. Few understand that the global economic tide shifted from the East to the West beginning about 600 years ago, and that it is currently shifting back from the West to the East. This shift is already influencing the global IT industry in dramatic ways.

INDIA AND CHINA: RIDING THE CREST OF THE THIRD WAVE

Prestowitz (2005) says that the third wave of economic globalization began in the year 2000, and that India and China are riding its crest, "coming back into their own after six hundred years" thanks to technological innovations that have negated time and distance, as well as the "rapid transfer of technology from advanced to developing countries" (p. 16). The three primary drivers of this rapid globalization are: (1) containerized cargo shipping since 1956 ("the Box"); (2) continuing advances in global communications; and (3) cheap labor made available since the opening of China, the former Soviet Union, and India (Aronica & Ramdoo, 2006, p. 32). Many of the same forces that led to U.S. dominance during the second wave are now contributing to the shift of wealth to the East.

Meanwhile, the U.S. emphasis on consumption over any real economic policy has led to a trade deficit of over $600 billion, with Americans consuming more than we produce at about 6% of GDP annually (Prestowitz, 2005, p. 17). Eisler (2007) explains that "overconsumption and wastefulness by those on top is a perennial feature of dominator cultures" (p. 130). While other countries have economic policies that focus on saving and reinvesting in their own economies, the U.S. continues to emphasize consumer spending. In their critical analysis of Thomas Friedman's *The World is Flat*, Aronica and Ramdoo (2006) argue that perhaps:

the real issue is that America does not have a national industrial policy that identifies and strengthens the industries in which it wants to be the master in the twenty-first century. America's economic policies are, by and large, set by transnational corporations who wield excessive power in Washington. (p. 66)

The lack of any real economic policy becomes a far more serious concern in the context of a dominator economic system in which trans-national corporations

(TNCs) are 50 of the world's 100 largest economies, making them wealthier than most nations. Two-thirds of international trade is accounted for by just 500 TNCs, and 40% of the trade they control is between different parts of the *same* TNC. Korten (1995) explains that "the world's 500 largest industrial corporations, which employ only 0.05 of 1 percent of the world's population, control 25 percent of the world's economic output. The top 300 transnationals . . . own some 25 percent of the world's productive assets" (p. 221). Today's TNCs make a joke of the notion of a "free market" since only a few very large companies have tremendous influence on the global economic market (Eisler, 2007, p. 161).

TNCs also contributed to sustaining an economic policy based on consumption worldwide. Korten (1995) describes the negative social impact of this focus which results in a downward spiral of deepening alienation: 1) the quest for money widens the gap between ourselves, our families, and our community; 2) deepening alienation creates an inner sense of social and spiritual emptiness; 3) advertisers assure us that their products will make us whole; and 4) buying these products to make ourselves whole requires more money which takes us back to step #1 (p. 267). U.S. Americans are not only encouraged to consume, they are also encouraged to do it on credit, moving us into a state called "financialization" where financial services become the dominant component of GDP and assume a leading role in cultural and political economies (Aronica & Ramdoo, 2006, p. 102). This idea is supported by the fact that four of the top five wealthiest companies in the world are in banking: #1 Citigroup (U.S. owned); #2 Bank of America (U.S. owned); #3 HSBC Holdings (United Kingdom); and #5 JPMorgan Chase (U.S. owned) (DeCarlo, 2007).

One vivid example of the global economic influence of a TNC lies in the Wal-Mart story. In the 50 years since its founding, Wal-Mart's emphasis on cost-cutting in order to provide the lowest possible costs to consumers has made it one of the world's wealthiest corporations. Wal-Mart was one of the first corporations to invest in China, forging a successful combination of the company's logistical and distribution knowledge with China's tax-free zones and seemingly endless cheap labor. The partnership was so successful that in 2004, "Wal-Mart's Xu Jun told the *China Business Daily*, 'If Wal-Mart were an individual economy, it would rank as China's eighth-biggest trading partner, ahead of Russia, Australia and Canada'" (Aronica & Ramdoo, 2006, p. 44). Prestowitz (2005) notes that if "Wal-Mart were an independent country . . . it would rank ahead of Germany and Britain as an importer from China" (p. 68). So, what is the problem? Prestowitz (2005) describes the non-unionized working conditions at one Chinese factory, the Shenzhen Baoan Fenda Industrial Company:

2,100 workers labor amid deafening machinery and clouds of sawdust to turn out 360,000 stereo sets for Wal-Mart each month. No one wears ear plugs or protective

goggles as screeching band saws carve wood for the stereo cabinets. Many of the
women stuffing circuit boards have bandaged hands, but few wear gloves. (p. 67)

These jobs pay about $120 per month, but because workers frequently work 6 days
per week, this amounts to about $0.50 to $0.60 per hour. Another problem is that
Wal-Mart's "success" encourages other U.S. producers to outsource more of their
production to China in order to offer lower prices and have their products stocked
by Wal-Mart. "Some complain that these kinds of prices are precisely what is
driving the U.S. trade deficit to unprecedented and perhaps unsustainable heights"
(Prestowitz, 2005, p. 58).

Consolidating so much economic power into a few large TNCs has a variety of
negative consequences that are directly relevant to the IT industry. Consider the
recent battle for network neutrality between consumers and TNCs over the U.S.
Telecommunications Act (called the Communications Opportunity, Promotion and
Enhancement Act in 2006). TNCs such as AT&T, Verizon, Comcast, Time-Warner,
and BellSouth spent more than $175 million to lobby for a new price structure that
would allow them to pay for the expense of building faster, better communication
networks. The problem is that the new price structure also meant greater controls
on delivery and content, compromising the current open and "neutral" state of the
Internet. In a perhaps ironic twist, the power of the Internet itself contributed to
the volume of consumer voices in sustaining network neutrality; over a million
concerned citizens contacted Congress to oppose "any bill that didn't protect Net
Neutrality" ("Frequently asked questions," 2007; Stern, 2006). Meanwhile, the lack
of an explicit national policy for promoting economic development in broadband
technology has meant that the U.S. has rapidly lost global ground, ranking 16th
globally in broadband penetration (Aronica & Ramdoo, 2006; Friedman, 2006).
In contrast, the national economic policy in Korea, which included an emphasis
on developing wireless broadband and Korea's WiBro technology, has led them to
be ranked #1 globally in broadband penetration including VDSL technology that
averages "four times faster than the fastest U.S. broadband connections that companies like Comcast, Time Warner or the Baby Bells provide over cable modems"
(Aronica & Ramdoo, 2006, p. 48).

Offshoring

The absence of a U.S. national economic policy combined with TNCs making
decisions in their own best economic interest has also contributed to the increase
in offshoring IT jobs. In *Communications of the ACM*, UC Davis computer science professor Norm Matloff (2004) paints "a gloomy picture for U.S. IT workers,
projecting that the only major sector of the U.S. economy likely to shrink over the

next decade as a result of offshoring will be IT" (Aronica & Ramdoo, 2006, p. 65). Intel's Chairman Andy Grove at a policy advisory board meeting said, "America is in danger of following Europe down the tubes, and the worst part is that nobody knows it. They're all in denial, patting themselves on the back as the *Titanic* heads for the icebergs full speed ahead" (Prestowitz, 2005, p. 8).

The U.S. was supposed to have an edge in the global IT business thanks to the abundance of so-called "knowledge workers." However, IBM already has 45,000 workers in India, and other IT companies are rapidly following suit in order to compete in the global economic marketplace. Some predict the loss of at least 3.3 million IT jobs from the U.S. to low-wage countries by 2015 (Aronica & Ramdoo, 2006, p. 109). With only three or four very large semiconductor makers still investing in their own plants by the late 1990s, the hardware industry had already largely moved offshore, and the software industry seems to be rapidly headed in the same direction (Prestowitz, 2005).

In addition, "underemployment in Silicon Valley since the dot-com bubble burst . . . may have disproportionately hit women and minorities" (Bartol & Aspray 2006, p. 408). Contrary to most social perceptions that women in other countries have better access to IT education and employment, women remain underrepresented cross-nationally. "With their strong emphasis on abstract logic, mathematical reasoning, and interaction with machines, the stereotypically masculine task profiles associated with computer science programs and IT jobs exhibit marked similarities to those for engineering, a strongly male-dominated field world wide" (Anker, 1998; Charles & Bradley, 2002). One global exception lies in three former Soviet states (i.e., the Czech Republic, Hungary, and the Slovak Republic) which "show substantially stronger female representation in engineering than in computer science programs" (Charles & Bradley, 2006, p. 191). The authors propose that this is likely the remnant of Soviet educational policy that placed students according to academic performance (and as a vehicle for national advancement) not according individual interest (which due to the influence of gender stereotypes may be less strong in women).

Prestowitz (2005) explains how knowledge work is able to shift from the U.S. to China, India, and the former Soviet Union: "Although these people are mostly poor, the number having an advanced education and sophisticated skills is larger than the populations of many first world countries" (p. 3). Nations with much larger populations than the U.S. can offer an endless supply of skilled labor, and offshoring has also been more viable by the ways in which the Internet and global air delivery have all but eliminated time and distance. In addition, skilled workers in India and China:

are not thinking about thirty-five-hour work weeks or whether the value of a Ph.D. in computer science is worth the effort. For them anything less than eighty hours a

week is a vacation, and not getting the Ph.D. constitutes a devastating setback. This
energy and drive make the third wave of globalization revolutionary and dynamic.
(Prestowitz, 2005, p. 42)

Knowledge Workers in India

Prestowitz (2005) offers a brief history of the climate that made India a viable site
for offshoring IT jobs from the U.S. In India, "education has historically been important to the Hindus, the inventors of zero," and the legacy of British colonialism
has been "a large English-speaking population and a leadership class educated along
Western lines" (p. 29). IBM was one of the first companies to bring its business to
India; in the 70s, IBM controlled nearly 75% of the Indian market. After the imple-
mentation of a new policy that sought to limit foreign investment, IBM left India
and the "immediate effect was to severely handicap the whole Indian economy"
(p. 85). However, that did not last long as former IBM staff "set up companies to
service the old computers and develop software" (p. 85). The free and open Unix
operating system became "India's system of choice" (p. 85). In 1984, Rajiv Gandhi
became Prime Minister of India, and his "government set the goal of becoming
to software in the 1990s what Taiwan and South Korea were to hardware in the
1980s" (Prestowitz, 2005, pp. 86-87). In the 1990s, three other factors contributed
to the massive movement of U.S. business to India: (1) because they developed
expertise in old systems, Indian programmers were a great asset in handling Y2K;
(2) the U.S. dot-com bubble burst; and (3) the development of high-speed Internet
made communication between the U.S. and India vastly more practical (Prestowitz,
2005, pp. 92-93).

Today, Bangalore's pleasant climate and good universities have made it the
"heart of the Indian high-tech industry"—the Silicon Valley of India (Prestowitz,
2005, p. 98). "The ten-acre Infosys campus with its gym, library, grasslands, and
video conference center" sounds very much like the Microsoft campus in Redmond,
Washington (p. 99). The major U.S. IT companies with offices in India include
Microsoft, Oracle, HP, IBM, Compaq, Dell, Siemens, Canon, Sony, Ericsson, and
Cisco (Aronica & Ramdoo, 2006, p. 69). The huge growth of customer service call
centers in India is a boon to the Indian economy while it also reifies the cultural
divide. Over 200 million Indians speak English, and 40 million speak it as their
first language (Prestowitz, 2005, p. 79). For those who do not speak English without an Indian accent, there are "accent neutralization" classes. Indian call center
workers are also encouraged to take on Western screen names such as "Megan,"
and taught to use "power words" such as "trust me" or "believe me." Megan's real
name is Nishat, and she works at the AOL Retention Center in Delhi where she

earns $300/month compared to the $3,000-4,000/month salary a U.S. counterpart might earn (Prestowitz, 2005, pp. 79-81).

Manufacturers in China

The reasons for offshoring IT jobs to China are slightly different. An aggressive national economic policy set the stage for China to surpass the U.S. GDP within a few decades (if they sustain the current rate of growth). The Chinese are helping their economy grow by reinvesting in it "from 42 to 45 percent of GDP . . . To put this figure in context, U.S. investment is 19 percent of GDP. Japan's is 24.2 percent, and the EU's is 19.9 percent" (Prestowitz, 2005, p. 74). During the late 70s:

a series of measures establishing special economic zones in coastal cities, free trade zones, and special high tech zones were introduced...hundreds of thousands of students were sent to the United States and other countries for foreign study. Today China is graduating over 2 million students from college annually. (Prestowitz, 2005, p. 27)

While an increasing number of Chinese students have earned degrees, students in the U.S. have not kept pace. According to U.S. Census data from 2006, even after decades of better access to higher education for women and people of color, only 24% of U.S. Americans had completed a bachelor's degree ("Table 13," 2006). Further, that is an aggregate number that does not account for differences in gender and race.

China also dramatically increased their foreign investments which grew from "less than $20 billion in 1980" to "$200 billion in 1990" and "well over $500 billion" in 2005—"exports climbed from $18 billion to nearly $600 billion" (Prestowitz, 2005, pp. 27-28). Worker productivity in China is also tremendously high. This is due in part to a cultural work ethic, and in part because of the education and skill of the workers. Also, unlike their counterparts in the U.S., Chinese workers are:

effectively nonunion with little ability to strike, complain, or take legal action against the employer . . . accustomed to grindingly long hours and prepared to work under difficult conditions . . . When this labor force is combined with modern production technology and techniques, good transportation and communications infrastructure, a currency managed to remain weak against the dollar, and substantial tax and financial incentives, the total manufacturing package is extremely powerful. (Prestowitz, 2005, p. 75)

On June 11, 2006, an article titled "iPod City" described how anyone over 16 is encouraged to apply at Foxconn's Longhua facility where "workers labor 15 hours a day building iPods, for which they usually earn about $50 per month . . . they live in secluded dormitories that each house 100 people and prohibit visitors" (Aronica & Ramdoo, 2006, p. 85). In the context of a dominator global economics, Indian and Chinese workers may be cheaper and more productive than U.S. workers. However, in a partnership economic context, these trends raise serious questions about the social, cultural, and moral costs of such unidimensional, bottom-line oriented economic decisions.

Globalization and Poverty

So far, I have focused on the loss of jobs in the U.S. to educated workers in India and China, which is certainly of concern to U.S. workers. However, even in these two countries where many IT jobs are being offshored, they are only going to the most educated and economically privileged in these societies. Poverty rates in India and China have not been significantly reduced by the presence of IT businesses, and poverty rates worldwide have actually grown, as Eisler (2007) comments:

In 2005, the United Nations reported that the globalization of an unregulated market system was actually a major factor in the creation of poverty . . . in 2003, the United Nations Human Development Report found that compared to 1990, fifty-four countries had become poorer, and in twenty-one countries the number of poor people increased rather than decreased. (p. 146)

Aronica and Ramdoo (2006) explain that "the high-tech sector employs just 0.2 percent of the workforce in India" and that current market policies in India "have failed to reduce poverty any faster than the state-oriented policies before them" (p. 23). Given this data on global poverty, one must consider the question of who even has access to IT worldwide:

99.5% of [Thomas Friedman's] 3 billion new flat worlders simply don't have access to the Internet and to Friedman's plug and play playground . . . 1.35 billion sweatshop workers doing duty 10 hours a day, 7 days a week for 20 cents an hour have been added to the transnational corporations' workforce—now they can sweat and play in Friedman's new neoliberal utopia. (Aronica & Ramdoo, 2006, p. 51)

Data on the global distribution of income further illustrate this point. Twenty percent of the world's wealthiest countries receive 82.7% of the world's income, while the 20% of the world's population who are in the poorest category receive only 1.4% of the world's income (Korten, 1995, p. 107). The gap between rich and poor promises to grow even larger as the global population expands. Depending on global fertility rates, estimates are that between 2005 and 2050 the global population will grow from 6.5 billion to 9.1-10.6 billion. Most of this growth will be in developing nations, which are expected to add 35 million annually, 22 million of whom will be in the least developed nations, while developed nations are expected to lose about 1 million annually ("World population prospects," 2005, p. 8).

Combining the dramatically unequal distribution of income data with the best estimates on global population growth raises some serious questions about our social responsibility to each other as a human community with regard to the direction of development efforts in the IT industry. Eisler (2007) suggests: "In our time, when high technology guided by values such as conquest, exploitation, and domination threaten our very survival, we need economic inventions driven by an ethos of caring" (p. 21). What might this new "caring economics" look like? How might we use technology to close the existing (and rapidly growing) gap between the haves and have-nots worldwide? How might we use IT in service of human need instead of placing humans in service to technology? What are the most critical global social concerns that technology might serve? Can we afford the either/or attitude of IT businesses that completely divorce profit-making IT development from broader social concerns? Clearly, the answer is no. As further evidence of why we must move away from our dominator economic model, I offer the cautionary tale of what resulted when one early IT corporate giant chose to divorce profit-making from a thoughtful consideration of the social context for technology they developed and the uses to which it was being put.

IBM AND THE HOLOCAUST

On a trip to the U.S. Holocaust Museum in 1993, Edwin Black saw an IBM Hollerith D-11 card sorting machine and decided to investigate the historical connection between this well-known American company and Hitler's Nazi Germany. In *IBM and the Holocaust: The Strategic Alliance Between Nazi Germany and America's Most Powerful Corporation* (2001), Black tells a cautionary tale about the potential dangers of developing technology for its own sake without concern for the social consequences of that technology. Black (2001) describes how IBM made its fortune by anticipating government and corporate needs and developing customized solutions without questioning the application of these solutions: "Solipsistic and dazzled by its own swirling universe of technical possibilities, IBM was self-gripped by a special amoral corporate mantra: if it can be done, it should be done" (Black, 2001, p. 8). In this case, IBM's technology became part of the "final solution" in Hitler's Nazi

Germany where customized punch card systems made it easier for the Germans to do things such as allocate food in order to starve Jews, manage slave labor, and run deportation trains (Black, 2001, pp. 10-12).

The history of the company we now know as IBM begins in the U.S. with a German immigrant and inventor named Herman Hollerith who developed his first prototype for a census tabulating machine in 1884, and then founded a company that was chosen by the U.S. government for the census in 1890. In 1910, Hollerith licensed patents to German businessman Willy Heidinger and a German company named Deutsche Hollerith Maschinen Gesellschaft (Dehomag) was born (Black, 2001, p. 30). One year later, Hollerith sold the U.S. company to industrialist Charles Flint, a man who had made his millions trading international commodities, including weapons (often selling to both sides of a conflict). Flint had also "perfected an infamous business modality, the so-called *trust*...the anti-competitive industrial combinations that often secretly devoured competition" (Black, 2001, p. 30).

Meanwhile, the man whose name would later become synonymous with IBM, Thomas J. Watson, was making his name as a salesman with National Cash Register (NCR) and learning a variety of competitive sales techniques from John Patterson. Watson stole clients from competitors and set up fake companies to put secondhand dealers in New York and Chicago out of business (Black, 2001, p. 32). In 1912, Watson, Patterson and several dozen executives of NCR were indicted for "criminal conspiracy to restrain trade and construct a monopoly" (p. 36). One year later, they were all found guilty and most were sentenced to one year in jail. However, Watson and others at NCR turned the public tide when they came to the aid of the dislocated citizens of Dayton, Ohio after the city was devastated by flooding immediately followed by a tornado; Watson was later pardoned for his crimes.

In 1914, Watson joined IBM (then CTR) as general manager; when his conviction was officially overturned, he became the company's president (Black, 2001, p. 39). In 1922, when the postwar economic depression was making business difficult in Europe, Watson convinced Heidinger to give 90% control of Dehomag to IBM New York and the German company became a subsidiary of U.S.-owned IBM. In 1924, Watson renamed the company International Business Machines (Black, 2001, pp. 40-41). Under Watson, the company was known for IBM spirit, IBM family, loyalty, revival-style sales meetings, and the now infamous IBM uniform, which consisted of a dark suit and a white shirt.

In the 1930s, while other companies were severing business ties with Nazi Germany and Americans were protesting in the streets, Watson was building his German subsidiary (Black, 2001, p. 46). Watson moved ahead in spite of: (1) evidence of barbarity in Germany; (2) vehement anti-Hitler sentiment (including mass protests) in the U.S. and worldwide; (3) the unpredictable business risk in Germany; and (4) knowing that helping Hitler was helping him prepare for war (p. 63). Evidence of the barbarity in Germany was regularly appearing in front page stories in the *New York Times* that chronicled a series of atrocities against Jews in Germany. One newspaper story described Hitler's plans for Jewish annihilation in his recently published *Mein Kampf* (pp. 63-66). Protests were beginning to be organized around the U.S. On March 27, 1933, anti-Hitler organizers collaborated for a 70-city protest of atrocities against Jews in Germany that was attended by 2 million U.S. Americans; schools and businesses were closed in many cities (p. 66).

If actions are any measure of beliefs, Watson did not seem concerned about doing business with Germany in spite of the mounting anti-Nazi tide in the U.S. In 1937, Watson wrote a letter to the Nazi Economics Minister, Hjalmar Schacht, praising the German leadership under Hitler and thanking the Germans for protecting Dehomag's assets so well during World War I (Black, 2001, p. 43). Black (2001) intimates that Watson ran his company like a fascist, which is why he may have been drawn to a fascist regime. Whether you are convinced of that argument or not, Watson's actions make it hard to deny that he saw an opportunity to make lots of money (regardless of the social cost) and he took it (pp. 69-70). Weeks after Hitler came to power, Watson and IBM-NY invested over $1 million to expand Dehomag's manufacturing; at the same time, Heidinger openly supported Hitler's plans to create a master race (p. 50). Black (2001) describes the situation as follows:

From the very first moments and continuing throughout the twelve-year existence of the third Reich, IBM placed its technology at the disposal of Hitler's program of Jewish destruction and territorial domination. IBM did not invent Germany's anti-Semitism, but when it volunteered solutions, the company virtually braided with Nazism. Like any technologic evolution, each new solution powered a new level of sinister expectation and cruel capability. When Germany wanted to identify the Jews by name, IBM showed them how. When Germany wanted to use that information to launch programs of social expulsion and expropriation, IBM provided the technologic wherewithal. When the trains needed to run on time, from city to city or between concentration camps, IBM offered that solution as well. Ultimately, there was no solution IBM would not devise for a Reich willing to pay for services rendered. One solution led to another. No solution was out of the question. As the clock ticked, as the punch cards clicked, as Jews in Germany saw their existence vaporizing, others saw their corporate fortunes rise. (pp. 73-74)

Ironically, at the IBM School in Endicott, New York, Watson had the following words engraved on the uppermost five steps: read, listen, discuss, observe, and think; "the word THINK was everywhere" (Black, 2001, p. 51).

After the U.S. declared war, Watson funneled information, management, and money through its subsidiaries in other countries such as IBM Paris and IBM Switzerland (Black, 2001, p. 73). As changing German laws made it harder for IBM to claim profits from Dehomag, Watson got increasingly creative with how profits were counted and/or funneled through other divisions in countries with fewer restrictions (p. 121). Although many other corporations were targeted by protestors for doing business in Germany, IBM was never identified because "Anti-Nazi agitators just didn't understand the dynamics of corporate multi-nationalism" (p. 69).

While serving as chair of the International Commerce Commission in 1937, Watson decided to host the annual conference in Berlin. He also accepted the Merit Cross of the German Eagle with Star from Hitler, the second highest award offered by the Third Reich (Black, 2001, p. 129-131). Meanwhile, IBM's automated technology was allowing the Reich to identify Jewish lineage (even down to $1/16^{th}$) back through several generations (p. 108). Black comments:

Understanding it possessed the technology to scrutinize an entire nation, Dehomag proudly advertised its systems...No one would escape. This was something new for mankind. Never before had so many people been identified so precisely, so silently, so quickly, and with such far-reaching consequences. The dawn of the Information Age began at the sunset of human decency. (p. 104)

In 1935, the U.S. Social Security Act required machines to track data and collate across data sets, and IBM got the contract (Black, 2001, p. 119). Due to such U.S. government contracts, IBM's income grew six-fold in several years, and the cross-referencing technology that they developed was transferred to their German subsidiary. In early 1938, Hitler invaded Austria. On November 10, 1938, 15,000 Jews were taken from their homes during the infamous Kristallnacht (so named because of all the glass that was broken while looting Jewish homes). Meanwhile, in the U.S., Watson was busy touting "world peace through world trade" (p. 148). In October 1939, after Hitler had occupied Poland, IBM/Dehomag machines counted 359,827 Jews in Warsaw in 48 hours (p. 190-191). The technology helped the war effort in other ways as well. In 1940, there were numerous censuses in Poland and Belgium including a cow census and a horse census, both done to help manage the German war effort (p. 206). Black further explains:

IBM had almost single-handedly brought modern warfare into the information age. Through its persistent, aggressive, unfaltering efforts . . . IBM organized the organizers of Hitler's war. Since IBM held the exclusive rights to print the cards that ran in their machines, customers were tied to doing business with IBM (and IBM continued to make money) long after they had purchased a machine. (p. 208)

In May 1940, Hoover's FBI began investigating Germans at IBM in the U.S., but they never questioned IBM's business interests *in* Germany (Black, 2001, p. 214-215). On June 6, 1940, Watson finally sent a letter to Hitler and returned his German Merit Cross (p. 217). This sparked a revolt over German ownership of Dehomag. Watson maneuvered to get three Germans who were loyal to him into positions of power to safeguard his assets during the war. Black (2001) points out that this was another moment when Watson could have easily gotten out of doing business with Hitler. During the "Dehomag revolt" one of the proposed solutions was to create a new company from the holdings of a couple of smaller competitors and build their own punch card technology. However, all of the German machines were built by IBM, and it would take years for other technology to catch up. Watson could have backed out and let the Nazi's data collecting operations fail, but he did not (p. 230). From 1933 through the summer of 1940, Watson micro-managed every Dehomag decision. However, from August 1940 through the end of the war, IBM-NY made sure it did not know the details of Hollerith uses (p. 236).

This is not a simplistic either/or story; it is complex and has many sides. IBM also helped the U.S. war effort. IBM machines (including mobile units that traveled with specially trained teams of soldiers) were used in the U.S. war effort for such tasks as tracking troops, issuing payrolls, and cracking codes. In addition, several IBM factories were converted to munitions factories at the outset of the war (Black, 2001, pp. 343-345). On the other hand, IBM technology also supported the U.S. Census of 1940, one result of which was to identify, track, and ultimately inter Japanese-Americans in concentration camps. From the evidence that Black provides, it seems clear that IBM was in the business of building its profits, no matter what the uses of its technology. Black (2001) summarizes it this way:

Perhaps IBM's business philosophy was best expressed by an executive of Belge Watson in an August 1939 letter to senior officers of IBM NY. The letter detailed the company's growing involvement in Japan's aircraft industry… 'It is none of our business to judge the reasons why an American corporation should or would help a foreign Government, and consequently Mr. Decker and myself have left these considerations entirely out of our line of thought…we are, as IBM men, interested in the technical side of the application of our machines.' (p. 395)

Ultimately, Watson's choice exists in stark contrast to the choice made by French counter-intelligence agent Rene Carmille. Carmille convinced the Nazis to let him run Occupied France's census operations on Holleriths which allowed him to create multiple schemes for providing inaccurate or false data that ultimately saved tens of thousands of French Jews. During the three years from 1941 to 1944 when he was arrested by the SS, Carmille's lack of cooperation meant that only 25% of the

Jews in France died. Carmille was subsequently tortured by the notorious Butcher of Lyon, Klaus Barbie, for two days, but he "never cracked"; Carmille was sent to Dachau where he died on January 25, 1945 (Black, 2001, pp. 322-332).

CONCLUSION

The story of IBM and the Holocaust is one example of an early TNC (a global IT company) whose actions reflected the values of a dominator economic model. You may think that it is a 60-year old story and we would never make such heinous decisions today. However, without a conscious recognition of the dominator values that undergird our global IT business relations today, we are prey to the same inhumane decisions. Dominator assumptions are so deeply embedded in our consciousnesses that few of us stop to question the core values guiding the global IT business.

I end this chapter where I began with questions about what we value. I have explored the values of our dominator economic model, the powerful influence of the historical legacy of colonialism on contemporary global economic relations, and the rising social and political significance of economic development in India and China in an effort to expose the core assumptions supporting the global IT business today. The rapid global distribution of IT has placed us at a crossroads. We have a choice to take the path of least resistance, or the road less traveled—the one that expresses our greatest human potential. We know where the path of least resistance has led us. Down the road less traveled lie the answers to such questions as: How might we use technology to close the rapidly growing gap between the haves and have-nots worldwide? How might we use IT in service of human need instead of placing humans in service to technology? What are the most critical global social concerns that technology might serve? Will you join me on the road less traveled? To paraphrase Robert Frost, it may make all the difference.

QUESTIONS FOR REFLECTIVE DIALOG

1. Technology is ubiquitous in daily life in the United States. Observe your interaction with technology over a 24-hour period. Write down all the technological assistance you get throughout your day, from the alarm clock ring that awakens you through setting that same alarm in the evening. Next, describe the type of assistance that you get from each piece of technology (for example, alarm clock=makes noise so that I wake up at a set time). Consider what your day would be like without electricity. According to the IEA World Energy Outlook, 2002, 35% of people in India have no access to electricity.

How does the U.S.'s relationship with technology influence our relationship with the rest of the world?

2. Developing technology to address a social need creates opportunities for partnership between rich and poor nations. Research the social conditions in a developing nation. Make a list of local non-government organizations working towards change in that nation. How might you partner with these organizations to use technology to address a locally-defined need?

3. What do you think of the idea of a global classroom in the future, an online version of kindergarten through university completion that would be conducted in a myriad of languages offered for free to the world? Who would design the curriculum? What would be taught? Who would be able to access it? What might be the benefits and drawbacks of such an idea?

4. Do you associate the word "modern" with the word "better"? Can you think of times in your life when the connection between innovation and improvement been assumed? Describe those circumstances.

5. Have you or anyone you know lost a job due to offshoring? Could your job be more cost-effectively done outside the U.S.? What jobs are safe from offshoring? Could parts of your current job be more effectively done without meeting face-to-face with clients? Why or why not?

6. Consider the conditions described in the Chinese iPod factory where employees as young as 16 years old work 15-hour days and are not allowed visitors in their living quarters. As technology consumers, what responsibility do we have to the individuals who assemble our products? How could increasing awareness of global working conditions contribute to, or complicate, our unexamined drive toward technological consumption in the U.S.?

7. Are corporations responsible for the ways that their products are used (as Black [2001] posits in his argument about IBM)? Consider an innovation that seems positive (nuclear energy) but has equally negative or dangerous applications (atomic weapons). How does this phenomenon reflect the dominator economic model?

REFERENCES[2]

Anderson, A., & Cottringer, A. (Producers/Directors). (1988). *Hell to pay* [Motion picture]. England: Women Make Movies.

Anker, R. (1998). *Gender and jobs: Sex segregation of occupations in the world.* Geneva: ILO.

Aronica, R., & Ramdoo, M. (2006). *The world is flat? A critical analysis of the New York Times bestseller by Thomas Friedman*. Tampa: Meghan-Kiffer Press.

Bartol, K. M., & Aspray, W. (2006). The transition of women from the academic world to the IT workplace: A review of the relevant research. In J. M. Cohoon & W. Aspray (Eds.), *Women and information technology: Research on underrepresentation* (pp. 377-419). Cambridge, MA: MIT Press.

Black, E. (2001). *IBM and the holocaust: The strategic alliance between Nazi Germany and America's most powerful corporation*. New York: Crown.

Charles, M., & Bradley, K. (2002). Equal but separate? A cross-national study of sex segregation in higher education. *American Sociological Review, 67*, 573-599.

Charles, M., & Bradley, K. (2006). A matter of degrees: Female underrepresentation in computer science programs cross-nationally. In J. M. Cohoon & W. Aspray (Eds.), *Women and information technology: Research on underrepresentation* (pp. 183-203). Cambridge, MA: MIT Press.

DeCarlo, S. (Ed.). (2007, March 29). The world's 2,000 largest public companies. *Forbes*. Retrieved December 16, 2007, from http://www.forbes.com/2007/03/29/forbes-global-2000-biz-07forbes2000-cz_sd_0329global_land.html

Eisler, R. (2002). *The power of partnership: Seven relationships that will change your life*. Novato, CA: New World.

Eisler, R. (2007). *The real wealth of nations: Creating a caring economics*. San Francisco: Berrett-Koehler.

Frequently asked questions: What's happening at congress? (n.d.). *Save the Internet. com*. Retrieved on August 26, 2007, from www.savetheinternet.com

Friedman, T. L. (2006). *The world is flat: A brief history of the twenty-first century*. New York: Farrar, Straus and Giroux.

Gill, D., & Levidow, L. (Eds.). (1987). *Anti-racist science teaching*. London: Free Association.

Harding, S. (1998). *Is science multicultural: Postcolonialisms, feminisms, and epistemologies*. Bloomington, IN: Indiana UP.

Harding, S. (2000). Should philosophies of science encode democratic ideals? In D.L. Kleinman (Ed.), *Science, technology & democracy* (pp. 121-138). Albany: SUNY.

Henderson, H. (1996). *Building a win-win world: Life beyond global economic warfare*. San Francisco: Berrett-Koehler Publishers.

Korten, D. C. (1995). *When corporations rule the world*. San Francisco: Berrett-Koeler.

Martin, K. (Producer) & Nash, T. (Director). (1997). *Who's counting?: Marilyn Waring on sex, lies & global economics* [Motion Picture]. Oley, PA: Bullfrog Films.

Matloff, N. (2004, November). Globalization and the American IT worker. *Communications of the ACM, 47*(11), 27-29.

Michaelson, M. (1987). Sickle cell anemia: An "interesting pathology." In D. Gill & L. Levidow (Eds.), *Anti-racist science teaching* (pp. 59-75). London: Free Association.

Our guiding principles. (n.d.). *The Bill and Melinda Gates Foundation*. Retrieved September 20, 2007, from http://www.gatesfoundation.org/AboutUs/OurValues/GuidingPrinciples/default.htm

Our values. (n.d.). *The Bill and Melinda Gates Foundation*. Retrieved September 20, 2007, from http://www.gatesfoundation.org/AboutUs/OurValues/default.htm

Pegoraro, R., & Noguchi, Y. (2007, January 8). Gates' CES keynote aims at 'connected experience.' *The Washington Post*. Retrieved January 8, 2007, from http://www.washingtonpost.com/wp-dyn/content/article/2007/01/08/AR2007010800053_pf.html

Prestowitz, C. (2005). *Three billion new capitalists: The great shift of wealth and power to the east*. New York: Basic Books.

Sarewitz, D. (2000). Human well-being and federal science: What's the connection? In D. L. Kleinman (Ed.), *Science, technology & democracy* (pp. 87-102). Albany: SUNY.

Shiva, V. (1997). *Biopiracy: The plunder of nature and knowledge*. Cambridge, MA: South End Press.

Shiva, V. (2005). *Earth democracy: Justice, sustainability, and peace*. Cambridge, MA: South End Press.

Stern, C. (2006, January 22). The coming tug of war over the internet. *Washington Post*. Retrieved August 26, 2007, from www.washingtonpost.com

Table 13: Educational attainment of the population 25 years and over, by state, including margin of error: 2006. (2006). Educational attainment in the United States: 2006. *U.S. Census*. Retrieved December 21, 2007, from http://www.census.gov/population/www/socdemo/education/cps2006.html

World population prospects. (2005, February 24). *Department of Economic and Social Affairs* (ESA/P/WP.193). New York: United Nations.

Young, R. (1987). Racist science, racist society. In D. Gill & L. Levidow (Eds.), *Anti-racist science teaching* (pp. 76-87). London: Free Association.

ENDNOTES

[1]   Interestingly, I wrote this chapter before Riane Eisler wrote her book on economics. However, using Eisler's earlier thinking about dominator systems, I had arrived at similar arguments citing many of the same authors that Eisler cited. When I discovered her latest book (which goes much farther down the trail than my thinking had led me), it affirmed the veracity of her systems level view of our current social system as a dominator model, as well as her vision of how we might shift to a partnership model.

[2]   Some portions of this chapter may have appeared in, and are reprinted with permission from Kirk, M. (2006). Bridging the digital divide: A feminist perspective on the project. In G. Trajkovski (Ed.), Diversity in information technology education: Issues and controversies (pp. 38-67). Hershey, PA: Information Science Publishing.

Section III
Perspectives on Partnership
Social Institutions

Section II explored how the values, attitudes, and beliefs of a dominator social model have been embedded in the following four primary social institutions: media, communication, education, and business. A partnership social model provides an alternative framework to our current dominator social organization. What are the characteristics of a partnership society and how might this contrast to a dominator system in direct relation to the participation of women as developers, users, and beneficiaries of technology?

Section III: Perspectives on Partnership Social Institutions (Chapters VIII through XI) offers ideas and examples for developing and teaching the values, attitudes, and beliefs of a partnership social model in specific relation to IT. These chapters offer examples in relation to the same four social institutions explored earlier—media, language, education, and business. I have separated a deeper exploration of the problem (in Section II) from suggestions for "solutions" (in Section III) for several reasons. One reason, and perhaps the most important one, is that I wanted to offer readers the opportunity to begin to envision their own solutions as we explore the problem more deeply together. Another reason is that although my suggestions emanate from my expert perspective on the available research in this area, they are not the only correct answers. My hope is that by allowing readers to begin to frame their own solutions as they read, my solutions will be viewed as less prescriptive and more as new perspectives from which to think about how to co-create more complex, systemic solutions together.

Chapter VIII: "Partnership Language and Media: Creating a New IT Culture" offers ideas for how we might shift away from a dominator social model to a partnership model in relation to language and media. This chapter explores the following ideas for how we can co-create the conditions that encourage partnership language and media: (1) identifying core components of a partnership culture that are particularly relevant to language and media; (2) developing partnership language and communication by understanding the cultural components of voice and silence, focusing on linkages in relationships in IT, practicing dialogic process, and practicing nonviolent communication; and (3) offering an example of new partnership media—connect! magazine.

Chapter IX: "Partnership Science and Technology Education" explores strategies for redefining education as a social institution. This chapter explores the following suggestions for shifting education (especially science and IT education) towards a partnership model by: (1) exploring partnership ways of knowing; (2) considering the needs and perspectives of users and beneficiaries of science and IT in education; (3) educating teachers from kindergarten through college to better understand how our current system works as well as how to co-create partnership; (4) redefining student-teacher relationships in terms of partnership; (5) co-creating collaborative learning environments; 6) developing partnerships systems of testing, evaluating, and measuring learning; and (7) offering examples of partnership curricula and programs.

Chapter X: "Partnership Global IT Business" introduces a partnership economic model and attempts to envision answers to questions about our social responsibility to each other as a human community with regard to the direction of development efforts in the global IT industry. For example: How might we use technology to close the existing (and rapidly growing) gap between the haves and have-nots worldwide? What are the most critical global social concerns that technology might serve? To address some of these questions, this chapter explores the following topics in relation to co-creating a partnership global IT business: (1) U.S. economic dominance in IT; (2) "partnerism" a new economic model; (3) global IT development ideas between developed and developing nations; (4) partnership IT policy making; and (5) examples of partnership science and IT.

Chapter XI: "A Concluding Pledge: With Technology and Justice for All" recaps the main themes of this book and offers suggestions for (1) future research; (2) where you can begin to co-create partnership; and (3) provides an epilogue from the author that demonstrates the ways in which social change is a lifelong learning experience.

Chapter VIII
Partnership Language and Media:
Creating a New IT Culture

OBJECTIVES

This chapter aims to help you understand the following:

- The core characteristics of a partnership social system that most closely relate to language and media as social institutions.
- How to apply the values of a partnership society to recreate language as a social institution (especially styles of communication).
- A new vision for partnership media.

INTRODUCTION

In Chapter IV, I discussed how language operates as a social institution to teach us the values, attitudes, and beliefs of our society. Our dominator legacy is deeply embedded in the language we use and the ways we have learned to communicate. Since language acts as such a powerful social institution, it is also a great place to begin to create a partnership culture. "We need a language that connects us to the heart of our human experience—our values, dreams, desires, and needs" (Hart, 2004, p. 115). We need language that liberates us from the limiting either/or perspectives of a dominator culture and inspires the unlimited both/and perspectives of a partnership culture. We need language (and styles of communication) that help us focus on the ways in which we are connected as human beings, more than the ways in which we are different (which serves the dominator values of ranking human beings).

In Chapter V, I discussed how media teach us the values, attitudes, and beliefs of a dominator culture via the persistent use of stereotypical images and messages. To create the climate for partnership in IT, we need new representations of women and people of color in relation to technology in books, magazines, television, film, and advertising. We need to break free of the "geek" stereotype and show more complex human beings portrayed as developers, users, and beneficiaries of technology. We need to move outside of a narrow Amerocentric lens regarding the ways in which we think about and envision technology and its uses.

Creating this kind of change may seem daunting, but it need not be. People often resist participating in change because they see society as a rigid mechanism that's "always been this way" or "just the way things are." However, we need to shift away from this dominator view of society as a machine in which people are "expendable cogs" (Eisler & Loye, 1990, p. 185); this attitude contributes to a lack of responsibility towards being part of the change. "If we deny our power to affect people, then we don't have to worry about taking responsibility for how we use it or, more significant, how we don't" (Johnson, 2006, p. 133). The truth is that individuals *interact* with the larger social institutions, and those social institutions can be changed by that interaction. To create a partnership society, you must adopt the view of society as a living organism that you are co-creating with others. This will make it easier to claim responsibility for your part in reifying our dominator system or moving towards partnership.

This chapter offers ideas for how we might create the conditions that encourage caring relations in language, communication, and media as social institutions. However, the ideas that I offer here are just that—ideas. As Riane Eisler (2002) wisely said, "I'm not going to preach that we should be more caring. I'm always going to focus on what I have learned about *creating the conditions that encourage rather than inhibit or prevent caring relations*" (p. 83). This chapter explores the following ideas for how we can co-create the conditions that encourage partnership: (1) identifying core components of a partnership culture that are particularly relevant to language and media; (2) developing partnership language and communication by understanding the cultural components of voice and silence, focusing on linkages in relationships in IT, practicing dialogic process, and practicing nonviolent communication; and (3) offering an example of new partnership media—*connect!* magazine.

In Chapter I, I contrasted the characteristics of dominator and partnership social systems. Table 1 describes the characteristics of partnership social systems that are particularly relevant to language and media as social institutions as they relate to

Table 1. Characteristics of partnership social systems linked to topics in this chapter

Partnership Characteristic	Related Topic in Chapter VIII
Trust- and respect-based	Cultural components of voice and silence
Hierarchies of actualization	Cultural components of voice and silence
Emphasis on linking	Linkages in relationships in IT
Win/win orientation	Dialogic process
Low degree of fear, abuse, violence, since they are not required to maintain rigid rankings	Nonviolent communication
Value traits that promote human development such as nonviolence, empathy, and caregiving	Dialogic process Nonviolent communication
Images of nurturance honored, institutionalized	Example of partnership media

the topics covered in this chapter (Eisler, 1987, 2002, 2007; Eisler & Loye, 1990; Eisler & Miller, 2004).

PARTNERSHIP LANGUAGE AND COMMUNICATION

How might language as a social institution operate differently in a partnership society? If we begin to see ourselves as co-creators of our society, we will begin to recognize the power for change that lies in each human communication. If we begin to value empathy and caregiving over fear and control, our language might change in a variety of ways. We might use myths and metaphors that honor nurturing and caring rather than valorizing violence and dominance as the actualization of heroism. If we focus on linking and connection, rather than ranking and difference, we might begin to use language that disassociates human behavior from gender altogether and simply describe the behavior itself. For example, we often use the "male-centric" term "brotherhood" but rarely use the term "sisterhood" in the same generic sense. Eisler and Loye (1990) recommend degendering our language to be more *de*scriptive of the behavior itself without being *pre*scriptive of gender. They offer the following terms as more descriptive of the attitudes and beliefs that "brotherhood" intends to convey without also being exclusive of gender: community, kinship, friendship, unity, or partnership (p. 190).

Language and communication exist together as different parts of an iceberg. We can think of the language that we use as the top 1/8th of the iceberg, since it is more explicitly visible; we can think of the communication style that we use as the bottom 7/8th of the iceberg, since it is often more implicit, and less visible. Therefore, shifting the style of our communication may present an even greater challenge than changing our language.

What forms might communication take in a partnership society? A perspective from Spender (1980) is useful to frame this discussion; she says that there "is no monodimensional, linear reality but a multidimensional, non-linear, interrelated reality in which either/or, right/wrong, subjectivity/objectivity are not useful distinctions" (p. 65). This is a great place to begin a discussion about changing our dominator communication style. It really was not an either/or to begin with. We are all humans with human characteristics. Some women interrupt others when they talk, and some men communicate to connect and build relationships. The fallacy is to believe (and to assert with our attitudes and behavior) that there is only one right way for a man or for a woman to communicate, and then to develop social systems that privilege one style of communication and suppress the other.

All men are not the same, any more than all women are the same, any more than all people from different cultures are the same. Somehow we have to hold the paradox that people may *both* communicate differently *and* share many things in common. We have to strike a balance between recognizing that there may be differences without assuming that those differences are based on particular aspects of stereotypes—based on gender, race, culture, class, and so forth. If we want to engage in partnership communication, we must focus on linkages rather than false rankings.

The following sections offer ideas for how to make the shift to a partnership communication style by: understanding the cultural components of voice and silence; focusing on linkages in relationships in IT; using dialogic process; and engaging in nonviolent communication.

Cultural Components of Voice and Silence

The field of intercultural communication offers additional perspectives from which to consider how we might shift communication from reflecting the values of a dominator social institution to a partnership model. Trefil's (1996) definition of cultural literacy "is that everyone carries around in his or her mind a matrix of information and knowledge, and that matrix plays a very active part in communication" (p. 546). However, in the case of our communication styles and the ways in which they reflect culture, this matrix is largely hidden for most of us; our attitudes, values, and beliefs are often implicit. Creating any lasting change requires both a shift in mindset and acquiring new skill sets, such as: (1) realizing that you have a culture, (2) becoming aware of your behavior, and (3) learning that your culture is not the only valid one.

One example of the way that culture influences communication style lies in the emphasis on voice vs. silence. To facilitate the shift from dominator to partnership communication, it is also important to understand different cultural values in relation to voice and silence. There are two important dimensions to this issue. One is that communication in dominator societies tends to privilege certain voices and silence others. This means that those who want to ally with groups who have previously been silenced often focus their energies on getting them to speak. However, although dominator communication privileges speaking (positively viewed as active and "male") over listening (negatively viewed as passive and "female"), these values are not shared across cultures. Some cultures value speech/voice and some value silence.

Further, some cultures and some individuals *choose* silence for very deliberate reasons, while others view claiming their voice as a way to counter systemic oppression. For example, many women in African-American culture claim their voice early by becoming "loud Black girls" (Goldberger, 1996, pp. 344-345). So for some individuals, some groups, speech is an act of political resistance—"a political gesture that challenges politics of domination that would render us nameless and voiceless" (hooks, 1989, p. 8). hooks, whose legal name is Gloria Watkins, explains that she adopted her lower-case pseudonym "bell hooks" because it was a family name—her maternal great-grandmother—and to "subdue all impulses leading me away from speech into silence" (hooks, 1989, p. 9). She shares the story of how she first heard the name as a young girl when she "talked back" to a grown up while buying bubble gum at the corner store. She (1989) writes:

Even now I can recall the surprised look, the mocking tones that informed me I must be kin to bell hooks—a sharp-tongued woman, a woman who spoke her mind, a woman who was not afraid to talk back. I claimed this legacy of defiance, of will, of courage, affirming my link to female ancestors who were bold and daring in their speech. (p. 9)

For those who choose silence, cultural stereotypes may negatively influence the perception of their silence as a choice; without empathic, active listening, we may miss the truth of a communication. Wanda, an Ojibwe woman, describes the experience of getting caught between different cultural notions of voice/silence:

Speech versus silence, for her, is 'wrapped up in identity and racism' (inside her Native community, she is considered a big talker; outside the community, she is seen as quiet and 'not enormously verbal'). If quiet, she is stereotyped as the stoic Indian; if voiced, she becomes the 'mouthy militant.' (Goldberger, 1996, p. 344)

Patrocinio Schweickart (1996) shares two aphorisms that express Filipina cultural attitudes around voice/silence: "*Speech is silver, but silence is gold*," and "*Silent waters run deep*" (p. 305). Schweickart adds that the "popular appeal of these proverbs among Filipinos suggests that for them silence often represents cognitive activity, and that thoughtful silence is a highly valued form of agency" (p. 306). Well-intentioned teachers or employers who try to "rescue" their students or staff from their silence may find themselves engaged in a different form of domination, enforcing the cultural value of speech over silence, and not appreciating that a lot may be going on in the silence.

Hurtado (1996) raises a different set of issues in her discussion of the ways that some women learn to use silence as a powerful survival tool, especially as disenfranchised members of a dominator social system:

Ultimately, the knowledge obtained by remaining silent is like a reconnaissance flight into enemy territory that allows for individual and group survival. Outspokenness is the complement of the strategy of silence. Knowing when to talk and just exactly what to say is especially effective if individuals are not expected to talk. (p. 382)

For members of disenfranchised groups in a dominator social system, there may be great risk involved in speaking vs. being silent. hooks (1989) says, "there are some folks for whom openness is not about the luxury of 'will I choose to share this or tell that,' but rather, 'will I survive—will I make it through—will I stay alive'" (p. 2). So, one dimension of the historical difference among many women of color is a sense that saying the wrong thing literally threatens survival. hooks adds that this is "a real race class issue 'cause so many Black folks have been raised to believe that there is just so much that you should not talk about, not in private and not in public" (p. 2).

hooks's description of her struggle to find her writer's voice is interesting in that she identifies the battle to claim her own voice against the popular notions of what people "want to hear" (p. 15). She explains how after a lifetime of systemic objectification, it was a challenge to learn to be the subject:

The struggle to end domination, the individual struggle to resist colonization, to move from object to subject, is expressed in the effort to establish the liberatory voice—that way of speaking that is no longer determined by one's status as object—as oppressed being. (p. 15)

Those who have been more privileged by the dominator social system in relation to communication may have different lessons to learn around silence: "the ability to remain silent out of respect for what you don't understand is often an intellectual achievement and political virtue as well as a practical necessity" (Goldberger, 1996, p. 254).

Linkages and Relationships in IT

Applying these communication practices in any environment will help co-create a partnership culture. However, there is a direct relationship between applying these communication practices in IT environments and increasing the participation of women and people of color. The importance of relationship (by definition a type of linkage or connection) as a factor in the attraction of women to IT (as well as their retention in education and success in the professions) is well-documented. Further, in an educational environment where teachers are committed to providing the most constructive learning experience, the nature of interactions between students and faculty takes on even more profound significance. "Faculty members act as gatekeepers and important sources of information about how to succeed in the discipline" (Cohoon & Aspray, 2006, p. 161). However, the character of these relationships takes on even more significance in a climate that is already inhospitable in a variety of other ways due to institutionalized sexism.

Faculty whose attitudes reflect confidence in students, who are receptive to questions, who make time for students, who encourage students to learn, and who encourage students to persist against obstacles can make a tremendous difference in the academic success and persistence of all students, but especially those who have been socially constructed as outsiders to computer culture (Kirk & Zander, 2002). Cohoon and Aspray (2006) demonstrate that faculty and same-sex peers "play a key role in the retention of women in postsecondary computing" and that "outcomes for women approach those of men" in departments where faculty "encourage students and mentor undergraduates because they want to eliminate underrepresentation" (p. 233). In fact, Seymour and Hewitt (1997) show that this kind of support can even "influence STEM students to persist despite a crisis of confidence" (p. 161).

Gender socialization (which teaches many women to define their identity more in relation to their success in relationships than their success in terms of individual achievements) causes successful and supportive teacher-student relationships to take on an even more powerful and mitigating positive influence on women students. Due in part to gender socialization, "women's self-perceptions are more influenced by evaluative feedback than men's, especially when the feedback is negative. Men often discount negative feedback" (Beyer & DeKeuster, 2006, p. 341). Other research has shown that this additive effect becomes especially significant in an environment that may cause individual women to tap into their internalized sexism daily:

Teachers' beliefs and attitudes about appropriate behaviors and roles for boys and girls, combined with their attitudes and beliefs about technology, can subtly influence girls to not study computers . . . For example, studies have found that teachers smile more, make more frequent eye contact with, and move physically closer to students they perceive as having high abilities than they do with students they perceive as having low abilities. (Barker & Aspray, 2006, pp. 20-21)

It is especially important for those in positions of authority in IT, such as teachers and administrators, to learn partnership communication.

The constructive influence on the retention of women in IT due to relationships with teachers and administrators (who can serve as role models and/or mentors) is also well documented. It is important for all of us to see "people who look like us" in the roles that we hope to assume (Cohoon & Aspray, 2006, p. 156). In relation to women in IT, the mainstream perspective that computer culture is for men combined with the low numbers of women in the field, make it especially important for women to see people who "look like them" in the field. Numerous studies have shown the positive influence of role models in attracting and retaining women in IT (Butler & Christensen, 2003; Seymour & Hewitt, 1997). However, it is even more important for that role model to exemplify the attitudes, values, and beliefs that we might aspire to in that role. Female graduate students "rejected women who had made it by following a 'male model' of being aggressive, competitive, and unconditionally devoted to work" (Cohoon & Aspray, 2006, p. 157).

Cohoon and Aspray (2006) distinguish role modeling from mentoring as "an active process of sponsorship by experienced members towards less experienced entrants or trainees" (p. 158). Mentors can serve as advocates for those new to an area of study in terms of helping them become IT professionals. In education, studies on both faculty and peer-to-peer mentoring have shown that students increase in self-confidence, career commitment, academic success, and retention, and the numbers of undergraduates who apply to graduate school also increase (Cohoon & Aspray, 2006, p.158). Although it can help if your mentor is also a role model, for women in IT their mentors are often not people who look like them. Campbell and Campbell (1997) show that although students were more satisfied with same-sex mentors, they "benefited regardless of their mentor's sex" (Cohoon & Aspray, 2006, p. 158). In fact, there is a long history of men serving to mentor women into fields of study and work not previously open to them. Historically, many women of achievement in science had a parent (most often their father) or a male coworker that mentored them into areas where there were few to no women (Bartol & Aspray 2006; Rossiter, 1982).

Dialogic Process

The work of Ellinor and Gerard (1998) on dialogic process offers another useful skill set to use in parallel with nonviolent communication to shift towards partnership communication. Using dialogic process in all kinds of group forums (from classrooms to business meetings) can help to deconstruct the confrontational, win-lose, discussion paradigm that often operates in dominator societies. Ellinor and Gerard (1998) define the conversation continuum with discussion/debate (a dominator style of communication) on one end, and dialogue (a partnership style of communication) on the other. In the traditional discussion process the emphasis is on: breaking issues into parts, seeing distinctions between the parts, defending ones own assumptions, focusing on persuading and telling, and striving to gain agreement on only one meaning.

In contrast, dialogic process emphasizes: seeking the whole among parts, seeking connections between parts, inquiring into your own assumptions, focusing on learning through inquiry and self-disclosure, and striving to create a shared meaning among many (Ellinor & Gerard, 1998, p. 21). hooks (1989) talks about dialogue in similar terms: "Dialogue implies talk between two subjects, not the speech of subject and object. It is a humanizing speech, one that challenges and resists domination" (p. 131). In part due to the fact that it is such a radical counterpoint to traditional dominator discussion/debate, like nonviolent communication dialogic process may seem deceptively simple at first glance, but requires commitment and practice to do well. Dialogue helps us to focus on listening, linking, and connecting in communication, which are core partnership practices.

Nonviolent Communication

In Chapter IV, I explored the idea that one of the core notions of dominator societies is the persistent assertion of power-over, which means that our communications are often focused on fear and control, rather than trust and respect. Partnership communication that values empathy and linkages also requires that we practice nonviolence in our communication. The work of Marshall Rosenberg (2005) in nonviolent communication offers a valuable skill set for creating a partnership communication style since it shifts us from "thinking in terms of *what* we are and what we *should* be, to thinking in terms of our deepest needs and values" (Hart, 2004, p. 125). Nonviolent communication focuses on empathically listening and honestly exchanging our observations, feelings, needs, and requests.

Rosenberg (2005) outlines the following four steps to nonviolent communication when you are the one speaking. First, observe the concrete actions that are affecting you. It is important not to characterize what you are observing with any form of evaluative language that suggests a judgment. Second, describe how you feel in relation to what you are observing. It is important to claim self-responsibility for what you are feeling which means avoiding the commonly used phrase "you made me feel," since this implies blaming the other rather than assuming self-responsibility for our feelings. Third, state what needs, values, or desires of yours are creating your feelings. Fourth, make a very specific request that provides the other person a concrete action with which to respond to your feelings and needs. Nonviolent communication is a fluid process in which we must also practice these same four steps as listeners: listening to observations without judgment; seeking out others' feelings; seeking out others' needs; and looking for a specific request to which we can potentially respond.

At first glance, this may sound like an easy enough shift to make in one's communication, but a closer look at some of the examples that Rosenberg offers makes it readily apparent how deeply different forms of violence are embedded in our daily discourse. Rosenberg (2005) describes several common communication patterns that block our ability to engage in nonviolent communication. He adds that these "life-alienating" forms of communication both stem from and support "hierarchical or domination societies" (p. 23). Moralistic judgments "that imply wrongness or badness on the part of people who don't act in harmony with our values" often take the form of blame, insults, put-downs, criticism, and comparisons (p. 15). The problem with judgment in communication is that this practice creates relationships where people are more likely to respond to your needs out of fear, guilt, or shame rather than out of the compassion that might allow us to build more constructive relationships.

In *New Vision, New Reality: A Guide to Unleashing Energy, Joy, and Creativity in Your Life* (2001), Donald Klein explains the cost of shame and humiliation as an element of human communication. Klein explains the role that humiliation, a persistent element of dominator societies, plays in the creation of our self-identity. Many of us learn patterns of communication and behavior that are focused on protecting the self from further humiliation. The stage is set early in our lives for a persistent "us vs. them," judging, and blaming approach to social interaction where the focus is more on defending our individual identity than on true connection or understanding of another. Rosenberg (2005) adds that denial of self-responsibility is another life-alienating communication pattern that is reflected in such common expressions as "have to" and "makes me feel," both of which deny personal responsibility for one's feelings and thoughts. Communicating our desires as demands is another form of life-alienating communication, yet it is "a common form of communication in our culture, especially among those who hold positions of authority" (Rosenberg, 2005, p. 22). This is easy to understand if we learn that our goal is to avoid humiliation at all costs; unfortunately, the cost in this case is authentic human connection.

AN EXAMPLE OF PARTNERSHIP MEDIA

In a partnership society, what might our new media look like? We need more images of all kinds of human beings in relation to technology. In order for more women and people of color to participate as developers, users, and beneficiaries of technology, they must envision the world of IT as one in which they belong. Therefore, we need new kinds of media with new ways of imaging people in relation to IT and new ways of imagining how IT relates to our human lives. Sandra Harding (1998) underlines the importance of engaging more perspectives from which to envision our scientific and technological worlds:

If women, the poor, and racial and ethnic "colonies" are kept illiterate, not permitted or encouraged to speak in public, and excluded from the design of the dominant institutions that shape their lives, they do not have the chance to develop and circulate their own politically and scientifically produced perspectives on nature and social relations. (p. 142)

Connect! The *Ms.* of the *Wired* World

As explored in Chapter V, the existence of the dominator culture that is displayed in *Wired* magazine serves to exclude and marginalize women and minority voices from the IT meta-conversation. An inclusive and innovative publishing venture could expand and focus the larger, society-wide exploration of the future of technology while nurturing tomorrow's innovators. What might a publication such as this look like? The magazine, titled *connect!*, could be the *Ms.* of the *Wired* world. The purpose, audience, and content of *connect!* would be informed by the historical legacy of attitudes about science and technology, and enhanced by a contemporary and candid examination of the two magazines that this magazine would position itself between. This section describes *connect!* in the context of how it amends and expands upon the discussion of women, computing, and culture that *Ms.* and *Wired* began.

The *Ms.* founders expressed their purpose as wanting to translate "a movement into a magazine" ("Ms. Herstory," 1999, p. 1). *Ms.* began as a sample insert in a December 1971 *New York* magazine, and the first real issue was published in July of 1972. Gloria Steinem, Pat Carbine, and Betty Harris formed Majority Enterprises in April 1971 to start the magazine, and *Washington Post* publisher Katharine Graham's $20,000 contribution helped launch the magazine (Samuel, 1997, p. 1). When the magazine premiered, skeptics made predictions that rapidly turned out to be ill-founded. Two of the most notable are cited by *Ms.* online in their "Ms. Herstory" column:

[T]he syndicated columnist James J. Kilpatrick jeered, it's 'C-sharp on an untuned piano. This is a note of petulance, of bitchiness, or nervous fingernails screeching across a blackboard.' And after the first regular issue came out in July, the network newsman Harry Reasoner announced to America, 'I'll give it six months before they run out of things to say.' (p. 1)

The members of the traditional media may have been more than a little skeptical, but the magazine's readers spoke for themselves. The original 300,000 copies sold out in 8 days, and generated 26,000 subscriptions and 20,000 letters from readers (Samuel, 1997; "Ms. Herstory", 1999). During its over 30-year life, *Ms.* has undergone numerous changes, including a period when they were advertising-free, which allowed the magazine a clearer editorial voice that better reflected women's diversity in features on international and national news, commentary, fiction, and poetry. What *Ms.* has done exceptionally well over the years is to sustain a strong and clear feminist standpoint that has allowed them to be the leading voice of the feminist movement since 1972. What *Ms.* has not done well enough for the purposes of this discussion is leave ample room in their generalist framework room for in-depth coverage on women in relation to technology.

Like the *Ms.* founders, the *Wired* founders wanted their magazine to be the voice of a movement—the digital revolution. I have discussed this vision in more detail in Chapter V. Also like *Ms.*, *Wired* was an instant success, with circulation topping 100,000 per issue and 23,000 subscribers by the end of the first year (Rossetto, 1993). However, although the media had a skeptical reaction to *Ms.*, they immediately loved and admired the content of *Wired*. What *Wired* did well was to be the first computing magazine to even attempt to discuss computing in relation to culture. What *Wired* did not do well was to establish an inclusive definition of "culture"—it was in fact a "youngish, White, male, highly educated and filthy rich" *sub*culture (Hudson, 1998).

connect! could be a computing magazine with a feminist agenda—the *Ms.* of the *Wired* world—and redress the history of negative stereotypes with positive images of women in relation to computing and with stories by and about women in computing. *connect!* could be a magazine in which computing is less about power, money, and consumption, and more about social issues, and the ways in which computing and the people of privilege who participate in its development can operate in service of society. *connect!* could be characterized by its questions rather than its answers; rather than attempting to provide simplistic explanations of very complex social issues, the magazine could "reveal critical convergences" (Harding, 1998, p. 12).

In contrast to *Wired* and in concert with *Ms.*, *connect!* could educate readers about feminist issues in relation to computing by introducing information from the scholarly world into mass media. Potential audiences could include those who currently work in technology companies or use computing at work, as well as those who are new to technology. The magazine could bring those who have been systematically marginalized as outsiders to computing to the inside; the magazine could also educate those who are computing insiders about issues through a feminist and multicultural lens.

The magazine could engage as many voices from diverse backgrounds as possible in its audience and in its creation, pushing the boundaries around issues by asking questions that no one else is asking and sharing perspectives that are currently not being heard in the discussion of computing. For example, topics of coverage might include: technology companies that are manufacturing in developing countries and use mostly female labor; environmentally-conscious technology companies; schools and universities creating programs to address race, gender, and class; and women IT innovators in the community, business, and education. Although there may be some discussion of these issues occurring in forums outside of the mainstream, there is currently no forum where they are all discussed in relation to each other.

From the time *Ms.* went advertising-free in 1990, they have not had any sexist advertising. *Ms.* has maintained its women-centered standpoint from its inception. What *Ms.* has not done as well is to include enough substantive discussion of women in relation to computing. *Ms.* has reported on computer technology since as early as December 1980, and during the late 90s the "techno.fem" department allowed the opportunity for more regular coverage. Although *Ms.* has consistently covered computers over the years, the assumption underlying most of the pieces has been that women are users, not developers, of technology and IT infrastructure. Topics of coverage have included the following broad areas: girls and computers; social influences; tips for buying and using; the Internet; alleviating fear; women entrepreneurs; and programming and employment in computing. Given the fact that *Ms.* is a generalist publication, they have done a good job of covering issues in the larger context of women's intersection with the IT industry. The more specific historic limitations of access to and engagement with technology-specific topics and the feminist paradigm (and how that relationship deeply impacts potential innovation) remains uncharted terrain.

What *Wired* magazine has done well, at least in contrast to other magazines about computing, is to *attempt* to discuss technology in the context of culture. Unfortunately, their definition of "culture" is almost never women-centered, only infrequently includes women, and when women are included, often stereotypes them in sexist or other negative terms. As I discussed in Chapter V, my research showed that in contrast to other computing magazines, women were represented in *Wired* magazine much more frequently, but *Wired* still fell far short of actual parity in terms of adequately representing women's participation in computing or even in the world at large.

connect! could combine the best of *Ms.* and *Wired.* Like *Ms.*, *connect!* could be advertising-free, thus avoiding the tension between sexist advertising and feminist copy. Like *Ms.* and unlike *Wired, connect!* could be women-centered and place voices of diverse women at the center of the discourse. Like *Wired, connect!* could place this feminist discussion of technology in the context of culture, but the definition of "culture" could be far more inclusive than that in *Wired.*

Like *Ms.*, the inside front cover might feature art by a woman working in digital media. Like *Ms.*, the editor's page and contents could appear at the beginning of the magazine. Like *Wired*, each issue could include a photo essay that spans several pages. As is the case in both magazines, letters to the editor could address a wide range of issues and many voices. In the philosophical tradition of *Wired*, *connect!* could include feature articles that discuss computing in relation to culture from diverse perspectives. Aligning with the future-focus of *Ms.*, *connect!* could highlight innovative programs that are involving girls and women in computing in local communities (non-profits), business, and education.

Ms. often revisits and explores women's history; *connect!* could feature a recurring section examining the history of women in computing. In an attempt to reach female users of technology, each issue could contain a how-to article that describes computer tasks in an accessible, jargon-free format. Like *Ms.* and *Wired, connect!* could include book reviews on books written by women about computing. In concert with the feminist mission to educate, "The F Word" could be a regular column that teaches about feminist theories and the historical development of feminist thought. Finally, like *Ms.*, the "No Comment" inside back cover could feature ads from computer technology companies that use particularly heinous stereotypes of women to advertise their products in computing magazines. Since there is very little attention paid to the demeaning vision of women that continues to assert itself in violent video games, this would be another source of visually disturbing material for this page of *connect!.*

One key tenet of feminist thought in terms of information delivery is broad accessibility. In a publication that is for and about social change, it is especially important that the ideas be accessible. bell hooks calls for feminist writers to make a greater "effort to write and talk about feminist ideas in ways that are accessible" and to find ways to help these voices reach a wider audience by participating in popular culture (hooks, 1994, p. 90). In *Talking Back*, hooks (1989) points to the ways in which "stylized" academic writing narrows and constricts thinking (p. 36). The computer world has the same kind of "insider jargon" that creates a similar exclusivity. *connect!* could be free of undefined computer jargon and continue to construct an increasingly open and accessible style of language.

Although *connect!* alone could not single-handedly remove the many barriers to women's participation in computing, it could help to give women a voice in the discussion and an image of themselves involved in the meta-conversation regarding technology and culture. A magazine like *connect!*, that represents women in the discussion of computing, could help women begin to "wake up to our magnificence and to the knowledge that our personal power is intensifying the fire of hope and change in which the world is being reborn" (Johnson, 1989, p. 124).

The exponential growth of digital information has presented us with an unprecedented opportunity to give birth to a new knowledge tradition, but only if the users and developers of computing are truly representative of human diversity. As a global community, we have a choice. The choice is whether or not to use this moment of profound cultural change that the information technology revolution has created as an opportunity. Without the full participation of women, we seem doomed to continue on the same narrow and exclusive path that we have so far trodden. The information revolution has created an unlocked gate allowing access into the "no trespassing" zone that represents social constructs in a dominator culture. It has established a conduit through which many more voices can participate in the discussion of the kind of world we create. We could *connect!*

This chapter offered a framework for co-creating partnership language, communication, and media. However, this is only a pencil sketch of some possibilities. The more we all commit to educating ourselves about these issues, and the more we all practice at partnership, the more we can co-create new and broader visions far beyond what I have suggested here.

QUESTIONS FOR REFLECTIVE DIALOG

1. Imagine what it might be like to work or learn in an IT environment that engaged in the language of linking and connecting, rather than ranking and competing. Envision day-to-day interactions. Brainstorm about new, nonviolent language that you might use to describe technology. What did you discover?
2. Write the words "loud" and "quiet" on a piece of paper and draw a line down the middle of the paper. Spend a few minutes brainstorming as many words as you can about each personality descriptor. Do you know anyone who is considered "quiet"? Describe this individual and explain what you mean by "quiet." Do you know any "loud" people who are considered "big talkers"? Describe these individuals and define what "loud" means to you. Would you describe yourself as one or the other? Why?
3. Socialization about gender, race, and class may influence how one accepts criticism. How do you handle criticism? Describe an instance where you had to accept criticism. Who gave you the negative feedback? How did you react?

Would you have handled the feedback better from a different person? How could that communication been handled in a partnership model?

4. Consider this premise of dialogue, that we suspend judgment and focus on listening. Spend one day thinking before speaking and pay close attention to your mental shortcuts. What types of thoughts race across your mind before you utter a word. Do you ever start a thought with the phrase "typical _____" as a shortcut to explain a person's behavior? Do you find yourself comparing your situation to others in a way that diminishes the other person's experience (e.g., "you think you have it tough")? When you pause to think before you speak, do you select different words?

5. Since we have often internalized dominator culture, nonviolent communication must begin with ourselves. Notice your internal conversations with yourself and about yourself. How do you approach an unfamiliar task? Do you enjoy puzzling out a method to approach a problem or conflict? How many times do you hear your inner voice say, "I'm not good at" or "I wish I was able to"? Try to suspend self-judgment for one day. What phrases did you come up with to reverse your negative self-talk?

6. If *connect!* magazine asked you to submit a story idea, what would you like to write about? Consider an image of women and technology that you could analyze. Who do you know who would benefit from a publication that explored the myriad of influences and voices involved in global IT? How could it be used as a tool to encourage young women to explore their love of science and math?

REFERENCES[1]

Barker, L. J., & Aspray, W. (2006). The state of research on girls and IT. In J. M. Cohoon & W. Aspray (Eds.), *Women and information technology: Research on underrepresentation* (pp. 3-54). Cambridge, MA: MIT Press.

Bartol, K. M., & Aspray, W. (2006). The transition of women from the academic world to the IT workplace: A review of the relevant research. In J. M. Cohoon & W. Aspray (Eds.), *Women and information technology: Research on underrepresentation* (pp. 377-419). Cambridge, MA: MIT Press.

Beyer, S., & DeKeuster, M. (2006). Women in computer science or management information systems courses: A comparative analysis. In J. M. Cohoon & W. Aspray (Eds.), *Women and information technology: Research on underrepresentation* (pp. 323-349). Cambridge, MA: MIT Press.

Butler, D. R., & Christensen, R. (2003). Mixing and matching: The effect on student performance of teaching assistants of the same gender. *Political Science and Politics*, *36*(4), 781-786.

CNVC. (2007). *Center for Non-violent Communication*. Retrieved September 1, 2007, from www.cnvc.org

Cohoon, J. M., & Aspray, W. (2006). A critical review of the research on women's participation in postsecondary computing education. In J. M. Cohoon & W. Aspray (Eds.), *Women and information technology: Research on underrepresentation* (pp. 137-180). Cambridge, MA: MIT Press.

Conduct Problems Prevention Research Group. (1999). Initial impact of the fast track prevention trial for conduct problems: I. The high-risk sample. *Journal of Consulting and Clinical Psychology*, *67*, 631-647.

Eisler, R. (1987). *The chalice and the blade: Our history, our future*. San Francisco: HarperSanFrancisco.

Eisler, R. (2002). *The power of partnership: Seven relationships that will change your life*. Novato, CA: New World.

Eisler, R. (2007). *The real wealth of nations: Creating a caring economics*. San Francisco: Berrett-Koehler.

Eisler, R., & Loye, D. (1990). *The partnership way*. San Francisco: HarperSanFrancisco.

Eisler, R., & Miller, R. (Eds.). (2004). *Educating for a culture of peace*. Portsmouth, NH: Heinemann.

Ellinor, L., & Gerard, G. (1998). *Dialogue: Rediscover the transforming power of conversation*. New York: John Wiley & Sons.

Goldberger, N. et al. (Eds.). (1996). *Knowledge, difference, and power: Essays inspired by women's ways of knowing*. New York: Basic.

Harding, S. (1998). *Is science multicultural?: Postcolonialisms, feminisms, and epistemologies*. Bloomington, IN: Indiana UP.

Hart, S. (2004). Creating a culture of peace with nonviolent communication. In R. Eisler & R. Miller (Eds.), *Educating for a culture of peace* (pp. 113-125). Portsmouth, NH: Heinemann.

hooks, b. (1989). *Talking back: Talking feminist, thinking black*. Boston: South End.

hooks, b. (1994). *Outlaw culture: Resisting representations*. Boston: South End.

Hudson, D. (1998, May 11). Snapped up by the jaws of the Mediasaurus. *Telepolis*. Retrieved April 27, 1998, from http://www.telepolis.de/tp/English

Hurtado, A. (1996). Strategic suspensions: Feminists of color theorize the production of knowledge. In. N. Goldberger et al. (Eds.), *Knowledge, difference, and power: Essays inspired by women's ways of knowing* (pp. 372-388). New York: Basic.

Johnson, A. G. (2006). *Privilege, power, and difference* (2nd ed.). Boston: Mc-GrawHill.

Kazan, E. (Director). (1947). *Gentleman's agreement* [Motion picture]. Hollywood: 20th Century Fox.

Kirk, M., & Zander, C. (2002, December). Bridging the digital divide by co-creating a collaborative computer science classroom. *Journal of Computing in Small Colleges, 18*(2), 117-125

Klein, D. (2001). *New vision, new reality: A guide to unleashing energy, joy, and creativity in your life*. Center City, MN: Hazelden.

Logan, J. (1993). *Teaching stories*. St. Paul, MN: Minnesota Inclusiveness Program.

Minnich, E. K. (1990). *Transforming knowledge*. Philadelphia: Temple UP.

Ms. Herstory. (1999). *Ms. Magazine*. Retrieved July 6, 1999, from http://www.msmagazine.com/msherstory.html

Rosenberg, M. B. (2005). *Nonviolent communication: A language of life*. Encinitas, CA: PuddleDancer.

Rossetto, L. (1993). Get wired (monthly). *Wired, 1*(5), 12.

Rossiter, M. W. (1982). *Women scientists in America: Struggles and strategies to 1940*. Baltimore: Johns Hopkins.

Samuel, S. (1997). Ideals and realities. *Women's Review of Books, 14*(2), 16-17.

Schweickart, P. (1996). Speech is silver, silence is gold: The asymmetrical inter-subjectivity of communicative action. In N. Goldberger et al. (Eds.), *Knowledge, difference, and power: Essays inspired by women's ways of knowing* (pp. 305-328). New York: Basic.

Seymour, E., & Hewitt, N. M. (1997). *Talking about leaving: Why undergraduates leave the sciences*. Boulder, CO: Westview.

Spender, D. (1980). *Man made language*. London: Routledge.

Trefil, J. (1996). Scientific literacy. *Annals of the New York Academy of Sciences: The Flight from Science and Reason, 775*, 543-550.

Walker, H. M., Colvin, G., & Ramsey, E. (1995). *Anti-social behavior in schools: Strategies and best practices*. Pacific Grove, CA: Brooks/Cole.

ENDNOTE

[1]   Some portions of this chapter may have appeared in, and are reprinted with permission from Kirk, M (2006). Bridging the digital divide: A feminist perspective on the project. In G. Trajkovski (Ed.), *Diversity in information technology education: Issues and controversies*. (pp. 38-67). Hershey, PA: Information Science Publishing.

Chapter IX
Partnership Science and Technology Education

OBJECTIVES

This chapter aims to help you understand the following:

- The core characteristics of a partnership social system that most closely relate to education as a social institution.
- How to apply the values of a partnership society to reshape education as a social institution, especially the ways we learn and teacher-student relationships.
- How examples of partnership curricula can help you envision education from new perspectives.

INTRODUCTION

Ultimately, creating lasting and long-term change in the participation of women as developers, users, and beneficiaries of technology necessitates addressing this change in all of our social institutions. However, as the social institution that is given explicit responsibility for teaching the next generation of citizens, education holds particularly significant potential to be a positive force for change. We need a fundamental shift in the culture of science and IT away from its dominator roots to a partnership perspective, and we all (i.e., teachers, students, parents, business-owners, and citizens) need to co-create this change together.

In *Tomorrow's Children: A Blueprint for Partnership Education in the 21ˢᵗ Century*, Riane Eisler (2000) calls for changes in content (what we teach—our curriculum), process (how we teach—our teaching methods), and structure (where we teach—our learning environments). In Chapter VI, I explored the first issue—what is missing from the content of our knowledge tradition. In Chapter III, I explored the second issue—process barriers that some learners face in due to the gendered philosophy of science and the ways in which certain learning styles are privileged over others. This chapter adds to the discussion of all three issues, but focuses primarily on the second and third—partnership methods of teaching and learning and how to create partnership learning environments.

This chapter explores the following suggestions for shifting education (especially science and IT education) away from a dominator and towards a partnership model: (1) partnership ways of knowing; (2) considering the needs and perspectives of users and beneficiaries of science and IT in education; (3) educating teachers from kindergarten through college to better understand how our current system works as well as how to co-create partnership; (4) redefining student-teacher relationships in terms of partnership; (5) co-creating collaborative learning environments; (6) developing partnerships systems of testing, evaluating, and measuring learning; and (7) offering examples of partnership curricula and programs. In Chapter I, I contrasted the characteristics of dominator and partnership social systems. Table 1 describes the characteristics of partnership social systems that are particularly relevant to science and technology education as they relate to the topics covered in this chapter (Eisler, 1987, 2000, 2002, 2007; Eisler & Loye, 1990; Eisler & Miller, 2004).

Table 1. Characteristics of partnership social systems linked to topics in this chapter

Partnership Characteristic	Related Topic in Chapter IX
Trust- and respect-based	Partnership teacher-student relationships Co-creating collaborative learning experiences Partnership evaluation measures
Hierarchies of actualization	Partnership teacher-student relationships Co-creating collaborative learning experiences Partnership evaluation measures
Emphasis on linking	Partnership ways of knowing Partnership teacher-student relationships Co-creating collaborative learning experiences Partnership evaluation measures
Win/win orientation	Partnership teacher-student relationships Co-creating collaborative learning experiences Partnership evaluation measures

continued on following page

Table 1. continued

Partnership Characteristic	Related Topic in Chapter IX
Low degree of fear, abuse, and violence, since they are not required to maintain rigid rankings	Partnership teacher-student relationships Co-creating collaborative learning experiences Partnership evaluation measures
Value traits that promote human development such as nonviolence, empathy, and caregiving	Partnership teacher-student relationships Co-creating collaborative learning experiences Partnership evaluation measures
Images of nurturance honored, institutionalized	Partnership teacher-student relationships Co-creating collaborative learning experiences Partnership evaluation measures
Leaders imaged as anyone who inspires others to collaborate on commonly agreed upon goals	Teacher, heal thyself Partnership teacher-student relationships
Society viewed as a living organism with people as involved co-creators	Inclusive science and IT education Teacher, heal thyself Co-creating collaborative learning experiences

PARTNERSHIP WAYS OF KNOWING

We all have different ways of learning that may be influenced by a variety of factors, but in dominator education we have emphasized one learning style to the near complete exclusion of others. Traditional dominator education "methods employ a kind of abstract theoretical knowing, divorced from the real world" (Bucciarelli, 2004, pp. 136-137). In Chapter III, I introduced ideas about how this unidimensional approach to teaching science and technology excludes many learners. The disciplines and their "ways of knowing" were created by a group of people whose circumstances and experiences of their world were not reflective of the broader population. Therefore, both the content of our knowledge tradition and the methods of teaching and learning that predominate in scientific and technical education today result from a narrow perspective. "Other groups, with a different set of experiences—in this case, women—were largely excluded from the identification of problems and the creation of disciplinary knowledge and tools of analysis" (Bucciarelli, 2004, p. 138).

The "separate knowing" characteristic of traditional disciplinary ways of thinking features a concerted effort to be "objective" by separating and suppressing the self, "taking as impersonal a stance as possible toward the object" under investigation (Belenky et al., 1986, p. 109). This is the type of "decontextualized, either-or thinking" that predominates in scientific and technical education today (Bucciarelli, 2004, p. 140). Not only does this privilege certain types of learners and learning styles over others, it often means that "the emotional and moral aspects of a problem are typically disregarded as irrelevant and are thought to get in the way of an adequate solution" (Bucciarelli, 2004, p. 137). We cannot afford to ignore the moral aspects of technology development, most especially as its global impacts are rapidly growing. Bucciarelli (2004) asks:

How can teachers help students learn to see in a morally engaged way, in a way that generates a deeper, more holistic understanding of the world and its people? In other words, how can teachers help students learn to analyze problems with connected disciplinary tools of analysis? (p. 149)

The answer may lie in "connected knowing," which was first described by Belenky et al. (1986). As the phrase suggests, "connected knowing" focuses on using connection via empathy and care to understand the object of study more deeply and is "rooted in everyday experience, intuitions, and feelings" (Belenky et al., 1986, p. 112; Bucciarelli, 2004, p. 141). Bucciarelli (2004) suggests that this approach to partnership education will help students explore what the subjects of their inquiry are telling them, the real-life concerns, relationships, and concrete circumstances in which a problem or question exists, and their concerns for the needs of others, which contributes to a "culture of peace in our schools" (pp. 137-150).

INCLUSIVE SCIENCE AND IT EDUCATION

It is important that we shift towards a more inclusive view of scientific and technical education that does not only serve those who expect to work in those fields. We need to begin talking and thinking about science and IT education in terms of the 99% of the population that will not be pursuing scientific or technical educations or careers, but who will be users and beneficiaries of IT. Since science and technology present themselves to the average citizen in terms of a problem or issue that needs to be addressed, more people need to be scientifically and technically literate in relation to the questions that will impact their lives. For example, "has global warming begun? Is it due to anthropogenic sources? . . . does the developed world have the right to tell developing countries not to cut down their forests? . . . are we really ready to shut down our economy to save the Kirtland's warbler?" (Trefil, 1996, p. 543). People who do not have, or do not know how to use a computer at home, are rapidly being closed out from aspects of their day-to-day lives, such as getting a bank statement or reserving a theatre ticket.

Making informed decisions about scientific and technical issues that impact our daily lives will increasingly require knowledge of "economics, politics, social policy" as well as science and technology (Trefil, 1996, p. 543). This suggests that: (1) we need to teach more science and technology; (2) we need to teach it in ways that are more broadly accessible; and (3) we need to expose students to scientific and technical knowledge earlier in their educations (Trefil, 1996, p. 544). This will help students build a matrix of knowledge that they can easily add to, and to begin to frame that knowledge in broader terms that encompass global cultural concerns. In a 21st century world in which technology figures to be a key player in our daily lives, we need a global "citizenry who has a sense of how the world works" (Trefil, 1996, p. 549). Margaret Mead made a similar case for a more inclusive approach to teaching about science as early as 1964:

If we look to 'clusters' of individuals rather than the lone (and ethnocentric) 'genius,' then we might expect them in every cultural and social context. Everyone on the planet, she reasoned, might have some vital contribution to make to the advancement of the sciences. (Trajkovski, 2006, p. 282)

Further, Trajkovski (2006) recommends that we move beyond "simply welcoming diversity into science education" towards including "students in the formation of research itself" so that they can begin to see the ways in which science and technology "are part of everyday life irrespective of culture, identity and academic discipline" (p. 283). Ensuring that citizens are educated enough to participate thoughtfully in the decisions that impact their lives is a critical component of any functioning democracy.

TEACHER, HEAL THYSELF

In Chapter VIII, I attempted to explain why we all need to commit ourselves to unlearning the dominator behaviors that we have internalized from our social institutions. Teachers are no exception. In fact, it may be even more important for teachers to do this deep interior work than for other professionals because teachers have the social authority to influence so many lives. If "we want to be true educators, we need to work on our own development and on our relationship with people, the knowledge, and the world around us so that we can be good role models" (Rocha, 2004, p. 101).

Teachers must start by cultivating their own power-within (or intuitive knowing); this will allow teachers to listen to students with their hearts, as well as their heads. Partnership education requires teachers who are not afraid to teach from their hearts and to have the courage to create classrooms "that welcome soul" (Kessler, 2004, p.65). Teachers must consciously and deliberately share power with students by allowing themselves to be human beings, not just subject experts.

Teachers should view their role as nurturing students' abilities to think, study, understand, and acquire knowledge by their own initiative, leading students through a process of discovery and invention, rather than filling them with knowledge from the "experts" (Bethel, 1994, p. 63). Teachers should not display a "know-it-all attitude" but should "share the learning experience with the students," clearly pointing out purpose and direction some of the time, and just being there to help some of the time (Bethel, 1994, p. 75). Teachers should not be an obstacle to student creativity but should facilitate their students' experience of the joy of discovery by helping them "develop internal discipline, perseverance, self-respect, and self-esteem" (Bethel, 1994, p. 75).

Teacher education needs to be redesigned to ensure that all teachers (from kindergarten through college) understand partnership practices. In the U.S., we have an imbalanced and bifurcated system where K-12 teachers must be certified in teaching practices and methods as well as having some subject expertise, while college and university teachers often have little-to-no teacher training, but far more subject expertise. This approach to teacher training is both a reflection of a flawed core philosophy of education and a contributor to the exclusivity of science and IT. If all teachers at all levels of education were trained in partnership education methods; we could all participate in co-creating a partnership society, rather than teaching the next generation how to sustain our dominator system.

Further, on the K-12 level, few schools have teachers who are equally skilled and trained at teaching methods and at technology. At the elementary level, the majority of "teachers are women, and many of them have low computing skills" (Barker & Aspray, 2006, p. 23). As a result of their dominator educations, female teachers often serve as negative role models to girls in relation to technology, passing along their own "gendered" attitude about computers. On the other extreme are teachers with a depth of knowledge as technologists, but who are often "ill prepared to communicate these ideas and concepts to students . . . [or to] call into question their gendered beliefs about what kinds of people do what kinds of tasks" (Barker & Aspray, 2006, p. 25). Without training in social science and in the broadly negative influences of our dominator society, these teachers are not likely to display attitudes and behaviors that continue to discourage girls from scientific and technical study.

The importance of early entrée into science and IT cannot be overemphasized. The inadequacies of K-12 education in these areas are well-documented and this is a key contributing factor to the low participation of women as developers, users, and beneficiaries of IT. Barker and Aspray (2006) explain that some schools "integrate the use of computing into subject areas . . . [and] are better at showing the wide applicability of IT and the social uses to which it is put, thus potentially increasing girls' interest" and familiarity. (p. 17) In contrast, other schools that allow students to choose electives are more likely to "provide a vehicle for gendered differences in preparation for college study of computing" due to the already powerful influences of gender socialization by the time they reach adolescence (p. 17). Of the fewer students who may sustain an interest in science and IT until their entry into higher education, they may then face instructors who teach science and IT in the way that they were taught, and who have little understanding of the diversity of learning styles and pedagogical methods that exist to better serve more students.

There are also structural entry barriers that differently influence men and women due to the forces of gender socialization discussed earlier in this book. For example, more women than men "develop an interest in computing as they mature" which means that they may have a very different academic and experiential background. This different preparation for studying IT at the college-level may negatively influence their entry due to a variety of barriers, including selection criteria, application processes, and "the tightly structured curricula typical of computing" (Cohoon & Aspray, 2006, p. 152). I will discuss issues regarding teaching methods and curricula in higher education in more depth later in this chapter.

PARTNERSHIP TEACHER-STUDENT RELATIONSHIPS

In education, the (usually unnamed) power-over, dominator structure keeps teachers captive to traditional, hierarchical visions of how classrooms and learning outcomes should be structured—with an almost exclusive emphasis on the rational, usually one-way communication of ideas, as an educator's primary job. Like all dominator social institutions, education is largely constructed around this either/or view that privileges the rational over the emotional, and usually to the complete exclusion and denigration emotion. Education as social institution is simply reflecting the privileging of "maleness" (associated with the rational or so-called objective) over "femaleness" (associated with the emotional or so-called subjective) that is the hallmark of dominator societies. Teacher-student relationships that honor emotion as well as rationality are at the heart of partnership education.

A primary key of partnership education is for teachers and students to establish healthy relationships. Teacher-student relationships need to shift away from the dominator power-over paradigm reflected in the traditional dialectical model of teaching which views the learner as an "empty, passive recipient who must be filled up by one who has been previously filled and who is in possession of knowledge" (Bethel, 1994, p. 18). To engage in partnership education, teacher-student relationships need to shift towards a dialogical model where the learner is "a dynamic organism" interacting with the student's environment and being changed in significant ways by that interaction. In the dialectical model the teacher is the "authoritative knower" while in the dialogic model the teacher is "a guide or facilitator who assists the learner in gaining the maximum benefit from his interaction with his environment" (Bethel, 1994, p. 18).

Creating an emotionally-safe learning environment is critical to the cultivation of each student's power-within; this is far less possible in a power-over, dominator teacher-student relationship. Partnership teachers create an environment where students feel safe to: "feel and know what they feel; tolerate confusion, uncertainty; express what they feel and think; ask questions that feel 'dumb' or 'have no answers'; take risks, make mistakes, and grow and forgive" (Kessler, 2004, p. 65). In order for students to claim their own power-within, teachers must create an environment in which students trust that they will not be "dominated." One way to reframe student expectations of teacher as dominator is to make sure that students know that you genuinely care about their learning experience. In *Teaching Community: Pedagogy of Hope* (2003), bell hooks says:

Committed acts of caring let all students know that the purpose of education is not to dominate, or prepare them to be dominators, but rather to create the conditions for freedom. Caring educators open the mind, allowing students to embrace a world of knowing that is always subject to change and challenge. (p. 92)

Creating a climate in which students feel safe to ask questions about what they do not already know is critical to any effective learning environment. To create a climate in which students begin to feel free to ask questions, teachers must consciously work to deconstruct their position as "the expert with all of the answers." Given the dominator educational training that most teachers have had, this can be very difficult. One place to begin is to step out of the role of expert-with-all-the-answers (even when you have them) and turn student questions back over to the class to answer. I do this frequently in my classes, and the possibilities for discovery that exist in this simple choice never cease to amaze me. We often go much deeper as a group in discovering the answer together than we might have gone if I had simply given the students my answer, venturing down trails of thought that I might never have considered. This is also an explicit sharing of power in the classroom; we are all co-creating knowledge together rather than sustaining the power-over expert-teacher, ignorant-student dynamic.

The potential for truly transformational learning that lies in shifting from teacher-centered, power-over, dominator practices to student-centered, power-within, partnership methods was affirmed for me at a recent faculty conference at my university. Mark Grunewald (a colleague who teaches statistics) and I hosted a workshop titled "The Compassionate Classroom: Stories from the Heart" to work with other faculty on exploring ways to create learning environments that develop the whole student (head and heart) (Kirk & Grunewald, 2006). Grunewald led the faculty participants through a guided meditation that took them back to their past and asked them to recall a life-changing moment in education with a favorite teacher. While visiting the past, they also were guided to find a treasure box containing three things: a photograph of their favorite teacher, a key to a room where this memorable learning event occurred, and a quote that epitomized this memory. Before they returned to the present, they had to choose only one of those items to bring back. After the meditation, my faculty colleagues shared their stories.

Here are some of the ideas they chose to bring back from the past: a teacher who told me "educate yourself, and that can never be taken away"; a teacher who created an environment where students could choose to transform themselves; a teacher who talked to students as if "we were capable of understanding difficult things"; a teacher who told me what I did well, no one had ever done that; a teacher who valued me, so that I could learn to value myself; and a kind and caring teacher who created an environment that was safer than my home was at the time. I was especially struck by the patterns apparent in their stories; all of them focused on "stories of the heart," none of them focused on a "rational" idea or subject.

Certainly, given the title of this particular workshop, such an outcome might be more likely. However, I remind you that participants were also told that they could bring back a quote that epitomized "a memorable learning event." One would think that at least one of the nearly 15 teachers in attendance would have wanted to share a great idea. However, when limited to only one thing that they could bring back, they all chose moments that emphasized the human or relational element of the teaching and learning experience. Doralice Lange de Souze Rocha (2004) shares a similar experience about how the undergraduates in her teacher training program responded when asked to write about "the experiences that marked them most in school": "It is interesting that none of them referred to situations in which they learned interesting things. They all focused on issues that directly related to the quality of being and behavior of their teachers" (p. 109). In both stories, the life-changing education experiences that students remembered decades later had to do with their hearts, not their minds. These two examples affirm the value of shifting from power-over, dominator teacher-student relationships to power-within partnership relations that honor the whole student (heart and head).

CO-CREATING COLLABORATIVE LEARNING EXPERIENCES

Partnership education necessitates a redefinition of the learning environment to move from "the single expert view to a more collaborative and engaging classroom" one that facilitates student understanding of complex IT issues from a variety of viewpoints (Dakers, 2006, p. 16). Teachers need to co-create learning with students by actively linking ideas/theories with feelings/experiences in meaningful ways. As a teacher, I know (and I mean *know* in the richest sense via linking theory and practice in ways that have now fundamentally shifted my perspective) that the more that I release traditional notions of power-over in the classroom, the richer my student's learning experiences become. Every semester in my classrooms, I observe what our founding university president David Sweet (1998) said: "Given freedom, students will opt for excellence." When you create a learning environment that implicitly and explicitly values students as whole people (with heads and hearts) who already know some things (rather than as empty vessels), they show up for the learning experience in a wholehearted and whole-*headed* way. They are *both* more deeply engaged in the questions that we are exploring *and* more significantly changed by their learning experience. When teachers cultivate an environment where students are empowered to co-create knowledge, they become better critical thinkers, self-reflective knowers, and life-long learners; just the kind of educated citizens our world needs in the 21st century.

Spender (1995) offers additional reasons for moving towards this type of partnership model of teacher-student relationships. She suggests that in a computer-based world where information (and increasingly reliable scholarly information) is more broadly available, the concept of professor/teacher as the "knowledgeable expert" becomes more questionable. Since it is increasingly easy for savvy students to seek out the information that is of interest to them, this raises some serious questions about how to redefine the teacher's role in the learning experience. It also suggests the increasing necessity for training students to be better critical thinkers and to be more skilled at scrutinizing, evaluating, and synthesizing ideas independently. Spender (1995) says that the "graded curriculum where students are to study a specific period or problem one year, and move on to another the next, looks increasingly absurd as kids dial up databases on whatever takes their interest, and become independent learners" (p. 103). As we move towards a model of education based on information technology, Spender sees subject lines crumbling, students becoming learners/doers, and teachers becoming "teachers of human beings, instead of teachers of a particular subject" (p. 115).

If we are to become teachers of human beings, not simply teachers of ideas, we must create a climate for collaborative learning that allows students to co-create knowledge— to think for themselves, not for the teacher. A competitive learning environment fosters the dominator attitude of ranking, and it is not well-suited to all learners. A collaborative learning environment fosters the partnership attitude of connecting and linking, and may better serve the needs of more learners. While many math, physics, and programming classes feature "timed tests and competitions to see who can solve the problem first at the blackboard," Rosser (1997) shows how "encouraging cooperative problem solving where everyone 'wins'" is more attractive to more students (p. 15). Namenwirth (1991) points to the emphasis on competition in science as problematic in terms of preparing students for careers: "While competition often is effective in augmenting motivation and dedication to one's scientific career, it is antithetical to a fundamental characteristic of science—the need to share one's methods and results" (p. 24).

In our 2002 paper titled "Bridging the Digital Divide by Co-Creating a Collaborative Computer Science Classroom," Carol Zander and I outlined several strategies for moving from competition to collaboration: "(1) guiding students toward collaborative problem solving in class; (2) supporting students toward success with accessible nonviolent examples; and 3) creating a positive climate for student questions in and out of the classroom" (p. 120). Cohoon and Aspray (2006) also include collaborative methods on their "things that work" list: collaborative methods such as pair programming where students take turns writing code, and structured labs that emphasize hands-on experience (p. 168). Cohoon and Aspray (2006) share the results of McDowell et al. (presented in 2003) who studied the effects of paired programming on 555 students (25% women) in an introductory programming course. They found that women's confidence increased with pairing (but remained lower than paired men's) and that both male and female paired students "were significantly more likely than unpaired students to declare a CSE major" (Cohoon & Aspray, 2006, p. 169). Trajkovski (2006) says that just "as management theory in IT has experimented with Taiwanese guanxi networks and various strains of Japanese-inspired 'quality circles,' science education has much to gain through experimentation in the transformation of pedagogies with the inclusion of cross-cultural diversity" (p. 282). Pedagogical methods that allow students more opportunities to collaborate rather than compete are much more likely to result in the understanding of cross-cultural diversity that will be critical in the global IT industry.

What kinds of adjustments in perspective and strategy might help teachers partner with their students in co-creating not just learning experiences, but deeply meaningful transformational ones? Shifting from a course design where the teacher holds power-over students to one in which students claim their own power-within as knowers is more easily facilitated when you allow students some choice over what is worth knowing. Certainly, this may seem tantamount to sacrilege for a traditional educator, but is it?

Piaget said that we learn best when we are able to hook the unknown to the known. Not all students have the right hooks set for the specific, detailed ideas one might cover in a class. But, if you establish broad, thematic course goals, and use a variety of methods to explore them, you are far more likely to facilitate a student's natural discovery of a hook that fits. This facilitates the kind of "aha" moments that represent fundamental perspectival shifts and the acquisition not just of ideas, but of knowledge that students will never forget. Logan (1993) talks about this teacher-student curriculum partnership in terms of balancing control over form/method and content (p. 14). She recommends a dynamic relationship in which there are times when the teacher controls the content and the student controls the form/method, and vice versa, constantly trading off control between teacher and student, but ensuring that the instructor only holds control of either form/method or content at one time, never both.

Building a partnership curriculum also necessitates listening to where students are in their learning experience and being willing to adapt the course or methods accordingly. Teachers need to discover where students are in their intellectual understanding as well as where they are emotionally. Since "transformative teaching arouses anxiety and fear," part of a partnership educator's job is to help students manage those emotions when necessary (Kuntz & Kaplan, 1999, p. 232). At first, it may seem frightening to do this and much more "comfortable" to stay with your plan. However, my experience as a teacher has been that when I released my own fear and was willing to respond to the present moment, the magic that occurred in that teachable moment provided reinforcement for taking the risk to do it again.

PARTNERSHIP EVALUATION MEASURES

Evaluation of student learning is another important area of consideration for educators who want to cultivate a power-within, partnership education experience. One transformational way to support student learning is through affirmative written responses on their work. For many students (perhaps especially women in science and IT), their previous education experiences are full of so many "no"s that for most of them the "shame" button is easily activated. Once that emotional state is engaged, no real knowledge can sink in. Marianne Williamson (1993) says: "People who are always telling us what's wrong with us don't help us so much as they paralyze us with shame and guilt. People who accept us help us to feel good about ourselves, to relax, to find our own way" (p. 162). The former describes the learning experience most students have had in dominator education; the latter describes partnership education.

In fact, students are far more likely to find their way to what they are ready to learn when teachers affirm their tentative steps towards that new knowledge. The power of shame to shut down learning, and the power of affirmation to transform is well-documented. In *New Vision, New Reality: A Guide to Unleashing Energy, Joy and Creativity in Your Life*, psychologist Donald Klein (2001) describes how shame and humiliation shut down our creative capacity and how appreciation opens up spontaneous channels of creative energy. Although Klein is speaking largely in terms of our inner emotional lives, these ideas apply equally well to learning environments. Criticism shuts down creativity, while praise inspires creativity. For partnership educators, the emphasis should be on affirming and appreciating who students are and where they are in their learning. However, that does not mean that teachers should never "correct" students. They should just adopt a partnership attitude of respect while asking questions that guide students away from places where they are stuck and begin to illuminate new perspectives. Partnership educators try to serve as a signpost on the road that guides students to new paths, rather than the dominator approach of handing them a map with only one path highlighted (implicitly suggesting that this is the only "right" path).

Tests and Journals

Partnership evaluation measures also necessitate a richer blending of so-called objective measures (such as tests) with so-called subjective measures (such as journals). In fact, some scholars have raised questions about the usefulness of testing in specific relation to 21st century education. Spender (1995) challenges the validity of teaching students to store information in their heads, which she sees as less useful in the computer era than facilitating their development as critical thinkers. She adds the following historical weight to her argument:

Socrates was against writing because it reduced the role of memory. The monks were against the book for the same reason. And some people today are against the computer because it further reduces the importance of memorization [sic]. All this tells us that there are those who have amnesia, who don't know their history, and who aren't prepared for change. (p. 106)

As an alternative, Spender (1995) suggests that "we move from content-based exams to the daily activity of doing research, learning, thinking, using . . . no matter how you label it, it's a method which doesn't lead to 'correct' answers or standardised [*sic*] responses" (p. 109). (This is also a way of co-creating a collaborative learning environment.)

Les Levidow (1987) challenges current methods of academic and intelligence assessment that privilege one sociocultural group. Levidow examines numerous studies of IQ tests and other standardized tests asking: What kind of power do these tests impose? What systems of thought do they perpetuate? He views this as a "class-based model of knowledge" that demands "a lone submission to rules of abstract thought which suppress certain associations with concrete experience," and adds that most tests merely test "the ability to take tests" which "entails the self-discipline to pursue formal rules of thought whose content bears no intrinsic interest for the testee" (Levidow, 1987, p. 236). Evidence that these tests may indeed be focused primarily on testing one's ability to take tests lies in the successful business that has developed in the recent years—selling courses to prepare students to take these standardized tests (which one supposedly cannot study for). Some have questioned the content of these broad standardized tests in relation to the cultural bias embedded in many questions that assume a particular social status and cultural knowledge. Campbell and Campbell-Wright (1995) examined the gender- and race-biased content of mathematical word problems and found that word problems still privilege very narrow views and values. For example, the authors' "survey of nine college algebra books with a 1992 copyright found 8 medical exercises and 100 radioactivity exercises" (p. 143). The authors explain that while these examples are only relevant to students who may already share those interests, examples that use food or nutrition are more broadly relevant to large groups of students because we all have to eat.

One of the best informal methods for evaluating student learning is the use of reflective journals. I have used reflective journals in every class that I have taught and have found them to be one of the best tools for assessing student learning and fostering the development of power-within learners. Journals benefit the teaching and learning experience in a rich variety of ways. Students benefit from reflective journals because they can: better prepare for in-class discussions; allow students to show what they know (vs. being tested and found "deficient"); explore ideas and clarify thinking informally while it is still under development; provide the opportunity for regular feedback/guidance from the teacher; and help students build a relationship of trust with the teacher. Teachers benefit from reflective journals because they can: demonstrate the new power relationship via affirmative, guiding comments; track student growth and development over time; incorporate topic questions linked to major themes as part of the journal requirements; regularly assess where students are individually and as a group in terms of their intellectual and emotional status; and adapt the class according to student needs.

Sharing Authority with Students

Another important way to communicate that you are co-creating a partnership, power-within learning environment with students is via assessment techniques that place more authority with students. Combine assessment methods that allow students to show you what they know (usually more informal methods) with methods that test them on what you think they should know (more formal methods). Rosser (1995) offers an innovative type of partnership evaluation measure in the design of tests:

We thought it important that students generate (and answer) their own questions. This would serve many purposes. It would provide practice in posing questions, involve students in their own learning, generate ideas for course content, and, for us instructors, provide a window into the world of our students. (p. 94)

This idea could be used in a variety of courses and contexts. It challenges students to thoughtfully reflect on what they consider the most significant components of their courses. It might help instructors recognize how well they have conveyed what they feel is important, and give them tools for redesigning their courses. It allows students to show what they have learned, not just what teachers think they *should* have learned. It gives students a way to demonstrate their capacity for complex synthesis of ideas. In the end, developing the test questions becomes a valuable assessment measure on its own.

Bonnie Kelly (1995) offers some creative and interesting frameworks that are sure to improve the educational experience of many students, not just women, in mathematics. Kelly developed a "four-component system" revising the traditional lecture format slightly with tools to help students: focus sheets summarize main lecture points on one page each day, forward homework combines reading with exercises that will be covered in the next lecture, recap quizzes are given at the end of each lecture to give students an ongoing sense of what they are understanding and still need to learn, and finally group tests (group problem solving sessions) are given every two weeks (pp. 114-118).

Another way to create partnership evaluation methods is to use multiple strategies to reduce (or eliminate) the power-over dynamic of hierarchically ranking student knowledge with traditional letter grades. For example, I encourage students to take my classes "credit-no credit" so that I am not forced to rank their knowledge on a so-called objective scale, but can measure their overall competence in a subject area. I allow students to demonstrate what they are learning in multiple informal and formal ways. Another strategy for evaluation of more formal assessment measures (such as research papers), is to ask students to write self-evaluations. Teachers can develop a self-evaluation form that contains a grading rubric and specific questions for students to address. Providing space for narrative commentary about what they have learned and/or what has influenced their learning experience becomes another opportunity both for students to learn and for teachers to gauge where students are in their development.

EXAMPLES OF INCLUSIVE CURRICULA AND PROGRAMS

Another key component of shifting towards partnership education is to develop curricula that are more inclusive. With regard to IT education, Cohoon and Aspray (2006) discuss two primary views on how to create curricular change. The first view considers it "more pragmatic to alter CSE for appeal to women than it is to attempt fundamental changes in gender-related values and stereotypes" (p. 154). The second view considers the "relationship between gender and technology to be socially defined and malleable;" therefore, they "resist changing the discipline to suit values and stereotypes that may fit the current definition of feminine yet not be inherent characteristics of women" (p. 154). I have several concerns with these views.

First, I find both of these views too narrow in scope. They reflect a classic sort of either/or that will not help us to solve such a deep-rooted and complex problem as institutionalized sexism, racism, and classism in IT. We need both/and solutions that recognize the dynamic nature of the challenge. The changes that we make to develop a more accessible curriculum today may need to be different in subsequent years. It is also important to understand that many of the proposed changes are not just beneficial to women; they are beneficial to many other students, some with racial/ethnic backgrounds outside of mainstream culture, and some men with different learning styles than the current system addresses. The changes we need to make in the IT curriculum are about being more inclusive of multiple perspectives, not just being more inclusive of women; we need partnership IT education.

Second, there is an implicit assumption in the second view that there *are* "inherent characteristics of women," which misses the whole point of gender socialization. The ways in which sex (biology) and gender (social behavior) interact are complex, multifaceted, and dependent on other interactions such as race, culture, and class, as well as family, local community, and so forth. There is no "monolithic" definition of "woman." We can only ever talk about these issues in terms of common propensities based on the pervasiveness of certain forms of gender socialization in mainstream culture. When we talk about individual women, each story will be slightly different, although there will likely be many shared themes.

Lastly, these views about curricular change also reflect the assumption that these changes are only needed to make computer science study available to more individual women. Although individual access to study and employment in IT is an important goal, it is not the only one. In the end, the larger work of feminist science studies is to ask questions about how we have come to think about technology. The power for constructive change lies in a more diverse community of knowledgeable citizens identifying, reflecting upon, and questioning the largely unnamed assumptions of the uses and benefits of the technologies that impact their lives. The goal is to be more inclusive on all levels in terms of education and employment as developers of technology, as well as to improve accessibility for users and usability for those who may benefit from technology.

To help readers envision more inclusive curricular models in science and technology, I offer a few examples from teachers of nutrition, biology, and chemistry, as well as several program-level projects, all of which attempted a variety of strategies to develop more inclusive curricula and programs.

Inclusive Science and Technology Courses

In a 2002 presentation titled "Bridging the digital divide by co-creating a collaborative computer science classroom" at the Consortium for Computer Sciences in Colleges, Dr. Carol Zander and I shared ideas for adapting an introductory computer programming course to be more inclusive. Our strategies included emphasizing collaborative problem solving and creating a positive climate for student questions, which I have addressed earlier in this chapter. Another strategy we shared was to develop nonviolent programming assignments. Adapting common programming assignments to eliminate the emphasis on domination and violence is simple to do, but can have a significantly positive impact on the climate of the learning community in an introductory programming course (where students are most likely to need, and therefore feel supported by, a sense of connectedness). One common early programming assignment, Hangman, can easily be adapted to an activity that "does not feature murder" by offering "students the option to reconstruct the exercise in a way that is more accessible for them. One computer science student developed an alternative game where the context was a garden; when the player lost, the garden turned to weeds" (Kirk & Zander, 2002, p. 121). Another common early programming activity is to kill a rat at the end of a maze; this can easily be adapted to a nonviolent exercise such as finding food at the end of the maze (Kirk & Zander, 2002). These types of suggestions do not require a major change to the structure of the course content, but can have a tremendously positive impact on building a partnership classroom climate.

Lindsay (1987) offers an example of how the way in which you frame the discussion can lead to particular kinds of answers. It is another example of the difference between a "blame-the-victim" approach to understanding the intersection of science, colonialism, and race vs. illuminating the systemic causes for a situation. Lindsay discusses how most texts portray the Third World as starving and the developed nations as exempt from these problems thanks to technology, but the same texts do not explain "that prosperous countries, comprising 25 per cent of the world's population, eat two-thirds of the world's food production or that much of the food imported by the affluent countries is produced by the poorer nations" (p. 95). Lindsay, who teaches in Great Britain, shares her approach to teaching about malnutrition, disease, and starvation in the Third World.

Lindsay (1987) begins by asking students to write down their own ideas about the causes. Next, she uses the Irish potato famine of 1846-50 as a starting point (since many students are from Ireland) and helps students discover that while 25% of the local population died, "farmers continued to produce cereals, cattle, pigs, eggs and butter—enough to feed twice the Irish population of the period—all of which were exported" (p. 95). Then, she asks students to work in groups to test their new hypotheses using books, pamphlets, and other materials with conflicting interpretations of the causes. This phase includes: having students read observations of visitors to Third World countries before Western colonization, where they discover "ordered societies"; having students observe where products that they buy come from; and sharing evidence about why birth control is not willingly practiced in many poorer countries (because of the high death rate among children and the need for security in old age) (p. 98-103). This model can be extrapolated to almost any area of science and technology, placing the scientific knowledge in a social context and facilitating student discovery of knowledge, not just transmission of ideas. The focus is on helping students generate new questions and exposing them to enough different source material to inspire new perspectives.

Gill, Patel, Sethi, and Smith (1987) describe their view of "good biology" that is antiracist and features the following characteristics: provides alternative perspectives to Western capitalist views; supports minority students' self-confidence and esteem; draws parallels between racism, sexism, and classism; and exposes the concept of race as void of scientific validity (p. 129). Green (1987) offers an example of "good biology" that exposes the ways in which colonial administrators damaged the relationship between the African people and wildlife by imposing conservation ideologies on the people of Africa that were rooted in other cultural experiences (p. 136). In this example:

colonial administrators sought to safeguard Kenyan wildlife without any consultation with the African communities that coexisted with them—an amazing arrogance when one considers how long the Africans had been custodians of the game before the Europeans set foot on the continent. (p. 138)

Both of these examples offer a vision of how to design courses around social issues by asking a question and covering broad sources to answer it. For example: "How do you solve the world food problem? Science and Technology may throw some light on the question, but essentially the answers lie in social, economic and political action" (Gill et al., 1987, p. 157). We might approach teaching about women in IT by designing curricula that help students answer a broad question, such as: What systems prevent more women from being involved in computing, as beneficiaries, users and developers? Teachers could facilitate students exploration of: the history of women in science as a way of identifying existing social patterns; the story of education from the past to the present as a way of understanding how the legacy of exclusion and limited access impacts the situation today; recent statistics and salary data as a way of pointing to institutionalized sexism, racism, and other isms; and finally, a science fiction novel and several films as a way of exploring how media shape our images of who belongs in IT. One of the greatest challenges that partnership educators may face with these new ideas for curricular design is to learn to be comfortable with the idea that not all questions have one right answer, and in fact some questions have many right answers. This, indeed, is a new approach to teaching about science and IT.

Middlecamp (1995) shares an interesting approach to creating cultural awareness in a Chemistry 101 course beginning with the first day of class. First, she puts a few categories on the board (credit/no credit, undergrad/grad) and asks students to generate more categories into which they fit. This activity helps students to examine what their responses reveal about the ways in which they have limited the scope of their questions, specifically the consequences of categories, role of questions, missing information, and freedom to experiment. Middlecamp (1995) explains that "categories reveal more about our conceptions of the world than they do about the actual nature of the world" (p. 81). She also shifts the power-over teacher-student dynamic by explicitly talking about the idea that the "right to ask questions is connected to power" (p. 82). In terms of the specifics of the chemistry curriculum she uses a variety of applied and locally relevant strategies, such as, studying the building and its occupants, reading graffiti, eavesdropping at vending machines, and so forth (pp. 79-87).

Inclusive Science and Technology Programs

There are many examples of programs nationwide that are working to increase the numbers of women and students of color in science, math, engineering, and technology (SMET). Following are just a few that encompass early education (kindergarten through high school) as well as higher education. Developing a new model for partnership education in science and technology requires change at all levels.

The Girls in Engineering, Mathematics, and Science (GEMS) program is a great example of a joint effort by Augsburg College and the Minneapolis Public Schools in Minneapolis, Minnesota. GEMS is a free 10-week summer program for girls in fourth through eighth grades (the peak years that girls are known to "disappear" from the sciences). GEMS focuses on engaging girls with science by making connections to topics of interest to them, such as teaching girls about the chemistry of cosmetics. The program has been tremendously successful in terms of both keeping girls interested in scientific and technical fields as well as increasing their academic knowledge. In 2004-2005, the 542 GEMS students were 46% White, 32% African-American, 14% Asian, 6% Hispanic, and 3% American Indian. In addition, 50% were eligible for free or reduced price lunches, and English was the second language for 11%. Table 2 demonstrates the positive influence that GEMS participation had on academic achievement; girls who participated in GEMS passed the Northwest Achievement Levels Test (NALT) and Minnesota Basic Skills Test (MBST) in much higher percentages than girls who did not attend GEMS (Kielbasa, 2005). GEMS seemed to make a difference for girls in one other way as well. Average school attendance data for 2004-2005 show that GEMS participants averaged 95.7% attendance, while other girls averaged 93.1%. This seems to indicate that GEMS helped girls be generally more engaged in school (Kielbasa, 2005).

A 2-year project in Austin, Texas that included 151 seventh grade math students (girls and boys) and their teachers focused on teaching about gender bias, especially with regard to computers. The "project was designed to challenge the view that technology is a male domain" (Gilbert, Bravo, & Kearney, 2004). The project included two parts: one for teachers and one for students. The teachers "participated in a 1-day interactive seminar called Broadening Technological Career Horizons for Girls" designed to help them understand gender bias and to develop specific strategies for addressing it in their teaching (p. 182). Students were guided through "three interactive skits that used role-play procedures and one collaborative group project" designed to help girls and boys understand about gender socialization. The project was a success with both teachers and students. Teachers reported that they "were better able to recognize and constructively counter gender stereotypic interactions" (p. 194). Girls reported "greater interest in future computer and technology involvement than girls in the control group" (p. 192). Boys also reported "finding the experience worthwhile and enjoyable and an increased awareness of stereotypes regarding technology" (p. 196).

The mission of an NSF grant program at the Community College of Baltimore: Essex Campus titled the *Grace Hopper Scholars Program (GHSP) in Mathematics*

Table 2. GEMS influence on percentage of girls passing 2005 NALT and MBST

	NALT, 2005		MBST, 2005	
	GEMS	**Non-GEMS**	**GEMS**	**Non-GEMS**
Math	62%	45%	72%	46%
Reading	61%	45%	89%	65%

and Computer Science is: "(1) to train women to become technicians in computer science and related fields, and (2) encourage women to pursue careers in computer science" (Dudley-Sponaugle, 2006, p. 139). The program focuses primarily on extra support systems, such as, advisors to locate financial aid, mentors to support students throughout their studies, tutors and bridge courses in math to better prepare students for computer science courses, helping students build employment skills via internships, and establishing a student network for peer support ("Unlocking," 2007).

Rosser (1997) describes a good example of a partnership project in the University of Wisconsin system that involved the whole statewide university system and established a "bottom up" organization at the outset. The project was "initiated by the UW Women's Studies Consortium so that it had the potential to affect every campus in the system" (Rosser, 1997, p. 30). Instead of dictating what changes should be made, Rosser requested that each campus "submit a proposal with specific objectives and aims, consistent with the overarching goals for the project, describing how they would use [her] as a faculty development consultant while [she] visited their campus" (p. 23). The UW System Women in Science Program that developed as a result of these efforts focuses on: increasing faculty expertise in inclusive and student-centered pedagogy; promoting science education that includes analysis of the social context in which science is practiced; providing role models of women and minority STEM professionals, scholars, and educators; promoting campus and classroom climates that attract and retain women and minority students in STEM disciplines; and fostering collaborative communities for UW System STEM educators and students (UW System, 2007).

A project at the University of South Carolina had many similar goals, but took a different approach. "Three plenary conferences formed the backbone of the project . . . including pedagogical methods and curricular content that provide more female friendly courses . . . [methods for] transforming science and mathematics classes to be more inclusive . . . evaluation and dissemination" (Rosser, 1997, p. 33). Both the UW and USC projects demonstrated the importance of individuals being the primary locus of change in order for a department to change, and demonstrated that most faculty are more willing to change their teaching approaches than their course content (Rosser, 1997, p. 36). This is further evidence of the fact that there is not an easy, quick-fix to a problem this systemic in nature. It requires a commitment to lifelong learning and reeducation on the part of faculty and administrators.

Margolis and Fisher (2002) report on a longitudinal project at Carnegie Mellon University to increase the enrollment and persistence of undergraduate women in computer science that included several primary focuses: (1) training high school teachers in gender equity to increase the participation of girls in high school computer science classes; (2) changing the curriculum to provide "first-year students with

four different ways to enter the curriculum, depending on their level of experience";
(3) broadening admissions standards to include factors such as community service
as well as excellence in math and science (not necessarily experience in computer
science); (4) educating graduate teaching assistants about gender equity and reas-
signing more experienced faculty (better teachers) to entry courses; (5) putting some
of the computer science courses into a cultural context; and (6) enacting a variety
of strategies to make the computer science culture more hospitable, including the
formation of a support and networking group called Women@SCS (pp. 130-134).
As a result of these comprehensive, multifaceted change strategies, Carnegie Mellon
increased the enrollment of undergraduate women in computer science from 7% to
42% in the 5 years from 1995 to 2000, and improved the persistence of women in
computer science after 2 years from around 40% in 1995 to around 85% in 2000, a
level nearly the same as that for men in the program (Margolis & Fisher, 2002, pp.
137-138). The Carnegie Mellon story is a great example of the potential for change
that is possible when organizations are willing to embrace multiple strategies for
change of the type that I have outlined in this book.

The Enhancing Diversity in Graduate Education (EDGE) program is a joint effort
of Bryn Mawr College and Spellman College to "increase the number of women
who successfully complete graduate programs in the mathematical sciences, with
a particular focus on women of color" (Bozeman & Hughes, 2004, p. 244). The
primary goals of the EDGE program are: (1) to provide a supportive community;
(2) facilitate adjustment from undergraduate to graduate education, especially the
first year; (3) establish supportive faculty relationships; (4) help students navigate
graduate school culture; and (5) broaden students' perspectives regarding mathematics and its connection to other disciplines (pp. 244-246). Major components
of the EDGE program are a four-week summer session followed by a mentoring
program. The success of EDGE lies in the numbers of women who complete their
graduate degrees. From 1998 to 2003, the 63 women who entered the EDGE program
included 49% underrepresented minorities and 44% had a liberal arts educational
background (Bozeman & Hughes, 2004, p. 249). "Of the first 50 EDGE students,
who made up the cohorts from the years 1998 to 2002, 45 (90%) persisted in their
graduate programs to earn M.S. degrees, continue studying in doctoral programs,
or both" (Bozeman & Hughes, 2004, p. 249).

All of these examples of inclusive programs in science and technology prove
the power of partnership educational practices. We need more efforts like these
that address girls and women at all levels of education. In the end, these student-
centered, partnership education strategies establish a learning environment that
benefits us all because we will be co-creating a society founded on trust and respect
rather than fear and control. Imagine what scientific and technological ideas such
a world might inspire.

QUESTIONS FOR REFLECTIVE DIALOG

1. Bucciarelli (2004) calls for us to begin "creating a culture of peace in our schools". In what other spheres of our lives could this partnership model help us enhance our understanding of each other? Could the culture of peace expand to our board rooms? How might a partnership model marked by concern for the needs of others influence daily interactions at your place of employment?

2. An emotionally safe learning environment is a necessity for partnership education. Define what the characteristics of an emotionally safe classroom are for you. Have you ever been in an emotionally unsafe classroom? Describe that environment and explain why the setting could be called "unsafe." What are the major differences between the two environments?

3. When did you first come to understand the subject of science? Did you ever want to be a physician? When you were a child were you or your friends interested in doing experiments (chemistry) or fascinated by dead creatures (biology)? Describe your earliest memory of a science teacher. Was your childhood science education enjoyable? Why or why not?

4. Consider some ways that you use science and technology in your daily life. If we assume that all citizens can have a beneficial input that enhances our understanding of science, what ideas might you contribute to our understanding based on your daily use of science and technology?

5. Many strategies for including more girls in science and technology education have also benefited male students. How might including more males and females of all races and cultures enhance early science and technology education? How does making science and technology a male-domain also limit male educational development?

6. Consider your own experience with collaborative learning. Have you had opportunities to do group work? Do you prefer to work in community or do you like to work on your own? Describe one positive and one negative group learning experience. Were either of these experiences collaborative?

REFERENCES[1]

Barker, L. J., & Aspray, W. (2006). The state of research on girls and IT. In J. M. Cohoon & W. Aspray (Eds.), *Women and information technology: Research on underrepresentation* (pp. 3-54). Cambridge, MA: MIT Press.

Belenky, M.F., et al. (1986). *Women's ways of knowing: The development of self, voice, and mind.* New York: Basic.

Bethel, D. M. (1994). *Makiguchi the value creator: Revolutionary Japanese educator and founder of Soka Gakkai*. New York: Weatherhill.

Bozeman, S. T., & Hughes, R. J. (2004). Improving the graduate school experience for women in mathematics: The EDGE program. *Journal of Women and Minorities in Science and Engineering, 10*, 243-253.

Bucciarelli, D. (2004). If we could really feel: The need for emotions of care within the disciplines. In R. Eisler & R. Miller (Eds.), *Educating for a culture of peace* (pp. 136-159). Portsmouth, NH: Heinemann.

Campbell, T. A., & Campbell, D. E. (1997). Faculty/student mentor program: Effects on academic performance and retention. *Research in Higher Education, 38*(6), 727-742.

Campbell, M. A., & Campbell-Wright, R. K. (1995). Toward a feminist algebra. In S. V. Rosser (Ed.), *Teaching the majority: Breaking the gender barrier in science, mathematics, and engineering* (pp. 127-144). New York: Teachers College.

Cohoon, J. M., & Aspray, W. (Eds.). (2006). *Women and information technology: Research on underrepresentation*. Cambridge, MA: MIT Press.

Dakers, J. R. (2006). Dialectic argumentation for promoting dialogue in IT education: An epistemological framework for considering the social impacts of IT. In G. Trajkovski (Ed.), *Diversity in information technology education: Issues and controversies* (pp. 15-37). Hershey, PA: Information Science Publishing.

Dudley-Sponaugle, A. (2006). Under-representation of African-American women pursuing higher-level degrees in the computer science/technology fields. In G. Trajkovski (Ed.), *Diversity in information technology education: Issues and controversies* (pp. 129-140). Hershey, PA: Information Science Publishing.

Eisler, R. (1987). *The chalice and the blade: Our history, our future*. San Francisco: HarperSanFrancisco.

Eisler, R. (2000). *Tomorrow's children: A blueprint for partnership education in the 21st century*. Boulder, CO: Westview.

Eisler, R. (2002). *The power of partnership: Seven relationships that will change your life*. Novato, CA: New World.

Eisler, R. (2007). *The real wealth of nations: Creating a caring economics*. San Francisco: Berrett-Koehler.

Eisler, R., & Loye, D. (1990). *The partnership way*. San Francisco: HarperSanFrancisco.

Eisler, R., & Miller, R. (Eds.). (2004). *Educating for a culture of peace*. Portsmouth, NH: Heinemann.

Gilbert, L. A., Bravo, M. J., & Kearney, L. K. (2004). Partnering with teachers to educate girls in the new computer age. *Journal of Women and Minorities in Science and Engineering, 10*, 179-202.

Gill, D., Patel, V., Sethi, A., & Smith, H. (1987). Science curriculum innovation at Holland Park School. In D. Gill & L. Levidow (Eds.), *Anti-racist science teaching* (pp. 145-174). London: Free Association.

Goldberger, N., et al. (Eds.). (1996). *Knowledge, difference, and power: Essays inspired by women's ways of knowing*. New York: Basic.

Green, M. (1987). Kenya: The conservationists' blunder. In D. Gill & L. Levidow (Eds.), *Anti-racist science teaching* (pp. 136-146). London: Free Association.

hooks, b. (2003). *Teaching community: A pedagogy of hope*. New York: Routledge.

Kelly, B. (1995). The four-component system: A nontechnological interactive learning environment where women count. In S. V. Rosser (Ed.), *Teaching the majority: Breaking the gender barrier in science, mathematics, and engineering* (pp. 113-126). New York: Teachers College.

Kessler, R. (2004). Education for integrity: Connection, compassion, and character. In R. Eisler & R. Miller (Eds.), *Educating for a culture of peace* (pp. 57-79). Portsmouth, NH: Heinemann.

Kielbasa, L. (2005, April 26). GEMS 2004-2005. *Presentation in PRSP 330: Women in Math, Science and Technology Course*. St. Paul, MN: Metropolitan State University.

Kirk, M., & Grunewald, M. (2006, April 22). *The compassionate classroom: Stories from the heart*. Workshop facilitated at the Workshop at the Metropolitan State University Spring Faculty Conference, St. Paul, MN.

Kirk, M., &, Zander, C. (2002, December). Bridging the digital divide by co-creating a collaborative computer science classroom. *Journal of Computing in Small Colleges, 18*(2), 117-125.

Kirk, M., &, Zander, C. (2004, December). Narrowing the digital divide: In search of a map to mend the gap. *Journal of Computing in Small Colleges, 20*(2), 168-175.

Klein, D. (2001). *New vision, new reality: A guide to unleashing energy, joy, and creativity in your life*. Center City, MN: Hazelden.

Kuntz, S., & Kaplan, C. (1999). Gender studies in god's country: Feminist pedagogy. In M. Mayberry & E. C. Rose (Eds.), *Meeting the challenge: Innovative feminist pedagogies in action* (pp. 229-247). New York: Routledge.

Levidow, L. (1987). 'Ability' labeling as racism. In D. Gill & L. Levidow (Eds.), *Anti-racist science teaching* (pp. 233-267). London: Free Association.

Lindsay, L. (1987). Nutrition and hunger: Two classroom approaches. In D. Gill & L. Levidow (Eds.), *Anti-racist science teaching* (pp. 94-106). London: Free Association.

Logan, J. (1993). *Teaching stories*. St. Paul, MN: Minnesota Inclusiveness Program.

Margolis, J., & Fisher, A. (2002). *Unlocking the clubhouse: Women in computing*. Cambridge, MA: MIT Press.

Middlecamp, C. H. (1995). Culturally inclusive chemistry. In S. V. Rosser (Ed.), *Teaching the majority: Breaking the gender barrier in science, mathematics, and engineering* (pp. 79-97). New York: Teachers College.

Miller, R. (2004). Introduction. In R. Eisler & R. Miller (Eds.), *Educating for a culture of peace* (pp. 1-10). Portsmouth, NH: Heinemann.

Namenwirth, M. (1991). Science seen through a feminist prism. In R. Bleier (Ed.), *Feminist approaches to science* (pp. 18-41). New York: Teachers College.

Rocha, D. (2004). On being a caring teacher. In R. Eisler & R. Miller (Eds.), *Educating for a culture of peace* (pp. 101-112). Portsmouth, NH: Heinemann.

Rosser, S. V. (Ed.). (1995). *Teaching the majority: Breaking the gender barrier in science, mathematics, and engineering*. New York: Teachers College.

Rosser, S. V. (1997). *Re-engineering female friendly science*. New York: Teachers College.

Spender, D. (1995). *Nattering on the net: Women, power and cyberspace*. North Melbourne, Australia: Spinifex.

Sweet, D. E. (1998). Freedom of choice and the wisdom of the elders. In T. B. Jones & C. Meyers (Eds.), *The educated person: A collection of contemporary American essays* (pp. 75-89). St. Paul, MN: Metropolitan State University.

Trajkovski, G. P. (2006). Training faculty for diversity infusion in the IT curriculum. In G. Trajkovski (Ed.), *Diversity in information technology education: Issues and controversies* (pp. 280-309). Hershey, PA: Information Science Publishing.

Trefil, J. (1996). Scientific literacy. *Annals of the New York Academy of Sciences: The Flight from Science and Reason, 775*, 543-550.

Unlocking doors, unlocking potential. (2007). *Grace Hopper Scholars Program.* Retrieved September 21, 2007, from http://www.ccbcmd.edu/ghsp/index.html

UW System Women and Science Program. (2007, March 15). Retrieved September 21, 2007, from http://www.uwosh.edu/programs/wis/

Williamson, M. (1993). *A return to love: Reflections on the principles of a course in miracles.* New York: HarperPerennial.

ENDNOTE

[1]   Some portions of this chapter may have appeared in, and are reprinted with permission from Kirk, M. (2006). Bridging the digital divide: A Feminist Perspective on the project. In G. Trajkovski (Ed.), *Diversity in information technology education: Issues and controversies* (pp. 38-67). Hershey, PA: Information Science Publishing.

Chapter X
Partnership Global IT Business

OBJECTIVES

This chapter aims to help you understand the following:

- The core characteristics of a partnership social system that most closely relate to the global IT business as a social institution.
- How global IT businesses in the U.S. need to shift from dominator to partnership perspectives.
- Why we need a new global economic model, such as Riane Eisler's (2007) "partnerism."
- How developed nations can work in partnership with developing nations regarding the global IT business in a way that does not reify our historical dominator colonial relations.
- How to begin to envision partnership policy making in the global IT business.
- How one individual can contribute to co-creating partnership in the global IT business as a social institution.

INTRODUCTION

In Chapter VII, I asked how our knowledge about the dramatically unequal distribution of global income combined with the estimates on global population growth might raise questions about our social responsibility to each other as a human community with regard to the direction of development efforts in the IT industry. How might we use technology to close the existing (and rapidly growing) gap between the haves and have-nots worldwide? How might we use IT in service of human need instead of placing humans in service of the technology? What are the most critical global social concerns that technology might serve? Can we afford the either/or attitude of IT businesses that completely divorce profit-making IT development from broader social concerns? What might a partnership philosophy of science look like? What might a partnership global IT business look like? This chapter outlines a few starting points for answering these questions by exploring the following topics in relation to co-creating a partnership global IT business: (1) U.S. economic dominance in IT; (2) "partnerism" a new economic model; (3) global IT development ideas between developed and developing nations; (4) partnership IT policy making; (5) examples of partnership science and IT; and (6) ideas for where you can begin to co-create partnership.

In Chapter I, I contrasted the characteristics of dominator and partnership social systems. Table 1 describes the characteristics of partnership social systems that are particularly relevant to the global IT business as a social institution as they relate to the topics covered in this chapter (Eisler, 1987, 2002, 2007; Eisler & Loye, 1990; Eisler & Miller, 2004).

Table 1. Characteristics of partnership social systems linked to topics in this chapter

Partnership Characteristic	Related Topic in Chapter X
Trust- and respect-based	Partnerism: A caring economics
Hierarchies of actualization	Are you going to eat that? Partnerism: A caring economics
Emphasis on linking	Partnerism: A caring economics
Win/win orientation	Partnerism: A caring economics
Low degree of fear, abuse, violence, since they are not required to maintain rigid rankings	Partnerism: A caring economics
Value traits that promote human development such as nonviolence, empathy, and caregiving	Partnerism: A caring economics
Images of nurturance honored, institutionalized	Partnerism: A caring economics
Leaders imaged as anyone who inspires others to collaborate on commonly agreed upon goals	Partnerism: A caring economics Sharing nicely with the other children
Planning includes short- and long-term concerns for present and future generations	Are you going to eat that? Partnerism: A caring economics Sharing nicely with the other children Partnership in IT policy making

continued on following page

Table 1. continued

Partnership Characteristic	Related Topic in Chapter X
Emphasis on sustainability, sharing	Are you going to eat that? Partnerism: A caring economics Sharing nicely with the other children Partnership in IT policy making
Society viewed as a living organism with people as involved cocreators	Are you going to eat that? Partnerism: A caring economics Partnership in IT policy making
Earth imaged as a living organism of which we are all a part	Partnerism: A caring economics

ARE YOU GOING TO EAT THAT? GLOBAL GLUTTONY AND IT

In the U.S., we have learned to view business in very individualistic terms; it's okay for a business to just be focused on profits and not to be concerned with the social context in which that business is done; after all, it's a *business,* not a non-profit organization. The defensive argument often goes something like this: "I have worked hard to build this business, and I am entitled to make money any way I want." Yes, you are absolutely entitled to make money in any way that you want; that is how capitalism works. However, that entitlement is the very issue that I would like to raise questions about. I simply want to ask the citizens of the wealthiest country in the world—whose transnational corporations are wealthier than most nations, whose citizens represent only 5% of the world's population, who represent 30% of the world's production, and 40% of its consumption—to authentically consider how we might use our global economic privilege *both* in service of ourselves *and* in service of our world (Prestowitz, 2005, p. 1). For example, might we consider how to use our privilege to manifest the core values of The Bill and Melinda Gates Foundation—all people have value, and to whom much has been given, much is expected? "Of the world's 1,000 largest corporations, 423 are American, and the New York and Nasdaq stock exchanges account for 44% of the value of all the stocks in the world" (pp. 1-2). What might those facts imply for U.S. Americans operating in a global IT business?

Would it be possible to invest at least *some* of our efforts toward developing technology that better serves the serious human needs that exist in the U.S. and worldwide? Can we find ways to better share access to some of that technology? Can we focus on ways to better educate others about technology so that they can actually use it? Can we include more people in the decisions about the development of technology? Rather than focusing on the vast predominance of new, more interesting "toys" (most of which only the privileged few have access to), might we focus some of our energy on efforts towards an inclusive IT industry that addresses a few of our shared global human needs? If we want to create a partnership global IT business, these are the types of questions we must consider.

A partnership perspective—one that values empathy and caregiving, views good leaders as those who collaborate on commonly agreed upon goals, sees good planning as including short- and long-term goals, and values sustainability and sharing—might help us begin to envision answers to some of these questions. Unfortunately, the shift away from a dominator to a partnership model is little in evidence in IT since the primary development mindset is to privilege the machines over the humans they are meant to serve. Most IT development occurs in a power-over, top-down fashion from industry to users in the marketplace. Very little IT development occurs in response to collaborative engagement with human communities who are requesting a particular technology to meet their human need. The technology that has resulted from this process reflects a dominator orientation to development. When we place the IT industry in a global context, this general practice becomes even more questionable. Certainly, the Internet and the concurrent explosion of information technology holds the potential to link us together, but how relevant is that link for people who cannot read or who do not have clean water to drink? How else might we view IT development in relation to, and in service of, our global human needs?

In 2000, former U.S. president and Nobel Peace Prize winner Jimmy Carter was invited to speak on the question: "What is the world's greatest challenge in the new millennium?" His answer: "The growing chasm between the rich and poor people on earth" (Carter, 2005, p. 179). There is general agreement on this issue as our primary global concern among several of the richest philanthropic foundations in the U.S.; most share similar goals such as ending poverty, improving healthcare, and improving access to education worldwide. With over $33 billion[1] in assets as of December 31, 2006 (ranking #1 on the list of wealthiest foundations), the Bill & Melinda Gates Foundation chose education and health as its top global issues. With over $11 billion in assets as of September 30, 2005 (ranking #2), the Ford Foundation lists ending poverty as one of its top two goals (the other is spreading democracy). With over $8 billion in assets as of December 31, 2006 (ranking #5), The William and Flora Hewlett Foundation focuses on global economic development, education, and global population as part of its core mission ("Top funders," 2007). Clearly, some of the most influential global non-profit organizations (two of which were founded by members of the IT community) have a shared vision about their top global priorities and about where their vast resources should be invested. Couldn't some of the even greater resources of the world's largest global profit-making organizations (trans-national corporations) be similarly invested in developing IT solutions that serve greater human needs?

The people at the table choose the menu. Due to the power-over dynamics of a dominator social system, simply inviting more people to the IT table is not likely to change the menu. As I have explored in previous chapters, the new dinner guests are likely to eat the food that was already ordered. And, they are likely to eat it the way the others do. We have established a kind of global gluttony in IT that has to stop. It is time to put our forks down, listen carefully, and redefine both the menu and the ways in which we consume the sumptuous delicacies that could be available for us all.

For partnership to flourish in global IT, we need more people (enlightened women and men) representing more nations (developed and developing) to engage in a broader dialog, identifying needs that are local to their communities. If those currently holding power do all of the deciding, we are likely to simply create a new kind of colonialism with the global IT business. The answer lies in dialog, in *discovering* in partnership together. If we engage in this process to solve global problems, we may discover ways to do what global economist Hazel Henderson (1996) describes as turning our current "breakdowns" into "breakthroughs" (p. 12). She adds that "the new confusion also leads to the possibility of rapid paradigm shifts, social innovation, and learning" (p. 12). It is time for transnational corporations (TNCs) in the global IT business (most of which are in the U.S.) to quit hogging all of the technological goodies and to use this time of rapid paradigm shift that the IT revolution has offered towards real social innovation.

PARTNERISM: A CARING ECONOMICS

In order for the global IT business to shift away from domination towards partnership, we must also reexamine the economic systems that have developed in dominator social systems. The global IT business is currently guided by the assumptions of a dominator economic system, which Eisler (2007) describes as follows:

The main motivations for work are fear of pain and scarcity. People cannot be trusted. "Soft" qualities and activities are inappropriate for social and economic governance. Caring and caregiving are impediments to productivity, or at best irrelevant to economics. Selfishness will lead to the greater good of all. (p. 34)

In my discussion of research funding in Chapter VII, I explored the idea that if you want to identify what a culture values, all you have to do is follow the money. Since dominator cultures value fear and control, "policymakers always seem to find money for control and domination—for prisons, weapons, wars. But we're told there's no money for caring and caregiving—for 'feminine' activities, such as caring for children and people's health, for nonviolence and peace" (Eisler, 2007, p. 42). Granted, in the climate of fear that is prevalent in dominator cultures, it is hard to convince people that the resources spent on defense might be better spent on activities that contribute to our human development, such as education. However, how necessary would most wars be in a world where people had plentiful access to clean water, safe housing, good healthcare, and free public education? If we were not driven by fear, domination, and a belief in scarcity, perhaps we might make different economic choices. However, in a dominator economic system we continue to choose fear over caregiving. Here is where our money *could* be going:

According to World Military & Social Expenditures, the cost of a U.S. intercontinental ballistic missile would feed 50 million children, build 160,000 schools, or open 340,000 health centers. According to a UNICEF report, the cost of one nuclear submarine would provide low-cost rural water and sanitation facilities for 48 million people, and the cost of eleven radar-evading bombers could provide four years of primary education for 135 million children. (Eisler, 2002, p. 131)

It is difficult to reach this understanding when one of our primary economic measures, gross domestic product (GDP), reflects dominator values in relation to measuring actual economic development. Multiple scholars have explained how GDP does not count substantial and positive contributions to the society such as the unpaid subsistence farming that women do to sustain their families (in large numbers in developing nations), and the volunteer work that women do to sustain their communities (in large numbers in developed nations). However, "the billion dollar cost of the 1989 Exxon-Valdez" oil spill was included in the U.S. gross national product rather than being listed as an "economic liability" (Eisler, 2007, p. 63). The GDP was simply established to measure economic growth in terms of profit-making activities; the social value of those activities is not included in the equation.

One reason that economics matters in relation to the global IT business is that the communication technologies offered by the Internet have fostered further development of our current uncaring economics. For example, from 1992 to 2002, the "illicit arms trade, which supplies terrorists and guerilla fighters in Africa, Asia, the Middle East, and Latin America" grew by $100 billion (Eisler, 2007, p. 157). In *Terror on the Internet: The New Arena, the New Challenges* (2006), Gabriel Weimann reports on 8 years of research on hundreds of terrorist Web sites on the Internet that "present their case, disseminate propaganda, and recruit followers and supporters" (p. 49). The paradox here lies in the fact that these groups who criticize modernity in the West are using our most sophisticated technology to purvey messages against us, and most of these Web sites are hosted on U.S. servers. One must ask: Would these attitudes thrive, or even be possible, in a partnership cultural climate that did not emphasize the dominator ethos of fear and control?

The international sex trade has also been aided and abetted by the Internet, with Web sites ranging from legitimate but questionable choices such as "mail order brides," to paid pornography, to "sex" vacations. "One of the fastest growing and most lucrative illicit trades is trafficking in people. Hundreds of thousands of people, including children, are sold into slavery in the international sex trade and other forms of servitude every year" (Eisler, 2007, p. 157). In a dominator cultural context where there continues to be dramatic economic disparity between men and women worldwide, women's bodies continue to be traded like commodities. Economic globalization has "heightened these disparities. New regions and countries enter into the sex trade as their economic fortunes wax or wane" (Seager, 2003, p. 56). Seager (2003) further explains:

The global sex trade is sustained by astounding levels of coercion, torture, rape, and systemic violence. Women are often lured into the sex trade under false pretences—hired as waitresses or maids and then forced into prostitution. Girls are often sold into prostitution by poor families and, increasingly, girls and women are simply kidnapped, often from poverty-stricken regions, to be traded globally as sex slaves and prostitutes. (p. 56)

In some cases, these activities actually count as part of GDP. "Prostitution and sex trafficking represents 2% of GDP in Indonesia and 14% in Thailand" (Seager, 2003, p. 57). From 2001 to 2002, minimum estimates of women trafficked out of these regions were: Southesast Asia (225,000), South Asia (150,000), Latin America/Caribbean (100,000), Eastern Europe (75,000) and Africa (50,000). Following are minimum estimates on where these women and children were trafficked to: United States (50,000) and Western Europe (500,000) (p. 57).

The dominator values underlying our current economic model have helped create a climate where such violence is more likely than not. In *The Real Wealth of Nations: Creating a Caring Economics*, Riane Eisler (2007) explains what was missing from the previous economic models, capitalism and socialism, both of which arose from a dominator social framework:

Neither capitalist nor socialist theory recognized . . . that a healthy economy and society require an economic system that supports optimal human development . . . As Amartya Sen notes, the ultimate goal of economic policy should not be the level of monetary income per person, but developing the human capabilities of each person. (p. 148)

What might a new partnership economic model—that emphasized empathy and caring rather than fear and control—look like?

Partnerism

Eisler (2007) proposes a new economic model called "partnerism" that "incorporates the partnership elements of both capitalism and socialism but goes beyond them to recognize the essential economic value of caring for ourselves, others, and nature" (p. 22). Developing partnerism will require fundamental changes in "economic measurements, institutions, and rules" (p. 43). Eisler (2007) outlines seven steps toward partnerism—a new "caring economics":

1. *Recognize how the cultural devaluation of caring and caregiving has negatively affected economic theories, policies, and practices.*
2. *Support the shift from dominator to partnership cultural values and economic and social structures.*
3. *Change economic indicators to give value to caring and caregiving.*
4. *Create economic inventions that support and reward caring and caregiving.*
5. *Expand the economic vocabulary to include caring, teach caring economics in business and economics schools, and conduct gender-specific economic research.*
6. *Educate children and adults about the importance of caring and caregiving.*
7. *Show government and business leaders the benefits of policies that support caring and caregiving, and work for their adoption.* (p. 43)

Eisler (2007) describes how this new caring economics supports "caregiving on the individual, organizational, social, and environmental levels" and replaces the fear-, control-, and scarcity-based ethos of dominator economic systems. Further, partnerism considers "the full range of human needs, not only our material needs for food and shelter but also our needs for meaningful work and meaningful lives" (p. 21). Partnerism also makes good business sense, as the example of The SAS Institute demonstrates.

The SAS Institute, "the world's largest privately held software company," offers an example of the potential for success that results from a partnership approach to business, featuring a participatory management style and support for "employees' well-being on all levels" (Eisler, 2007, p. 47). Some unique features of the company that reflect caring for their workforce include: a seven-hour work day; the "largest on-site daycare operation in North Carolina"; fully-paid healthcare for employees and their domestic partners and on-site medical facilities; "unlimited sick days, which may be used to care for sick family members"; and on-site exercise facilities that include a swimming pool and gym, with workout rooms and yoga classes, as well as two basketball courts, and softball and soccer fields (p. 47).

Caring for employees clearly pays since the company regularly earns a spot on *Fortune* magazine's list of "100 Best Companies to Work For," has an employee turnover rate of only 4% (compared to the industry average of 20%), and has experienced "nearly twenty consecutive years of double-digit growth" (Eisler, 2007, pp. 47-48). Eisler (2007) shares other examples of how a caring economics results in a variety of financial returns: one 2001 study showed that companies with "paid parental leave had 2.5 percent higher profits" than those that did not; companies rated among *Fortune*'s best "also yielded shareholder returns on investment of 27.5 percent, much higher than the Russell 3000 stocks, which only had average returns of 17.3 percent" (p. 51). Partnership pays.

SHARING NICELY WITH THE OTHER CHILDREN

Both the wealth and global reach of the IT industry make it a prime candidate for partnership economic practices. However, the potential of IT to link our world together is seriously limited by global disparities in wealth and education. In *Disconnected: Haves and Have-nots in the Information Age*, William Wresch (1996) demonstrates the profound contrast between the information-rich and information-poor worldwide and demonstrates the severity of the global chasm of inequity. From the perspective of the "haves," many believe that the answer is to give "them" (more often, sell them) what we have. This is certainly one place to begin, but these plans often reflect the top-down, dominator perspective that obscures local limitations and local needs.

One Laptop Per Child

The One Laptop Per Child (OLPC) project, now housed under a non-profit foundation headed by Nicholas Negroponte, involved academic researchers and business leaders in the U.S. with teachers, global policy makers (including the United Nations), and politicians in other countries. The goal was to design a durable, easy-to-use, easily networked, $100 laptop that runs on open source software in order to improve access to education for children worldwide. Mass production began in November 2007 and the laptops are currently being sold to governments in countries as diverse as Thailand, Uruguay, and Rwanda, who have committed millions of dollars to purchase the laptops. ("One," n.d.)

On its face, this seems like a great way to share technology from developed nations to developing ones; educating children gives them the tools to build better lives for themselves and their communities. Without a doubt, the OLPC project is a step in the right direction in terms of its goals and intentions. However, in the absence of a broader consciousness about the dominator social context from which it emerged, the project functions largely top-down. It did not arise from local needs and does not address them for the most part. One primary issue is that the laptop's actual cost of $200 is not affordable in most developing economies. Another issue is the lack of other kinds of infrastructures (such as government, education, and technology) in some of the countries that have committed to the project.

Further, some citizens of nations being courted by OLPC have objected to their governments spending money on computers rather than more urgent social needs. The Indian government's response to Negroponte's invitation to join the OLPC project was to organize plans to develop their own $10 laptop using Indian-owned companies and IT professionals (Mukul, 2007). (This raises an interesting question regarding global development. If India can develop a laptop for 1/20th of what it will cost in the U.S., why is OLPC not partnering with Indian developers?) However, even this "local" proposal from the Indian government received criticism from some citizens. One article raised concerns that digital "dependency is just a click away, and the transformation from couch to mouse potato needs no great evolution"; the same article also suggested that government monies would be better spent improving the infrastructure of government-run schools rather than paying for laptops; "many have no drinking water, toilets, classrooms or even electricity" ("Counter view," 2006).

In spite of some of the obvious challenges, several nations in Africa have committed to the OLPC project. However, they have educational and technical infrastructure problems to deal with in order to make the laptops accessible and broadly viable for education. Perhaps even more important than infrastructure is cultural structure. A study of six countries in Africa showed that "women have one third less chance than men to benefit from the information society" due in large part to their second class status which means that there are "still more boys than girls in school in Africa" (Daniel, 2006). Simply putting laptops in the hands of girls cannot bridge this type of cultural divide. It takes a broader commitment at the local level to create this kind of change.

What Can Developed Nations Do?

Henderson (1996) suggests that one way to close the huge global economic chasm between developed and developing nations is to develop a "grassroots globalism" that would represent a "bubble up" framework for networking organizations worldwide who are finding creative solutions to their own socioeconomic challenges (Henderson, 1996, p. 187). Here is an explicit way that IT could be used in service of a better world, linking organizations that are already working locally, to share information globally. Technologists in developed nations might commit some of their energy and resources to support local efforts towards closing this type of technological gender gap. For example, Uganda was one of the first countries to commit to developing their information and communication technology infrastructure nationwide. As part of their efforts, they developed a series of strategies using a variety of media to be more inclusive of women. "This included training, opening a women's cybercafé, collecting women's stories and basing content on real urgent needs" as well as "radio talk shows on violence against women, especially war victims and refugees" (Daniel, 2006). One way to serve the vision of a partnership global IT industry is to make ourselves available to support local development efforts such as this.

The World Summit on the Information Society (WSIS) (organized by the United Nations) was a major step in the direction of this vision of global partnership in IT. The WSIS "provided the world community as a whole with a first opportunity to participate in an inclusive dialogue on a broad range of issues associated with the global information society" (Drake, 2005). The WSIS was held in two phases and laid "the foundation for long-term progress" in terms of developed nations working with developing nations regarding their self-defined technology needs (Drake, 2005). The first phase, hosted by the Government of Switzerland in Geneva on December 10-12, 2003, had more than 11,000 participants from 174 countries including 158 government leaders (i.e., heads of state, ministers, and vice ministers) ("Basic", 2006). The second phase, hosted by the Government of Tunisia in Tunis on November 16-18, 2005, had more than 19,000 participants from 174 countries including 247 government leaders ("Basic," 2006).

Certainly, we all have a lot to learn about each other in order for a project on a global scale such as this to be successful, especially in terms of operating with partnership rather than dominator values. Drake (2005) explains what WSIS participants had to learn: "Business and civil society participants accustomed to open and fast-moving debates have had to adjust to formalistic and heavily structured intergovernmental procedures" and government representatives had to "learn how to deal with civil society counterparts that . . . usually show up with laptop computers, demand wifi connections and full transparency, and e-mail or blog the details of the discussions to readers around the world in real time" (p. 13). However, progress towards a "bubble up" partnership approach that respects local perspectives was early evidenced by the fact that the agenda was not restricted "to just a few issue-areas, as the United States in particular had proposed" (Drake, 2005, p. 5). Leaving a "wide range of topics on the table . . . meant that many more issues could be added to the mix" (Drake, 2005). As long as those with more technical expertise practice partnership communication and really listen to the needs of those who have less expertise (or simply fewer resources), the WSIS has the potential continue to build partnership global IT relations.

Marilyn Waring's suggestions for a partnership global economics parallel Henderson's "bubble up" economic framework. Waring's vision includes: systems that offer more immediate feedback from governed to government (another powerful possibility for IT to be of real service); using the United Nations as a locus point for shifting global economics (the WSIS project reflects this idea); "time use" surveys that offer alternative ways to record economic trade that does not involve money, such as women's subsistence farming; and the Women's Aboriginal Network that links together First Nation women worldwide (another constructive use of IT that only works in populations that have the money and education to use computers). Waring adds:

If women, the poor, and racial and ethnic "colonies" are kept illiterate, not permitted or encouraged to speak in public, and excluded from the design of the dominant institutions that shape their lives, they do not have the chance to develop and circulate their own politically and scientifically produced perspectives on nature and social relations. (Martin & Nash, 1997, p. 142)

As some of these scholars suggest, IT could be used to link people who are already working on change together in relation to information alone, as well as for many of the organizing functions required for such large scale social change. This approach might be one of the best demonstrations of a partnership IT where the concerns arise from local populations but the resources and ideas to support solutions are shared globally. In the U.S., we already have a cultural ethos of wanting to help that we could potentially build upon. Carter (2005) points out that many Americans are eager to help when there is a disaster, such as the 1999 tsunami that resulted in 200,000 fatalities in 11 nations. However, we need to help in an ongoing way, and technology could be a source for action in relation to the *monthly* deaths worldwide of 165,000 from malaria, 140,000 from diarrhea, and 240,000 from AIDS (Carter, 2005, p. 187). Carter claims that "$2.50 a year from each American and European citizen could mount an effective global fight against malaria" (p. 187). How might IT be mobilized in broader service of such a human need?

The research of Stockard, Akbari, and Domooei (2006) examines how increasing the diversity of IT users can lead to increased confidence and self-esteem as well as empowering users to see IT as a tool for social change. They also recommend expanding the conception of "diversity in IT" into a global context, arguing for a sustainable diversity that embraces the Industrialized North as well as the countries of the South. In *Tectonic Shift: The Geoeconomic Realignment of Globalizing*

Markets, Jagdish Sheth and Rajendra Sisodia (2006) also predict that globalization will require a geoeconomic restructuring from our current East-West trade relations to new North-South relations between three major regional blocks:

a US/American block, a European/African bloc, and an Asian bloc... The emergence of this tri-polar system promises a more stable world economy than is possible when there is only one superpower, or when two superpowers are locked in irreconcilable conflict with each other. (Aronica & Ramdoo, 2006, p. 55)

Nobel Prize winning economist Joseph Stiglitz (2003) shares his vision of how we might reshape the practices for economic globalization that have not equally benefited all:

When it is properly, fairly run, with all countries having a voice in policies affecting them, there is a possibility that it will help create a new global economy in which growth is not only more sustainable and less volatile but the fruits of this growth are more equitably shared. (p. 22)

For example, Stiglitz (2003) suggests that "the tide of illegal immigration into the U.S. from Mexico could be reversed by making infrastructure investments in Mexico" such as a "regional retirement program" that would include:

a series of measures aimed at facilitating and promoting the voluntary relocation of retired US and Canadian citizens to Mexico. In the next thirty years, more than 100 million Americans will turn 65. Many will have a hard time affording a comfortable US retirement. One cheap and relatively easy part of the solution would be to let retirees follow the sun over the border by extending their Medicare coverage to Mexico, where the cost of living is much lower. (Aronica & Ramdoo 2006, p. 97)

The "economic boost of their spending and Medicare payments alone would be roughly equal to 50 percent of Mexico's current GDP. Mexico would also gain from an increased demand for both skilled and unskilled healthcare workers" (Aronica & Ramdoo 2006, p. 98). The IT industry could serve this type of project in a variety of ways from basic information sharing to database technologies to track and transfer payments. These scholars offer just a few views of how a new perspective on our global IT relationships might inspire creative and mutually fruitful directions for economic development. However, for any of these ideas to work, we must practice partnership communication and be grounded in partnership economic values both of which implicitly respect that the emphasis is on building relationships of respect and trust that are founded in mutual empathy and care, not fear and control.

PARTNERSHIP IT POLICY MAKING

To achieve partnership relations in science and technology requires a reconsideration of economic and research policy-making regarding the global IT industry. Harding (2000) suggests "that those who bear the consequences of decisions should have proportionate shares in making them" (p. 127). Grassroots research designs that are bottom-up, such as participatory action research and other methods for giving users a central voice in the design of scientific and technological projects, can result in scientific, technological, and political benefits (p. 127). However, in the U.S., "science and technology policies are customarily framed by representatives of just three groups: business, the military, and universities" (Sclove, 2000, p. 33). Richard Sclove (2000) shares the results of two projects in Denmark and the U.S. designed to involve citizens in scientific and technological policy making and to challenge the notion that "nonexperts are ill-equipped to comment on complex technical matters" (p. 33).

In the late 80s, the Danish Board of Technology (DBOT) pioneered the "consensus conference" concept and this practice has been explored in other countries in Europe (as well as Japan and the U.S.) since then. Here is how the process works: (1) The DBOT selects a topic for consideration; (2) The DBOT appoints a steering committee that may include "an academic scientist, an industry researcher, a trade unionist, a representative of a public-interest group, and a project manager from the board's professional staff"; (3) The DBOT advertises for lay participants who must write a letter describing their background and reasons for participating; (4) Fifteen participants are chosen that represent "the demographic breadth of the Danish population"; (5) The lay group meets with a facilitator for a weekend to study an expert background paper and pose questions to be addressed during a public forum; (6) Based on these questions, the DBOT assembles an expert panel that includes technologists and social scientists; (7) The lay group meets for a second weekend to study more background readings, refine previous questions, and pose additional ones; (8) Based on the resulting questions, the DBOT makes any necessary adjustments to the expert panel; (9) The expert panel prepares short oral and written responses to the questions; (10) A 4-day public forum is held that includes the lay group, expert panel, members of Parliament, media, and Danish citizens (the forum includes presentations by experts, cross-examination by the lay group, the experts leave and the lay group prepares a report, and the experts return on the final day to correct any errors of fact); and (11) "The lay group presents its report to a national press conference" (Sclove, 2000, pp. 35-36).

A further benefit of this process is that in contrast to studies produced by experts that tend to focus on the technology and contain a separate section on "ethics," "the lay reports can be incisive and impassioned" as well as demonstrating a central concern with social issues that are integrated throughout the report (Sclove, 2000, p. 37). Sclove (2000) describes the social benefit of this approach over the "conventional politics of technology":

The public's first opportunity to react to an innovation can occur years or even decades after crucial decisions about the form that innovation will take have already been made. In such a situation, the only feasible choice is between pushing the technology forward or bringing everything to a halt. And no one really wins. (p. 39)

The U.S. National Institutes of Health (NIH) attempted a similar partnership approach to policy making in the mid-80s when they:

initiated a program to include consumers on advisory panels responsible for reviewing research proposals...First, scientists determined the technical merits of proposals and then an advisory council composed of scientists and laypeople decided whether a particular research project should be supported based on the prior scientific assessment as well as NIH priorities and social considerations. (Kleinman, 2000, p. 141)

This decision-making model reflected partnership values since it included the perspectives of technical experts (whose primary role was to evaluate the science) and so-called laypeople (whose primary role was to evaluate social concerns and priorities).

In 1997, a group of public policy scholars and technologists decided to explore the Danish concept by hosting a Citizen's Panel in Boston to explore "telecommunications and the future of democracy" (Sclove, 2000, p. 40). The "15-member citizen's panel issued a call to protect First Amendment rights and personal privacy on the Internet, mandating community involvement in telecommunications policy-making, and returning a percentage of high-tech corporate earnings to communities and non profit organizations" (p. 40). Their report also contained specific recommendations such as establishing "volunteer citizen groups at the local level to address appropriate restriction of access to certain (e.g., pornographic) Internet sites at public libraries, schools and community centers," and "legally prohibiting the use of private individual data without prior notification and approval" (p. 41). Other examples of communities of laypeople who have organized to encourage particular research agendas include AIDs activists in the U.S. in the 80s and the local residents of Woburn, Massachusetts who convinced Harvard researchers to investigate the link between the water in their neighborhood and an increased incidence of cancer (Kleinman, 2000, pp. 146-148).

Strategies for overcoming the obstacles to citizen participation in science include: offering a small per diem and/or fellowships to increase the participation of community members across all social strata in issues of concern to them; developing more inclusive practices for educating all citizens about science and technology so that they can be more informed participants in decisions that effect their lives; encouraging the participation of scientific experts by validating this type of community-based research as a recognized part of promotion and tenure decisions for university faculty, and/or increasing the grant monies available for this type of research (Kleinman, 2000, pp. 153-157).

EXAMPLES OF PARTNERSHIP SCIENCE AND IT: THE NEW PRISM

In a column titled "Hold on science hides religious zeal," syndicated editorial columnist Ellen Goodman (1989) characterized American interest in keeping up with the latest developments in science and technology as an obsession with cult-like religious overtones. This cult-like devotion to technology is now being purveyed worldwide. However, without a consciousness of whose needs, whose ideas, and whose voices are represented in the information and the technology, our global IT efforts may simply result in a new type of global colonialism. In order to engage a diversity of perspectives, Visvanathan calls for a kind of "cognitive justice" where there is "a truly creative, innovative dialog of knowledges" that encourages "a sustainable diversity of people and communities" (Stockard et al., 2006, p. 123). If we hold the theory of cognitive justice in the forefront of our IT development decisions "the knowledge of indigenous peoples, women, the old, the young and various communities will be privileged, not just technoscientific knowledge" (p. 123). What if such a diversity of perspectives were brought into the consideration of IT development decisions? What might that look like? Here are just a few examples of the scientific and technical innovation that such diverse perspectives have inspired.

In *Teaching Science for Social Justice*, Angela Calabrese Barton (2003) and others demonstrate what a redefinition of science to be "science for all" might look like by sharing stories of urban youths living in homeless shelters in Texas and New York. In after school science clubs at their homeless shelters, these youth use science to solve problems in their lives and the lives of their communities and share the value that science is something that helps "to beautify and change your community, to make it a better place" (pp. 134-135). This is a far cry from the traditional notion of good scientific research as existing apart from any social context, and often any social purpose.

In *Searching for Life: The Grandmothers of the Plaza de Mayo and the Disappeared Children of Argentina*, Rita Arditti (1999) chronicles the tale of how a group of women—who self-identified as "simply housewives" and who had "never done anything outside the home"—helped change both science and the face of a nation. The Grandmothers worked with scientists to develop a genetic blood test to identify biological affiliation even when the parents were dead—a "grandparentage" test. In 1987, the National Genetic Data Bank was established in Argentina and by 1996, "2,100 individuals had deposited their blood in the bank, representing about 175 family groups" and over 30 children of the disappeared had reclaimed their birth identities (Arditti, 1999, p. 73). As mass graves began to be unearthed in the mid-80s, the Grandmothers also engaged internationally renowned forensic scientists to identify remains, inspiring one of the first uses of this science as a tool in human rights investigations.

In *Diversity in Information Technology Education: Issues and Controversies*, Stockard et al. (2006) explore ways that IT professionals are participating in closing the digital divide by serving as resources for underserved communities and contributing to solve "such problems as unequal performance on SAT and AP tests by high school students of color, elevated high school dropout rates among Latinos and high levels of community youth violence" (p. 102). They share information about constructive projects, such as: networking between a local neighborhood and Pennsylvania State University; TASH, an organization dedicated to equity and inclusion for people with disabilities (see www.tash.org); organizations such as Global NetCorps and the Trust for the Americas; FLOSS (Free/Libre Open Source Software), an organization that supports open software and operates "on the assumption that information technology use and development can be applied to the creation of a society based on co-operation, equality and sharing"; and the collaboration between Sarai (a Delhi-based initiative that encourages people in poor neighborhoods to record events around them using local computer centers) and Waag Society (an Amsterdam-based research and development organization that works to link technology and culture) (Stockard et al., 2006, pp. 102-109).

Joint global projects like The Literacy Project (www.google.com/literacy)—launched by Google in collaboration with LitCam (a non-profit literacy organization) and UNESCO's Institute for Lifelong Learning—offer an example of partnership in the global IT business. The project features a Web site with resources for teachers and literacy organizations worldwide and includes scholarly articles, books, videos, and blogs available in English, German, and Spanish. Since the vast majority of current Web content is in English, they are also working to expand and include other languages (The Literacy Project, 2007).

The new partnership model of global IT development that I am proposing in this chapter is best envisioned as a kind of prism. When projected through a prism, white light reflects all of the colors:

White Light will only return to the planet when every human being recognizes every other human being as an individual frequency of the White Light. As long as we keep eliminating or devaluing other human beings we have decided we don't like, that is, destroying frequencies of the spectrum, we will not be able to experience the White Light. Our job is to protect and nurture each human frequency so that the White Light can return. (Lipton, 2005, p. 194)

A partnership approach to global IT development offers the potential for information technology to serve as the prism through which the white light that reflects all of our human colors is projected.

QUESTIONS FOR REFLECTIVE DIALOG

1. Write a letter to the Bill and Melinda Gates foundation addressing an area of social concern that you feel should be better funded. Develop an argument for action that includes specific information about the situation and asks for well-defined needs to be met. Send it.

2. Consider Eisler's (2007) list of positive social programs that cost the same as some of our most sophisticated weaponry. How might we be safer if we built schools instead of bombs? How might technology be used to enable the most desperate global communities to have fresh drinking water?

3. Consider your own community. How could science or technology help "beautify and change" it to "make it a better place" (Barton et al., 2003)? What do the people who you consider "your community" need? Is there a way that technology could enhance their lives? Is there a way for them to be a proactive part of the process? What are their needs and what tools might meet those needs?

4. The concept of white light (all colors are reflected in its prism) is a great metaphor for the interdependency that exists in our human community and in our relationship with nature. What is another good image that could represent the links that bind us? Try to draw the visual and write an explanation for the metaphor. How could this visual be used to promote a global portrait of IT?

5. "Partnerism" is dependent on creating links on an individual and cultural level. How could you look to see and celebrate the connections you have in your daily human interaction with others? Consider phenomena like "road rage," where complete strangers have resorted to violence because they do not

see each other as humans, but as impediments. How does seeing ourselves as dependent on and connected to others feed into the cultural connectedness of society as a whole?

6. Anwar Sadat wrote that his experiences in prison allowed him to change the "fabric" of his thoughts. How do we go about weaving a new fabric for our thoughts? What educational settings allow us to experience transformational learning? What ideas in this chapter made you feel you repaired, added to, or expanded the fabric of your thoughts?

REFERENCES[2]

Arditti, R. (1999). *Searching for life: The grandmothers of the Plaza de Mayo and the disappeared children of Argentina.* Berkeley: U of California P.

Aronica, R., & Ramdoo, M. (2006). *The world is flat? A critical analysis of the New York Times bestseller by Thomas Friedman.* Tampa: Meghan-Kiffer Press.

Barton, A. C. et al. (2003). *Teaching science for social justice.* New York: Teachers College.

Basic information: About WSIS. (2006). *World Summit on the Information Society.* Retrieved December 29, 2007, from http://www.itu.int/wsis/basic/about.html

Carter, J. (2005). *Our endangered values: America's moral crisis.* New York: Simon & Schuster.

Counter view: HRD ministry and tech experts devise plan for $10 laptops. (2006, September 27). *The Times of India.* Retrieved December 26, 2007, from http://timesofindia.indiatimes.com/articleshow/2029815.cms

Daniel, P. (2006). Africa: Tools of liberation. *openDemocracy.net.* Retrieved December 25, 2007, from http://www.opendemocracy.net/democracy-africa_democracy/technology_liberation_4124.jsp

Drake, W. J. (2005, May). World summit on the Information Society (working paper). *Computer Professionals for Social Responsibility.* Retrieved December 27, 2007, from http://www.cpsr.org/pubs/workingpapers/2/Drake

Eisler, R. (1987). *The chalice and the blade: Our history, our future.* San Francisco: HarperSanFrancisco.

Eisler, R. (2002). *The power of partnership: Seven relationships that will change your life.* Novato, CA: New World.

Eisler, R. (2007). *The real wealth of nations: Creating a caring economics*. San Francisco: Berrett-Koehler.

Eisler, R., & Loye, D. (1990). *The partnership way*. San Francisco: HarperSan-Francisco.

Eisler, R., & Miller, R. (Eds.). (2004). *Educating for a culture of peace*. Portsmouth, NH: Heinemann.

Goodman, E. (1989, February 5). Hold on science hides religious zeal. *The Austin-American Statesman*. Editorial page.

Harding, S. (1998). *Is science multicultural? Postcolonialisms, feminisms, and epistemologies*. Bloomington, IN: Indiana UP.

Harding, S. (2000). Should philosophies of science encode democratic ideals? In D. L. Kleinman (Ed.), *Science, technology & democracy* (pp. 121-138). Albany: SUNY.

Henderson, H. (1996). *Building a win-win world: Life beyond global economic warfare*. San Francisco: Berrett-Koehler Publishers.

Kleinman, D. L. (Ed.). (2000). *Science, technology & democracy*. Albany: SUNY.

Lipton, B. H. (2005). *The biology of belief: Unleashing the power of consciousness, matter and miracles*. Santa Rosa, CA: Elite.

The Literacy Project. (2007). Retrieved September 10, 2007, from http://www.google.com/literacy/

Martin, K. (Producer), & Nash, T. (Director). (1997). *Who's counting? Marilyn Waring on sex, lies & global economics*. Oley, PA: Bullfrog Films.

Mukul, A. (2007, May 4). HRD hopes to make $10 laptops a reality. *The Times of India*. Retrieved December 26, 2007, from http://timesofindia.indiatimes.com/Business/HRD_hopes_to_make_10_laptops_a_reality/articleshow/1999828.cms

One Laptop Per Child. (n.d.). Retrieved December 30, 2007, from http://laptop.org

Prestowitz, C. (2005). *Three billion new capitalists: The great shift of wealth and power to the east*. New York: Basic Books.

Sclove, R. E. (2000). Town meetings on technology: Consensus conferences as democratic participation. In D. L. Kleinman (Ed.), *Science, technology & democracy* (pp. 33-48). Albany: SUNY.

Seager, J. (2003). *The Penguin atlas of women in the world.* New York: Penguin.

Stiglitz, J. E. (2003). *Globalization and its discontents.* New York: W.W. Norton.

Stockard, R., Akbari, A., & Domooei, J. (2006). Dimensions of sustainable diversity in IT: Applications to the IT college major and career aspirations among underrepresented high school students of color. In G. Trajkovski (Ed.), *Diversity in information technology education: Issues and controversies* (pp. 92-128). Hershey, PA: Information Science Publishing.

Top funders: Top 100 U.S. foundations by asset size. (2007). Retrieved September 8, 2007, from http://foundationcenter.org/findfunders/topfunders/top100assets.html

Weimann, G. (2006). *Terror on the Internet: The new arena, the new challenges.* Washington, D.C.: United States Institute of Peace.

Wresch, W. (1996). *Disconnected: Haves and have-nots in the information age.* New Brunswick, NJ: Rutgers UP.

ENDNOTES

[1]   In June 2006, Warren Buffet committed to donate 83% of his wealth (about $30 billion) to the Gates Foundation.

[2]   Some portions of this chapter may have appeared in, and are reprinted with permission from Kirk, M. (2006). Bridging the digital divide: A feminist perspective on the project. In G. Trajkovski (Ed.), *Diversity in information technology education: Issues and controversies* (pp. 38-67). Hershey, PA: Information Science Publishing.

Chapter XI
A Concluding Pledge:
With Technology and Justice for All

This book has offered one feminist's perspective on how a deeper understanding of our dominator social system might clarify why women are underrepresented as developers, users, and beneficiaries of technology. I have suggested that we move beyond the attitude of simply providing access to the more encompassing goal of co-creating a partnership social system. This approach will increase the participation of women, as well as other currently underrepresented populations, in information technology. In the end, co-creating a partnership global IT industry is about building relationships founded in an attitude of empathy and caring that informs all of our human relations. Although I have attempted to offer a vision of what partnership in IT might look like in relation to media, language, education, and business, the best efforts to increase the participation of women as developers, users, and beneficiaries of technology will be broad-based, multifaceted, include many more perspectives than mine, and involve all of our social institutions.

In earlier chapters, I have suggested some places to begin. Breaking through false assumptions about the purpose and relevance of women's studies and feminist science studies, along with perspectives from many other disciplines, is a key to exploring a rich mine of ideas about how our current social system operates and how we might work together to co-create a more hospitable social climate for all.

Undoing the damage done by dualistic thinking and stereotypes will take us a long way towards a richer understanding of our shared human experience. Reframing some of the core assumptions of the philosophy of science—primarily the founding assumption that science is male and nature is female—will offer new perspectives from which to understand our increasingly complex scientific and technical knowledge tradition. Citizens of the United States of America have learned to think of themselves as members of the world's greatest democracy. We call our nation the "land of opportunity" and we rely on the "myth of meritocracy" (the idea that anyone can achieve anything by their own efforts) without any acknowledgement of the institutionalized barriers that make it much harder for some. However, we have yet to live up to a true democratic ideal as a nation, and one of the reasons for this is the power of unnamed stereotypes.

Learning more about the power of media as a social institution to shape our views about ourselves and one another is a critical component of any lasting social change. Henderson (1996) describes the global mass information system as a new kind of "government" that she calls a "mediocracy" run by large businesses and financial interests (p. 112). At the same time, Henderson also shares my hope for what the media could do if we all participated in information technology: "Mass media could become a national feedback mechanism by providing a random-access conduit for all the wisdom, creativity, and diversity of our citizens" (Henderson, 1996, p. 117). That is the potential that a partnership approach to information technology can help us manifest.

Using partnership perspectives to reform education—a social institution with critical responsibility for enculturating the next generation of citizens—will encourage more to have a voice in our increasingly global society. We need to include the stories and the voices of women and people of color in our knowledge tradition and we need to teach differently. In *Re-Engineering: Female Friendly Science*, Sue Rosser (1997) asked, "What would be the parameters of a feminist or women-centered science?" and proposed the kinds of pedagogical changes that have proven more supportive for many more learners, not just women. Rosser (1997) names the following constructive pedagogical changes, encompassing a range of issues from curriculum redesign to classroom practices: (1) teachers who guide rather than solely challenge; (2) shifting from competitive to collaborative learning models; (3) placing computer science in a social context; and (4) using combinations of qualitative and quantitative evaluation methods (p. 9). Robert Young (1987), a scholar writing about anti-racist science, also emphasizes the importance of taking "a historical and social approach to knowledge" that examines "the social forces and connections (or articulations) of scientific and technological disciplines and research problems" (p. 22).

Educating ourselves about the historical legacies of colonialism and contemporary global economics will create possibilities for the global IT industry to be of better service in relation to critical human needs. Eisler (2007) offers this perspective:

Globalization and the shift to the postindustrial age are bringing great economic and social dislocation. This dislocation is a source of fear for many people. But it also offers an unprecedented opening for new and better ways of thinking and living. It offers us the opportunity to use our vision and ingenuity to help create the social and economic conditions that support our evolution as individuals, as a species, and as a planet. (p. 24)

The global IT industry could participate in our human evolution in vastly more productive ways if we adopt a partnership perspective.

What might we ask from ourselves as individuals and from each other as a society? In *Our Endangered Values: America's Moral Crisis*, former U.S. President Jimmy Carter (2005) cites Reinhold Niebuhr who described the difference between a person and a society: "The expectations from a person are a much higher standard. A person should have as our goal complete *agape*, self-sacrificial love. The most we can expect from a society is to institute simple justice" (p. 59). The 21st century will be dominated by the fast-paced sharing of digitized information and many other technologies. It seems that the least we could ask of our society is the "simple justice" of including all of our global citizens as developers, users, or beneficiaries of the technologies that will increasingly impact their lives. However, I also believe that Riane Eisler's (1987, 2000, 2002, 2007) concept of partnership offers us a way to achieve far more than simple justice. Contributing to the development of a partnership society—one that holds empathy and caring as one of its highest values—might actually lead us towards our highest potential as human beings, the manifestation of agape. Perhaps, in pledging ourselves to creating a digital world with technology and justice for all, we might find our way to the experience of *agape*. What a world that might be.

This chapter offers a few ideas for co-creating this kind of partnership world by exploring: (1) ideas for future research, (2) ideas for what one individual can do, and (3) my own story of learning about partnership. However, these ideas are only a pencil sketch of some possibilities. The more we all commit to educating ourselves about these issues, and the more we all practice at partnership, the more we can co-create broader visions far beyond what I have suggested here.

IDEAS FOR FUTURE RESEARCH

The major reasons that girls and women do not participate in science and technology (as users and beneficiaries, but especially as developers of it) have been well-documented over time by multiple scholars (e.g., Brainard & Carlin, 2001; Camp, 1997; Cohoon & Aspray, 2006; Margolis & Fisher, 2002; Seymour & Hewitt, 1997;

Table 1. Reasons women leave correlated with issues and chapter where discussed

Reason girls, women leave	Core issues involved	Chapters where discussed
male-centered culture of science	dualisms, stereotypes, and male-centered IT culture	II, V, VIII
different cultural values, ignored or unacknowledged	dualisms, stereotypes, male-centered IT culture, media, communication, education, business	All
gender constraints on assertiveness	dualisms, stereotypes, male-centered IT culture, media, communication	I, II, III, IV, V, VIII
internalization of negative stereotypes	dualisms, stereotypes, male-centered IT culture, media, communication, education	I, II, III, IV, V, VI, VIII
discrimination and sexual harassment	dualisms, stereotypes, male-centered IT culture, media	I, II, III, IV, V, VIII
perceived "hardness" of science	dualisms, stereotypes, male-centered IT culture, history, education	II, III, V, VI
few women role models, mentors	male-centered IT culture, communication, history, education	V, VI, VIII, IX
inadequate high school preparation	dualisms, stereotypes, history, education	II, III, V, VI, IX
limited pedagogical approaches	history, education	VI, IX
competitive weed-out tradition	education	IX
emphasis on grades over learning	education	IX

Sonnert, 1995). Table 1 lists the major reasons that girls and women leave science and technology in association with the core issues involved and where these issues have been addressed in this book.

Clearly, multiple factors influence women's choices not to participate in science and IT, which is why we need complex, multifaceted solutions that address change on multiple levels. We cannot create lasting, long-term change with narrowly focused single-solution approaches. Research that attempts to prove that "x" is (or is not) "the problem" will not take us far enough in resolving questions about women's participation in IT. For example, McKenna (2006) attempted to test the relationship between gender and abstract vs. concrete learning styles, concluding that "there is no gendered difference in attitudes to black boxes in programming, and that the reasons for female under-representation in computing lie elsewhere" (p. 68).

This only answers questions about the learning styles of those who have already succeeded enough in the current educational environment to make it to a college-level computer programming class; this research tells us nothing about the learning styles of those who dropped out of this study much earlier. We know nothing more about why certain people are not there or about what learning environment might make it more possible for them to succeed. Their voices are silent. Rosser (1995) suggests that this type of single-focused research may lead us to fallacious debates about whether we should change our teaching methods for "them" instead of asking questions about whether some of these changes might be better for many more learners, not just women. We must design research agendas that engage in more complex, multifaceted, meta-approaches to answering the remaining questions about creating an inclusive culture in IT.

In "Under Western Eyes: Feminist Scholarship and Colonial Discourses," Chandra Talpade Mohanty (1991) gives concrete examples of how to generate this kind of "both/and" scholarship which requires true interdisciplinarity, crossing traditional scholarly boundaries to understand the interlocking issues that contribute to a particular social situation. Mohanty (1991) describes this type of feminist research as "context specific differentiated analysis" (p. 67). "Context specific" analysis begins with a *thorough* understanding of the context from which a social situation arises. "Differentiated" analyses include issues and perspectives from multiple traditional disciplines, such as history, politics, social science, and so forth. Mohanty (1991) also advises particular attentiveness to avoiding the flawed assumption of the universal "woman," of "women as an already constituted, coherent group," and adds that sisterhood "cannot be assumed on the basis of gender; it must be forged in concrete historical and political practice and analysis" (p. 58). This is the multidisciplinary and multicultural perspective that is essential in order to engage in any analysis of the global IT industry and how it might better serve real human need.

The wealth of data on why girls and women do not participate in science and technology certainly suggests viable approaches to better encourage their participation. However, some future research could focus more deliberately on what encourages girls and women of color to stay in science and technology. For example, many scholars have observed that historically Black colleges and universities (HBCUs) seem to have fostered the development of African-American women in math, science, and technology. A research project at the University of Pennsylvania's Graduate School of Education is attempting to document the truth of these mostly anecdotal observations. The project—titled Increasing the Representation of African-American Women in Science, Technology, Engineering, and Math (STEM) Education: The Role of Historically Black Colleges and Universities (HBCUs)—seeks to understand both individual and institutional factors that "contribute to the success of Black colleges in advancing African-Americans along one segment of the STEM education pipeline: completion of a bachelor's degree in a STEM discipline and enrollment in a graduate school program in STEM" (Gasman, 2007). The project includes a survey of students studying science, technology, engineering, and mathematics (STEM) that attempts to understand more about their experiences as well as what factors influence their choices to pursue STEM-related fields. The solutions yielded by this type of research might be directly applied to social action projects.

The greatest potential for future research lies in projects that both take action to encourage participation and document the results of such actions. For example, the University of Michigan's Health Sciences House, Pennsylvania State University's Engineering House, and Purdue University's Wood, Water, and Wild Wonder program are examples of living-learning programs in STEM fields. These living-learning programs involve a variety of strategies such as "residential colleges, linked courses and first-year interest groups" meant to foster the development of faculty-student and peer-to-peer relationships (Johnson, et al., 2006, p. 2). These types of active interventions are known to encourage student retention and positively influence student learning. We might engage in more action-oriented research of this type that simultaneously attempts to create change while documenting the effectiveness of these strategies on women's participation over the long term (Johnson, et al., 2006).

Whatever future research we engage in, must begin with individuals educating themselves about how our current dominator social model contributes to the exclusion of some and inclusion of others on all levels of society, not just in relation to IT. In a dominator society in which fear, control, and power-over pervade our lives on a daily basis, it can be a challenge to root these attitudes out of our own behavior. However, it is not impossible; it just takes time and patience to peel back all of the layers of the onion that have developed as we have grown in this field of domination.

WHAT CAN ONE INDIVIDUAL DO?

Plenty. The relationship between individuals and their social institutions is interactive. By changing your individual behavior, you can impact all of the social institutions with which you engage. The weight of our dominator legacy is heavy, and that is why it can feel so freeing to lay that burden down.

With regard to language as a social institution, individuals can make a tremendous impact just by adopting non-sexist language and partnership communication styles. With regard to education, it is important that we all participate in creating the climate for partnership because a healthy democracy depends on an educated citizenry—a population that has learned to think for themselves and that has learned to manifest and actualize their best selves. Further, the challenges that we face as global citizens today require people who are functioning at the top of their capabilities.

With regard to the global IT business, know that whatever your role in life, you participate in global economics. Even if you do not work in the global IT business, you can contribute to change right where you are. It's a matter of adopting partnership perspectives through which to reconsider the life you are already living. What do you notice about how the IT industry is portrayed? What do you notice about the latest products technology has to offer? What do you notice about how those products are marketed? What might you do to share a partnership perspective with these businesses?

This section suggests the following ways that one individual can begin to create change: (1) commit to adopting a partnership perspective; (2) start with yourself; (3) slow down and be mindful; (4) become a lifelong learner; and (5) take action.

Commit to Adopting a Partnership Perspective

Allan Johnson (2006) says that the "greatest barrier to change is that dominant groups . . . don't see the trouble as *their* trouble, which means they don't feel obliged to do something about it" (p. 127). My hope is that the previous chapters have clarified some of the ways in which our social systems reflect the values of a dominator society so that readers have also come to appreciate how we are all part of these social systems, albeit often in unconscious and nondeliberate ways. Table 2 contrasts the characteristics of a dominator social system with a partnership social system (Eisler, 1987, 2002, 2007; Eisler & Loye, 1990; Eisler & Miller, 2004).

Table 2. Characteristics of dominator and partnership social systems

Dominator	Partnership
Fear- and control-based	Trust- and respect-based
Hierarchies of domination	Hierarchies of actualization
Emphasis on ranking	Emphasis on linking
Win/lose orientation	Win/win orientation
High degree of fear, abuse, violence	Low degree of fear, abuse, violence, since they are not required to maintain rigid rankings
Value so-called "male" traits such as control and conquest over so-called "female" traits	Value traits that promote human development such as nonviolence, empathy, and caregiving
Images of heroic violence sanctified, institutionalized	Images of nurturance honored, institutionalized
Leaders imaged as men who give orders and have subordinate followers	Leaders imaged as anyone who inspires others to collaborate on commonly agreed upon goals
Planning is short-term with little thought for future generations	Planning includes short- and long-term concerns for present and future generations

continued on following page

Table 2. continued

Dominator	Partnership
Emphasis on scarcity, hoarding	Emphasis on sustainability, sharing
Society viewed as a machine with people as expendable cogs	Society viewed as a living organism with people as involved cocreators
Earth imaged as an object to be conquered, exploited	Earth imaged as a living organism of which we are all a part

Making the commitment to adopt partnership perspectives is a great place to begin to create change, especially with regard to increasing the participation of women as beneficiaries, users, and developers of IT.

Trust and Respect

If you assume an attitude of trust and respect for others, rather than the fear and control you have learned from our dominator system, you will make a dramatic contribution to creating a partnership culture wherever you go. Assuming an attitude of trust and respect is especially important in dealing with individual differences, both in terms of actual behavior and in terms of perception. In addition, fear and control are so pervasive in our dominator society that their absence will provide a psychic oasis that holds tremendous transformational power.

Hierarchies of Actualization

If you focus on hierarchies of actualization rather than hierarchies of domination, you can contribute to creating environments in which learning can be about our growth as human beings as well as our growth as scholars and critical thinkers. "In hierarchies of domination, power is defined as *power over*: a means of imposing and maintaining top-down control . . . In hierarchies of actualization, power is defined as *power to* or *power with*. Parenting, teaching, and leading are designed to empower rather than disempower, to inspire others to realize their potentials" (Eisler, 2004, p. 20). Unfortunately, in our current dominator education environment a "basic lesson children learn in dominator settings is strict conformity to orders" (Eisler, 2002, p. 7). Over time this can breed learning environments in which students become passive recipients of information instead of active seekers of knowledge. Further, Eisler (2002) suggests that "when people are truly loved rather than abused, they are more likely to be empathic, caring, and creative—to develop their noblest spiritual qualities" (p. 188). We will need to engage at the level of our best selves to face the challenges of the global IT industry in the 21st century.

Linking and Connecting

Focus on linking or connecting with others rather than ranking yourself in relation to others. Adopting this approach in your communication style (as opposed to a win-lose, ranking, dominating style) can make a significant contribution to more inclusive interpersonal communication and to shifting away from a dominator culture in IT. A focus on linking or connecting, rather than ranking, might reshape education in a variety of ways. It could foster better teacher-student relationships, and it could redefine the climate of our classrooms (or other learning environments) as a participatory environment where teachers and students co-create knowledge.

In our increasingly interconnected global community, it is especially important that education fosters the development of learners who can think for themselves. Miller (2004) explains the problem with sustaining our current "education-as-trans-mission" of knowledge dominator system: "When education-as-transmission is transplanted from its heritage within the archaic, local, tradition-bound community to the modern nation-state and multinational corporation, powerful elites obtain compelling influence over the ideas and attitudes of huge masses of people" (Miller, 2004, p. 3). Partnership education that fosters the development of free-thinking individuals is a key to sustaining democratic societies that honor and respect the local contexts in which knowledge is created.

Nonviolence, Empathy and Caregiving

If you practice valuing traits and behaviors that promote human development such as nonviolence, empathy, and caregiving over traits such as control and conquest, you will move rapidly towards creating a partnership culture wherever you go. You will also be actively participating in direct social resistance to sexism which has inappropriately and inaccurately assigned these human traits exclusively to one gender—empathy and caregiving to women, control and conquest to men. Focusing on empathy and caring (rather than control and conquest) also contributes to a creating a climate in which violence is less likely to occur. Eisler (2002) explains that empathic relations release "the chemicals dopamine and serotonin into areas of the brain" and that "these chemicals also strengthen the capacity to control aggressive impulses" (p. 38). Further, if you consciously practice the attitudes and behaviors of nonviolence, you will be making an implicit contribution to ending systems of domination as well as an explicit contribution to building a partnership culture. Partnership cannot thrive in a climate of violence.

Given the dramatic changes and challenges our global community currently faces, we need educated global citizens who have used education to develop into their highest manifestation of self. To foster caring citizens who can co-create a partnership culture, Eisler (2004) suggests that "a thread running through the entire curriculum from preschool to graduate school should be *caring for life*: caring for self, for others, and for our natural habitat" (p. 32).

Leaders Who Inspire

If you redefine good leaders as those who inspire others to collaborate on commonly agreed upon goals, rather than as "men who give orders and have subordinate followers," you will create a partnership perspective from which to consider our global business relations—a perspective that honors the needs and contributions of local communities over the current top-down approach to global IT business. A partnership business organization "naturally facilitates the emergence of more leaders with real leadership ability" which means that "larger numbers of employees are able to use their knowledge and abilities to meet new business challenges" (Eisler, 2002, p. 70).

We might also begin to envision good teachers as leaders who inspire others to collaborate on commonly agreed upon goals, rather than as those who give orders and have subordinate followers, creating more democratic learning environments. Eisler (2004) says that teaching and leading should be "designed to empower rather than disempower, to inspire others to realize their potentials" (p. 20). This approach to teachers as leaders and guides, rather than autocratic experts, is more likely to awaken student "awareness of the huge moral and cultural choices that lie before them," which is an especially important goal in the context of the global IT industry (Miller, 2004, p. 5).

Imagining the Earth as a Living Organism

If you can imagine the Earth as a living organism of which we are all a part, it will be easier to understand the significance of efforts towards global sustainability, and why we need to move away from dominator attitudes of scarcity and hoarding in our global relations, especially with regard to the global IT business. "We need economic models, rules, and policies that support caring for ourselves, others, and our Mother Earth" (Eisler, 2007, p. 8). If you live in a developed nation, this perspective might help you understand why some have called for developing a "need-based" rather than "desire-based" lifestyle (Henderson, 1996, p. 187). The world cannot support everyone living at the same standard as the developed nations. If those in the developed nations do not develop a less consumptive lifestyle by choice, global economic shifts may force us to. Of course, if we do as Eisler (2007) suggests and adopt "partnerism" as a new economic model, our choices will be guided by a fundamental respect for global sustainability. In the meantime, you might ask yourself these questions: What businesses does your money support? What values does your money implicitly support at these businesses?

Start With Yourself

Chapter II explored the deeply-embedded stereotypes that influence how we have learned to perceive ourselves and each other. One of the first steps to building a partnership society is to free ourselves from stereotypical thinking. Since we also may have internalized these messages, it is important to examine and understand your own identity and social location, especially in terms of the interrelationships of gender, race, and socioeconomic class. How might you apply partnership practices to liberate yourself and others from stereotypes that focus on difference?

In *The Power of Partnership: Seven Relationships that Will Change Your Life*, Riane Eisler (2002) suggests that we begin by ending our dominator attitudes towards ourselves; we should begin to treat ourselves with empathy and compassion, trust and respect, and especially nonviolence. Eisler suggests that you apply the golden rule to yourself: "do unto yourself as you would do unto others" (p.10). This may be more difficult for some than others. Many of us have learned to view self-care as selfishness. However, Eisler (2002) offers a helpful clarification: "Selfishness is being insensitive to others. Partnership with yourself means being sensitive to both yourself and others" (p. 10).

Unfortunately, dominator family systems have taught many of us to disassociate from ourselves. We learn an attitude of fear and control towards our own psyches rather than trust and respect. We attempt to gain dominance over our inner selves rather than connecting with and being in partnership with our interior. Emotions (female) are bad, and rationality (male) is good. The problem is that those pesky emotions keep cropping up. However, our dominator culture has made it increasingly hard to have the quiet necessary to really reflect on our inner lives. Eisler (2002) describes how technology plays a part in this disassociation from self:

The speed and omnipresence of today's communication technologies—from the Internet to cell phones to fax machines to e-mail to voicemail—is out of sync with the natural rhythms of our bodies. We can't keep pace with it all. This makes it hard for us to reflect on our lives and our world. (p. 18)

Before you can free yourself from stereotypes, you must identify which ones are holding you captive. This can be very difficult because stereotypes are so ubiquitous and because we have been trained not to see them. Judy Logan (1993) offers an interesting guided meditation that she uses with her students to try to develop awareness of gender stereotypes:

Today I will be taking you on a journey back through time. This is not a real journey, it is a journey of the imagination. First, step out of your body and see yourself at your desk with your head down. Now, travel back through time until you are in the fifth grade . . . What are you wearing? Who is your teacher? What are you doing? Who are your friends? . . . Now see yourself as a kindergartener . . . who are you playing with, what are you doing . . . Now you are two . . . beginning to really talk . . . Travel back again to being a baby . . . Now, travel back some more, and here you are, ready to be born!!! Everyone is so excited, so anxious, so happy, waiting for your birth . . . and here you are!! Only this time, imagine that you are born as the opposite sex. (p. 22)*

Logan (1993) then guides students back through the same ages and stages as the opposite sex. Lastly, students write a list of the ways in which their lives seemed different as the opposite sex. This meditation is a useful way to reveal internalized individual perceptions about sex and gender—the ways in which you may think men and women have it better or worse—and to begin to scrutinize what gender stereotypes you have adopted. This same technique might be used to reveal attitudes and beliefs about race, socioeconomic class, disability, and so forth.

A Meditation on Difference

In *Truth or Dare: Encounters with Power, Authority, and Mystery,* Starhawk (1987) provided another valuable tool for identifying your own internalized perceptions about gender, race, class, and other stereotypes based on difference. Starhawk (1987) suggests the following meditation as an exercise for discovering how we have learned to see ourselves and others in relation to our hierarchically-defined social locations:

Close your eyes. Breathe deep, and relax. Imagine yourself walking down a street. People pass you by, and you look into their eyes, and you feel fear, because you know that if they knew how different you really are, they might hate you or kill you. The street is lined with billboards advertising things you have no use for, selling images of what is sexy and beautiful and desirable, and you know that you are different from the images and always will be.

Breathe deep, and walk on down the street. You pass a school, and you know that inside the walls of its classrooms the name for who you are is never even mentioned. None of . . . your poets, your writers, your artists, your scientists or studies are named: or if they are, their differences are concealed.

Breathe again; keep walking. You pass a church, and you know that from its pulpit your differences are denounced. You walk past shops and workplaces, knowing that if your difference became visible, no one would hire you or sell to you.

You enter your home. See your family; greet them. Do they know who you are? Do they share your difference? Do they strengthen you? Or if they knew who you were, would they hate you? Would they be ashamed?

Breathe deep, and open your eyes. Notice how you feel. Talk about it; write it down. When have you experienced a taste of this reality?

Now close your eyes again. Relax. Imagine yourself back on the street. This time, everything fits. Everything reflects who you are. You walk along, and the eyes of the people you meet reflect pride and appreciation of you. Along the sides of the road are billboards, and the images of beauty and desirability they project look just like you. You know that the schools teach your history and extol the lives of your great artists and thinkers. You glance inside the church: the God they worship is in your image. Enter your own house; greet your family. Know that they are like you, take pride in you, wouldn't have you be any different from how you are. Open your eyes.

Talk about the meditation. What was it like? How do you feel now? When have you tasted this reality? How as it different? (pp. 322-323)

Slow Down and Be Mindful

Simply being aware of the stereotypes we have learned is not enough to eliminate them from our thinking and behavior. The next step is to make the committed and mindful effort to change, which is a life's work for most of us. Eradicating stereotypes from our thinking is challenging in part due to the way that our brains learn and organize information. Our brains like to categorize and stereotypes are just a form of categorization gone wild. The following exercise demonstrates how powerful established patterns of thought can be. Try these steps out loud:

*   Repeat the word "shop" six times quickly.
*   Answer this question: "What do you do at a green light?"

If you said "stop," go back and reread the question (by the way, you are not alone). If you said "go," you may already be skilled at the mindfulness required to begin eradicating stereotypes from your thinking, judgments, and behavior. We are trained to try to guess the correct answer to a given question as quickly as possible. We all take mental shortcuts. Being mindful requires that we slow down and truly listen in order to engage our intellects in the moment. Okay. Now, try these steps out loud:

- Repeat the word "folk" six times quickly.
- Answer this question: "What do you call the white of an egg?"

If you answered "yolk," you just learned how difficult mindfulness can be. When you combine the efficient ways in which our brains organize and access information with the persistent messaging systems that purvey stereotypes in our daily lives, the degree of conscious, mindful effort required to eradiate stereotypical thinking becomes readily apparent.

Ironically, today's communication technologies can contribute to "further alienating us from consciousness of ourselves and the world around us. Increasingly, we find ourselves controlled by the very technologies that are supposed to free us" (Eisler, 2002, p. 19). We must consciously choose to slow down and take the time to reflect and to be mindful.

Become a Lifelong Learner

In order to participate in the shift towards a partnership social model, you must educate yourself. Further, you must commit to the fact that educating yourself about these issues is really a lifelong learning project because truth is "complex and elusive" (Johnson, 2006, p. 139). Make a point of studying history so that you can know that the world we have created so far is not "just the way things are." While social systems may seem large and static, they are really fluid systems directly subject to the shifting influences of those who participate in them. Johnson (2006) describes it this way:

No social system lasts forever, and this fact holds especially for oppressive systems of privilege. We can't know what will replace existing social systems, but we can be confident that they will go, that they are going at every moment. It's only a matter of how quickly, by what means, and toward what alternatives, and whether each of us will do our part to make change happen sooner rather than later and with less rather than more human suffering in the process. (p. 130)

You might begin with some of the resources listed in this book's Appendix: Recommended Resources. This appendix offers some resources for further study organized in the following categories: Feminism and Partnership; Feminist Science Studies; Media Studies; Language and Communication; Education; Her-Story; Global Economics and Partnership Science; Films; and Organizations Working Towards Change.

There is also a great deal more to Marshall Rosenberg's ideas on nonviolent communication than I could cover in the few paragraphs in Chapter VIII. Learn more at the Center for Nonviolent Communication (www.cnvc.org), which was established by Rosenberg in 1984 and has since become "a global organization whose vision is a world where all people are getting their needs met and resolving their conflicts peacefully" (CNVC, 2007). In addition to the training, workshops, and lectures featuring Rosenberg, the CNVC has regional teams of trainers and organizers in Eastern Europe, the Middle East, Western Europe, Africa, Asia, and Latin America. With over 200 CNVC-certified trainers throughout the world, the organization estimates that they trained over 500,000 people in NVC worldwide in 2005 and 2006 alone.

Seek Alternative Media

As you educate yourself, be sure to seek alternative views and different voices than those you find in mainstream media. Do not rely solely on mass media (or mass market bookstores) to teach you more about dominator societies and how systems of privilege work. As I explored in Chapter IV, large scale mass media operate as social institutions that typically purvey the ideas of the status quo. "As large capitalist enterprises, the media have a vested interest in ignoring . . . anything that seriously questions the status quo" (Johnson, 2006, p. 139). Therefore, with a few exceptions, most mass media take the "path of least resistance." In fact, those that do not are often marginalized in very deliberate ways.

For example, films that focus on relationships (emotion=female) rather than ideas (rational=male), or those that feature small intimate stories rather than large action-packed stories, are typically referred to with the derogatory term "chick flick." I remind you of Elizabeth Minnich's (1990) idea that the "modifier" identifies who lies in the marginalized group; since the group at the center is assumed, it need not be defined. The term "chick flick" points to the fact that so-called "women's concerns" are marginalized and so-called "male concerns" are at the center. That's why you'd never see the term "dick flick," because maleness is assumed to be at the center and so it does not need to be called out in language.

Book publishing and book selling has also changed profoundly in recent years. The move toward larger corporate ownership over publishers and sellers has made it more difficult for some ideas to be published at all, and you may have to do a little digging to find alternative sources. Following are a few suggestions for learning more about alternative media:

- Center for Media and Democracy at www.prwatch.org
- Fairness and Accuracy in Reporting at www.fair.org
- Sut Jhally's books or videos at www.sutjhally.com
- Jean Kilbourne's books or videos at www.jeankilbourne.com

- Media Education Foundation at www.mediaed.org
- Media Watch at www.mediawatch.com
- Yes! Magazine at www.yesmagazine.com

Look, Listen, Learn

As you move through your day, adopt the attitude of a lifelong learner and live like an anthropologist or participant-observer; watch and listen for "patterns that come up again and again in social life" (Johnson, 2006, p. 140). Pay special attention to listening attentively and respectfully to members of those groups that you may have been socialized not to listen to—women, people of color, people who are disabled, people who are working class, and so forth. Work to listen without the defensiveness that sometimes results when a person who is used to experiencing privilege encounters criticism. Johnson (2006) stresses:

If someone confronts you with your own behavior that supports privilege, step off the path of least resistance that encourages you to defend and deny . . . Assume for the time being that it's true, because given the power of paths of least resistance, it probably is. And then take responsibility to do something about it. (p. 141)

You can practice as an anthropologist in many other ways in your daily life aside from real human interaction. Try adopting this perspective as a conscious observer while you are consuming mass media—noticing advertising on the bus bench, driving by billboards, listening to radio ads in your car, observing how odd it is that the women on CSI are wearing miniskirts and stilettos at bloody crime scenes, or noticing how many White males are pictured in the technology section of your newspaper.

You might be surprised what you may notice in your regular daily environment once your consciousness has been raised by more knowledge of our social systems. I recall a male women's studies student who told me that our class had "spoiled" one of his favorite movies. He said, "Now, that my perspective on gender has been expanded by our class, I can't enjoy watching my favorite movie anymore. The sexism in it makes me cringe. I can't believe it because I've watched that movie 100 times and never noticed before." I told him I was sorry, but I really wasn't. I was proud of him.

Take Action

Creating change requires us to recognize that racism, sexism, classism, and all of the other members of the dysfunctional "ism" family[1] interrelate to such an extent that one may be privileged by race and oppressed by gender, or privileged by class and oppressed by race. It's not possible to separate these different influences from each other in terms of our individual experience of them. Ultimately, although our individual experience matters, what matters most are the attitudes, values, and beliefs reflected by our social institutions. So, while it is important to understand our own individual experiences and stereotypical perceptions regarding others, it is also important to commit to reshaping our social institutions in ways that benefit us all.

Be Brave

Allan Johnson (2006) suggests that we focus on thinking about change in terms of actions that are "small, humble, and doable rather than large, heroic, and impossible" (p. 152). I would add that we need to redefine "heroism" by shifting from win-lose, control-based dominator models, to win-win, respect-based partnership models. When you emphasize empathy and caring rather than control and conquest, bravery can take on new forms. You can start to see how being brave does not need to involve some large-scale heroic deed, but can happen right where you are in small ways and in relationships with others. Hmm? Maybe there is something worth watching in those "chick" flicks after all.

You can be brave right where you are by choosing not to follow the path of least resistance in day-to-day social situations. In this context, being brave may mean having enough empathy for the suffering caused by our dominator thinking not to allow your fears of being perceived as a "radical" to deter you from speech or action. Being brave may mean not being afraid to make people uncomfortable by challenging their stereotypical and/or dominator thinking and/or actions. Our dominator social system does "a lot more than make people feel uncomfortable" and "discomfort is an unavoidable part of any meaningful process of change" (Johnson, 2006, p. 145). With this in mind, be brave enough not to tolerate any of the following in your environment: anti-feminist backlash (educate others about the "F" word); woman-bashing, by men or women; male-bashing, by women or men; and sexist, racist, homophobic, xenophobic, classist, or any other "ist" comments, images, or actions.

Take Small Risks

While we may not live to witness some broader social changes in our lifetimes, we can influence the perceptions of those we interact with on a daily basis by taking small risks. A 1947 Hollywood movie starring Gregory Peck and Dorothy McGuire called *Gentleman's Agreement* offered a thoughtful exploration of anti-Semitism in New York society (Kazan, 1947). In a powerful scene at the end of the film, Dave (who is Jewish) confronts Kathy (who is not) about her anti-Semitism. Even though she has not displayed bigotry in any explicit or blatant ways, Dave confronts Kathy about the times that she has been offended by anti-Semitic jokes or slurs, but chosen to remain silent. These seemingly small, insignificant social moments hold great potential for change when those with privilege use their social authority to challenge the status quo.

Allan Johnson (2006) describes how most of us have been socialized to choose "the path of least resistance" in such situations. However, he adds that when "we openly pass up a path of least resistance, we increase resistance for other people around that path, because now they must reconcile their choice with what they've seen us do, something they didn't have to do before" (p. 134). Demonstrating the courage to change ourselves, can inspire change in others. However, the goal is not simply individual change; ultimately, the goal is institutional change. Taking small risks can encourage the shift away from attitudes, values, and beliefs that support a dominator model and contribute to those beliefs losing their legitimacy over time.

Model Different Behavior

Observing positive behavior has the power to encourage it. This fact has been documented by scholars of "prosocial modeling" who have found it to be a powerful antidote to violence in our dominator system (Conduct, 1999; Walker et al., 1995). Mares and Woodard (2005) conducted a meta-analysis of 34 other studies on the positive effects of television on children's social interactions, levels of aggression, altruism, and levels of stereotyping. Their research shows that children who watched prosocial content in experimental settings were significantly more likely to behave in positive ways in real situations compared to control groups or those who watched antisocial content (Mares & Woodard, 2005, p. 301).

Other prosocial modeling researchers have also demonstrated the correlation between watching positive media and constructive human behavior. Flannery et al. (2003) documented the positive results of prosocial modeling using a program called PeaceBuilders that "focuses on individual behavior change . . . [and] incorporates an ongoing, long-term strategy to alter the climate and culture of a school" (p. 3). This research is particularly interesting because the goal was a deep, systemic, *cultural* change in an educational institution. Rather than being presented solely as a time- or subject-limited curriculum (more of a top-down, dominator approach), the PeaceBuilders activities and strategies are woven into the daily routine of the entire school on a daily basis. The PeaceBuilders program attempts to change:

characteristics of the setting (antecedents) that trigger aggressive, hostile behavior, and it increases the daily frequency and salience of both live and symbolic prosocial models. If there are more prosocial cues and models in a school and these behaviors are consistently reinforced and rewarded, then over time, child social competence will increase and the frequency and intensity of aggressive behaviors will decline. (Flannery et al., 2003, p. 3)

The broad success of the PeaceBuilders program is a living example of the possibilities that lie in modeling partnership behavior, rather than simply "punishing" or ignoring violence. You might openly choose to model alternative behavior by: promoting awareness of our dominator social system; speaking out for constructive alternatives to how things already are in your workplace or educational institution; refusing to support businesses that do not model partnership behavior; openly supporting others who choose the path of greatest resistance; and being an ally with women, people of color, and others working towards a partnership society.

Be Patient

Unlearning the habits of a lifetime in a dominator society takes time; therefore, we must be patient with ourselves and with others. With regard to changing ourselves, Eisler (2002) suggests that the attitudes of partnership begin with ourselves, that we express empathy and care toward ourselves as well as others: "Remember not to blame, shame, or punish yourself if you sometimes 'lose it' and revert to dominator ways of relating" (p. 32). With regard to changing social systems, "we have to let go of the idea that change doesn't happen unless we're around to see it" (Johnson, 2006, p. 131). While social systems are not static, they are large and can be slow-moving; research "on men's changing attitudes toward the male provider role . . . shows that most of the shift occurs *between* generations, not within them" (Johnson, 2006, p. 135). This means that certain kinds of fundamental shifts may take a confluence of many factors over many years in order for change to be observable on a broader scale. This is a particularly important idea to keep in mind in relation to increasing the participation of women in IT. No simple individual solution is likely to dramatically increase rates of inclusion. It is more likely to require a combination of solutions at multiple levels to begin to create a lasting shift in women's participation across education and the industry. So, we must set both short-term goals (that are more easily achieved and whose success inspires us to keep going), and long-term goals (that we literally may not see in our lifetimes). Johnson (2006) put it this way:

We need faith to do what seems right without necessarily being sure of the effect that will have. We have to think like pioneers who may know the direction they want to move in or what they would like to find, without knowing where they will wind up . . . If pioneers had to know their destination from the beginning, they might never go anywhere or discover anything. (p. 132)

This seems to be a particularly fitting stance from which to think about changing our social systems in order to increase the participation of women in IT. How many inventors, scientists, and technologists were true pioneers who had to commit to a process without definitively knowing the outcome of their lifelong efforts? They just took step one.

Ideas for Step One

Sometimes we hesitate to act towards social change because we do not know where to begin and sometimes it is because we do not know where our actions will lead. However, taking step one will lead to step two. Table 3 offers some ideas for step one in relation to the four social institutions discussed in this book.

Table 3. Ideas for step one in relation to language, media, education, and the global IT business

Social institution	Ideas for step one
Language and communication	• Listen for ways that dominator language polarizes and separates us. Practice using partnership language.
	• Practice more respectful ways of communicating, such as nonviolent communication and dialogic process to create opportunities for a richer exchange of ideas and experiences.
	• Study *The Handbook of Nonsexist Writing* (2001) by Kate Swift and Casey Miller. Their many (often humorous) examples will help you develop partnership in your spoken language as well.
Media	• Inventory the media in your home. What ideas do your books, films, magazines express? Share these ideas with others, especially those close to you.
	• Start a study group to learn more about feminism, our dominator society, and partnership. Focus on both/and rather than either/or discussions that move "past old categories such as right versus left, capitalism versus communism" (Eisler, 2002, p. 120).
	• Help others understand the links between violence in the U.S. and dominator social values.
	• Create partnership media (e.g., textbooks, children's books, stories, radio, television, film, and Web content).

continued on following page

Table 3. continued

Social institution	Ideas for step one
Education	• Create accessible information about feminism and partnership.
	• Work to develop media literacy programs in your schools.
	• Join organizations that are committed to building a partnership society, such as The Partnership Way at www.partnershipway.org.
	• Learn more about what is going on in schools in your community and find ways to contribute to the educational institutions in your community.
	• Start a reading group and educate yourself and others about access issues regarding science and technology.
	• Share the ideas in this book with others.
	• Volunteer to teach others about how to use computers at your local community center. You will learn more about real issues of access and who the technology insiders and outsiders really are.
	• If you are an educator, Chapter VIII outlined a variety of places to create a climate for partnership education. Start an action team with colleagues at your school to devise strategies for creating a partnership learning environment.
	• When attending meetings, leave your laptop in your office and listen to the human beings who are present.
Global IT Business	• Learn more about global economics in general.
	• Learn more about Riane Eisler's new economic model called "partnerism," and how to create a partnership global IT business.
	• Learn more about the business you work for (and the businesses where you spend your money) and its global relations.
	• Learn more about what other people and organizations are already doing to make a difference regarding the global IT business.
	• Vote for political candidates whose policies and actions reflect a partnership perspective, especially with regard to policies that relate to IT and global business relations.
	• If you work in the global IT industry, you can use the ideas from Chapter X as a model for rethinking your business.

Can you think of other first steps in relation to other social institutions such as law, government, and family? You can make a difference in relation to the participation of women in IT just by taking step one.

EPILOGUE: DARING TO LIVE IT

There is an old adage that we teach what we most need to learn, and maybe we also write what we most need to understand. My story of writing this book illustrates how deeply internalized sexism can be coded in one's psyche. As I suggested in Chapter I, internalized oppression may be the most damaging effect of our dominator system; when the message of those hierarchical social rankings become internalized, we act in negative ways to diminish our*selves*. Internalized thinking—such as "You can't do that," or "That's not good enough," or "Nice girls, don't . . ." (fill in the blank with just about anything because apparently "nice" girls don't do a whole lot of things)—can limit one in ways far more severe than external factors. In spite of my accomplishments as a teacher and a scholar, in writing this book, I still had to confront the deeply-embedded belief that apparently "nice" girls also don't "write good books." Teaching continues to foster my own growth and development in remarkable ways, and writing this book has shown me what I still need to learn. Here is what this experience has taught me.

Ever since I began teaching about social systems, I have challenged myself to confront any internalized attitudes of my own that may contribute to a negative learning environment for students. I have worked to be a caring and empathic educator rather than manifesting the fear and control-based models that predominated in my previous schooling. The more I taught, the more I realized the value of helping students understand gender, race, and class in terms of both individual development and social institutions. I have worked to help them understand how our individual identities and behaviors cooperate with what we learn from (and how we participate in) social institutions that shape our society. My compassion grew as I observed students courageously confronting their fears and struggling to understand. It became increasingly easy to move away from the dominator practices of shaming and blaming students towards the partnership practices of empathy and care. The more I engaged in this empathic practice with students, the more they learned, and the more deeply they were transformed by that learning. The more I saw the profound results of these partnership relations with students, the more convinced I became that this was the path to take in all of my relationships. I knew that my understanding of partnership relations would continue to grow and deepen through practice and I knew that I had a lot to learn, but I was surprised by what resulted from writing this book.

When I began writing this book, Eisler's (1987) dominator-partnership continuum deeply informed my thinking about social systems. However, I was well into the book's creation before I clarified that this was really the primary message—how to shift IT from a dominator to a partnership system. I discovered the value of this framework in helping others understand how to increase the participation of women in information technology as I was writing the book. In fact, my early thinking about the participation of women in technology began during my doctoral studies before I had read Riane Eisler's work. I was so busy reading feminist science studies scholars that I did not read Riane Eisler's (1987) *The Chalice and the Blade* until after I finished my doctorate in 2000. I remember being glad that I had not read this book until then because my depth of knowledge allowed me to see the brilliance in Eisler's dominator-partnership continuum in a way that I might not have so fully appreciated earlier. As a result of my education, I also knew that all of the elements of the story Eisler told were richly supported by many other scholars. However, Eisler (1987) provides an invaluable "big picture" framework that none of the others do, and I especially liked the way that the dominator-partnership continuum liberated discussion of social systems from an "either/or" gender-war standpoint. So, as I developed the first draft of this book, Eisler's voice grew increasingly loud.

After I delivered the first draft to the publisher to be read by three anonymous reviewers, my friend and mentor Dr. Catherine Warrick reminded me of Eisler's most recent book on global economics. Knowing it would add to my chapter on a partnership global IT business, I eagerly read Eisler's (2007) *The Real Wealth of Nations: Creating a Caring Economics*. My first response was panic. My thinking in Chapter X on what a partnership global IT business might look like so closely paralleled Eisler's that I worried about having developed a "shadow" book. Without having read Eisler's recent work, I had arrived at a similar vision of how to co-create a partnership global IT business. I remembered the wise advice that Dr. Judith Arcana offered when I was deep into my doctoral research and found another scholar who had arrived at similar conclusions. In response to my disappointment at not being "the first" to explore these ideas, Dr. Arcana replied, "Mary, How do you think our knowledge tradition was created? We all add to each other's thinking. Now, you can add your voice to the conversation that another scholar began." But, this is when the sticky goo of internalized sexism rose up to bob on the surface of my consciousness. As a woman in a society where there are still so many messages that contribute to my feeling "voiceless," it was a challenge to believe that my voice was worth hearing. So, I spent a few weeks consumed with self-doubt about the veracity of and quality of my work in this book, before I was able to hear the truth. Using Riane Eisler's (1987) early thinking about dominator and partnership social systems as a guide, I manifested a similar vision of what a partnership society might look like in relation to information technology. I see now that that fact actually makes this book serve as further evidence of the profound significance of Eisler's ideas about dominator and partnership societies.

I believe in Eisler's (1987, 2000, 2002, 2007) vision of partnership. I hope that I have honored it with this book, as I will strive to honor it with my life. I still have a lot to learn about partnership relations, but the only way to learn is to dare to push ourselves beyond what we already know or believe to be true. If we are ever to achieve our true human potential, we must dare ourselves to live it. I hope some day we will have co-created a world where we can share this poem with our grand-children. They will ask, "How did you create a partnership society in the midst of so much domination?" We will answer:

So you say
    Tell me, old ones
    How did you do it?
    How did you change it?
And they smile

Listen
Hear what they say to you

    We struggled
    We held out our hands and touched each other
    We remembered to laugh
    We went to endless meetings
    We said no
    We put our bodies on the line
    We said yes
    We invented, we created
    We walked straight through our fears
    We formed the circle
    We danced

    We spoke the truth
    We dared to live it   (Starhawk, 1987, p. 344)

REFERENCES

Brainard, S. G., & Carlin, L. (2001). A six-year longitudinal study of undergraduate women in science and engineering. In M. Lederman & I. Bartsch (Eds.), *The gender and science reader* (pp. 24-37). London: Routledge.

Camp, T. (1997). The incredible shrinking pipeline. *Communications of the ACM, 40*(10), 103-110.

Carter, J. (2005). *Our endangered values: America's moral crisis.* New York: Simon & Schuster.

CNVC, the organization. (2007). *Center for Nonviolent Communication.* Retrieved September 1, 2007, from www.cnvc.org

Cohoon, J. M., & Aspray, W. (Eds.). (2006). *Women and information technology: Research on underrepresentation.* Cambridge, MA: MIT Press.

Eisler, R. (1987). *The chalice and the blade: Our history, our future.* San Francisco: HarperSanFrancisco.

Eisler, R. (2000). *Tommorrwow's children: A blueprint for partnership education in the 21st century.* Boulder, CO: Westview.

Eisler, R. (2002). *The power of partnership: Seven relationships that will change your life.* Novato, CA: New World.

Eisler, R. (2004). Education for a culture of peace. In R. Eisler & R. Miller (Eds.), *Educating for a culture of peace* (pp. 11-41). Portsmouth, NH: Heinemann.

Eisler, R. (2007). *The real wealth of nations: Creating a caring economics.* San Francisco: Berrett-Koehler.

Eisler, R., & Loye, D. (1990). *The partnership way.* San Francisco: HarperSanFrancisco.

Eisler, R., & Miller, R. (Eds.). (2004). *Educating for a culture of peace.* Portsmouth, NH: Heinemann.

Flannery, D. J. et al. (2003). Initial behavior outcomes for the PeaceBuilders Universal School-Based Violence Prevention Program. *Developmental Psychology, 39*(2), 292-308. Retrieved August 31, 2007, from http://www.apa.org/journals/releases/dev392292.pdf

Gasman, M. (2007). *Black women in the STEM fields at black colleges.* Retrieved January 5, 2008, from http://www.gse.upenn.edu/~mgasman/blackwomen.htm

Henderson, H. (1996). *Building a win-win world: Life beyond global economic warfare.* San Francisco: Berrett-Koehler Publishers.

Johnson, A. G. (2006). *Privilege, power and difference.* Boston: McGrawHill.

Johnson, D. et al. (Eds.) (2006, June). *Facilitating success for women in STEM through living-learning programs.* Paper presented at the National Conference on Women in Engineering Programs and Advocates Network, Pittsburgh, PA. Retrieved

January 5, 2008, from http://www.engr.utexas.edu/wep/wepan2006/Presentations/WhitePaper_FacilitatingSuccess.pdf

Kazan, E. (Director). (1947). *Gentleman's agreement* [Motion picture] Hollywood, CA: 20th Century Fox.

Mares, M., & Woodard, E. (2005). Positive effects of television on children's social interactions: A meta-analysis. *Media Psychology, 7*(3), 301-322. Retrieved August 25, 2007, from www.ebscohost.com

Margolis, J., & Fisher, A. (2002). *Unlocking the clubhouse: Women in computing.* Cambridge, MA: MIT Press.

McKenna, P. (2006). Gender and programming: Mixing the abstract and the concrete. In G. Trajkovski (Ed.), *Diversity in information technology education: Issues and controversies* (pp. 68-91). Hershey, PA: Information Science Publishing.

Miller, R. (2004). Introduction. In R. Eisler & R. Miller (Eds.), *Educating for a culture of peace* (pp. 1-10). Portsmouth, NH: Heinemann.

Mohanty, C. T. (1991). Under western eyes: Feminist scholarship and colonial discourses. In C.T. Mohanty et al. (Eds.), *Third world women and the politics of feminism* (pp. 51-80). Bloomington, IN: Indiana UP.

Rosenberg, M. B. (2005). *Nonviolent communication: A language of life.* Encinitas, CA: PuddleDancer.

Rosser, S. V. (Ed.). (1995). *Teaching the majority: Breaking the gender barrier in science, mathematics, and engineering.* New York: Teachers College.

Seymour, E., & Hewitt, N. M. (1997). *Talking about leaving: Why undergraduates leave the sciences.* Boulder, CO: Westview.

Sonnert, G. (1995). *Gender differences in science careers: The project access study.* New Brunswick, NJ.

Starhawk. (1987). *Truth or dare: Encounters with power, authority, and mystery.* San Francisco: Harper & Row.

Swift, K., & Miller, C. (2001). *The handbook of non-sexist writing.* Retrieved May 6, 2008, from www.iuniverse.com

ENDNOTE

[1] Gloria Yamato coined this expression "the ism family" in Yamato, G. (1998). Racism: Something about the subject makes it hard to name. In P. S. Rothenberg et al. (Eds.), *Race, class and gender in the U.S.* (pp. 150-153). New York: St Martin's.

Appendix:
Recommended Resources

Educating ourselves about the complexity of the issues is a great way to begin to co-create viable solutions to the absence of women as developers, users, and beneficiaries of IT. This appendix offers some resources for further study in the following areas: feminism and partnership; feminist science studies; media studies; language and communication; education; her-story; global economics and partnership science; films; and organizations working toward change.

FEMINISM AND PARTNERSHIP

Anzaldua, G. (1987). *Borderlands/La frontera: The new mestiza*. San Francisco: Spinsters.

Brumberg, J. J. (1997). *The body project: An intimate history of American girls*. New York: Random House.

Cofer, J. O. (1998). The myth of the Latin woman: I just met a girl named Maria. In P. S. Rothenberg (Ed.), *Race, class, and gender in the United States: An integrated study* (4th ed., pp. 292-296). New York: St. Martins.

Collins, P. H. (1990). *Black feminist thought: Knowledge, consciousness, and the politics of empowerment*. New York: Routledge.

Edut, O. (Ed.). (1998). *Adios, Barbie: Young women write about body image and identity*. Seattle: Seal Press.

Eisler, R. (1987). *The chalice and the blade: Our history, our future.* San Francisco: HarperSanFrancisco.

Eisler, R. (2000). *Tommorrow's children: A blueprint for partnership eduation in the 21ˢᵗ century.* Boulder, CO: Westview.

Eisler, R. (2002). *The power of partnership: Seven relationships that will change your life.* Novato, CA: New World.

Eisler, R. (2007). *The real wealth of nations: Creating a caring economics.* San Francisco: Berrett-Koehler.

Eisler, R., & Loye, D. (1990). *The partnership way.* San Francisco: HarperSanFrancisco.

Eisler, R., & Miller, R. (Eds.). (2004). *Educating for a culture of peace.* Portsmouth, NH: Heinemann.

Faludi, S. (1991). *Backlash: The undeclared war against American women.* New York: Crown.

Faludi, S. (1999). *Stiffed: The betrayal of the American man*

Fausto-Sterling, A. (2000). *Sexing the body: Gender politics and the construction of sexuality.* New York: Basic.

Feinberg, L. (1996). *Transgender warriors: Making history from Joan of Arc to Dennis Rodman.* Boston: Beacon Press.

Gilbert, S. M., & Gubar, S. (1984). *The madwoman in the attic: The woman writer and the nineteenth-century literary imagination.* New Haven: Yale UP.

hooks, b. (1984). *Feminist theory: From margin to center.* Boston: South End.

hooks, b. (1989). *Talking back: Thinking feminist, thinking black.* Boston: South End Press.

hooks, b. (1992). *Black looks: Race and representation.* Boston: South End.

hooks, b. (2000). *Feminism is for everybody: Passionate politics.* Cambridge: South End.

Johnson, A. G. (1997). *The gender knot: Unraveling our patriarchal legacy.* Philadelphia: Temple UP.

Johnson, A. G. (2006). *Privilege, power and difference.* Boston: McGrawHill.

Johnson, S. (1989). *Wildfire: Igniting the she/volution.* Albuquerque, NM: Wildfire Press.

Kadi, J. (1996). *Thinking class: Sketches from a cultural worker.* Boston: South End.

Kesselman, A. et al. (Eds.). (2003). *Women images and realities: A multicultural anthology.* Boston: McGrawHill.

Kimmel, M. S. (2000). *The gendered society.* New York: Oxford UP.

Kimmel, M. S., & Messner, M. A. (1989). *Men's lives.* New York: Macmillan.

Kirk, G., & Okazawa-Rey, M. (2004). *Women's lives: Multicultural perspectives* (3rd edition). New York: McGraw-Hill.

Lorde, A. (1984). *Sister outsider: Essays and speeches.* Berkeley, CA: Crossing Press.

McIntosh, P. (1998).White privilege: Unpacking the invisible knapsack. In P. S. Rothenberg et al. (Eds.), *Race, class and gender in the U.S.* (pp. 165-169). New York: St Martin's.

Minnich, E. K. (1990). *Transforming knowledge.* Philadelphia: Temple UP.

Mohanty, C.T. et al. (Eds.). (1991). *Third world women and the politics of feminism.* Bloomington, IN: Indiana UP.

Morrison, T. (1992). *Playing in the dark: Whiteness and the literary imagination.* New York: Vintage.

Northrup, C. (1998). *Women's bodies, women's wisdom: Creating physical and emotional health and healing.* New York: Bantam.

Ogawa, D. M. (1971). *From Japs to Japanese: An evolution of Japanese-American stereotypes.* Berkeley, CA: McCutchan.

Pipher, M. (1994). *Reviving Ophelia: Saving the selves of adolescent girls.* New York: Putnam.

Rich, A. (1986). *Of woman born: Motherhood as social institution.* New York: Norton.

Seagar, J. (2003). *The Penguin atlas of women in the world.* New York: Penguin.

Spencer, S. J., & Steele, C. M., & Quinn, D. M. (1999). Stereotype threat and women's math performance. *Journal of Experimental Social Psychology, 35,* 4-28.

Starhawk. (1987). *Truth or dare: Encounters with power, authority, and mystery.* New York: Harper.

Steele, C. M., & Aronson, J. (1995). Stereotype threat and the intellectual test performance of African-Americans. *Journal of Personality & Social Psychology, 69*(5), 797-811. Retrieved July 24, 2007, from the EBSCOhost database.

Stice, E. (1998). Modeling of eating pathology and social reinforcement of the thin-ideal predict onset of bulimic symptoms. *Behaviour Research and Therapy, 36*(10), 931-944.

Stice, E., & Shaw, H. E. (1994). Adverse effects of the media portrayed thin ideal on women and linkages to bulimic symptomatology. *Journal of Social and Clinical Psychology, 13*(3), 288-308.

Striegel-Moore, R. H. et al. (1986). Toward an understanding of risk factors for bulimia. *American Psychologist, 41*(3), 246-263.

Tavris, C. (1992). *The mismeasure of woman.* New York: Touchstone.

Taylor, J. M. et al. (Eds.). (1995). *Between voice and silence: Women and girls, race and relationship.* Cambridge, MA: Harvard UP.

Williams, P. J. (1991). *The alchemy of race and rights.* Cambridge, MA: Harvard UP.

Williams, P. (1997). *The rooster's egg: On the persistence of prejudice.* Cambridge, MA: Harvard.

Wolf, N. (1992). *The beauty myth: How images of beauty are used against women.* New York: Doubleday.

Wollstonecraft, M. (1996). *A vindication of the rights of woman. 1792.* Mineola, NY: Dover.

Yamato, G. (1998). Racism: Something about the subject makes it hard to name. In P. S. Rothenberg et al. (Eds.), *Race, class and gender in the U.S.* (pp. 150-153). New York: St Martin's.

FEMINIST SCIENCE STUDIES

Ambrose, S. A., Dunkle, K. L., Lazarus, B. B., Nair, I, & Harkus, D. A. (1997). *Journeys of women in science and engineering: No universal constants.* Philadelphia: Temple UP.

Arditti, R. (1980). *Science and liberation.* Boston: South End.

Bix, A. S. (2000). Feminism where men predominate: The history of women's science and engineering education at MIT. *Women's Studies Quarterly, 28*(1/2), 24-45.

Bleier, R. (1991). *Feminist approaches to science.* New York: Teachers College.

Camp, T. (1997). The incredible shrinking pipeline. *Communications of the ACM, 40*(10), 103-110.

Cassell, J. (in press). Genderizing HCI. In J. Jacko & A. Sears (Eds.), *The handbook of human-computer interaction.* Mahwah, NJ: Lawrence Erlbaum. Retrieved July 30, 2007, from http://web.media.mit.edu/~justine/publications.html

Cassell, J., & Jenkins, H. (Eds.). (1998). *From Barbie to mortal kombat: Gender and computer games.* Cambridge, MA: MIT.

Cherny, L., & Weise, E. R. (Eds.). (1996). *Wired women: Gender and new realities in cyberspace.* Seattle: Seal.

Cohoon, J. M., & Aspray, W. (Eds.). (2006). *Women and information technology: Research on underrepresentation.* Cambridge, MA: MIT Press.

Cooper, J., & Weaver, K. D. (2003). *Gender and computers: Understanding the digital divide.* Mahwah, NJ: Erlbaum.

DeBell, M., & Chapman, C. (2006, September). Computer and Internet use by students in 2003. *National Center for Education Statistics* (NCES 2006-065). U.S. Department of Education: Institute of Education Sciences. Retrieved September 5, 2007, from www.eric.ed.gov.ezproxy.metrostate.edu

Faulkner, W. (2000). Dualisms, hierarchies and gender in engineering. *Social Studies of Science, 30*(5), 759-792. Retrieved on January 16, 2007, from www.jstor.org

Figueroa, R., & Harding, S. (Eds.). (2003). *Science and other cultures: Issues in philosophies of science and technology.* New York: Routledge.

Furger, R. (1998). *Does Jane compute? Preserving our daughters' place in the cyber revolution.* New York: Warner.

Gross, P. R. & Levitt, N. (1994). *Higher superstition: The academic left and its quarrels with science.* Baltimore: Johns Hopkins UP.

Harding, S. (1998). *Is science multicultural? Postcolonialisms, feminisms, and epistemologies.* Bloomington, IN: Indiana UP.

Harding, S. (2000). Should philosophies of science encode democratic ideals? In D. L. Kleinman (Ed.), *Science, technology & democracy* (pp. 121-138). Albany: SUNY.

Harraway, D. J. (1991). *Simians, cyborgs, and women: The reinvention of nature.* New York: Routledge.

Hawthorne, S., & Klein, R. (Eds.). (1999). *CyberFeminism: Connectivity, critique and creativity.* North Melbourne, Australia: Spinifex.

Henrion, C. (1997). *Women in mathematics: The addition of difference.* Bloomington, IN: Indiana UP.

Huff, C., & Cooper, J. (1987). Sex bias in educational software: The effect of designers' stereotypes on the software they design. *Journal of Applied Social Psychology, 17,* 519-532.

Jasanoff, S. et al. (Eds.). (1995). *Handbook of science and technology studies.* Thousand Oaks, CA: Sage.

Jenkins, H., & Cassell, J. (2007). From Quake grrls to desperate housewives: A decade of gender and computer games. In Y. Kafai, C. Heeter, J. Denner, & J. Sun (Eds.), *Beyond Barbie and Mortal Kombat: New perspectives on gender and computer games.* Cambridge, MA: MIT Press. Retrieved September 1, 2007, from http://www.soc.northwestern.edu/justine/publications/Jenkins_Cassell%20BBMK_Forward.pdf

Keller, E. F. (1985). *Reflections on gender and science.* New Haven, CT: Yale UP.

Keller, E. F. (1992). *Secrets of life, secrets of death: Essays on language, gender and science.* New York: Routledge.

Keller, E. F. (2002). *Making sense of life: Explaining biological development with models, metaphors, and machines.* Cambridge, MA: Harvard UP.

Kirk, M., &, Zander, C. (2002, December). Bridging the digital divide by co-creating a collaborative computer science classroom. *Journal of Computing in Small Colleges, 18*(2), 117-125.

Kirk, M., &, Zander, C. (2004, December). Narrowing the digital divide: In search of a map to mend the gap. *Journal of Computing in Small Colleges, 20*(2), 168-175.

Kramer, P. E., & Lehman, S. (1990). Mismeasuring women: A critique of research on computer ability and avoidance. *Signs, 16*(11), 158-172.

Lederman, M., & Bartsch, I. (Eds.). (2001). *The gender and science reader.* London: Routledge.

Margolis, J., & Fisher, A. (2002). *Unlocking the clubhouse: Women in computing.* Cambridge, MA: MIT Press.

Mayberry, M., Subramaniam, B., & Weasel, L.H. (Eds.). (2001). *Feminist science studies: A new generation.* New York: Routledge.

Merchant, C. (1980). *The death of nature: Women, ecology and the scientific revolution.* San Francisco: HarperSanFrancisco.

Rosser, S. V. (Ed.). (1995). *Teaching the majority: Breaking the gender barrier in science, mathematics, and engineering.* New York: Teachers College.

Rosser, S. V. (1997). *Re-engineering female friendly science.* New York: Teachers College.

Rosser, S. V. (2000). *Women, science & society: The crucial union.* New York: Teachers College.

Schiebinger, L. (1993). *Nature's body: Gender in the making of modern science.* Boston: Beacon.

Schiebinger, L. (1999). *Has feminism changed science?* Cambridge, MA: Harvard.

Seymour, E., & Hewitt, N. M. (1997). *Talking about leaving: Why undergraduates leave the sciences.* Boulder, CO: Westview.

Sonnert, G. (1995). *Gender differences in science careers: The project access study.* New Brunswick, NJ.

Spender, D. (1995). *Nattering on the net: Women, power and cyberspace.* North Melbourne, Australia: Spinifex.

Turkle, S. (1984). *The second self: Computers and the human spirit.* New York: Touchstone.

Turkle, S. (1995). *Life on the screen: Identity in the age of the Internet.* New York: Touchstone.

Vesgo, J. (2007, July 31). CRA Taulbee trends: Female students & faculty. *Computer Research Association.* Retrieved September 18, 2007, from http://www.cra.org/info/taulbee/women.html

Ware, M. C., & Stuck, M. F. (1985). Sex-role messages vis-à-vis microcomputer use: A look at the pictures. *Sex Roles, 13*(3/4), 205-214.

Wilson, F. (2003). Can compute, won't compute: Women's participation in the culture of computing. *New Technology, Work, and Employment, 18*(2), 127-142.

Women, minorities, and persons with disabilities in science and engineering: 2004. (2004). *National Science Foundation, Division of Science Resources Statistics* (NSF 04-317). Retrieved September 23, 2007, from http://www.nsf.gov/statistics/wmpd/

Wyer, M. et al. (Eds.). (2001). *Women, science, and technology: A reader in feminist science studies*. New York: Routledge.

MEDIA STUDIES

Balnaves, M. et al. (Eds.). (2001). *The Penguin atlas of media and information*. New York: Penguin Putnam.

Cialdini, R. B. (1993). *Influence: The psychology of persuasion*. New York: Quill.

Dates, J. L., & Barlow, W. (Eds.). (1993). *Split image: African-Americans in the mass media* (2nd ed.). Washington, D.C.: Howard UP.

Douglas, S. J. (1995). *Where the girls are: Growing up female with mass media*. New York: Times Books.

Erens, P. (1990). *Issues in feminist film criticism*. Bloomington, IN: Indiana UP.

Kang, M. (1997). The portrayal of women's images in magazine advertisements: Goffman's gender analysis revisited. *Sex Roles, 37*(11/12), 979-996.

Kilbourne, J. (1999). *Deadly persuasion: Why women and girls must fight the addictive power of advertising*. New York: The Free Press.

Kitch, C. L. (1998). *The girl on the magazine cover: Gender, class, and the emergence of visual stereotypes in American mass media, 1895-1930*. Diss. Ann Arbor, MI: Temple University. 9838498.

Lazier, L., & Kendrick, A. G. (1993). Women in advertisements: Sizing up the images, roles, and functions. In P. J. Creedon (Ed.), *Women in mass communication* (pp. 199-219). Newbury Park: Sage.

Lester, P. M. (1996). *Images that injure: Pictorial stereotypes in the media*. Westport, CT: Praeger.

MacGregor, R. M. (1989). The distorted mirror: Images of visible minority women in Canadian print advertising. *Atlantis: A Women's Studies Journal, 15*(1), 137-143.

MacKay, N. J., & Covell, K. (1997). The impact of women in advertisements on attitudes toward women. *Sex Roles*, *36*(9/10), 573-583.

McClelland, J. R. (1993). Visual images and re-Imaging: A review of research in mass communication. In P. J. Creedon (Ed.), *Women in mass communication* (pp. 220-234). Newbury Park: Sage.

Millar, M. S. (1998). *Cracking the gender code: Who rules the wired world?* Toronto: Second Story.

Nelkin, D. (1995). *Selling science: How the press covers science and technology.* New York: Freeman.

Quart, A. (2003). *Branded: The buying and selling of teenagers.* Cambridge, MA: Perseus.

Rapping, E. (1994). *Media-tions: Forays into the culture and gender wars.* Boston: South End.

Robinson, L. (1996). *Media myth, media reality: A primer of racism in America.* Diss. The Union Institute, Ann Arbor: UMI. 9633792.

LANGUAGE AND COMMUNICATION

Aires, E. (1996). *Men and women in interaction: Reconsidering the differences.* New York: Oxford UP.

CNVC. (2007). *Center for Nonviolent Communication.* Retrieved September 1, 2007, from www.cnvc.org

Creedon, P. J. (Ed.). (1993). *Women in mass communication.* Newbury Park: Sage.

Eisler, R. (2002). *The power of partnership: Seven relationships that will change your life.* Novato, CA: New World.

Eisler, R., & Loye, D. (1990). *The partnership way.* San Francisco: HarperSanFrancisco.

Ellinor, L., & Gerard, G. (1998). *Dialogue: Rediscover the transforming power of conversation.* New York: John Wiley & Sons.

Klein, D. (2001). *New vision, new reality: A guide to unleashing energy, joy, and creativity in your life.* Center City, MN: Hazelden.

Lakoff, R. T. (1990). *Talking power: The politics of language*. New York: Basic.

Mares, M., & Woodard, E. (2005). Effects of television on children's social interactions: A meta-analysis. *Media Psychology, 7*(3), 301-322. Retrieved on August 13, 2007, from www.ebscohost.com

Mulvaney, B. M. (1994). *Gender differences in communication: An intercultural experience*. Retrieved on August 9, 2007, from http://www.cpsr.org/prevsite/cpsr/gender/mulvaney.txt

Rosenberg, M. B. (2005). *Nonviolent communication: A language of life*. Encinitas, CA: PuddleDancer.

Spender, D. (1980). *Man made language*. London: Routledge.

Swift, K., & Miller, C. (2001). *The handbook of non-sexist writing*. Retrieved May 13, 2008, from www.iuniverse.com

Tannen, D. (2001). *You just don't understand: Women and men in conversation*. New York: Quill.

Van Fossen, B. (1996). Gender differences in communication. *Institute for Teaching and Research on Women, Towson University*. Retrieved August 5, 1997, from http://midget.towson.edu/itrow

Williamson, M. (1993). *A return to love: Reflections on the principles of a course in miracles*. New York: HarperPerennial.

Wood, J. T. (1999). *Gendered lives: Communication, gender, and culture* (3rd ed). Belmont, CA: Wadsworth.

EDUCATION

Barton, A. C. et al. (2003). *Teaching science for social justice*. New York: Teachers College.

Belenky, M. F., et al. (1986). *Women's ways of knowing: The development of self, voice, and mind*. New York: Basic.

Bethel, D. M. (1994). *Makiguchi the value creator: Revolutionary Japanese educator and founder of Soka Gakkai*. New York: Weatherhill.

Campbell, T. A., & Campbell, D. E. (1997). Faculty/student mentor program: Effects on academic performance and retention. *Research in Higher Education, 38*(6), 727-742.

Cooper, J. et al. (1990). Situational stress as a consequence of sex-stereotyped software. *Personality and Social Psychology Bulletin, 16*, 419-429.

Eisler, R. (2000). *Tomorrow's children: A blueprint for partnership education in the 21ˢᵗ century.* Boulder, CO: Westview.

Eisler, R., & Miller, R. (Eds.). (2004). *Educating for a culture of peace.* Portsmouth, NH: Heinemann.

Fung, Y. H. (2002, November). A comparative study of primary and secondary school students' images of scientists. *Research in Science & Technological Education, 20*(2), 199-213.

Gill, D., & Levidow, L. (Eds.). (1987). *Anti-racist science teaching.* London: Free Association.

Goldberger, N., et al. (1996). *Knowledge, difference, and power: Essays inspired by women's ways of knowing.* New York: Basic.

Greenbaum, J. (1990). The head and the heart: Using gender analysis to study the social construction of computer systems. *Computers and Society, 20*(2), 9-17.

hooks, b. (2003). *Teaching community: A pedagogy of hope.* New York: Routledge.

Kirk, M., & Grunewald, M. (2006, April 22). *The compassionate classroom: Stories from the heart.* Workshop facilitated at the Workshop at the Metropolitan State University Spring Faculty Conference, St. Paul, MN.

Kirk, M., &, Zander, C. (2002, December). Bridging the digital divide by co-creating a collaborative computer science classroom. *Journal of Computing in Small Colleges, 18*(2), 117-125.

Logan, J. (1993). *Teaching stories.* St. Paul, MN: Minnesota Inclusiveness Program.

Mayberry, M., & Rose, E. C. (Eds.), *Meeting the challenge: Innovative feminist pedagogies in action.* New York: Routledge.

Riger, S. (1992). Epistemological debates, feminist voices. *American Psychologist, 47*(6), 730-740.

Rosser, S. V. (Ed.). (1995). *Teaching the majority: Breaking the gender barrier in science, mathematics, and engineering.* New York: Teachers College.

Sadker, M., & Sadker, D. (1995). *Failing at fairness: How our schools cheat girls.* New York: Touchstone.

Stanley, A. (1995). *Mothers and daughters of invention: Notes for a revised history of technology.* New Brunswick, NJ: Rutgers UP.

Walker, H. M., Colvin, G., & Ramsey, E. (1995). *Anti-social behavior in schools: Strategies and best practices.* Pacific Grove, CA: Brooks/Cole.

HER-STORY

Ajzenberg-Selove, F. (1994). *A matter of choices: Memoirs of a female physicist.* New Brunswick: Rutgers UP.

Amott, T., & Matthaei, J. (1996). *Race, gender, and work: A multicultural economic history of women in the United States.* Boston: South End.

Estrin, T. (1996). Women's studies and computer science: Their intersection. *IEEE Annals of the History of Computing, 18*(3), 43-46.

Fritz, W. B. (1996). The women of ENIAC. *IEEE Annals of the History of Computing, 18*(3), 13-28.

Jordan, D. (2006). *Sisters in science: Conversations with black women scientists on race, gender, and their passion for success.* West Lafayette, IN: Purdue UP.

Keller, E. F. (1983). *A feeling for the organism: The life and work of Barbara McClintock.* San Francisco: Freeman.

Lerner, G. (1986). *The creation of patriarchy.* New York: Oxford.

Lerner, G. (1993). *The creation of feminist consciousness: From the Middle Ages to eighteen-seventy.* New York: Oxford.

McGrayne, S. B. (1993). *Nobel prize women in science: Their lives, struggles, and momentous discoveries.* Secaucus, NJ: Carol.

Osen, L. (1974). *Women in mathematics.* Cambridge: MIT P.

Reynolds, M. D. (1999). *American women scientists: 23 inspiring biographies, 1900-2000.* Jefferson, NC: McFarland & Co.

Rossiter, M. W. (1982). *Women scientists in America: Struggles and strategies to 1940.* Baltimore: Johns Hopkins.

Rossiter, M. W. (1995). *Women scientists in America: Before affirmative action 1940-1972.* Baltimore: Johns Hopkins.

Sayer, A. (1975). *Rosalind Franklin & DNA*. New York: W.W. Norton.

Stanley, A. (1995). *Mothers and daughters of invention: Notes for a revised history of technology.* New Brunswick, NJ: Rutgers UP.

Takaki, R. (1993). *A different mirror: A history of multicultural America*. Boston: Little, Brown & Co.

Tolley, K. (2003). *The science education of American girls: A historical perspective.* New York: RoutledgeFalmer.

Toole, B. A. (1992). *Ada, the enchantress of numbers: A selection from the letters of Lord Byron's daughter and her description of the first computer.* Mill Valley, CA: Strawberry.

Warren, W. (1999). *Black women scientists in the United States*. Bloomington, IN: Indiana UP.

GLOBAL ECONOMICS AND PARTNERSHIP SCIENCE

Amott, T. L., & Matthaei, J. (1996). *Race, gender, and work: A multicultural economic history of women in the United States.* Boston: South End.

Arditti, R. (1999). *Searching for life: The grandmothers of the Plaza de Mayo and the disappeared children of Argentina.* Berkeley: U of California P.

Aronica, R., & Ramdoo, M. (2006). *The world is flat? A critical analysis of the New York Times bestseller by Thomas Friedman.* Tampa: Meghan-Kiffer Press.

Black, E. (2001). *IBM and the holocaust: The strategic alliance between Nazi Germany and America's most powerful corporation.* New York: Crown.

Bronfenbrenner, U. (Ed.). (2005). *Making human beings human: Bioecological perspectives on human development.* Thousand Oaks, CA: Sage.

Carter, J. (2005). *Our endangered values: America's moral crisis.* New York: Simon & Schuster.

Eisenstein, Z. (1998). *Global obscenities: Patriarchy, capitalism, and the lure of cyberfantasy.* New York: New York University Press.

Eisler, R. (2007). *The real wealth of nations: Creating a caring economics.* San Francisco: Berrett-Koehler.

Enloe, C. (1989). *Bananas, beaches, and bases: Making feminist sense of international politics.* Berkeley, CA: U of California P.

Friedman, T. L. (2006). *The world is flat: A brief history of the twenty-first century.* New York: Farrar, Straus and Giroux.

Harding, S. G. (1998). *Is science multicultural: Postcolonialisms, feminisms, and epistemologies.* Bloomington: Indiana UP.

Henderson, H. (1996). *Building a win-win world: Life beyond global economic warfare.* San Francisco: Berrett-Koehler Publishers.

Kleinman, D. L. (Ed.). (2000). *Science, technology & democracy.* Albany: SUNY.

Korten, D. C. (1995). *When corporations rule the world.* San Francisco: Berrett-Koeler.

Lipton, B. H. (2005). *The biology of belief: Unleashing the power of consciousness, matter and miracles.* Santa Rosa, CA: Elite.

Lukacs, J. (2001). Heisenberg's recognitions: The end of the scientific world view. In M. Lederman & I. Bartsch (Eds.), *The gender and science reader* (pp. 225-230). London: Routledge.

Prestowitz, C. (2005). *Three billion new capitalists: The great shift of wealth and power to the east.* New York: Basic Books.

Roy, A. (2004). *An ordinary person's guide to empire.* Cambridge, MA: South End.

Sclove, R. E. (2000). Town meetings on technology: Consensus conferences as democratic participation. In D. L. Kleinman (Ed.), *Science, technology and democracy* (pp. 33-48). Albany: SUNY.

Shiva, V. (1997). *Biopiracy: The plunder of nature and knowledge.* Cambridge, MA: South End Press.

Shiva, V. (2005). *Earth democracy: Justice, sustainability, and peace.* Cambridge, MA: South End Press.

Stiglitz, J. E. (2003). *Globalization and its discontents.* New York: W.W. Norton.

Stockard, R., Akbari, A., & Domooei, J. (2006). Dimensions of sustainable diversity in IT: Applications to the IT college major and career aspirations among underrepresented high school students of color. In G. Trajkovski (Ed.), *Diversity in information technology education: Issues and controversies* (pp. 92-128). Hershey, PA: Information Science Publishing.

Trajkovski, G. (Ed.). (2006). *Diversity in information technology education: Issues and controversies*. Hershey, PA: Information Science Publishing.

Weimann, G. (2006). *Terror on the Internet: The new arena, the new challenges*. Washington, D.C.: United States Institute of Peace.

Wresch, W. (1996). *Disconnected: Haves and have-nots in the information age*. New Brunswick, NJ: Rutgers UP.

FILMS

Anderson, A., & Cottringer, A. (Producers/Directors). (1988). *Hell to pay* [Motion picture]. England: Women Make Movies.

Frenkel, K. (Executive Producer & Director). (1995). *Minerva's machine: Women in computing* [Motion picture]. Association for Computing Machinery.

Jean Kilbourne's books or videos at www.jeankilbourne.com

Kazan, E. (Director). (1947). *Gentleman's agreement* [Motion picture] Hollywood: 20th Century Fox.

Lazarus, M. (Director). (1987). *Still killing us softly: Advertising's image of women* [Motion picture]. Cambridge, MA: Cambridge Documentary Films.

Martin, K. (Producer), & Nash, T. (Director). (1997). *Who's counting?: Marilyn Waring on sex, lies & global economics* [Motion picture]. Oley, PA: Bullfrog Films.

Sut Jhally's books or videos at www.sutjhally.com

ORGANIZATIONS WORKING TOWARD CHANGE

AllAfrica Global Media at allafrica.com

Anita Borg Institute for Women and Technology at www.iwt.org

Association for Computing Machinery's (ACM) Committee on Women in Computing, ACM-W at women.acm.org

Association for Progressive Communications at www.apc.org

Association for Women in Computing at www.awc-hq.org

Association for Women in Science (AWIS) at www.awis.org

Center for Media and Democracy at www.prwatch.org

Center for Partnership Studies at www.partnershipway.org

Center for Women and Information Technology at www.umbc.edu/cwit

Committee on Women in Science and Engineering at www7.nationalacademies.org/cwsem

Computer Professionals for Social Responsibility at www.cpsr.org

Computing Research Association's (CRS) Committee on the Status of Women in Computing research (CRA-W) at www.cra.org/Activities/craw

Fairness and Accuracy in Reporting at www.fair.org

International Development Research Center at www.idrc.ca

Media Education Foundation at www.mediaed.org

Media Watch at www.mediawatch.com

Society of Women Engineers at www.swe.org

TechnoServe: Business Solutions to Rural Poverty at www.technoserve.org

United Nations Information and Communication Technologies (ICT) Task Force at www.unicttaskforce.org

WiTEC, the European Association for Women in Science, Engineering and Technology at www.witec-eu.net

Women in Engineering Programs & Advocates Network at www.wepan.org

Women in Technology International at www.witi.com

WorldChanging at www.worldchanging.com

World Summit on the Information Society (WSIS) Outcome Documents at www.itu.int/wsis/index.html

About the Author

Mary Kirk is an associate professor in the Individualized, Interdisciplinary & Lifelong Learning Department at Metropolitan State University where she also teaches in the women's studies program. She also taught at the University of Washington, Bothell for 4 years in the computing and software systems program. Kirk has convened panels on women in science and technology at conferences such as the Grace Hopper Celebration of Women in Computing, National Women's Studies Association, and the Conference on Computing in Small Colleges. She has published articles on women in science and technology in journals such as the *Journal of Computing in Small Colleges* and the *NWSA Journal*, and a chapter in Goran Trajkovski's (2006) *Diversity in Information Technology Education: Issues and Controversies*. This is her first book.

Index

CPSIA information can be obtained at www.ICGtesting.com
Printed in the USA
BVOW09*2051170915

417682BV00019B/75/P